The Theatre Riggers' Handbook

Delbert L. Hall, Ph.D.

and

Q. Brian Sickels

Spring Knoll Press
Johnson City, Tennessee 37601

Copyright and Liability

The Theatre Riggers' Handbook

Written by
Delbert L. Hall, Ph.D. and Q. Brian Sickels

Published by
Spring Knoll Press
Johnson City, Tennessee
www.SpringKnollPress.com

Copyright © 2016 Delbert L. Hall and Q. Brian Sickels

ISBN-10: 0997874600

ISBN-13: 978-0-9978746-0-0

Printed in the United States of America

Cover Photo: Walnut Street Theatre, Philadelphia, PA

Table of Contents

<u>Acknowledgements</u>

We would like to thank the following for their assistance:

Frank Cortez - The Long Center
Reid Neslage - H & H Specialties Inc.
Patrick Finn - J.R. Clancy
Mark T. Black - InterAmerica Stage, Inc.
Dave Vick - IATSE, Local 274
Scott C. Parker - IATSE, Local 8
Bill Sapsis - Sapsis Rigging
Chad Doherty – IATSE, Local 8
Katheryn McCumber – Walnut Street Theatre
Louis Peter – RoseBrand
Mountain Productions
David Carmack - Columbus McKinnon
Jonathan Deull
Tim Sidebottom – T&M Stage Supplies

Introduction

In preparing to write this book, we began by looking at many books available on theatre rigging. Some primarily focused on rigging hardware. Other books, those that primarily discuss stagecraft, had good information on how the use the hardware. We wanted to write a book that both explained the hardware and rigging systems, as well as explain how to use it and how to be a rigger. And we took our inspiration from books by Jay Glerum and A.S. Gillette, just to name two.

We also wanted to discuss some of the things that riggers should know: rigging math, how to tie knots, work with fiber and wire rope and do a rigging inspection. We wanted to cover training and safety, so we wrote about fall protection, ladders and lifts, and discussed some of the OSHA regulations that affect theatre rigging. In short, we wanted to write a comprehensive book on how to be a theatre rigger.

Most importantly, we used our decades of experience working in theatres as riggers, technical directors, rigging inspectors and consultants, to try to write a textbook for entry level riggers, as well as a reference book for experienced rigging.

Various manufacturers and vendors of stage rigging equipment will be mentioned in this book. We use these as examples of types of equipment and hardware, please do not take this to be an endorsement of any brand over another, it is not.

We hope we have succeeded in accomplishing our goals and that you will find this book informative. After all, helping riggers be safe and more productive is the real goal of this book.

-Delbert L. Hall and Q. Brian Sickels

Part I:
The Mechanics of Rigging

Chapter 1:
Static and Dynamic Forces

Introduction

Dynamic forces occur when an object accelerates or decelerates. Essentially, these forces are multiplying factors of the static load, which are always a constant. If an object is moving at a constant speed (no matter what the speed) there is no dynamic force created. A static load is simply a load that is neither accelerating nor decelerating. Forces remain stable. As soon as the load is raised, the rate of acceleration or deceleration becomes a key factor, as forces are created necessary to overcome *inertia* (*inertia* being the tendency of objects to resist a change in a state of motion and/or direction). The faster the acceleration, the greater the dynamic force created. Shock loads are an extreme example of this. Once the force has overcome *inertia*, there is no more dynamic force.

Think of an airplane sitting on the runway waiting to take off. The airplane is *static*- not moving. The pilot applies thrust to the engines. The force exerted by the engines begins to accelerate the plane to overcome inertia. You can feel this *dynamic* force as you are pressed back into your seat. It may seem like your weight is increasing, but your weight remains a constant. What you are experiencing is simply the *dynamic* force being exerted on your body by the acceleration. This *dynamic* force is experienced as the plane continues to accelerate until it reaches its cruising altitude. Once at its cruising speed, you and the plane are traveling at the same rate. There is no more inertia to overcome. You and the plane are *static*. As the plane begins its descent and the throttles are cut back, you may feel lighter in your seat. *Dynamic* forces are once again at work as the plane slows, lands and then ultimately comes to a stop (*static* again).

Shock loads are an extreme example of dynamic forces at work. A *shock load* is an excessive *dynamic* force created by the sudden acceleration or deceleration of an object. A sudden deceleration of a moving object can create a very great dynamic force. Understanding the rate of acceleration or deceleration is a key factor in the creation of dynamic forces.

This chapter will examine these *static* and *dynamic* forces. We will especially focus on truss and battens rigged with two or more rigging points. We will also look at the differences between *determinate* and *indeterminate* structure and specifically how *indeterminate structure* can radically affect dynamic forces on rigging points.

Standing Rigging (Static) vs Running Rigging (Dynamic)

Let's begin by defining the two types of rigging. *Standing rigging* is rigging that does not move- it is static. It is attached at both ends. Essentially, it is rigging that is used to hold something in place. Guy-wires are a good example of *standing rigging*. But understand, *all static rigging will become dynamic at some point*. The same static guy wires become dynamic as soon as they take up the force loads they were asked to support.

Running rigging, on the other hand, is rigging that moves. It becomes dynamic as it moves to overcomes inertia. Just like our airplane example above, it is static only if it is not moving or has attained its maximum velocity. Lift lines on battens can be said to be *static* as long as they are not in motion. As soon as the batten is raised or lowered, it becomes *dynamic*.

What is a Determinate and Indeterminate Structure?

Statics

Statics is the branch of mechanics that deals with loads and forces. Relatively speaking, statics involves simple math - math that can be done with paper and pencil and a calculator (in the old days a slide rule was used in place of a calculator). However, to keep the math simple, statics assumes that all structures are rigid. This is not true; you may have heard the phrase "everything is a spring." Everything is a spring and it deflects under a load, but statics cannot take this into account so the calculations are not as accurate as they could be.

To get the calculations more accurate you must understand strength of materials. With this knowledge you can use *Finite Element Analysis* (FEA) to calculate the load or force on the structure. The problem with this, at least for us in the entertainment industry, is that this math is very complicated and requires not only a lot more knowledge about strength of materials than we possess, but it requires sophisticated computer software to do all of the math involves - so we stick to statics.

Before you get too concerned about using statics, you should realize that, depending on the rigidity of the structure, statics can be pretty accurate. In fact, the engineering of most buildings, bridges, airplanes, etc. built before the 1980's were engineered using statics. For those of us involved in entertainment rigging, statics works just fine for most problems. For example, we can very accurately determine the load on the points supporting a truss, if the number of points is two. On the other hand, if three or more points are used to support a truss, statics falls short of being able to accurately calculate this force, which is why this type of loading is called a *Statically Indeterminate Structure*.

Determinate Structure

A structure is considered to be *determinate* if the equilibrium of the structure can be *determined* by mathematical equations that analyze the forces and reactions within that structure. A batten or truss, suspended by **two** *static* points IS considered to be *determinate* and the loads on the two points CAN be accurately calculated. The examples below show truss in four separate configurations where the loads on the rigging points can be found. Regardless if the suspension points are angled or vertical, or the truss is horizontal, cantilevered or angled, as long as there are **two** *static* points and the weight of the structure is known, then the load on the points can be calculated.

A determinate UDL. The total load is 50% on the first leg and 50% on the other

A non-UDL. The load on the points *can* be determined

A cantilevered, determinate UDL

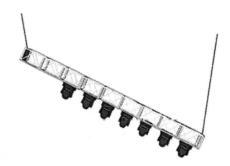

An angled, determinate non-UDL with angled bridles

Examples of Determinate Structures

Indeterminate Structure

A structure is statically *indeterminate* if the equilibrium of the structure CANNOT be calculated mathematically using statics. In other words, there is no way to analyze the forces and reactions with that structure without an understanding of the strength of the materials and using *Finite Element Analysis*. Trusses are considered to be indeterminate, if three or more points support them.

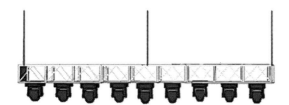

An indeterminate UDL

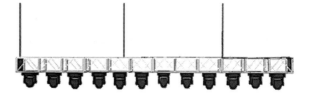

An indeterminate, cantilevered UDL

Examples of Indeterminate Structures

Uniform Distributed Loads (UDL) and Indeterminate Structure

When the loads are evenly distributed across the entire length of a truss or batten, we call this a "uniformly distributed load" or UDL. Figuring out how much of the load is on each supporting line is very easy when only two lines are supporting the batten/truss. As we see in the first line of the Load Diagram Chart below, 50% of the total load is on each supporting line.

As we noted before, this is condition is called a *determinate structure*, because the loads on each point can be calculated using statics. However, it gets more complicated when three or more lines support a truss or batten. The table below shows how a uniform load is *theoretically* distributed. When three or more lift lines support it, the structure becomes *indeterminate*. Note the term "theoretical" is used because, in order to be accurate, four conditions **must** exist:

1) The lift lines must be equally spaced.
2) The outer lift lines must be at the ends of the truss/ batten to match the diagram shown below
3) The load must be uniformly distributed
4) The batten or truss must be completely level

This is almost never the case. There are many factors that prevent a batten or truss, support by more than two points, from being perfectly level or the load from being perfectly distributed. Real world tests have proven that it is nearly impossible to "eye" a batten or truss and accurately level it or evenly distribute the load - even for the most experienced rigger.

The Load Diagram Chart shown below is theoretical at best. The first example shows the load distributed on two points. The load can be calculated because it is distributed on two points. It is the only example of a *statically determinate structure*. All the remaining examples are *indeterminate!* The only way these percentages could be achieved is by monitoring each point with load cells and adjusting each point individually.

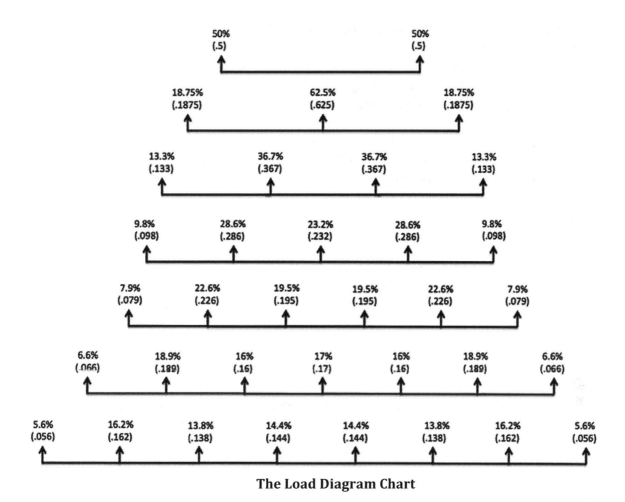

The Load Diagram Chart

Reprinted with permission from Jay Glerum, Stage Rigging Handbook (Carbondale: Southern University Press, 2007), 86.

The Force Diagram

So why bother? Why do we even concern ourselves with load diagrams if all this is theoretical anyway? The answer is - it provides us with a useful *load approximation* when comparing these loads to the Working Load Limits of hardware and a building's structure [1].

To better explain this, let's take a look at a *Force Diagram*. The illustration on the following page is for an eight-line set counterweight system in a theatrical application. The illustration shows the forces on the loft blocks calculated on the percentages from the illustration above. In addition, it shows the *static* and *resultant* forces on both the head block and the loft blocks. Even though these forces are in close approximations, they can be helpful when comparing data to the Working Load Limits (WLL) of the hardware. In the case of the loft blocks, these have WLL of 725 lb. The head block has a WLL of 2,700 lb[2]. Even though the vertical forces are shown, the resultant forces are far more important to know because these are what approach the Working

[1]Working Load Limits will be explained in depth in Chapter 3.
[2]Rated Load Limits are based on manufacturer's data.

Load Limits. Look at Sheave #4 in the Force Diagram. It has a horizontal force of 274 lb, and a vertical force of 274 lb. The angle is 90 degrees. Using the formula for Resultant Loads[3], the resultant force on the loft block is calculated to be 387 lb. If the WLL of the loft block is 725 lb, we are well within the operational limits of the hardware. Adding up all the vertical loads on the loft blocks, we get 1,900 lb horizontal force on the head block, and 1,900 lb. horizontal force needed to counterweight the load[4]. Working out the resultant forces for the head block, we get 2,687 lb - just under the WLL of 2,700 lb for the head block. One last point to remember; these load calculations are for *static* loads. Dynamic forces will be greater.

[3]The formula for is Resultant Force = Load (Sin of Angle/ (Sin of (Angle/2)). Resultant forces will be explained in Chapter 2.
[4]The structural engineer has set a maximum load for the batten of 1,900 lb based in part by the load capacity of the arbor.

Force Diagram Reaction Loads

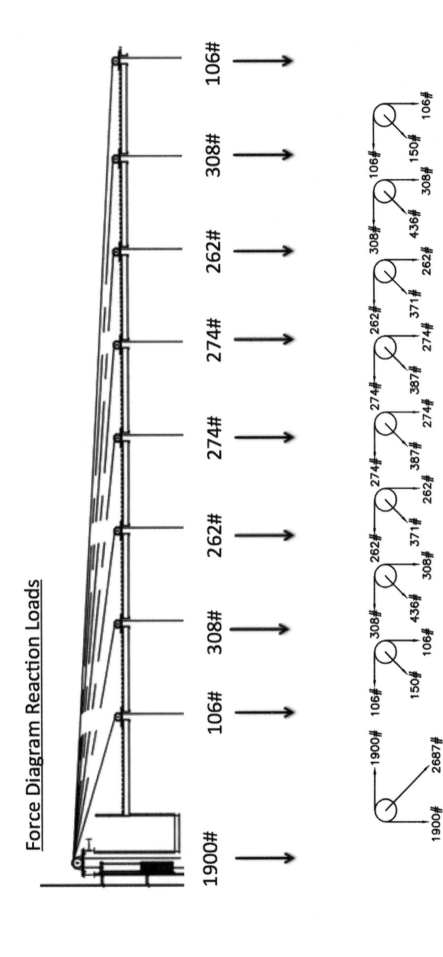

	Head Block Forces	Loft Block #1	Loft Block #2	Loft Block #3	Loft Block #4	Loft Block #5	Loft Block #6	Loft Block #7	Loft Block #8
Horizontal Force	1900#	106#	308#	262#	274#	274#	262#	308#	106#
Vertical Force	1900#	106#	308#	262#	274#	274#	262#	308#	106#
Resultant Force	2687#	150#	436#	371#	387#	387#	371#	436#	150#

Indeterminate Structure

When truss is rigged to three or more chain hoists, the phenomenon of *indeterminate structure* can be even more problematic. Counterweight battens are attached to lift-lines, then to arbors, and move at the same speed. Chain hoists, on the other hand, are rigging to the truss *independent* of any arbor and generally run at 16 fpm. However, chain hoist motors never run *exactly* at 16 fpm. There is always some variance due to voltage and loading. As noted earlier, this is NOT a concern if there are only two rigging points. But if there are MORE than two, great concern has to be taken to avoid overloading the truss on any given point. What happens is this:

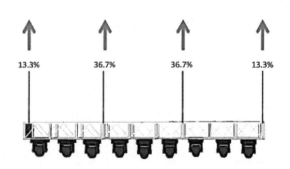

A truss with four rigging points could look like this.

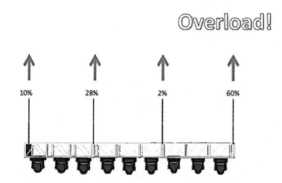

When raised, hoists running at slightly different speeds could cause the truss to look like this where one hoist overtakes the others and an "overload" situation may be created.

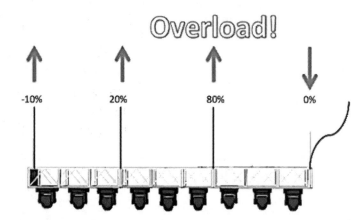

A chain reaction can follow as one overloaded point breaks, followed by the others. Recent concert stage rigging failures can ultimately be traced to failures such as this.

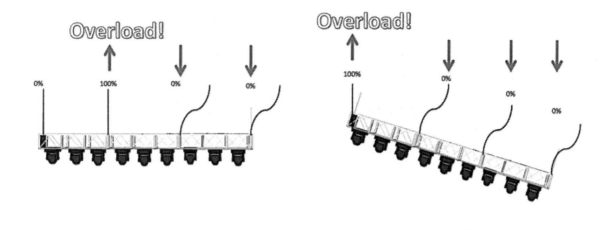

Ooops!

Even if the hoists are run as a group and LOOK horizontal, one hoist still has the possibility of overtaking the others. Visually checking the truss for horizontal (or with a level) WILL NOT insure that the loads are where they should be. The only way to insure the loads are distributed uniformly is by the use of *Load Cells.*

Shackled Load Cells
Photo courtesy of Ron StageMaster and Eilon Engineering Ltd

What do Load Cells do?

Load cells usually connect between the hoist hook and the truss round sling. What they do is monitor the dynamic loads on each point as the truss is being raised. If one hoist starts ascending faster or slower than the others, the stage technician can re-adjust the trim on each individual hoist so that the read-out is uniform across the truss. In other words, if the total UDL is 8400 lb., the trim on each hoist can be adjusted to be 1400-lb per hoist. This now makes every rigging point equal to each other and under the equipment Working Load Limits.

Rigging Truss in a Theatrical Venue

Due to dynamic forces, chain hoists should not be rigging off the battens. Hoists should be rigged off the grid as dead-hangs. Truss can be attached to battens only if they are attached *directly* to the battens with attachment points made as close to the lift-lines as possible.

Load data for each of the rigging points and their location is crucial to accurately plan for and safely suspend each point from the grid. In the case of extremely heavy loads, such as video walls, the rigging points should be attached directly to structural I-beams and not directly to the grid. In any case, a structural engineer should be consulted. Most production designers try and create plots using only two rigging points. However, in the case of video walls and some lighting truss, three or more rigging points are often unavoidable. A portion of a six-point video wall from a rigging plot is shown below.

| V1 | V2 | V3 | V4 | V5 | V6 |
| 856 lb. | 2094 lb. | 1830 lb. | 1830 lb. | 2094 lb. | 856 lb. |

A portion of a rigging plot, with a six-point truss showing static loads

The hanging points are labeled V1, V2, V3, V4, V5 and V6 and the load on each point is shown below the number. The video wall and truss itself is a UDL so the weight of the wall is distributed evenly over the entire length of the 40 ft. span. Even though the structure is indeterminate, some calculation can be made. To begin, the total load of the video wall is 8,000 lb. The 40-ft truss weighs 400 lb. That will give us a UDL of 8,400 lb. Using the **Loading Diagram Chart** for a span with six points, we get V1 at 663.6 lb, V2 at 1,898.4 lb, V3 at 1,638 lb, V4 at 1,638 lb, V5 at 1898.4 lb, and V6 at 663.6 lb. Taking the total UDL and multiplying by the percentage of each point will give us these numbers. Next, we add to each point the weight of the hoist and chain. For our rigging plot, each hoist weighs 112 lb and the chain weight is 1 lb. per foot. So 80 feet of chain weighs 80 lb. The total hoist and chain weight added to each point will be 192 lb. This will give us the loads shown on each rigging point on the rigging plot above.

Example:
To find the load on V1, we take the total load of 8,400 lb x 7.9% = 663.6 lb. We do this for each point based on the percentage for each point on the **Loading Diagram Chart**. Check your math by adding the loads on all of the lift lines together. The sum should be equal to the total load being supported – 8,400 pounds in this case. Next, add the weight of the hoist and chain to each point, 192 lb.

So, with hoist and chain weight added, we get for each point:
V1= 855.6, V2= 2,090.4, V3= 1,830, V4= 1,830, V5= 2,090.4, V6= 855.6

Additional considerations are as follows:

1. **Hoist and hardware selection.** Typical hoists available are 1-Ton and 2-Ton. Because rigging points V2 and V4 are 2,090.4 lb each, it is obvious that we will choose 2-Ton hoists over 1-Ton hoists for our plot. With 2-Ton hoists, we generally select ½" steel for the legs and baskets with ¾" shackles.

2. **Dynamic Loading.** Loads increase when raised. How will this affect the rigging plot? We need to take this into consideration in our equipment selection.

3. **Truss loading on the spans and rigging point spacing.** The truss is 40 feet long and made up of 8-foot sections. Load data charts will need to be consulted to see if additional rigging points will need to be added to support the dynamic weight. For this example, we assume that we are good to go.

Most production designers add an additional 25% to each rigging point to account for dynamic forces. Assuming our 6-point, 40-foot truss passes manufacturer's load data for 8-foot sections, our revised rigging plot for the six-point video wall will now have 25% added to each point along with 2-Ton hoists.

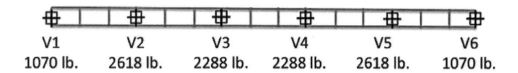

| V1 | V2 | V3 | V4 | V5 | V6 |
| 1070 lb. | 2618 lb. | 2288 lb. | 2288 lb. | 2618 lb. | 1070 lb. |

The same six-point rigging plot with a 25% dynamic increase on each point

In the revised rigging plot shown above, we have added 25% to account for dynamic forces. We've included the hoist and chain weight to this because these will also be part of the dynamic forces. (Note that on points V3 and V4, we are still 1,382 lb. well under the WLL for a 2-Ton.) But how do we account for *indeterminate* structure to our plot? The answer is, we can't. The only action available to us is the use of load cells. However, some touring productions still do not want to absorb these additional rental costs. (It is this author's opinion that if you compare rental costs to the expense of accident related lawsuits and litigation, you will soon see that load cells are *extremely* affordable!)

Some productions not using load cell during their tour, will use them during their technical rehearsals only. During tech rehearsals, technicians will monitor the load cell readings and record the averages for each point as the truss or video wall is being raised. If the truss/ video wall is only being raised to a height of 35 feet, they note the most extreme load variance on each hoist. As long as these readings fall well below the WLL of the hardware, then they will maintain the truss level by measurement alone. They will assign specific hoists with known, limited speed variances to that truss. Still, this can be risky. Load cells are recommended.

Calculating Accurate Dynamic Loads

Previously, we simply added 25% of the load onto each rigging point to account for dynamic loads. This is a fairly quick method, but it lacks accuracy. Let's compare the 25% method to a more accurate calculation of dynamic forces. Learning to calculate the dynamic forces on a rigging point is not as hard as it may seem.

Example:
A 180-lb man steps into an elevator and presses the button for the 15th floor. It takes 5 seconds for the elevator to overcome inertia and attain a speed of 16 feet-per-minute. How much force is exerted during acceleration? Let's first calculate the *rate of acceleration*. It takes the elevator 5 seconds to reach a speed of 16 fps.

16 fps / 5 sec = 3.2 fps^2

Next, we will use Newton's Second Law of Physics, Force = Mass X Acceleration.

Inserting these values into the formula, we get:

F = 180 pounds X ((32-feet + 3.2-feet/sec^2)/acceleration of gravity [*32 feet-per-sec^2*]) = 198-pounds.

or

F= 180 x ((32+3.2)/32) = 198

The man weighs 180-pounds at rest but 198-pounds due to force exerted during the 5 seconds upward acceleration at 16 fps. But it is not the man's weight that increased because his weight is a constant; it was the dynamic forces exerted that caused the increase.

Inversely, there would be less force on the person during deceleration. Reversing our formula, we get:

F = 180 pounds X ((32-feet - 3.2-feet/sec^2)/acceleration of gravity [*-32 feet-per-sec^2*]) = 162 pounds.

or

F= 180 x ((32-3.2)/-32) = 162

Since we are more concerned with upward acceleration forces on a truss, than deceleration forces, let's look at the upward acceleration of a chain hoist.

 Example:
A 500-lb load is to be raised by a 112-lb chain hoist. The total load to be raised will be 612 lb. The hoist ascends at a rate of 16 feet-per-minute or 0.266666 feet per sec (16 fpm / 60 sec. = 0.266666). It takes less than 1 second for the hoist to overcome inertia.
0 .266666 fps / 1 sec = 0.266666 fps^2

Next we calculate the dynamic load to the rigging point during its upward acceleration. Force = Mass X Acceleration.

F = 612 pounds X ((32-feet + .266666-feet/sec^2)/acceleration of gravity [32 feet-per-sec^2]) = 617.09-pounds.

or

F=612 X ((32+.266666)/32) = 617.09

This may not seem like a lot, but remember, we do this for each rigging point. Let's compare this quotient of 617 pounds to our 25% example.

612 x 25%= 765

The 25% seems to add a substantial safety factor to our point, but there is another factor we have yet to consider: *shock loads*.

Shock loads

In the introduction to this chapter, we commented that dynamic forces are simply a multiplying factor of the static load, which is a constant. A shock load is an excessive dynamic force created by the sudden acceleration or deceleration of an object. The formula for a shock load is:

Shock load = Weight ((Free Fall Distance / Stopping Distance) + 1)

Example:
A 50 lb. object falls 20 ft. to the ground. The stopping distance is a *sudden* 0.03 ft. Plugging these numbers in to our formula, we get:

Shock load = 50 ((20 / .03) + 1) = 33383.333 lb force.

Wow! That's a lot. But the stopping distance of 0.03 feet is essentially the "sudden" deceleration distance. If we use the same example, but lengthening the deceleration distance to 2 feet, we get:

Shock load = 50 ((20 / 2) + 1) = 550 lb force.

Look how the force dropped from 33383.333-lb force to 550-lb force simply by lengthening the deceleration distance.

Shock loading on Truss

As you've seen by the sudden deceleration of loads above, similar forces can be experienced when "bumping" a chain hoist(s). It is important to limit this sudden loading especially when raising a truss for the first time. Truss should be raised slowly at first to take up any slack on the bridle legs and round slings. "Bumping" once or twice will settle everything in and avoid sudden loading on the system. However, every time a hoist is "bumped" resonances momentarily resound in the rigging connections. Continuous "bumping" will compound those resonances by compounding the load. It is best to wait a few seconds before "bumping" the hoist again so as to let the resonances settle. The illustration below shows what happens when a 200-lb load is dropped 2 feet. The load was measured using a load cell and graphed. The shock load measured 2,168 lb. of force; note the oscillations that followed. Had the same load been dropped too soon, that same 2,168 lb would have added itself onto the oscillations.

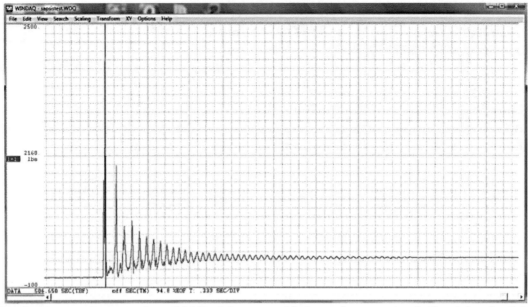

Here's what happens when you drop 200 lb, 2 feet on cable hung from a tripod. Shock load = 2,168 lbs. Note the oscillations that follow.

photo courtesy of Jonathan Deull

Summary

This chapter examined static and dynamic loads and forces. Dynamic forces occur when objects accelerate or decelerate. These forces are multiplying factors of the static load, which are always a constant. Remember, if an object is moving at a constant speed there is no dynamic force created. So, a static load can be either a load that is stationary or a load that is neither accelerating nor decelerating. Dynamic forces are created necessary to overcome *inertia*. *Shock loads,* on the other hand, are extreme examples of dynamic forces at work. A *shock load* is an excessive *dynamic* force created by the sudden acceleration or deceleration of an object. Understanding the rate of acceleration or deceleration is a key factor in the creation of all dynamic forces.

Chapter 2:
Pulleys and Forces

Introduction

Before we get into the permanent rigging systems that we typically see in theatres, we think that an understanding of the mechanics of rigging, particularly an understanding of pulleys and how they affect forces, will be beneficial. This chapter will begin by looking at a simple rigging system and advance to compound rigging systems. We will also look at how the loads on pulley systems affect the beams that support them.

A Pulley

A pulley is a simple device that uses a rotating wheel, called a sheave, to change the direction of a line (fiber or wire rope). The sheave rotates around an axle that is supported by side-plates. Often, friction between the sheave and the axel is reduced by a bushing (sometimes called a "common bearing"), which is a slick material between the sheave and the axel, or bearings (needle bearings, roller bearings or ball bearings). Because friction between the sheave and the axel makes the sheave more difficult to turn, it is important that the bearings be as efficient as possible. This is especially true when the pulley is used to lift a heavy load or when many pulleys are used in a system. A pulley is also referred to as a "block," hence the term "block and tackle," referring to pulleys and rope. A pulley typically has a means of mounting to a beam, an eye, a hook or mounting holes. A pulley might also have a secondary attachment point, called a becket, where a line can be attached.

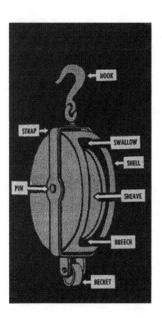

The designs for pulley blocks can vary greatly, depending on their use. Some pulleys only allow the end of the line to be fed over sheave, while other pulleys, often referred to as "snatch blocks" open to allow the middle of the line to be inserted over the sheave. Below are examples two different types of snatch blocks.

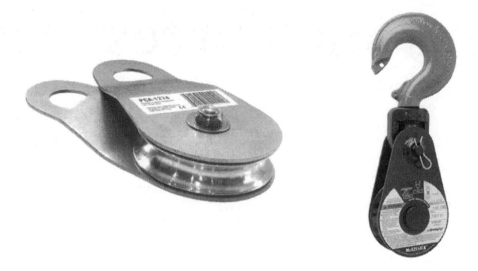

A pulley, or more specifically, the pulley's sheave, is intended to be used with a specific type of line, (either fiber or wire rope), as well as a specific size of line. To understand this this better, we look at the D:d of the sheave and the line.

When we speak of the D:d ratio, we are speaking of the diameter of the sheave's tread (D) compared to the diameter of the fiber or wire rope that runs over the sheave (d).

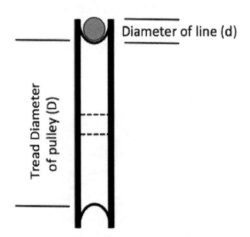

This ratio affects the strength of the line, as well as its lifespan. The smaller the D:d ratio, the sharper the bend and the greater the stress on the line. Both fiber and wire rope manufacturers have "Recommended D:d Ratios" for their products.

Most manufacturers of fiber ropes recommend a minimum D:d ratio of 8:1, although it is common to see ropes passing over sheaves with a D:d ratio of 4:1 or smaller. The minimum recommended D:d ratio for 7x19 and 6x19 construction wire ropes (the most common constructions used in entertainment rigging) is 30:1. Wire ropes with 7x7 construction are stiffer and have a recommended minimum D:d ratio of 40:1. Several sheave manufacturers make sheaves for wire ropes that have D:d ratios of 40:1, 20:1, and smaller. Ratios of 16:1 and smaller significantly decrease the lifespan of the cable. Using a sheave with a D:d ratio that is greater than the recommended minimum D:d ratio will give the rope a greater lifespan.

The sharpness of the bend on the rope also decreases the breaking strength of the rope. The listed breaking strength of a rope is based on a "straight pull." When a rope is forced to bend around a sheave, the tension on the outside of the bend is greater than the tension at the core of the rope, thereby reducing the breaking strength. The table below shows the strength efficiency rating of 7x19 and 6x19 construction wire ropes, based on various D:d ratios.

D:d Ratio	Strength Efficiency	D:d Ratio	Strength Efficiency
40:1	95%	6:1	79%
30:1	93%	8:1	83%
20:1	91%	4:1	75%
15:1	89%	2:1	65%
10:1	86%	1:1	50%

To determine the minimum recommended diameter of sheave for a particular diameter of wire rope, use this equation:

Sheave diameter (in inches) = "D" factor of the D:d ratio × diameter of the rope

Example: What is the minimum recommended sheave diameter that should be used with a ¼" diameter 7x19 GAC?

Sheave diameter = 30 × 1/4"
Sheave diameter = 30/4
Sheave diameter = 7.5 inches

Just as important as the D:d ratio is the diameter of the rope compared to the size of the groove in the sheave. This is particularly important for wire rope. The groove in the sheave should be slightly larger than the diameter of the rope. The groove should support between 120 and 170 degrees of the circumference of the rope. If less than 120 degrees of the rope's circumference is supported (the groove is too large), the rope will "flatten" on the sheave's tread, and damage the rope. Be sure that the groove is properly sized for the diameter of rope that you are using.

A pulley block can contain more than one sheave, typically up to four sheaves. The conventional arrangement of these sheave is on a single axel, with each sheave on its own plane. However, a "fiddle block" arranges the sheaves on multiple axles, all on the same plane.

Convention pulley   Fiddle pulley

Although they both types of blocks serve the same purpose, the line is reeved very differently when they are used in a block and tackle system.

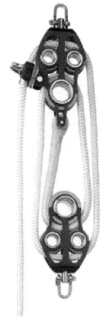

Both systems above have a 4:1 MA

Simple Pulley Systems

A typical block and tackle rig is a simple pulley system, meaning that it uses a single line and it typically used to create a mechanical advantage (although later we will discuss mechanical disadvantage). In a block and tackle rig, one block is attached to a structural member and does not move, while the other block, to which the load is attached (although not always directly to this pulley), moves at the same rate as the load. These moving pulleys are sometimes called "running" pulleys. Look at the two examples below and ask yourself, "Is there a pulley in motion (is there a running pulley)?" If the answer is "No" then there is no mechanical advantage. If the answer is "Yes" then there is a mechanical advantage, and you will need to figure out how much.

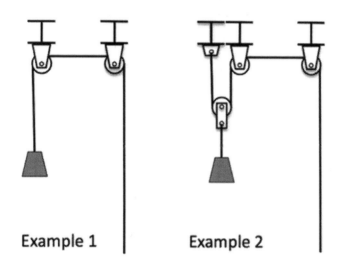

Example 1   Example 2

Before we learn to figure out how much mechanical advantage exists, let's look at how mechanical advantage is expressed. Typically, mechanical advantage is expressed as a ratio, such as 2:1. The number on the left is the "result" of the "effort" of the number on the right. In this example, 2 pounds can be supported for every 1 pound of effort. So, 300 pounds of load can be supported with only 150 pounds of effort. If the mechanical advantage (MA) is 5:1, 300 pounds can be supported with only 60 pounds of effort.

Wow, mechanical advantage is great. But not perfect. You do not get something for nothing. What you give up is speed of lifting. With a 5:1 MA the person doing the lifting must pull 5 feet of rope in order to lift the load 1 foot. So, mechanical advantage is wonderful if you need to lift a heavy load, but DO NOT have to lift it quickly.

Sometimes you see mechanical advantage listed as a single number, such as 2 or 5. These are simplified version of 2:1 and 5:1. Think of them as 2 divided by 1 equals **2**, and 5 divided by 1 equals **5**. This abbreviation works well until you get to complex mechanical advantages such as 3:2 (3 pounds can be supported for every 2 pounds of effort, which we will discuss later in this lesson).

Computing Mechanical Advantage

Computing mechanical advantage is almost as easy as counting, but first you have to know "what" to count. The "what" is the number of parts of the lift line that are applying a force on the running pulley. Because mechanical advantage is created by the running pulley, that is where you must look.

A helpful "Rule of Thumb" for quickly determining mechanical advantage is to count the number of parts of the lift line that are applying force on the running block. Remember, it does not matter if the load being lifted is connected directly to the running pulley or to a secondary line that is connected to the running pulley (and that line passes over other pulleys). The mechanical advantage is created by the number of lift line parts (the one the operator pulls) acting upon the running pulley.

Look at the three examples below. Identify the running block in each example and count the number of parts of the lift line that are acting upon it. Despite the number of pulleys in each system, they are all examples of 2:1 MA because the running pulley is acted upon by only two parts of the lift line.

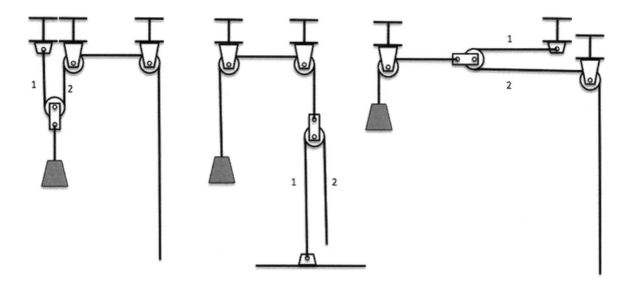

Note: All of the systems above are simple pulley systems because there is only one pulley in motion.

A 2:1 MA is about as simple as you can get. When you have an "odd" amount of MA, one part of the lift line must connect directly to the running pulley. See the examples of a 3:1 MA and 5:1 MA below.

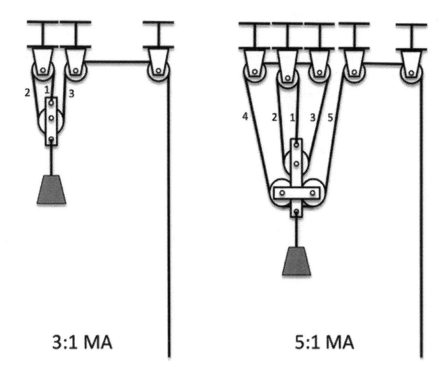

3:1 MA   5:1 MA

Below are two examples of more complex 3:1 mechanical advantage rigging systems.

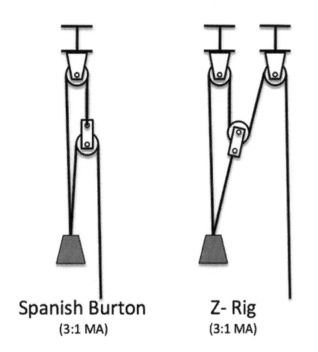

Spanish Burton
(3:1 MA)

Z- Rig
(3:1 MA)

To figure out the MA of these systems you need to think of each one as a two-part system that is interlinked (the MAs added to reveal the total MA). Below is a diagram of the two parts of the Spanish Burton. What is confusing is that some components are used in both sub-systems in different ways but at the same time.

The pulley shown in the diagram in the left (below) functions as a stationary pulley, so the line passing through it and to the load has a 1:1 mechanical advantage. The diagram on the right shows this same pulley as a moving pulley and the two parts of the line passing through it. This creates a 2:1 mechanical advantage that acts upon the line attached to the top of this pulley. This line travels to the load to create a second lifting line with its own mechanical advantage. Since both of these actions are occurring at the same time, we have to add the two mechanical advantages. Therefore, the total mechanical advantage is 3:1.

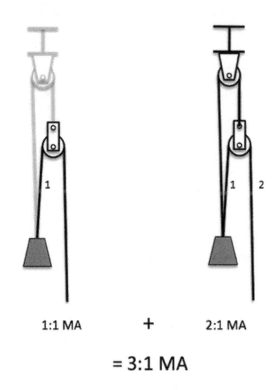

1:1 MA   +   2:1 MA

= 3:1 MA

After you have studied this system, try to figure out how the Z-Rig works.

Compound Rigging Systems

Compound rigging systems use two or more lines, and moving pulleys, to create the mechanical advantage. They are essentially two separate MA systems where the moving pulley for one system pulls the operating line of the second system, and so on. It is possible to chain these systems together to create systems with very large mechanical advantage. Look at the example of a two-part compound system below.

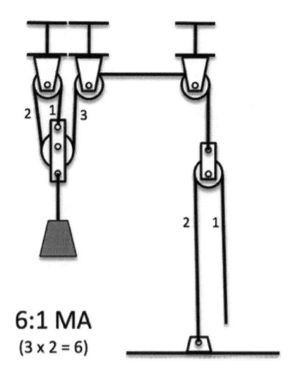

6:1 MA

(3 x 2 = 6)

Mechanical Disadvantage

Earlier, I described the MA ratio by saying, "The number on the left is the 'result' of the 'effort' of the number on the right." This implies that there are two parts to every MA system. When we wanted to create a simple mechanical advantage (2:1, 3:1, 4:1, 5:1 etc.), we were only concerned with creating the "result" since our natural effort is 1. What if 2:1 is too much MA (too slow) but 1:1 is not enough MA? Is there a way to rig something in between (1.5:1)? Of course we would not express it this way, since "1.5" is not a whole number and there is no way to rig a "half" of a MA. But 3:2 is the same ratio as 1.5:1, and we can rig a 3:2 MA.

To understand these ratios a little better, let's look at it graphically. Look at the drawing below. Remember when I said, "Because mechanical advantage is created by the running pulley, that is where you must look." Well, what is the dividing line between the two parts of the system? It is the colon (:). On one side is a 3:1 MA and on the other is a 1:1 MA (no mechanical advantage). When you combine these halves (multiply the two left halves of the ratios together and then the right halves of the ratios together), the result is 3:1.

Note: Anytime you multiply any ratio by 1:1, you get the original number.

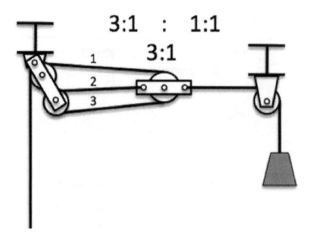

So, to get a 3:2 MA, we need to have a 3:1 MA on one side and 1:2 MA on the other (3 x 1 = <u>3</u> and 1 x 2 = <u>2</u>, so 3:2).

What is a 1:2 MA? It is a mechanical disadvantage (MD) – where the result is less than the effort. In this example, it means that 1 pound of load can be supported for every 2 pounds of effort. In effect, it divides our efforts in half. And half of 3 is 1.5, exactly what we wanted. This system would look like:

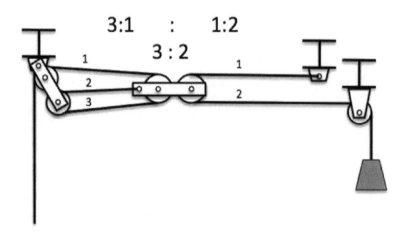

This is an example of a "compound" mechanical advantage system. A compound mechanical advantage system is where you have one simple mechanical system acting upon another simple mechanical advantage system. Sometimes one of the systems is mechanical disadvantage, as above, and sometimes it just multiplies the mechanical advantage of the first system.

While mechanical disadvantage is not as common as mechanical advantage, is still commonly used in some theatrical rigging systems. For example, double-purchase mechanical counterweight systems, which you will learn about in Chapter 6, uses both mechanical advantage and mechanical disadvantage. The 1:2 mechanical disadvantage allows the batten to move twice as fast as the arbor and the mechanical advantage makes it easier to move the arbor and the load being lifted.

Resultant Forces

We have already stated that a pulley is used to change the direction of a rope or cable. What is less understood is the load that is exerted on a pulley and beam to which the pulley is attached when a pulley system is used in lifting a load. The term "resultant force" is commonly used to refer to the load on the pulley and its supporting beam. It should be understood that the load/force on the beam is seldom equal to the load being lifted. This force can be a fraction of the load being lifted or as great as twice the load being lifted.

In Chapter 1, we looked a force diagram showing the tension on the lift lines of a mechanical counterweight system. We also showed the resultant force on each loft block and the head block (and the structure supporting them). Now, let's look at how these resultant forces were calculated.

The determining factors of the resultant force is 1) the tension on the line (the Load) and how much the line bends around the sheave of the pulley as it changes direction (the inclusive angle).

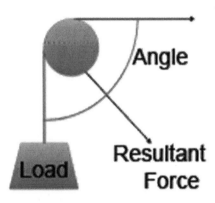

Also, note that the direction/angle of the resultant force bisects the two lines. So if the angle of the cable is 90 degrees, the resultant force is at 45 degrees. The equation for computing the resultant force is:

$$Resultant\ Force = Load \times \frac{sine\ of\ angle}{sine\ of\ (angle/2)}$$

Don't let this formula scare or confuse you. This equation can be broken into two parts: The first part is the load being lifted, and the second part, the scary and confusing part, is the multiplying factor (MF). The MF is the sine of the angle divided by the sine of half the angle as shown by the formula:

$$\frac{sine\ of\ angle}{sine\ of\ (angle/2)}$$

This MF is based on the angle of the rope/cable going into the sheave compared to the angle of rope/cable after it exits the sheave. Below are some examples of "angles" in order to help you understand them better.

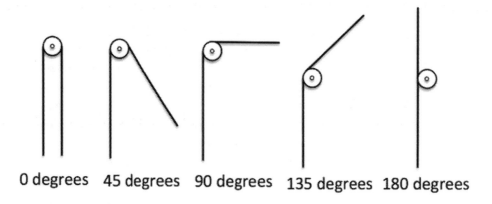

0 degrees   45 degrees   90 degrees   135 degrees   180 degrees

So, using this equation, let's work through a problem.

Example: What is the resultant force on a beam when the load being lifted is 200 lb and the angle of the cable is 90 degrees?
First, let's compute the multiplying factor (using a TI-30XA scientific calculator).

[ON/C] 90 [SIN] [÷] 45 [SIN] [=] **1.41**

Note: Since I could calculate $\frac{90}{2}$ *in my head (45), I did.*

Now, I multiply the MF (the result of my last calculation) by the Load.

[X] 200 [=] **282.84 lb**

Note: Since I wanted to use the result of my last calculation in this one, I did not press the [ON/C] to clear that result.

Using the same Load, try different angles. You will discover that the greater the angle, the lower the MF; and the smaller the angle, the greater the MF.

Note: If the angle is zero degrees, this formula does not work since you cannot divide by zero. Luckily, anytime your angle is zero degrees, your MF is automatically 2, which is easy to remember. In fact, you should "know" the MFs for many of the common angles. Here is a list:

Angle (degrees)	MF
0	2.0
90	1.41
120	1.0
180	0.0

IMPORTANT: Do not confuse the Resultant Force (the tension on the pulley and the structure supporting the pulley) with the tension on the rope/cable. If the load that is being lifted weighs 200 pounds, then 200 pounds is the tension on the rope/cable, even if the Resultant Force on a pulley and supporting beam is different.

One last thing: if you do not know the angle, you can calculate it using the formula:

$$Angle = Arctangent\ of\ \left(\frac{Offset}{Distance}\right)$$

Resultant Force at Zero Degrees

When the angle of the line is zero degrees, such as with a block-and-tackle, use the following rules to find the resultant force on the beam:

- If the working end of the line is coming off of a <u>stationary</u> pulley, then

  Resultant Force = Load + force need to support the load

- If the working end of the line is coming off of a <u>moving</u> pulley, then

  Resultant Force = Load - force need to support the load

Let's look at some examples.

Example 3   Example 4

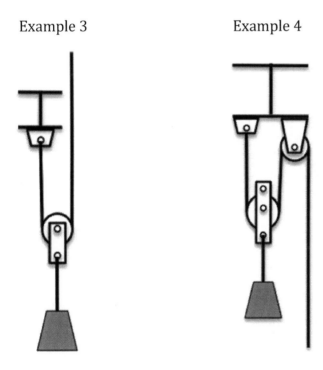

In both of these examples we have a 2:1 mechanical advantage, but the result forces on the beams are considerable different. Assuming the load in both examples are 100 pounds, let's calculate the load on the beam.

In Example 3, the working end of the line is coming off a moving pulley, so we use the formula: *Resultant Force = Load - force need to support the load.* Because this is a 2:1 MA, the force needed to support the load is 50 pounds. *So,*
Resultant Force = 100 - 50
Resultant Force = 50 pounds

In Example 4, the working end of the line is coming off a stationary pulley, so we use the formula: *Resultant Force = Load + force need to support the load.* Again, the force needed to support the load is 50 pounds. *So,*

Resultant Force = 100 + 50
Resultant Force = 150 pounds

Let's look at two more examples.

Example 5   Example 6

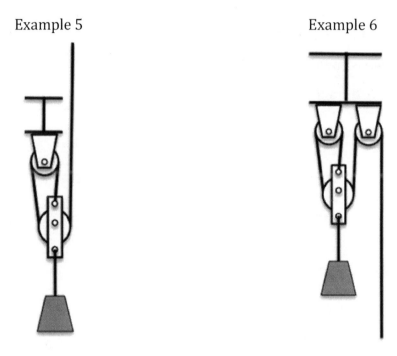

In both of these examples we have a 3: 1 MA. If the load is 100 pounds, then it take 33.33 pounds to support the load. Let's calculate the Resultant Force on the beams for these examples.

In Example 5, the working end of the line is coming off a moving pulley, so:

Resultant Force = 100 - 33.33
Resultant Force = 66.67 pounds

In Example 6, the working end of the line is coming off a stationary pulley, so:

Resultant Force = 100 + 33.33
Resultant Force = 133.33 pounds

Note: http://www.thecrosbygroup.com/html/default.htm#/en/calc/snatchblockrigcalc.htm contains a calculator that can be used to determine the force on a beam in these types of rigs.

Horizontal and Vertical Forces on an Anchor Point
Earlier I said, "the direction/angle of the resultant force bisects the two lines. So if the angle of the cable is 90 degrees, the resultant force is at 45 degrees." This is very important here because

30

you need to know the angle of the Resultant Force in order to calculate the Horizontal and Vertical forces that the Resultant Force puts on the anchor point (the beam supporting the pulley).

Let's look at two examples:

Example 7.

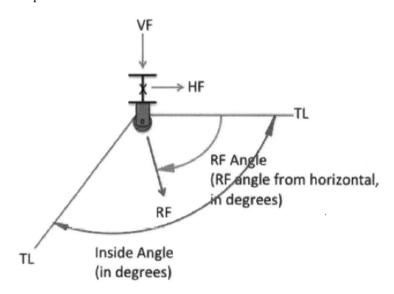

Below is the legend for this diagram.
TL - Tension on Line (Equal to the weight of the Load on Line)
RF - Resultant Force
HF - Horizontal Force on point
VF - Vertical Force on point

The two equations you need are:
$$HF = RF \times COS \ of \ RF \ Angle$$
and
$$VF = RF \times SIN \ of \ RF \ Angle$$

So, let's solve Example 7.

If *Load* = 100 lb and RF *Angle* = 50 degrees
TL = 100 lb
RF = 128.55 lb
HF = 82.63 lb
VF = 98.48 lb

Example 8.

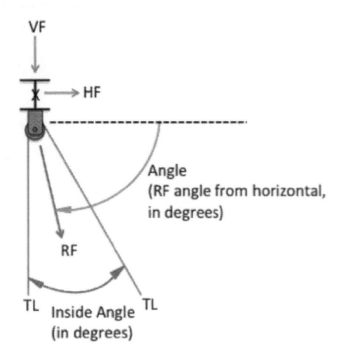

VF

HF

Angle
(RF angle from horizontal,
in degrees)

RF

TL   TL
Inside Angle
(in degrees)

If *Load* = 100 lb and RF *Angle* = 75 degrees
TL = 100 lb
RF = 193.185 lb
HF = 50 lb
VF = 186.6 lb

Note: For this type of problem, you must always measure the RF angle from the horizontal line that is on the same side of the pulley as the RF.

While you may not commit these formulas to memory, knowing the Horizontal and Vertical forces can be very useful in many rigging situations, so remember where they are found in this book so that you can find them when you need them.

Summary

All theatre rigging involves pulleys and lines (fiber or wire rope). Sometimes the pulleys are simply used to change the direction of the line and sometimes it is used to create mechanical advantage or mechanical disadvantage. No matter how it is used, all of the parts must work together, as a system to accomplish the desired task. An accomplished theatre technician must understand the role that each component in the system and how the components work together. Further chapters with describe various types of rigging systems and how we use them in productions.

Part II:
The Stage and Its Equipment

Chapter 3:

Stage Equipment and Rigging Installations

Introduction

All equipment and hardware has limitations. The equipment and hardware we use in the theatre is no exception. One reason catastrophic failures occur is because the load placed on a structural member or a piece of hardware exceeds the breaking strength of the structural member or hardware. While a structural engineer must determine the strength of the structural members and the manufacturers determine the strength of the hardware, the rigger and technical designer are responsible for knowing the forces that will be exerted on each rigging point and piece of hardware. These forces are determined not only by the weight of the object (its static load) but also how the rigging is installed and dynamic forces each object will sustain. Theatre Riggers as well as Technical Designers must be able to calculate all of these loads/forces successfully.

This chapter will focus on *stage equipment*, how it is installed, examine *Working Load Limits (WLL)*, *Minimum Breaking Strengths*, *Design Factors*, *Fleet Angles*, and *D:d ratios.* Let's begin by looking at *Minimum Breaking Strengths* and *Working Load Limits*, what they are, and how they are determined. Automated stage equipment will be explained separately in Chapter 12.

Working Load Limits and Design Factors
Most of the hardware we use in the entertainment industry falls into one of two categories: industrial hardware (i.e. shackles and slings) and recreational hardware (i.e. carabineers and climbing loops). Most industrial hardware is stamped with a *Working Load Limit (WLL)* or *Safe Working Load (SWL)*, whereas recreational hardware is mark with it *Minimum Breaking Strength (MBS),* usually expressed in kiloNewtons (kN). To understand the WLL of a piece of hardware, you must first understand its MBS, and how it is derived.

Most hardware manufacturers use a statistical method called "3 sigma" to determine the MBS of their products. Cancord Inc., a manufacturer of fiber rope, explains 3 sigma this way,

This means the minimum breaking strength is calculated by taking the mean or average breaking strength of 5 rope samples, and subtracting 3 standard deviations. Statistically, this creates a confidence level of 99.87% that any sample of rope will actually be stronger than the quoted minimum breaking strength.

Got it? Probably not, so let's look at the theoretical results of a destructive test done on five samples of a fictional new product - a "Rigging Widget."

Sample #	BS (kN)
1	31
2	31
3	30
4	30
5	29.5

Now that we have the results of the five samples, we need to find the <u>Mean</u> (average) of these tests.

Mean = 30.3

Next, we find the <u>Variance</u>. To find the Variance, we need to do several things. First, find the difference from the Mean for each sample. We do this by subtracting the Mean from the BS. Next, we square each difference (BS-Mean)^2. Third, we total this column for the five samples - giving us 1.8. See table below.

Sample #	BS (kN)	BS - Mean	(BS - Mean)^2
1	31	0.7	0.49
2	31	0.7	0.49
3	30	- 0.3	0.09
4	30	- 0.3	0.09
5	29.5	- 0.8	0.64

Total = 1.8

The final step is to divide this total by the number of samples.

Variance = 0.36

The Standard Deviation is the square root of the Variance, so
Standard Deviation = 0.6

Since Standard Deviation is often denoted by the Greek letter sigma, 3 sigma is three times the Standard Deviation.

3 Sigma = 1.8

Now that we know 3 Sigma we can calculate the Minimum Breaking Strength. It is the Mean minus 3 Sigma (three Standard Deviations).

Minimum Breaking Strength = (30.3 - 1.8) or **28.5 kN**

Since manufacturers always round to a whole number when listing the MBS, we would round this down and stamp **MBS 28 kN** on our rigging widgets.
It may seem odd that the rated MBS on our rigging widget is **28 kN**, while our lowest test result was **29.5 kN**, the Mean was **30.3 kN**, and just under half of our samples broke at **31 kN**, but that is how the MBS is calculated. It is possible for there to be test results that are lower than MBS derived with the 3 sigma method, but statically it is a very small number.

Now, the manufacturers of industrial hardware will assign their equipment a *Working Load Limit (WLL)* or *Safe Working Load Limit (SWL)* based on the calculated MBS and what they determine to be a safe operational margin or *Design Factor.*

The *Design Factor* creates a margin of safety to compensate for normal wear and less than optimal working conditions. *Design Factors* do NOT compensate for extreme shock loads, extensive wear/damage, or other factors that might cause the hardware to fail. All hardware used in rigging should be inspected before every install to ensure that it is not damaged.

All hardware does not have the same *Design Factor.* Below is a list of common *Design Factors* that are used by manufactures of different types of hardware for determining the *Working Load Limit.* Keep these in mind as we examine the stage hardware.

- Synthetic Slings: 5:1
- Wire rope slings: 5:1
- Stage rigging (counterweight rigging system, including the wire rope): 8:1
- Shackles: 6:1
- Base mounted drum hoists: 7:1
- Personnel lifts: 7:1 to 10:1
- Fiber ropes: 7:1 to 12:1
- Chain (except grade 43): 4:1
- Grade 43 chain: 3:1
- Ratchet straps: 3:1
- Most Sailing hardware (including stainless steel shackles): 2:1

The *Design Factor* that the WLL is based on is not commonly displayed on the hardware's packaging or even in literature from the manufacturer. Therefore, it is important that riggers be familiar with the common *Design Factors* above. If you are not sure of the *Design Factor* used to derive the WLL, you need to check with the manufacturer. Knowing the *Design Factor* for all rigging hardware is very important.

Whereas, the *Working Load Limit* is the maximum force that may be applied to the product, the *Design Factor* or DF is a number assigned by the manufacturer that determines the *Working Load Limit. Design Factors* are a percentage of the *Breaking Strength* and are often expressed as a ratio, such as 5:1 or sometimes as a single number, such as 5.

Example 1:
A piece of rigging hardware has a *Breaking Strength* of 1,400 lb. The manufacturer gives the hardware a *Working Load Limit* of 280 lb. What is the *Design Factor* being used?

To calculate this, simply divide 1,400 by 280. *Design Factor* is 5.

Example 2:
A shackle has a *Working Load Limit* of 6,500 lb. Using a *Design Factor* of 6, what is the *Breaking Strength* of the shackle?

6,500 x 6 = 39,000 lb

Remember, recreational hardware, such as carabiners, are marked with the *Breaking Strength* (usually in kiloNewtons) instead of a WLL. Note: Newtons and kiloNewtons are a measurement of Force. Sometimes weight and force are given in pounds, which can be confusing to the beginner or expert alike.

To convert kiloNewtons to pounds, multiply the MBS by 224.8. Example: If a carabineer has a rated MBS of 53 kN, it's MBS is 11,914.4 lb.

You now have to apply a *Design Factor* to the MBS. The General Rules of Thumb below are a good guideline.

General Rules of Thumb

- DF of 5:1 for Standing Rigging (i.e. rigging that does not move)
- DF of 8:1 for Running Rigging (rigging that moves)
- DF of 10:1 for rigging used in flying of people or moving over the heads of people

The Hardware

Now that we are familiar with *Working Load Limits (WLL)* and *Design Factors (DF)*, let's take a look at the stage hardware used on the stage. It was noted previously, that *counterweight rigging systems* have a *Design Factor* of 8:1. However, this factor is for loft blocks, head blocks, arbors, wire rope, and track. It does not include shackles, which will have a DF of 6:1; turnbuckles, which will have a DF of 5:1, or chain; which will have a DF of 4:1. This is why it is important for riggers to know *Design Factors*. As noted earlier, if in doubt, contact the manufacturer.

Battens and Batten Hardware

Battens and pipe grids are typically made from seamless Schedule 40 (sometimes Schedule 80) pipe with a matte black finish. They come in 21 ft. lengths with inside diameters of 1.25, 1.5 and 2 inches and then joined together to the desired length. Batten sections are spliced together using a couple of different methods. They are:

- Welding
- The 18" batten splice
- Mega-Quick pipe slice
- The Threaded Coupling (prohibited in most applications by ANSI E1.4–2014)

Of all the methods for joining pipe, welding is the more permanent method for joining. The problem with welding is that it requires a welder to be on hand during the installation and overall makes the installation process more complicated and expensive. Inversely, if a section of pipe needs to be replaced, it will require the damaged section to be "cut out" and removed. The reason for pipe splices and connectors is that it allows for ease and simplification during the install and avoids welding altogether. Today, the pipe splice is the most commonly means by which sections of the pipe batten are joined together[1].

The 18" batten splice shown below is made from an 18" section of pipe that can slide into an end of a batten section. It is joined together by 4 – grade 5, 3/8" bolts and *Nylock* nuts. The splice diameter will vary depending on the inside pipe batten diameter of the batten, but it is generally 1.5 inches. This method is commonly used, but demands that holes be pre-drilled into both the batten and the spice ahead of time. The bolt fasteners do stick out and can create problems with batten clamps or if a totally smooth pipe is required.

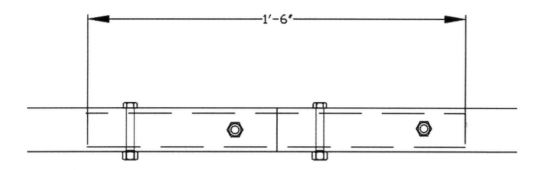

The standard batten splice

Mega-Quick splice is gaining in popularity because of its simplicity of design. It does not require any pre-drilling of holes, but simply slides into the pipe ends and is tightened in place by a single Allen key. This makes it very easy and cost effective on the installs. However, most installation companies prefer the *standard batten splice* to the *Mega-Quick* spice on *pipe battens* because of fear that the single Allen key could loosen with time. *The Mega-Quick* splice is excellent choice for pipe grids and other static installations.

---

[1]Note: Key Clamp sleeves are NOT to be used as batten connections because they do not support a load of 30 pounds per linear foot as recommended by ANSI E1.4-2014

The Mega-Quick pipe splice
-photo courtesy of Rose Brand

The Threaded Coupling Although threaded couplings can still be found in many older theatres, they are not a recommended for connecting pipe battens. In fact, they are prohibited for this purpose by ANSI E1.4-2014.

ANSI E1.4-2014 sec 3.9.1(b) says, in part, *"Battens exceeding one standard pipe length shall be joined using internal splicing sleeves. Threaded couplers shall not be permitted. Spliced battens shall have at least the same overall capacity, deflection, and strength as the component pipe."*

The Threaded Pipe Connector

Pipe Grid and other connections
When schedule 40 pipe is overlapped at 90 degree angles, connecting the intersection can be accomplished with:
- Cross Grid Connectors
- Roto-Locks
- Cheeseboughs

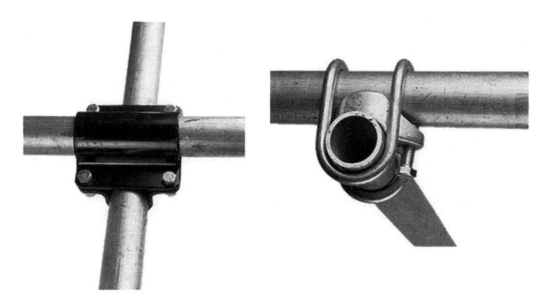

The Grid Cross Connector. RWL 1500 lb
-photo courtesy of JR Clancy

Roto Lock
-photo courtesy of Rose Brand

Cross Grid Connectors Pipe grids are comprised of schedule 40 - 1.5" steel pipe suspended in two levels. The first level is suspended from the building's structure while the lower level attaches to the upper level at a 90-degree angle forming a bay. The average bay measures 4 ft x 4 ft. These lower lever pipes are attached to the upper lever with *Cross Grid Connectors* and grade 5 bolts. What makes the *Cross Grid Connector* useful is the ease of installation. The lower level pipes are simply raised without having to slide them into position.

Roto-Locks can be used to secure short sections of pipe together. Because they require the lower pipe be slid through the *Roto-Lock,* it makes pipe grid installations impractical.

Cheeseboughs (scaffolding clamps) are often used for temporary pipe connections. They are both swivel and non-swivel.

A non-swivel cheesebough

Hanging the Pipe Batten
With the rope line system (hemp), lift lines were attached to pipe batten using a clove hitch followed by two half hitches (see Chapter 9). Later, when the counterweight system came into use, 6 x 7 wire rope sash cord was used for lift lines. Terminations to the batten were made using a clove hitch with the end of the sash cord wound around the standing part of the lift line. The ends were then taped. When these sash cord lift lines were exchanged for a more practical

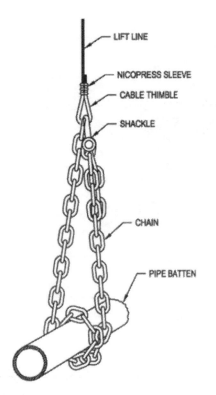

Labels on illustration:
- LIFT LINE
- NICOPRESS SLEEVE
- CABLE THIMBLE
- SHACKLE
- CHAIN
- PIPE BATTEN

Trim chain is an older but still acceptable way of attaching a batten to a lift line.

-photo courtesy of JR Clancy

7 x 19 galvanized aircraft cable, the terminations to the batten remained basically the same. This was not very efficient for trimming the batten, as the cable was not as flexible as rope and the kinks in the cable reduced the efficiency of the termination. Later, this was exchanged for a Grade 30 trim chain as seen in the illustration to the left. The trim of the batten was now easy to adjust as it could be done link by link with a shackle or quick link. Unfortunately, there was much contention over the use of Grade 30 chain as trim chain. Chain manufacturers state that Grade 30 chain is *"not to be used for overhead lifting."* Because the batten moves up and down, it was thought that the chain was being used in an overhead lifting application. We will discuss this problem later in Chapter 8 and Appendix 3.

Trimming the Batten

Another piece of hardware that is used for hanging and trimming a batten is a batten clamp.

The batten clamp

- photo courtesy of Rose Brand

With the *batten clamp*, lift lines can be trimmed with one or two methods. The first illustration below shows the batten clamp secured to the pipe batten. The lift line is attached to the clamp by means of a *turnbuckle*. The ends of the lift lines are terminated with a thimbled eye splice. A *jaw-to-jaw turnbuckle* attaches the lift line to the batten and allows for fine-tuning the batten trim. The *turnbuckle* is then *moused* to prevent rotation after the batten is in trim. *Mousing* involves securing the sleeve with a zip tie or wire to the jaw so as to prevent rotation.

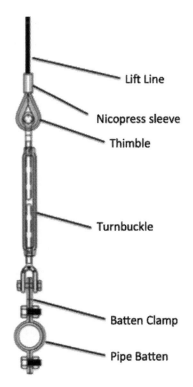

Lift Line

Nicopress sleeve

Thimble

Turnbuckle

Batten Clamp

Pipe Batten

Lift lines are best attached to the batten using a batten clamp and turnbuckle. The turnbuckle adjustment, but should be moused after adjustment to prevent rotation.

The other method for trimming the batten involves the *batten trim clamp* shown below. This system is used when the batten must be flown out close to the ceiling. The batten trim clamp runs the lift line through a pulley an over to a batten clamp. Moving the batten clamp thereby lengthens or shortens the lift line.

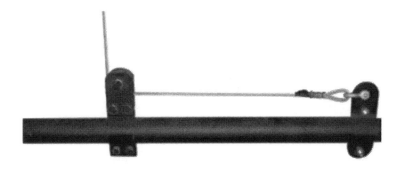

The batten trim clamp is used when headroom is at a premium

-photo courtesy of JR Clancy

Trim Plates

Another method of trimming a batten is with a trim plate. By changing the hole on the trim plate that is connected to the batten clamp, it is possible to adjust the trim up or down.

Kidney shaped trim plate

Load distribution on a pipe batten

According to the information on pipe battens that is part of ANSI E1.4-2014 Entertainment Technology — Manual Counterweight Rigging Systems. Section 3.9.1(c). This standard states,

> *"The batten shall be capable of supporting at minimum 45 kg/m (30 lbs/ft) of uniformly distributed load. Battens shall be capable of sustaining a point load of 45 kg (100 pounds) at mid-span between any two lift lines with a maximum span deflection of 1/180 of the span."*

This tells us two things: 1) when the pipe is uniformly loaded, it should hold a minimum of 30 pounds per linear foot without permanently bending; and 2) the force, placed on the center point of any span required to deflect the pipe 1/180 of the Span distance must be at least 100 pounds. Now that we know what requirements we are attempting to meet, let's look at how we calculate these numbers.

Before we start looking at equations, we need to know the physical/structural properties of pipe. Specifically, we need to know the pipe's Modulus of Elasticity (psi), Section Modulus (In³), Moment of Inertia (in³), Weight of pipe (per linear inch) and Yield Strength (psi).

Luckily, it is not as complicated and confusing as it all sounds. In fact, pipe manufacturers supply this information in tables, so you just have to look it up. The ASTM A53 pipe that is typically used for pipe battens, has a **Modulus of Elasticity (E) of 29,000,000 psi**, and a **Yield Strength (Fy) of 30,000 psi**.

Below is a table that contains most of the other information you need for commonly used sizes of pipe.

Schedule 40 Pipe

ID	Weight per ft	Weight per inch (W)	Section Modulus (S)	Moment of Inertia (I)
1"	1.68	0.14	0.13	0.09
1-1/4"	2.27	0.192	0.23	0.19
1-1/2"	2.72	0.2267	0.33	0.31
2"	3.65	0.3042	0.56	0.67

Schedule 80 Pipe

ID	Weight per ft	Weight per inch (W)	Section Modulus (S)	Moment of Inertia (I)
1"	2.17	0.1808	0.161	0.106
1-1/4"	3.0	0.25	0.291	0.242
1-1/2"	3.65	0.3042	0.412	0.391
2"	5.02	0.4183	0.731	0.868

Now that we have the data, let's look at how to calculate the maximum force, per linear foot, that we can put on a Span of pipe without permanently deforming it. Since we do not want to load the pipe to its yield point, because that is the point when it will permanently deform, it is common to calculate the load at two-thirds (0.6667) of the yield point. So, the equation to do this is...

$$UDL = (12 \times Fy \times 8 \times S / (W\texttt{\^{}}2) \times 0.6667) - Weight\ of\ pipe\ per\ foot$$

Using the information from the table above, let's calculate the UDL for 1-1/2" Schedule 40 pipe with a Span of 10.

$$UDL = ((12 \times 30{,}000 \times 8 \times 0.326 / ((10 * 12)\texttt{\^{}}2)) \times 0.6667) - 2.72$$

$$UDL = ((938{,}880 / 120\texttt{\^{}}2) \times 0.6667) - 2.72$$

$$UDL = ((938{,}880 / 14{,}400) \times 0.6667) - 2.72$$

$$UDL = (65.2 \times 0.6667) - 2.72$$

$$UDL = 43.47 - 2.72$$

$$UDL = 40.7\ pounds$$

Since 40.7 pounds is greater than 30 pounds minimum specified in this standard, a 10-foot Span is an acceptable span distance for this size pipe. Also, this calculation tells us the UDL that we can place on this pipe.

The second requirement of this standard is that the force, placed on the center point of any span, needed to deflect the pipe 1/180 of the Span distance, must be at least 100 pounds. Before we do this calculation, let's discuss the "1/180" part of it.

This number sets the stiffness required of the beam (or pipe, in this case). The higher the denominator, the stiffer the beam. For most beams, the denomination is either 120, 180, 240, 360 or higher. This number is not a safety matter. Rather, it is selected to ensure that the beam is rigid enough for the purpose it is used for. For example, a beam supporting a plaster ceiling or a tile floor needs a stiffness of at least L/120 in order to prevent the plaster or tile from cracking when the the beam bends under a load. (Note: "L" stands for "Length"). Stone needs a "fraction of deflection" of at least L/720. In this case, 180 was most likely selected because the pipe does not need to be exceptionally stiff. Jay Glerum discusses the allowable load for battens based on 1/240 of the span and J.R. Clancy's Allowable Batten Load table uses 1/360 of the span. Both of these allow less deflection than ANSI E1.4-2014.

The equation for calculating the max CPL on a pipe is:

$$Max\ CPL = \left(Fraction\ of\ deflection - 5 \times W \times (Span \times 12)^3 / (384 \times E * I)\right) \times 48 \times E \times I / (Span \times 12)^2$$

So, using the same 1-1/2" Schedule 40 pipe with a Span of 10 feet, let's calculate the maximum Center Point Load that can be placed on the beam when the deflection is 1/180 of the Span.

$$Max\ CPL = \left(0.005556 - 5 \times 0.226667 \times (120)^3 / (384 \times 29,000,000 \times 0.31)\right) \times 48 \times 29,000,000 \times 0.31 / (120)^2$$

$$Max\ CPL = \left(0.005556 - 5 \times 0.226667 \times 1,728,000 / (384 \times 29,000,000 \times 0.31)\right) \times 48 \times 29,000,000 \times 0.31 / 14,400$$

$$Max\ CPL = (0.005556 - 1,958,402.88 / 3,452,160,000) \times 431,520,000 / 14,400$$

$$Max\ CPL = (0.005556 - 0.000567298) \times 431,520,000 / 14,400$$

$$Max\ CPL = 0.004988702 \times 431,520,000 / 14,400$$

$$Max\ CPL = 2,152,724.687 / 14,400$$

$Max\ CPL = 149.5$ pounds

Because our result is greater than 100 pounds, that spacing of the lift lines allows the CPL to exceed the minimum requirement of ANSI 1.4, so it is "good to go."

If you know the CPL or UDL that you need to hang on a horizontal pipe, you can use the equations above to help you determine the size of pipe and the minimum spacing (span) between the lift lines for your needs.

Like other problems, this is one that would benefit greatly from being in a spreadsheet. You can download PipeLoad.xls from http://www.springknollpress.com/RiggingMath/downloads/.

Counterweight Rigging Systems and Hardware

There are many types of counterweight rigging systems. Each utilizes a variety of different rigging hardware and methods. A structural engineer and theatre consultant will best decide upon which system is best for that particular facility. The structural engineer will examine the structural framework of the building and determine what the building can support; a theatre consultant will help determine the specific needs of venue. Multi-use facilities must accommodate the needs of theatre, music, and dance events as well as serve classroom functions. These spaces must be adoptable for every function. This is where a theatre consultant can work together with the structural engineer to insure that the needs of the client are met.

In this section, we will be discussing the typical hardware used in *counterweight rigging systems* and the installation of that hardware. Later chapters will discuss the operation of these systems. Some of the terms we will be using are:

- **Grid or Gridiron:** an open framework of steel located above the stage for the support of stage rigging equipment and hardware. The grid provides access to head and loft blocks for inspection and maintenance as well as a framework for the attachment of spot lines and dead-hangs.
- **Loft Block:** a single grooved sheave assembly used in groups for the support of pipe battens.
- **Idler Blocks:** are small blocks that are attached to the sides of loft blocks that limit the sag of horizontally running lift lines.
- **Sag Bars** are bars support sagging lift lines. They run perpendicular to the lift lines supporting the longer running lines.
- **Mule Block**: a multi sheave block designed to change direction of the lift line between the loft block and head block.
- **Head Block:** a multi-grooved sheave assembly whose purpose is to gather all the lift lines from the loft blocks and reeve them toward the arbor.
- **Arbor:** A framed carriage designed to hold counterweight bricks so that the amount of counterbalance on the arbor is proportional to the load on the pipe batten.
- **Tension Block:** A single grooved sheave assembly mounted under the counterweight arbor. It reeves the purchase line from the bottom of the arbor carriage to the head block.
- **Rope Lock:** A device used to lock the purchase line thereby locking a balanced counterweight arbor at its required trim position in the fly loft.
- **Purchase Line:** A 3/4" diameter manila or synthetic rope that is reeved from the bottom of the arbor carriage, down through a floor block, up to a locking rail, up over the head block and back down to where it is tied off at the top of counterweight arbor. The purchase line controls the arbor.
- **Lift Lines:** 7x19 galvanized aircraft cable used to support a pipe batten at intervals of approximately ten feet on center. Cable diameter is 3/16" or 1/4".
- **Pipe Battens:** Typically, Schedule 40 - 1.5" inside diameter steel pipe.
- **Single Purchase System:** A counterweight system where one foot of arbor travel equals one foot of batten travel. When loading the arbor, the counterweight is equal to the batten weight.

- **Double Purchase System** A counterweight system where one foot of arbor travel equals two feet of batten travel. When loading the arbor, twice the amount of counterweight will be needed to offset the load on the pipe batten.
- **Wire Guide Systems:** A system which uses wire rope guides, instead of a rigid track, to direct the counterweight arbor. The Wire Guided System is economic to install but requires space between arbors and limits wire cable guides to 30 ft.
- **Rigid Guide Systems:** A system whereby steel tracks (J-track or T-track) are mounted to the wall of the theatre. The arbors guide in the tracks by means of shoes. The track height can be of any length.

Let's begin by looking at each of the components of the counterweight system. The details of the operation of counterweight systems will be discussed in Chapter 8. We will start with the *head and loft blocks* and how they are positioned in the over-hung and under-hung, *single* and *double purchase* counterweight systems.

Head and Loft Blocks

There are several types of *head* and *loft blocks* available on the market. A few of these are shown in the illustrations that follow. However, the choice of blocks will depend on how the blocks can be attached to the structural steel of the building, the load bearing capacities of the structural steel, and whether there is a gridiron or not. In each case, a theatre consultant along with a structural engineer will decide what type is feasible based on a structural analysis of the building. In the case of existing facilities, the choice of equipment may need to be adapted to suit field conditions. In new construction, an under-hung system with a gridiron is sometimes the easiest as the loft blocks can attach directly to the I-Beams that support the roof. A gridiron provides easy walking access to the blocks. With the over-hung system, the loft blocks are attached to the channel steel located at "wells", while separate I-Beams are installed for the *head blocks*.

One type of under-hung loft block. Note the addition of the idler block on the side

Typical over or under-hung single sheave loft block. Mounting can be to either one or two I-Beams

-photos courtesy of JR Clancy

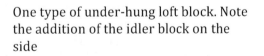

A typical over-hung or under-hung multi-sheave head block

The installation of *upright head and loft blocks* will require a steel gridiron with a series of *wells* for the attachment of *loft blocks*. The number of wells will usually dictate how many *loft blocks* will be used per line set. Separate raised steel I-Beams will be positioned to the off-stage wall for the attachment of *head blocks*. The illustration below shows a typical steel gridiron, wells and I-Beams. The next illustration shows typical *loft* and *head block* installation attached to the steel.

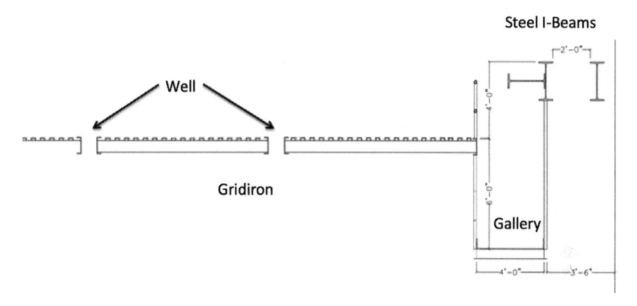

Loft blocks will be positioned over each well. Head blocks will be mounted over the steel I-Beams.

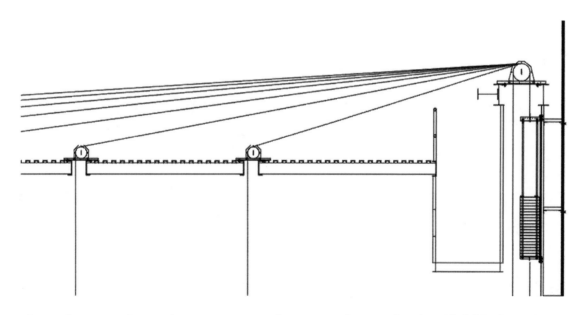

A typical over-hung, single purchase counterweight system showing head and loft block configuration.

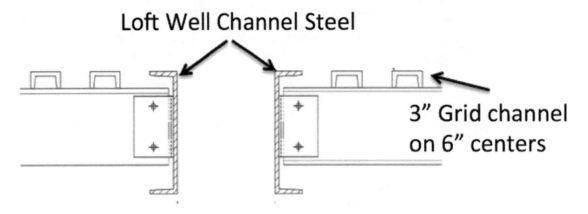

Loft Well Channel Steel

3" Grid channel on 6" centers

Detail of the well channel steel and grid channel

The *head* and *loft block* illustrations below details the installation and shows the direction of the resultant forces that were explained in Chapter 1.

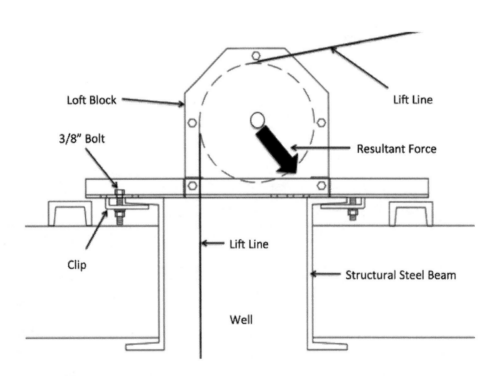

Loft Block

Lift Line

3/8" Bolt

Resultant Force

Lift Line

Clip

Structural Steel Beam

Well

A typical over-hung loft block installation. The use of "clips" holds the loft block to the structural steel. The arrow shows the direction of the resultant forces that will be placed on the block. For this reason, the clips need to be tight to the channel steel.

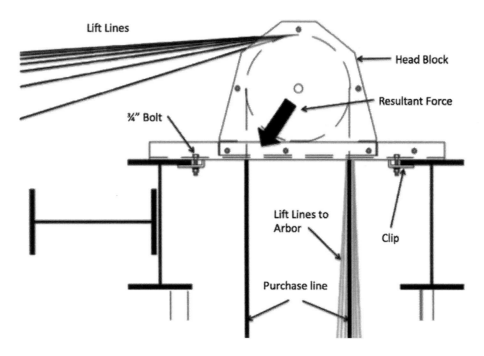

A typical over-hung head block installation. Again, the use of "clips" holds the head block to the structural steel. The arrow shows the direction of the resultant forces that will be placed on the block. For this reason, the clips need to be tight to the I-Beams.

Now, let's look at a typical under-hung *head* and *loft block* installation with two types of *loft blocks*. Under-hung arrangements are usually for venues with limited fly space or no gridiron. The illustrations below show two different styles of *loft block* in under-hung configurations.

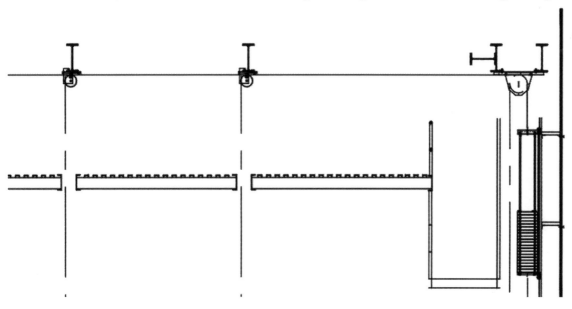

A typical under-hung, single purchase system. Note that the bottom flanges of the I-Beams must be on the same level. The under-hung system can be done with or without a grid, but the grid makes access to the head and loft blocks easer for inspections and servicing.

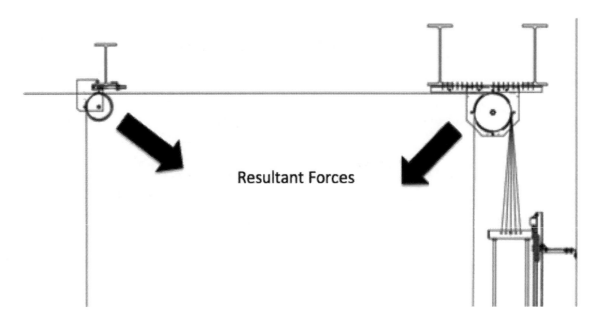

Resultant Forces

The resultant forces on an under-hung system.

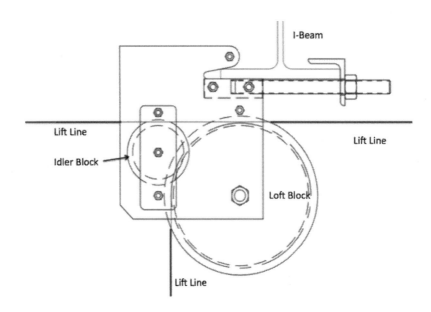

The attachment detail of the loft block shown above. Note the idler block.

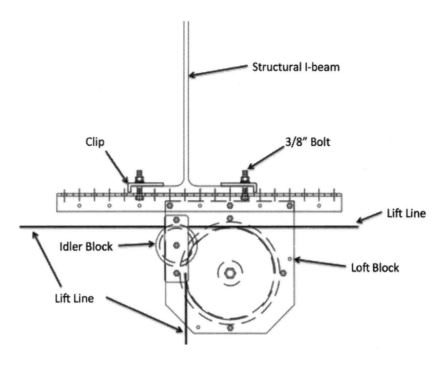

Another typical under-hung loft lock. Note that the lift line running to the batten lines up to the center web of the I-Beam. The idler block supports the lift line running to the next block.

Idler Blocks

Idler blocks are small blocks that attach to the sides of the loft blocks and are designed to reduce cable sag and noise. Each lift line is supported by the idler block as they pass to adjacent loft blocks.

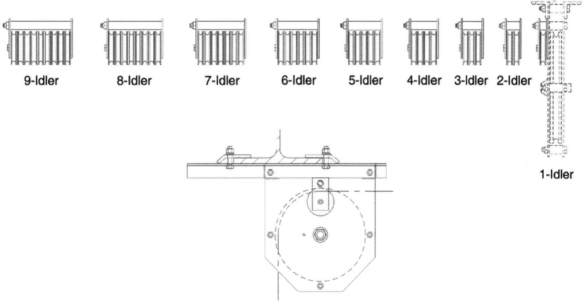

Typical idler blocks have anywhere from 1 to 9 sheaves and guide liftlines past adjacent loft blocks.

-graphics courtesy of H and H Specialties

53

Sag Bars

Sag Bars are usually found in older theatres and that pre-date the idlers. Their purpose is to prevent lift line sag as the cables run across the stage to each consecutive loft block. Made from wood or steel pipe, they are suspended from the ceiling above the grid.

Head Block Pitch

The grooves in the sheave of a head block are designed to receive the correct size wire rope and the correct size purchase (operating) line. The pitch diameters MUST be in the same plane. The illustration on the next page shows the smaller grooves of the wire rope linesets in the same plane (or pitch) as the larger groove of the purchase line. Unequal pitch will often cause the purchase line to slip around the sheave causing the line to wear faster and put additional friction into the system. This slippage can be felt when the lineset is being lifted under load. The heavier the load on the batten, the more friction will be felt in the system and the more difficult the lineset will be to move. The illustration on the right shows uneven pitch to the grooves of the sheave. *Head Block Pitch* is something that should be checked during a rigging installation and inspection. It can only be fixed by having the head block itself replaced or the sheaves re-tooled.

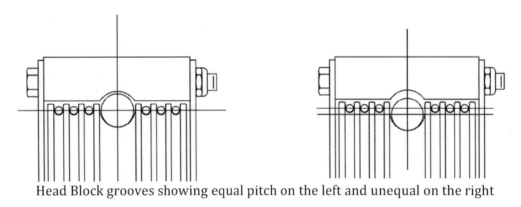

Head Block grooves showing equal pitch on the left and unequal on the right

Types of I-Beams

There are two basic types of I-Beams encountered by the rigging installer; the S-Beam and the W-Beam. I-beams are usually made of structural steel are found in both construction and civil engineering. The diagrams below show the parts of the beam.

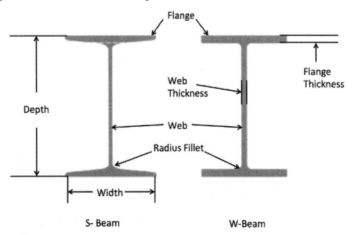

The basic types and dimensioned parts of an I-Beam

There are two basic parts to the I-Beam; the web and the flanges. The web resists *shear* forces and the flanges resist *bending* forces. The design of the I-Beam is very efficient for carrying both of these forces in one plane. When choosing the correct clip hardware for head and loft block attachment, it will be important for the engineer to know which type of I-Beam is installed as well as *all* the I-Beam dimensions shown above.

Choosing the Correct Hardware

Stage rigging hardware must support both the vertical and horizontal forces on the head and loft block I-Beams. The head block I-Beams must support not only the entire horizontal batten load from *all* the loft blocks, but also the vertical load of counterweighted arbor. As we learned in Chapter 1, individual loft block loads will vary depending upon distribution of the loads on pipe batten (see the diagram on page 7). These forces can best be "summed up" as the resultant forces on the Force Diagram. The structural engineer along with the theatre consultant will decide on the correct type of the equipment to be installed; the installation contractor usually choses the equipment manufacturer.

As noted in that chapter, the load limits on the arbor affected the load limits that could be placed on the head block. This load data was determined to be at 1,900 pounds. For this theoretical installation, we will use the H and H Series 50, 12" head block for eight 1/4" wire rope linesets with a Nylatron GSM sheave. The load chart from H and H shows that the Series 50 head block has a WLL of 2,400 lb or 500 pounds over the WLL.

The Force Diagram

The following illustration shows the single purchase *Force Diagram* that we discussed in Chapter 1. As noted in that chapter, the load limits on the arbor affected the load limits that could be placed on the head block. This load data was determined to be at 1,900 pounds. For this theoretical installation, we will use the H and H Series 50, 12" head block for eight 1/4" wire rope linesets with a Nylatron GSM sheave. The load chart from H and H shows that the Series 50 head block has a WLL of 2,400 lb. or 500 pounds over the WLL.

Model No.	Sheave Diameter	Sheave Material	Cable Groove Quantity	Groove Size	Standard Bearing	Working Load Limit*
6850N19	8"	Nylatron GSM	6	3/16"	1" BB	1200
7850C25	8"	Cast Iron	7	1/4"	1" TRB	1800
7850N25	8"	Nylatron GSM	7	1/4"	1" TRB	2000
61050N19	10"	Nylatron GSM	6	3/16"	1" BB	1400
71250C25	12"	Cast Iron	7	1/4"	1" TRB	1800
71250N25	12"	Nylatron GSM	7	1/4"	1" TRB	2400
101250C25	12"	Cast Iron	10	1/4"	1" TRB	1800
101250N25	12"	Nylatron GSM	10	1/4"	1" TRB	2400
71650C38	16"	Cast Iron	7	3/8"	1-3/8" TRB	2500
91650C25	16"	Cast Iron	9	1/4"	1-3/8" TRB	2500

BB - Sealed precision ball bearings   All sheaves include one groove for 3/4" purchase line.
TRB - Tapered roller bearings   *Weight in pounds @ 300 ft/min

Load Table for the H and H Series 50 head blocks. The head block that has a WLL of 2,400 lb.

Next we will select our loft blocks. The engineers have specified an 8" Nylatron GS loft block. Since the liftline cables are ¼", this will leave us with the H and H Series 40 loft block as shown in the load chart below. Its WLL is 725 lb.

Model Number	Sheave Diameter	Sheave Material	Groove Size	Standard Bearing	Working Load Limit*
640N19	6"	Nylatron GS	3/16"	5/8" BB	400
640N50	6"	Nylatron GS	1/2"	5/8" BB	250
840C25	8"	Cast Iron	1/4"	5/8" BB	450
840C75	8"	Cast Iron	3/4"	5/8" BB	400
840N19	8"	Nylatron GS	3/16"	5/8" BB	525
840N25	8"	Nylatron GS	1/4"	5/8" BB	725
1040C25	10"	Cast Iron	1/4"	5/8" BB	550
1040C31	10"	Cast Iron	5/16"	5/8" BB	690
1040C75	10"	Cast Iron	3/4"	5/8" BB	500
1040N25	10"	Nylatron GSM	1/4"	1" BB	875
1040N31	10"	Nylatron GSM	5/16"	1" BB	1150
1240C25	12"	Cast Iron	1/4"	1" BB	700
1240C38	12"	Cast Iron	3/8"	1" BB	1025
1240N25	12"	Nylatron GSM	1/4"	1" BB	875
1240N38	12"	Nylatron GSM	3/8"	1" BB	1500

BB - Sealed precision ball bearings. Tapered roller bearings available.
*Weight in pounds @ 300 ft/min

Load Table for the H and H Series 40 loft blocks. The loft block that supports our system has a WLL of 725 pounds.

Now that we know how the head and loft block hardware is determined, let's move on to some other equipment.

Arbors
Arbors are steel carriages that hold counterweight bricks thereby balancing the load on the pipe batten. They typically ride in tracks or are guided by steel cables. A properly loaded arbor allows the operator to easily raise and lower the battens.

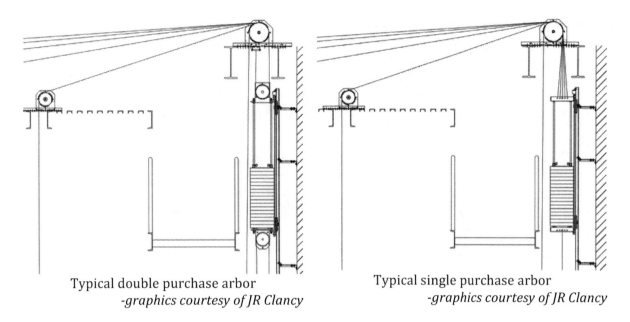

Typical double purchase arbor
-*graphics courtesy of JR Clancy*

Typical single purchase arbor
-*graphics courtesy of JR Clancy*

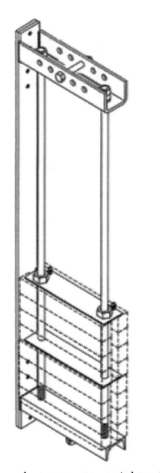

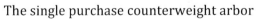

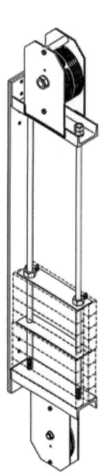

The single purchase counterweight arbor

The double purchase counterweight arbor
-*graphics courtesy of Hand H Specialties*

The top of a single purchase arbor showing lift lines and purchase line attachment.

As noted earlier, there are two basic types of counterweight systems, the *Single Purchase* and *Double Purchase*. The *Single Purchase System* is a system where one foot of arbor travel equals one foot of batten travel. When loading the arbor, the counterweight is equal to the batten weight. The *Double Purchase System* is a counterweighted system where one foot of arbor travel equals two feet of batten travel. When loading the arbor, twice the amount of counterweight will be needed to offset the load on the pipe batten.

Arbors have Working Load Limits based upon the length of the arbor and brick size capacity. The arbor chart below shows the load capacities for H and H Series 991 single purchase arbors.

Model Number	Rod Length	Empty Weight	Capacity* 4" Wide Weights	Capacity* 6" Wide Weights	Spreader Plate Quantity
991x4	4 feet	50 lbs.	565 lbs.	835 lbs.	2
991x5	5 feet	67 lbs.	740 lbs.	1100 lbs.	3
991x6	6 feet	74 lbs.	915 lbs.	1365 lbs.	3
991x7	7 feet	81 lbs.	1090 lbs.	1630 lbs.	4
991x8	8 feet	89 lbs.	1265 lbs.	1895 lbs.	4
991x9	9 feet	96 lbs.	1440 lbs.	2160 lbs.	5
991x10	10 feet	104 lbs.	1615 lbs.	2425 lbs.	5
991x11	11 feet	111 lbs.	1790 lbs.	2690 lbs.	6
991x12	12 feet	118 lbs.	1965 lbs.	2955 lbs.	6

* Capacities include the empty weight of the arbor and are calculated based on an industry average for cut steel counterweights. Actual capacities may vary by as much as 5%.

-photo courtesy of H and H Specialties

Tension Blocks and Purchase Lines

A *tension block* is a single grooved sheave assembly mounted under the counterweight arbor. Its purpose is to float in a track maintaining tension on the *purchase line*. The *purchase line* is a ¾" or 1" hemp or synthetic rope that attaches to the top of the arbor carriage, runs over the head block, down through the rope lock, around the tension block, and back up to the arbor under-carriage. In a double purchase system, it will reeve around additional arbor blocks. It enables the operator to raise and lower the load on-stage with relative ease.

The purchase line should be tied to the arbor ends with either a bowline or two half hitches with the rope ends fixed to the standing part of the rope with zip tie wraps. This will be important as the purchase line will stretch under load with time and need to be adjusted. Polyester rope will not stretch as much as hemp and will not need the same amount of frequent adjustment.

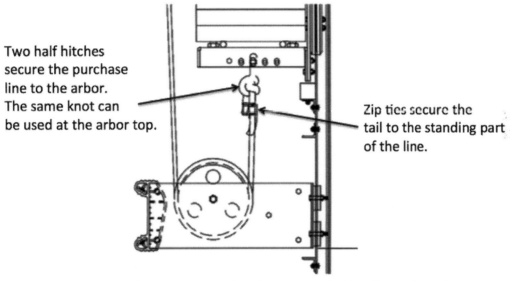

Two half hitches secure the purchase line to the arbor. The same knot can be used at the arbor top.

Zip ties secure the tail to the standing part of the line.

The purchase line is secured to the arbor with a bowline or two half hitches. The tail is then secured to the standing part of the line with zip ties. The knots are used rather than an eye splice in order to periodically adjust the tension on the purchase line.

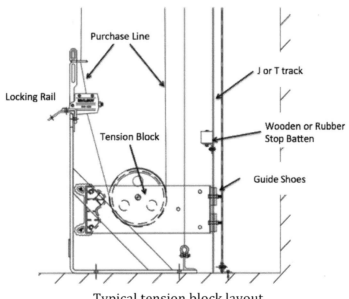

Purchase Line

Locking Rail

J or T track

Tension Block

Wooden or Rubber Stop Batten

Guide Shoes

Typical tension block layout

Fixed Floor Blocks

Due to the limited travel of the wire guided system, these floor blocks are fixed at the base of the lineset. They are non-adjustable which means that slack in the purchase line must be taken up and adjusted by the operator.

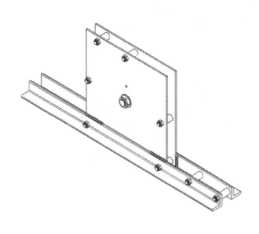

A Fixed Floor Block

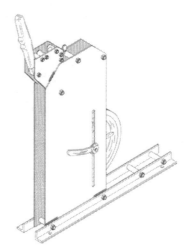

A Combination Floor Black
-*graphics courtesy of H and H Specialties*

Combination Floor Blocks

Combination Floor Blocks are adjustable floor blocks that maintain proper tension on the purchase line. These blocks are generally found with wire guided, rigid guided, or lattice track installations that require an integral rope lock as part of the system.

Mule Blocks

Mule Blocks are multi sheave blocks designed to change the direction of the lift line running between the loft block and head block. The rigging for a curved cyclorama would be a good example of a system that would use mule blocks. Lift lines running from the head block would need to be redirected by the *mule blocks* to the various loft blocks supporting the curved batten.

Three sheave mule blocks redirecting the liftlines from the head block. These mule blocks appear to be welded to the beams, which will make changing them out difficult.

-photo courtesy of J. Lillian Gray

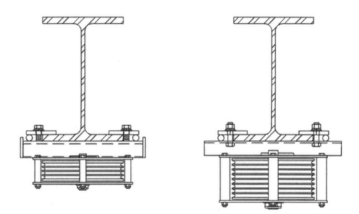

One method of mule block mountings. Note the clips and how they are attached to the I-Beams
-graphics courtesy of H and H Specialties

Rope Locks and Locking Rails

Rope locks are levers that use a cam device to secure the purchase line. As the levered is lowered, pressure is released off the rope. As the lever is lifted, pressure locks the operating line into position. Once locked, a retaining ring is placed over the rope and lock handle, preventing the lock from accidently releasing. It should be noted that the rope lock is designed to secure a load that is "in balance". It should never be used to "lock off" and secure a load that is "unbalanced". More on the operation of the counterweight system will be discussed in Chapter 8.

The *locking rail* is a structural steel frame that is used to mount the rope locks. It is located on either the stage level or on a fly floor gallery. In either case, the *locking rail* must be structurally anchored to the building in order to withstand uplift and lateral forces.

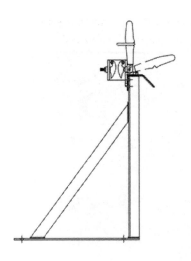 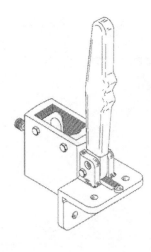

A sectional view of the locking rail is shown right. The rope lock itself is shown top. The framework of the locking rail must be anchored to the structure of the building due to lifting and lateral forces.

-graphics courtesy of H and H Specialties

The two basic types of locking rails are the T Guide and the Wire Guide Locking Rails. Both rails have an index card strip for index cards that identify each lineset and what it controls.

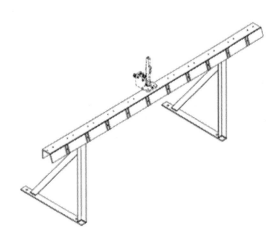 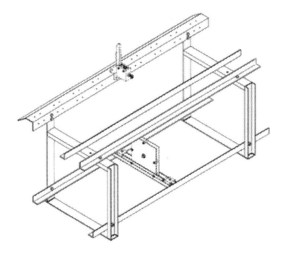

The T Guide Locking Rail is designed to be used with the T or J track systems.

The Wire Guide Locking Rail is designed to be used with the wire-guided systems.
-graphics courtesy of H and H Specialties

The completed locking rail. Numbers start down stage and run up stage.
-photo courtesy of InterAmerica Stage, Inc.

Track and Arbor Guides

Counterweight arbors must be guided in their vertical travel by either a wall mounted track or a wire-guided system. This is to direct them from too much lateral movement. This section will examine three basic guide systems; the *T and J track*, the *wire-guided system*, and the *lattice track*. We will also look at the means by which arbors are attached to the tracks and the tracks are anchored to the building's structure.

T and J Track Guide System

These systems are called *Rigid Guide Systems*. The illustration below shows a typical system with the *J and T track* in plan view. These systems are found in venue installations that exceed 30 feet in height. The arbors are captured and ride in the track by *guide shoes. The aluminum J and the steel T bar tracks* are held in place by *horizontal wall battens* which set the distance between the *J or T bar* at 6, 8, 10 or 12 inch centers. Splicing of the track pieces occurs at the *wall batten* insuring an even transition between splices. *Horizontal wall battens* are normally spaced every 5 feet.

Knee braces anchor the entire track frame assembly to the venue wall. They are made from a two-piece adjustable strut is bolts to the *wall batten* on one end, and is anchored to the venue wall on the other. The installer can adjust the distance of the frame to the wall insuring the entire frame is plum to vertical.

Steel arbor stops (humorously called *crash bars*) are mounted at the top and bottom of the steel frame. Their purpose is to limit the travel of the arbor both at the top of the frame and the bottom. Attached to the arbor stops are wooden battens that partially absorb the contact of the arbor with the steel stop.

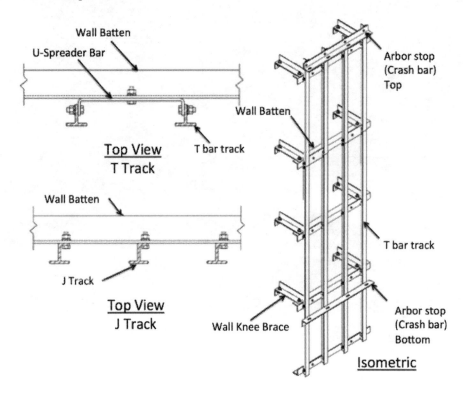

A typical Rigid Guide System showing both the J and T track in plan view.
-graphics courtesy of Hand H Specialties

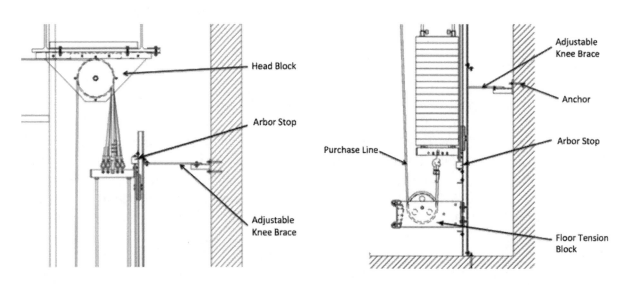

Rigid track mounting at top of track   Rigid track mounting at track bottom

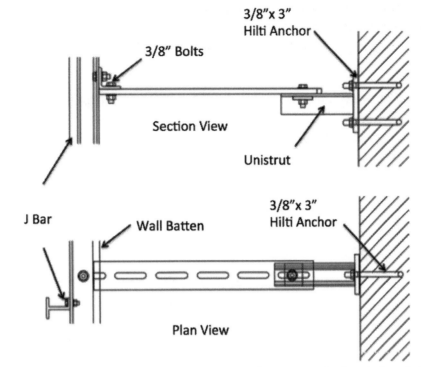

The adjustable wall knee brace allows for the track to be leveled in field.

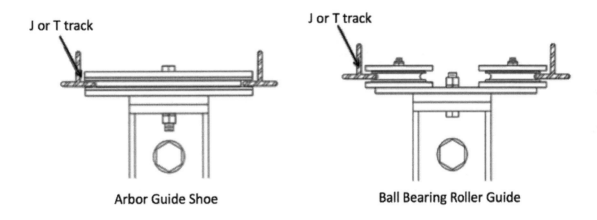

Typical Arbor Guide Shoes

-graphics courtesy of H and H Specialties

Arbor Guide Shoes are attached to the arbor and allow it to ride inside the J or T channel. There are two basic types of shoes; one is *Ball Bearing Roller Guide* and the other is a high density *Polyethylene Guide Shoe*. Both allow the arbor to ride effortlessly inside the track.

Wire Guided Systems

Wire Guided Systems are recommended only as a cost saving measure and when ceiling height is less than 30 ft. Quarter inch wire rope cable guides run through the arbors from the ceiling to the floor. These guide the vertical travel of the arbor instead of a track. Because there is some lateral movement of the arbors due to the wire guides, adequate clearance must be designed into the system and maintained between the rear wall and adjacent arbors.

Lattice Tracks
Lattice Tracks are most often found with *act* and *fire safety curtains*. The arbor assembly rides flat against the proscenium wall between two opposing steel T tracks.

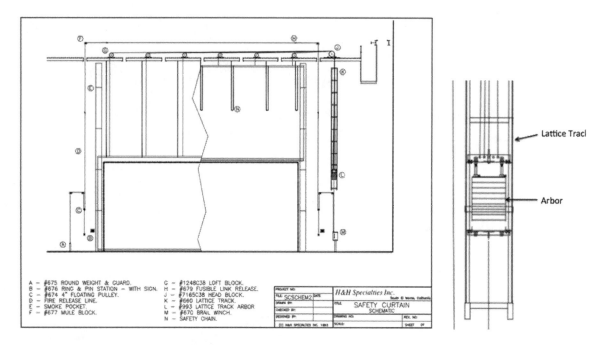

Elevation of Fire Safety Curtain with Lattice Track
-photo courtesy of H and H Specialties

Detail of Lattice
Track and Arbor

Positioning the Loft Blocks on the Gridiron
So far we have examined head blocks, loft blocks, floor blocks, idlers, arbors, track and their installation. Next, we will look at the problem of positioning and lining up loft blocks. If you recall, these can be installed either over-hung or under-hung on the grid or on I-Beams. Important to understanding how to line up loft blocks, we have to understand fleet angles and how this relates to our lining up the liftlines.

Fleet Angles
In an ideal world, when a cable runs over the sheave in a loft block (or any other type of block or pulley), the cable should be perfectly perpendicular to the axle. If this were true, then the cable would align perfectly with the groove in the sheave, and its fleet angle would be 0 degrees. We do not live in a perfect world, and when a cable runs between the head block and a loft block (for example), the cable might not be perfectly aligned with the groove in one or both sheaves. If this is the case, the cable can cause the groove to wear since the cable is harder than the sheave. The farther out of alignment (a fleet angle greater than zero), the more (and faster) the sheave will wear. Stage rigging manufacturers specify that the blocks or pulleys used in stage rigging should

be installed so that the fleet angle of the cable is no greater than 1.5 degrees. This raises the question, "How can you tell if the fleet angle is 1.5 degrees or less?" That is the subject of this lesson.

To start, we need to establish a line with a zero-degree fleet angle (the dotted line in the diagram below) to the groove of the sheaves – the dotted line in the diagram below. This assumes that both sheaves are parallel to each other. Once this is done, we compare the "Offset" (measurement) to the "Distance" between the sheaves.

A good rule of thumb (one that is easy to remember) is that you are allowed 1 unit of "Offset" for every 40 units of "Distance." A slightly better equation is:

Maximum Allowable Offset = Distance × .026 (which is the Tangent of 1.5 degrees).

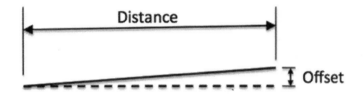

This will not tell you the fleet angle of the cable, just if it exceeds 1.5 degrees. Using this equation, let's work though a sample problem.
Example: What is the maximum allowable offset of a cable at 25 feet? The equation for solving this problem is: Maximum Allowable Offset = 25 × 0.026

[ON/C] 25 [X] 0.026 [=] (0.65) feet   By multiplying 0.65 [X] 12, you can convert feet to inches, which would give you a measurement

that might be a little easier to understand. So, the

Maximum Allowable Offset = 7.8 inches.

Computing the actual fleet angle
If you want to know the actual fleet angle (in degrees), you must know both the Offset Distance and the Measurement Distance. Then, plug these numbers into the following equation:

$$Angle = Arctangent \ of \ \left(\frac{Offset \ Distance}{Measurement \ Distance} \right)$$

So, if the Offset is 6" (0.5 feet) and the Distance is 25 feet, the fleet angle is:

$$Angle = Arctangent \ of \ \left(\frac{0.5}{25} \right)$$

Note: On the TI-30XA calculator, arctangent is denoted as "TAN-1" and is entered by using the [2nd] and [TAN] keys.

Angle = Arctangent of 0.02

Angle = 1.145 degrees

Lining up the Loft Blocks

Now that we have an idea of what *Fleet Angles* are, let's finish the installation. The diagrams below show two methods for aligning and reeving head and loft blocks with minimum acceptable fleet angles. With new installations, it will be especially important to plan everything out ahead of time. CAD can provide the best layout for positioning the blocks and liftlines while at the same time measuring the fleet angles against the 1.5-degree maximum for accuracy.

Batten spacing is usually on 6", 8", 10" or 12" centers and will follow the same spacing as the arbors. Since the lift lines run directly down to the battens, the loft blocks will remain in the same plane as the battens. Once determined, loft block positions do not change, but the angles of the lift lines running to the head block will. Small adjustments to the head block can be made, but the position of the head block is, for the most part, directly over the arbor/ track and cannot change. So, there is not a lot of room for error. Pre-planning is essential. Double-checking fleet angles against the plans will also be done during installation.

The drawings below show two separate methods for reeving the lift lines. Note that each method has the head blocks positioned directly over the arbor/ track. It is the position of the loft blocks/ batten that has shifted slightly.

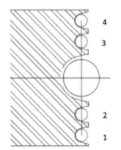

The method of reeving shown above will have the least fleet angle for all the blocks. The illustration to the left shows the order of lift lines coming off the sheave.

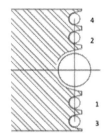

This method or reeving will have the greatest fleet angle for the long center lift line. The illustration left shows the order of lift lines coming off the sheave.

The position of the head block needs to be directly over the arbor/ track. The large purchase line groove in the head block needs to run directly down to, and align with, the center of the arbor/ track. The choice of which method of reeving to use is best determined in the planning stages.

Dead Hangs

Occasionally battens are suspended directly from an I-Beam and not the counterweight system. These are called *dead hangs*. The attachment points are made to I-Beams with beam clamps.

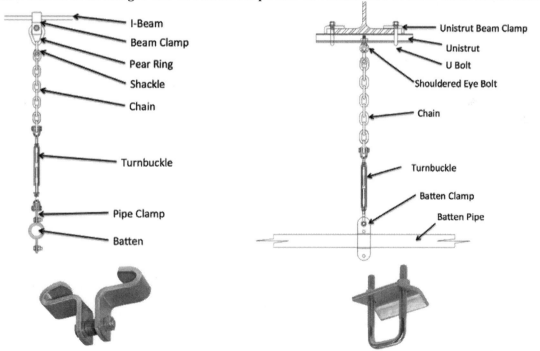

Standard beam clamp attached to I-Beam   Unistrut beam clamp attached to I-Beam

The beam clamps above are only two of the many styles of beam clamps available.

Summary

This chapter focused on just some of the stage equipment available and its installation. You should note that there are a wide variety of products on the market designed for a variety of different applications. Companies like JR Clancy, Thern Stage Equipment, and H and H Specialties, to name a few, manufacture reputable equipment for the theatre. Their catalogues, along with load rating charts, are available for download off the internet. When considering a renovation or installation, it is important to seek out the advice of a professional theatre consultant and structural engineer. As discussed earlier, the theatre consultant with the structural engineer will best determine the strength of the structural members in the building, while the manufacturer will determine the strength of the hardware. It is the installer and technical designer that will be responsible for knowing the forces that will be exerted on each rigging point and piece of hardware. These forces are determined not only by the weight of the object (its static load) but also how the rigging is installed and dynamic forces each object will sustain. Theatre riggers as well as technical designers must be able to calculate all of these loads/forces successfully.

Chapter 4:

Stage Curtains and Curtain Track

Introduction

Stage curtains can be a scenic element for a production or provide the masking for scenery, scene changes and equipment. These curtains come in many sizes, shapes, and colors. This chapter will describe many of the curtains found on many proscenium stages, but focus primarily on *act curtains, masking curtains, cycloramas, roller drops* and *kabuki curtains*. We will also discuss the hardware that is used, how it's rigged and how the curtains operate.

Stage Curtains – A General Overview

Let's begin with an overview of curtain terminology and where these curtains can be found.

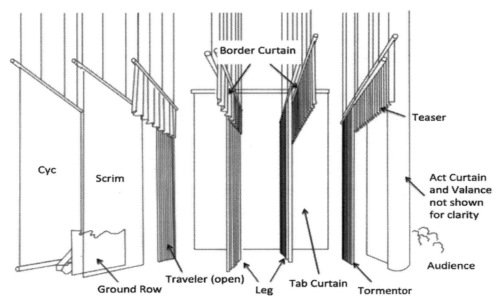

The location of stage curtains as seen from the wings. The Act Curtain is not shown for clarity, but it's location is just upstage of the proscenium arch.

The illustration above is a cross section of the stage and shows where these curtains are located. Each curtain can be defined as follows:

- **Act Curtain** *The act curtain* is a "show" curtain. It is often called the *main curtain, main drape or grand drape*. It hangs just upstage of the proscenium arch making it the first curtain the audience sees. It defines the proscenium and helps to frame the art that is to be revealed behind. In many cases, the act curtain takes on the look and style of the venue. It is sometimes extremely elaborate, colored and styled in such shapes as the *Brail (Austrian) Curtain, the Draw Curtain, the Tableau Curtain*, and the *Contour (Venetian) Curtain*. Each of these curtain styles will be discussed in this chapter. When raised, the act curtain often becomes the valance or teaser, the first horizontal masking curtain.

- **Valance** Essentially, the *valance* is a decorative, horizontal masking curtain, however it is considered a show curtain because it is often colored and styled to match the main *act (show) curtain*.

- **Teasers** The *teaser* is the first, black, horizontal, downstage masking curtain. Its purpose is to shape the proscenium by masking off the fly space and the *first electric lighting pipe. The first electric* is usually just upstage of the teaser.

- **Tormentors** The *tormentor* is the first downstage, black, vertical masking curtain. Just like the *teaser*, it shapes the proscenium arch by tormenting the sides of the arch and masking the wings.

- **Borders** *Border curtains* are horizontal black masking curtains located upstage of the *teaser*. Their purpose is to mask the equipment in the fly space.

- **Legs** The *legs* are black, vertical-masking curtains that are located upstage of the *tormenters*. They provide masking for the stage right and left (*wings*) areas of the stage.

- **Cyclorama (cyc)** The *cyclorama* is a light blue or muslin curtain. It may be hung on a straight or curved batten. It is used for sky effects or projections.

- **Tab (masking) curtains** *Tab* (not to be confused with *Tableau Curtain*) *curtains* are black curtains that are hung as additional side masking. They generally run perpendicular to the legs and mask the side backstage walls.

- **Black Traveler** The *black traveler curtain* is a full draw curtain that is usually found mid to upstage. It masks the back stage wall. If the theatre has a fly space, the curtain can open as a guillotine curtain, otherwise it opens and closes as a draw curtain.

- **Black out curtain** The *blackout (BO) curtain* generally has no fullness. It is a curtain that is used in conjunction with a *cyc* or scenery that is positioned mid to upstage. Often times, when the stage goes black, there is an afterglow on scenic elements upstage of the *B.O. curtain*. To achieve a complete B.O., the curtain is lowered in to the floor as the lights dim out.

- **Scrim** This curtain gets its name from the material that it is made from -typically *sharkstooth scrim*. Scrim is made a gauze-like fabric. When it is lit from the front, the curtain becomes opaque. When objects are illuminated from behind, it becomes transparent. Scrims come in basic colors of white, natural, light blue, and black.

A swatch of sharkstooth scrim showing the fabrics weave

- **Leno or Leno-filled Scrim** The white *Leno Scrim* is essentially a *sharkstooth scrim* with the holes filled in. It reflects lights making it ideal for sky effects and abstract projections. The texture, however, is not the best for high-resolution images.

Sightlines The quantity and dimensions of stage curtains will be determined by *sightlines*. The size and physical layout of the facility will determine how the curtains are to be positioned. *Floor plans* and *sectional drawings* can aid the scenic designer in choosing the placement and trim height of the *border curtains* and *legs*. *Sightlines* are the extreme audience seating positions and can be found on both the *floor plan* and the *section drawings*. They show how the masking curtains will effect what the audience can and cannot see of both the stage and the backstage and fly loft areas.

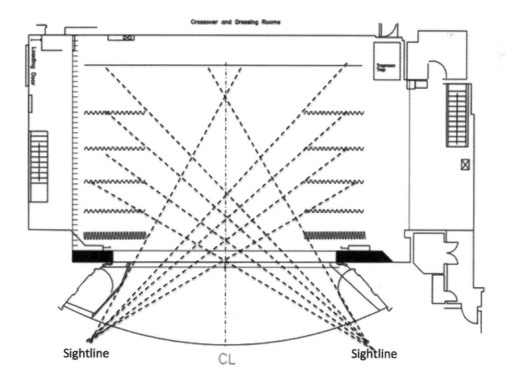

Sightlines as shown on the floor plan are the extreme downstage right and left audience seats.

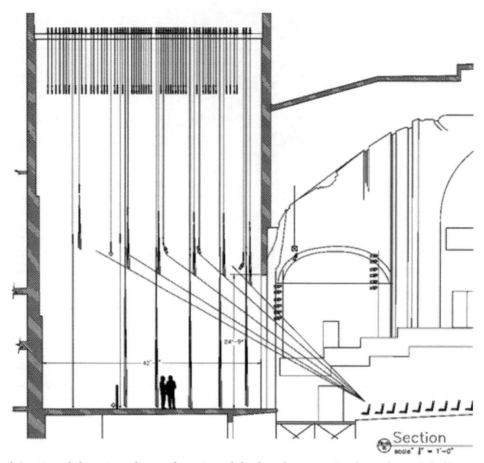

A Longitudinal Sectional drawing shows the trim of the border curtains based on sightlines and masks the equipment in the fly space.

Curtain Heights The height of the curtains will be dependent on the sightlines as seen in the sectional drawing above. A good rule of thumb is the have the height of the *traveler* and *legs* a minimum of 2 ft. above the height of the proscenium opening. If this can't be done, then the travelers and legs can be made at a lower height, but it will be necessary to have border curtains attach in front in order to mask the attachment of the traveler and legs to their battens.

Curtain Widths How wide a curtain is to be will be dictated by the sightlines and the physical width of the stage area on the floor plan. A *valance curtain*, for example, will extend 2 feet to 4 feet past each side of the proscenium opening. *Teaser* and *border* curtains will need to be sized according to what they are masking. The width of *the cyclorama, traveler curtains*, *tormentors, legs* and *scrims* will be based upon the sightlines as well as the track dimensions.

Stacking Space A *traveler (draw) curtain* that is fully opened should not be visible to the audience (although it sometimes is). This curtain, in its stored position, will take up what is known as "stacking" space. There are many variables that determine this space; fabric type, added fullness, linings and number of carriers to name a few. An unlined traveler panel, for example, suspended on an H and H Series 401S track with 28 carriers will need 64" of stacking space[1].

[1] This calculation is based on the H and H stacking space calculator downloadable from the Internet. Stacking space is determined by totaling the lengths of the master carrier, end pulley and single carriers, plus10%.

To account for the space needed for stacking, addition panel width is added to the curtain. When closed, the curtain will run the complete length of the track section. If for some reason an opened curtain cannot be hidden out of view, the traveler width can be shortened so that the remaining curtain will fit into the stacking space. When closed, the entire curtain will advance to the track overlap leaving a gap in the stacking space. To keep the offstage curtain edge attached to the track, a leash or tag line is attached that runs to the pulley. This will be shown later in the chapter when we look at special problems.

Lineset Schedule The *lineset schedule* is a spreadsheet that shows the total of linesets that are available in the theatre and which ones will be dedicated to curtains, electrics, scenery and drops. Starting down stage, each lineset is numbered. The distance from the plaster line to the lineset is noted along with whether the batten is empty or in use. The trim height of each scenic unit, border curtain and electric batten is also noted.

The Act Curtains and their Operation

Now that we have looked at masking curtains and how their location and trim are determined, lets examine act curtains and the types that are commonly available. As we noted earlier, the *act curtain* is a "show" curtain. It is the first curtain the audience sees when they enter the house. It defines the proscenium and, when it is opened, serves to reveal the scenery. In most cases, the act curtain serves the look and style of the venue.

- **The Guillotine, Draw and Combination** A *guillotine style curtain* is one that is tied to a pipe batten and rises up into the fly space. Most *fire curtains* will be of this type. The *draw curtain*, on the other hand, is one that opens and closes by a hand line that is either SR or SL of the curtain. *Draw curtains* are sometimes referred to as *travellers* as they operate on a traveler track system. This type of curtain is great for theatres with little or no fly space. The combination combines the elements of both the *draw and guillotine.* The illustration below shows a *combination* curtain. Both the *guillotine and combination curtains* will require a fly loft one and a third times the height of the curtain.

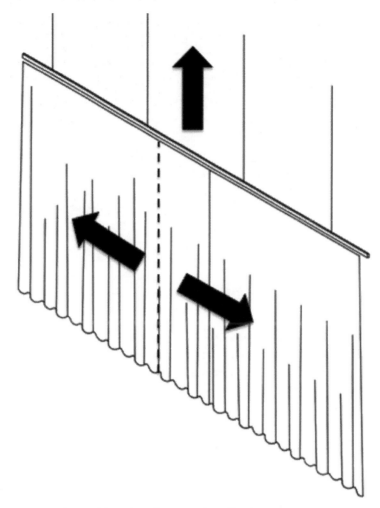

A combination draw and guillotine curtain

- **The Brail or Austrian Curtain** This curtain has horizontal scalloped pleats sewn into its shape. It is manufactured with 25% to 50% of fullness. While the brail curtain has no vertical fullness, the puffs in the curtain are created by adding 100% "sewn-in" vertical fullness. The curtain is usually mounted to a permanent position and is raised or lowered by a series of lift lines that run through rings sewn into the back of the curtain. The brail will always raise and lower the bottom edge of the curtain parallel to the floor.

  Because this curtain gets increasing heavy as it is raised, thereby picking up more fabric as it goes up, it is almost always lifted by a winch (either a single or multiple winches).

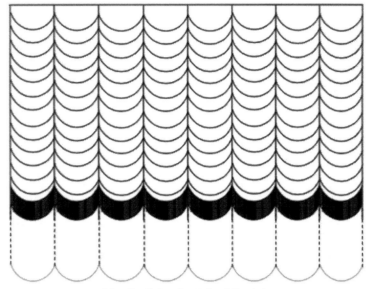

The Brail (or Austrian) Curtain

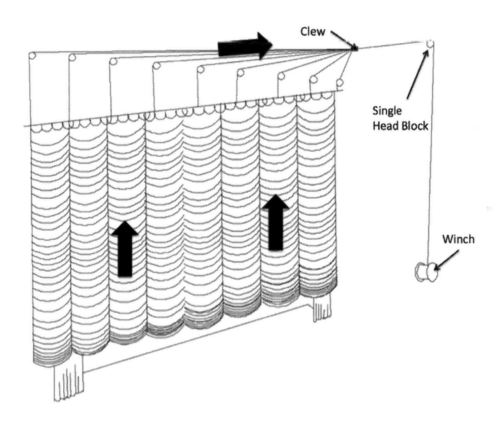

How the Brail Curtain works

- **The Contour or Venetian Curtain** Similar to the Brail curtain, the Contour Curtain is often scalloped in shape when raised. This type of curtain can be lifted by a single winch with different sizes of drums, so that it all lines are not raised the same amount, giving the bottom a very distinctive shape, or sometimes lifted by multiple winches, a separate winch for each line, allowing for different shapes to be created.

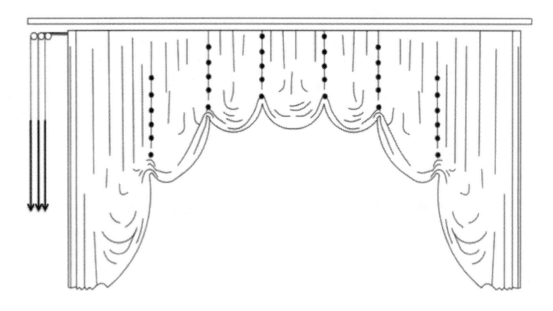

The Contour or Venetian Curtain

- **The Tableau Curtain** The Tableau Curtain (sometimes called "tab") is made in two sections similar to the draw curtain. It uses rings sewn diagonally to the curtain on the backside of each half. Lift lines run diagonally through the drape. How the stage is revealed when it is opened will be determined by the position and angle of the lift lines.

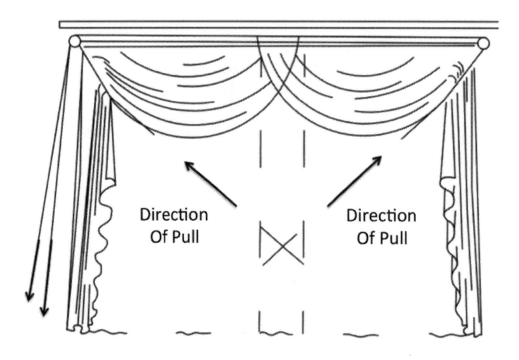

The Tableau Curtain

Other non- masking curtains

- **Kabuki Drop** The Kabuki drop is a lightweight curtain that is pre-hung on stage. Once released, it falls to the stage floor revealing what was hidden behind. Its design is relatively simple. A grommeted curtain is attached to pegs on a roller batten. Suspension ropes run from above the stage from a permanent batten. When the roller batten is rotated, the pegs roll down, releasing the curtain off the grommets.

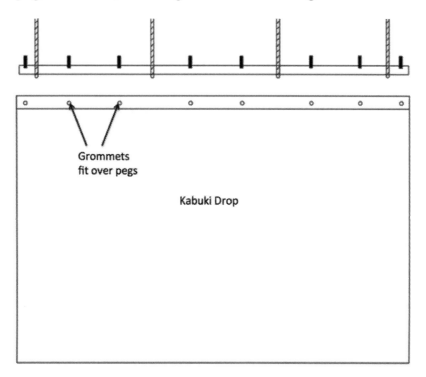

The manually rigged Kabuki Curtain is relatively simple.

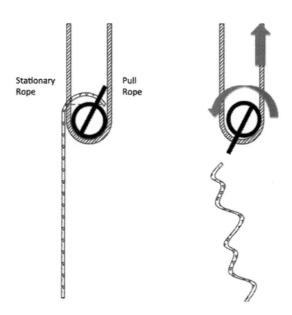

Once the operating line is pulled, the curtain falls off the pegs

Electronic solenoids can be rigging to a batten replacing the pegs. The curtain grommets are attached to the pins of the solenoid. Once power is sent to the magnetic coil, a plunger is pulled into a magnetic field and the curtain drops.

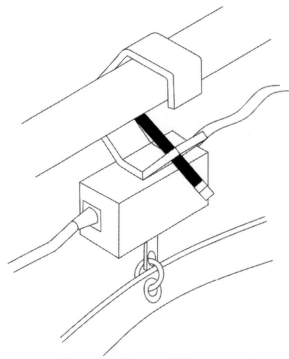

One of several solenoids connected to a pipe batten. When power is supplied to the solenoid, a plunger releases the drop

The Roll Drop The *roll (olio) drop* is used when fly space is at a premium. The term "Olio" is taken from the vaudevillian era when acts were performed mid-stage in from of a painted scenic drop. Today, the name "olio" has remained because many *roller drops* are painted and are suspended mid-stage.

Essentially, the *olio* or *roller drop* is rolled up on a lightweight and very stiff tube. There are several methods of rolling the drop including a motorized version. Let's look at two of the more basic methods.

- o Method 1. A scenic muslin drop is tied to a pipe batten with the bottom of the drop is attached to a 6" aluminum tube[2]. There must be an additional 12 or more of additional fabric to wrap and secure around the tube. The liftlines coil around the tube in the opposite direction that the drop will roll. The idea is that as the liftlines are pulled, they un-wrap as the drop rolls up.

[2] Aluminum tube is preferred, but depending on the length of the drop and budget, re-enforced Sonotube makes an inexpensive alternative.

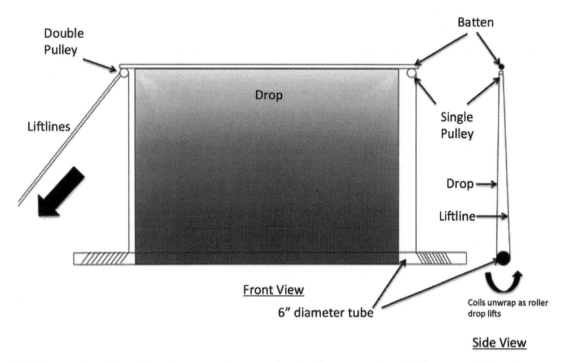

Method 1. The rigging the roller drop involves a ridged tube secured to the bottom of the drop. Liftlines are wrapped in the opposite direction of the roller drop. As the liftlines are pulled, the drop rolls up on the tube as the liftlines unwrap.

- o Method 2. With this second method, the roller tube is mounted to the top of the drop rather than the bottom. Liftlines can run to one end of the drop (as shown in the illustration below) or to both. Again, the liftlines wrap around the tube ends. As the liftlines are pulled they un-wrap as the drop is raised.

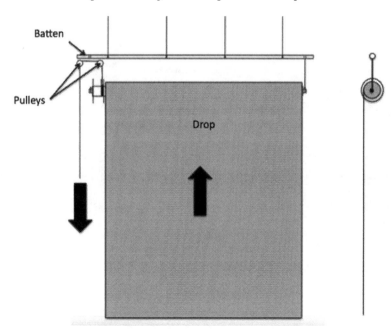

Method 2. With this method, the rigging of the roller drop has the tube mounted at the top near the batten. Again, the liftlines wrap around the tube. As the liftlines are pulled, the drop is raised.

Track Hardware

Rigging a curtain track is not as complicated as it may seem. This section will focus on the rigging of curtain track, basic parts and special problems. Because there is a wide variety of track sizes and components, it will be necessary to contact the manufacturer/ supplier to make sure you have the correct parts for your track.

How a Curtain Track Works The operation of the curtain track is the same as any other draw curtain track you may find in your home. To begin with, every draw track must have one or two *master carriers*. If the curtain is to draw in one direction, then only one *master carrier* will be required as the *master carrier* is attached to the *operating line*. If the curtain draws in both directions, then two will be necessary. The basic draw curtain (both directions) will have a track mounted to a batten or to a structure. The length of the track will be based on the area of the stage that needs to be covered.

Let's look at the operation of a traveler curtain.

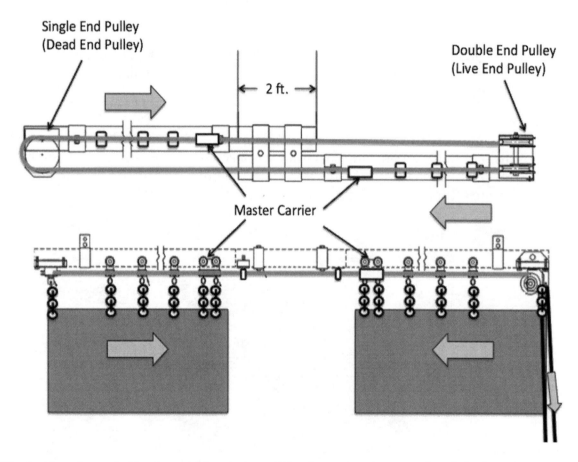

This illustration shows both a top and front view of the draw curtain operation. It is the master carriers that are secured to the rope. The end pulleys are often referred to as the *Live End Pulley* and the *Dead End Pulley.*

The illustration above shows the basic operation and rigging of the operating line.
Note that the *master carriers* are attached to the *operating line* so that as the line is pulled in any one direction, both carriers will follow with the direction of the line.

Track Components of the Straight Curtain Track

With any "two-way" straight *draw curtain*, there will need to have a 2 feet overlap of the track. This enables the curtain to overlap in the closed position. These illustrations show the track components necessary to rig the track. With many straight track sizes available, it is best to contact the manufacturer for the correct components for the size of track being used.

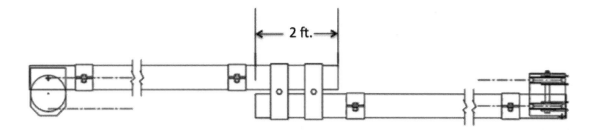

Plan View of Straight Track showing 2 ft. overlap

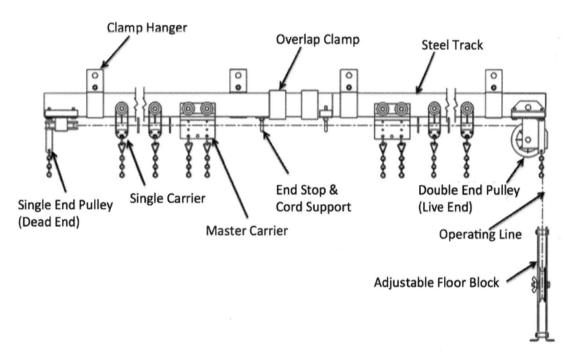

Elevation of Straight Track showing basic track components

The track shown above is for a typical H and H Specialties straight track. It shows the rigging of the components that follow in the illustrations below.

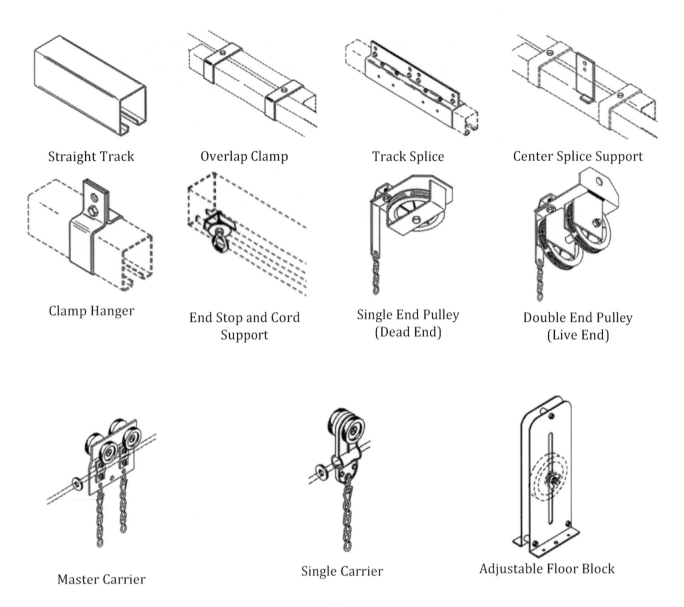

Straight Track

Overlap Clamp

Track Splice

Center Splice Support

Clamp Hanger

End Stop and Cord
Support

Single End Pulley
(Dead End)

Double End Pulley
(Live End)

Master Carrier

Single Carrier

Adjustable Floor Block

-graphics courtesy of H and H Specialties

Curtain tracks can be made from steel or aluminum. They are attached to a batten or mounted permanently to a structure. *Carriers* run inside the track. The number of *carriers*, including *master carriers*, should correspond to the number of grommets in the curtain. Trim chain is then attached to each of the carriers in 6" lengths. The grommeted curtains will have "*S-hooks*" or *curtain carriers* with *snaps* that will attach 3" down the *trim chain*. The reason for this is to allow for trim height adjustment in field. You will see that this will be especially important if the curtain track is hung to a permanent structure such as a wall, ceiling or I-Beam. With a counterweighted batten, raising or lowering the batten can adjust the trim of the curtain. But if the curtain track is permanently mounted to an I-Beam, ceiling, or wall, then trim adjustment has to be done by the trim chains. The 3" attachment "rule" will allow the curtain height to be "fine-tuned" (plus or minus links) to achieve trim. The manufacturer will construct the curtains to hang 2" off the floor. This also aids the installer in trimming out the curtain due to any irregularities in the building.

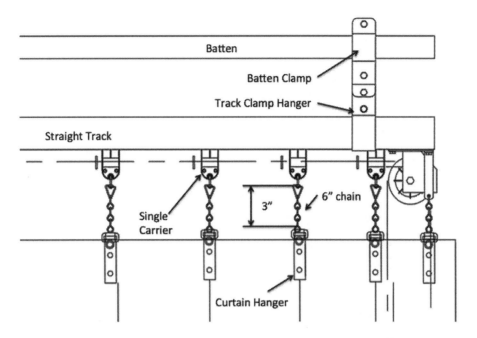

Track attachment is made to the batten by the use of batten clamps that are bolted to the Track clamp hanger. The view is shown from the *Live End Pulley*.

Sometimes the only way to hang a curtain is by dead hanging it to a structure. There are many methods to do this, and the manufactures' have the hardware necessary to adapt to any situation. The method below is commonly encountered on stage. In addition to the 3" rule for the curtain trim, fine-tuning track trim can be accomplished by means of the turnbuckle as shown below.

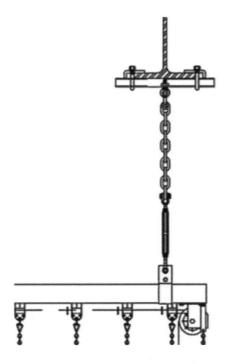

One of many methods by which a curtain track is "dead hung off a structure. This method uses the Unistut beam clamp to attach to an I-Beam with a chain and turnbuckle attached below.

Special Problems: The Curtain Leash

When there is inadequate track length needed for stacking, a leash or tag line may be attached to the top off-stage edges of the curtain and track pulley. This arrangement reduces the width of the curtain fabric and gives it room to be "stacked" or stored off-stage. These leashes are simply curtain trim chains, cut to length, and then attached to the off-stage edge of the curtain and then to the end pulleys as shown below.

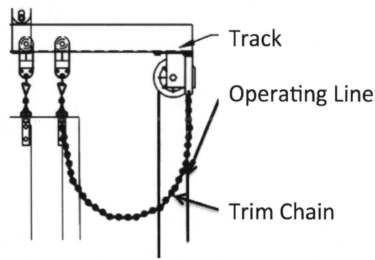

Trim chain leashes allow the curtain to be stored at the track ends, yet be pulled out when the curtain is closed.

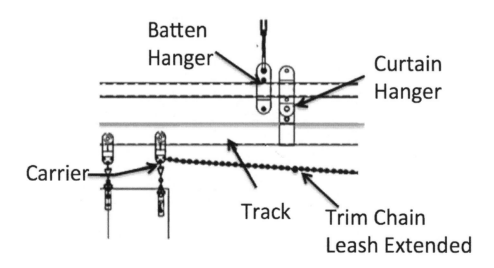

When the curtain is closed, the leash extends allowing the curtain to fully close. When the curtain is opened, the master carrier will pull the curtain all the way to the track ends.

Curved Curtain Tracks

Curved curtains use an extruded aluminum track similar to the one show right. The shape allows for the track to be easily bent conforming to the curve needed. The principle behind the opening and closing remain basically the same; it is the hardware that will be different.

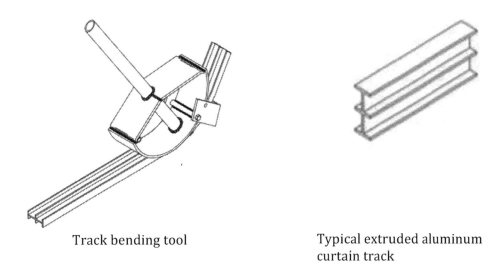

Track bending tool

Typical extruded aluminum curtain track

-graphics courtesy of H and H Specialties

The extruded aluminum track comes in a variety of different extrusions, weights and sizes; all depending upon the type, weight and use of the curtains. Again, it is always best to contact the manufacturer to find out which curtain track is best suited for your needs.

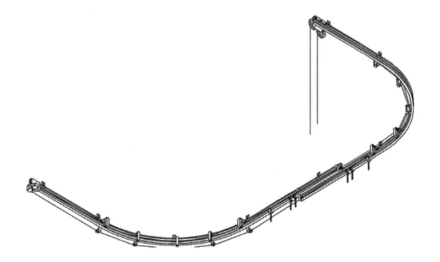

H and H Series 300 curtain track can be made straight or made curved.

Tracks can be made to be "walk along" (ie. without an operating line), or cord drawn. It is important to remember, with any curve track the more severe the curve the more effort will be needed to operate the curtain. Gentle curves are best. For this reason, the curve in a track should be no less than 4 feet in radius.

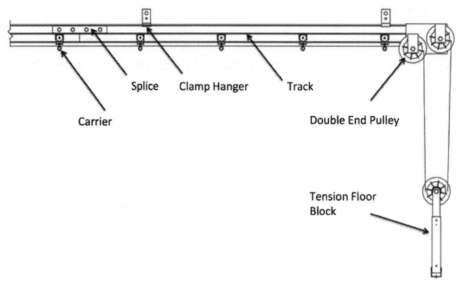

The operating end of a curved curtain track system.

The track shown above is for a typical H and H Specialties Series 300 track. It shows the rigging of the components that follow in the illustrations below.

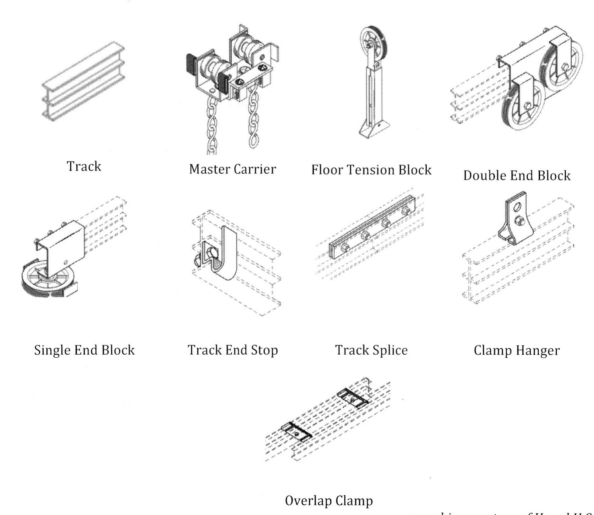

Track   Master Carrier   Floor Tension Block   Double End Block

Single End Block   Track End Stop   Track Splice   Clamp Hanger

Overlap Clamp

-graphics courtesy of H and H Specialties

Getting the operating lines to move around the corners is solved with spindles and idlers. Spindles and idlers serve as struts allowing the operating line to follow the curve in the track. The illustration below shows how these are attached and how the operating line is reeved.

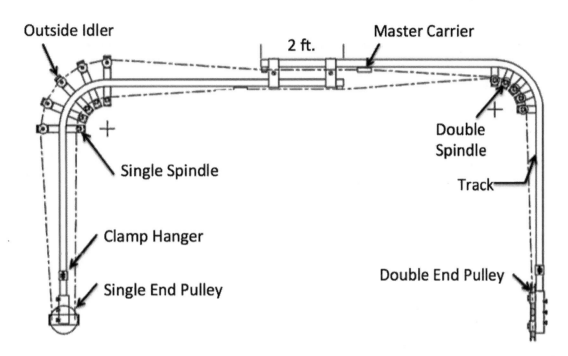

-graphics courtesy of H and H Specialties

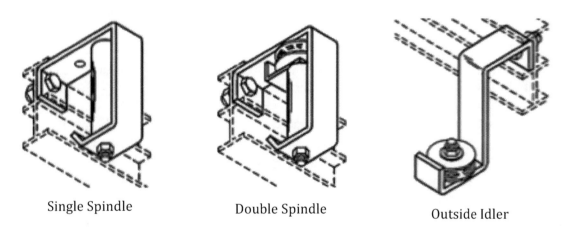

Single Spindle   Double Spindle   Outside Idler

-graphics courtesy of H and H Specialties

Care and Inspection of Curtains

Maintenance

Stage curtains can visually be inspected every time there is a turnover between productions. Inspections of borders, legs, scrims, and cycs can immediately check for rips, tears, and water damage as the curtains are brought in and/or changed.

If rips or tears are found, do not use gaffer's tape to repair the curtain. Gaffer's tape leaves a residue on the fabric that cannot be removed. It is best to repair the fabric by either hand stitching or by sewing machine.

Repair to the Fabric When repairing the fabric by hand, it is best to use a stitch that crosses over each side of the torn fabric so that the edges can be pulled together. Two stitches that do this are the *Herringbone and Cross Stitches*. When repairing scrims, you will need to keep the stitch as loose as possible so as not to pull the edges too close together.

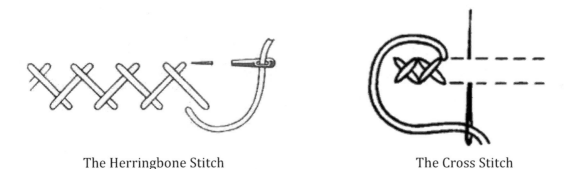

The Herringbone Stitch   The Cross Stitch

When using a sewing machine, set the stitch to a wide and long *zigzag stitch*, reversing over the stitch several times. This will lock the stitch while creating a strong repair. Unfortunately, this will tend to "mash" down the nap on velour fabrics. If this is a concern, repair the curtain by hand. Do not repair scrims on a sewing machine, as the sewing machine feed dogs and pressure foot do not support the loose weave of the scrim fabric.

Flame Proofing of Curtains Certain fabrics are treated with a flame retardant chemical and will require periodic re-treatment. Flame proofing certificates are issued when the curtain is purchased and should be kept on file. Check these certificates to see when your curtains were last inspected. Re-flame proofing is recommended every five years.

Liquids Keep all curtains away from water or any other liquid as the water will remove the flame retardant and leave a chalky white substance on the surface that can only be removed by dry cleaning.

Cleaning Never wash curtains in a washing machine as this will remove all the flame proofing and may shrink the fabric. Dry clean curtains only. Once curtain are dry cleaned, they will need to be re-flame proofed. Generally, this should be done every five years.

Changing out curtains from batten to batten Changing over from one show to the next often times involves moving curtains from one batten to the next. It is best to avoid dragging curtains across the floor. Moving a curtain with a chain in the bottom hem pocket can quickly destroy the hem edge of the curtain; plus the curtain will get dirty quicker. When changing out or moving curtains it is best to sweep the floor thoroughly making sure there are no nails protruding out of the floor that can catch and rip the fabric. The suggested method is to lay down muslin *"diapers"* on the stage floor so that as the curtain is lowered, it will land on the *diapers.* Once the curtain is un-tied and falls on the *diaper*, then the *diaper* can be dragged over to the new batten. This will save the wear and tear on the curtain and avoid dirt. As the curtain is raised up on the new batten, check for rips. Curtains also get very dusty or dirty with time. This may be a good time to sweep off any dirt as the curtain is being raised, but make sure your crews are wearing *dust masks* as this process raises a lot of dust, dirt and allergens.

Storing and folding curtains If curtains are to be removed from the stage and stored, it is best to fold them and store them in laundry hampers or canvas bags. This will keep dirt and moisture from collecting on the fabric. Do not store in plastic bags, as this will "seal in" any moisture and encourage the growth of mildew. Also, never try to steam out any wrinkles, as this will only create water stains. The best way to remove wrinkles is to simply *hang* the curtain. Lastly, always fold curtains before storage. Never just throw them into a hamper as this will create wrinkles. Since curtains are sewn from fabric panels, they should be folded seam-to-seam, face to face and then rolled – this is a two-person job. This method works for both flat curtains and pleated curtains.

Step 1 – Lay the curtain out face up on the stage.

Step 2 – Since the panels run top to bottom, position one person at the top of the curtain and one person at the bottom - on one end, opposite each other.

Step 3 – Each person finds the seam where the first and second panels are sewn together. Then, while pulling against each other, fold this seam over the first panel to the edge of the curtain.

Step 4 – Straighten this entire length of this seam so that it aligns with the edge of the curtain. The folded portion of the curtain will be one half of the width of one panel of fabric.

Step 5 – Repeat Steps 3 and 4 with each subsequent panel, folding the panels face to face, until the entire curtain has be folded.
Note: Pleated curtain will be in a trapezoid shape (wider at the bottom), whereas flat curtains will be a rectangular shape.

Step 6 – Now you can either roll the curtain, from the bottom up, or fold both the top and bottom to the middle (actually a little empty space so that you have room to make a final fold), and then repeat until you have a nice bundle.

West Coast (or East Coast) This term refers to the furling scrims and drops like sailors would furl sails on yardarms. The curtain is furled to the batten with its own ties , alternating ties every 3 feet. The first version is that it started on Hollywood sound stages where the drop being taken down was almost immediately put back up. There was no need to carefully fold the drop for long storage. Another version says that shows mostly toured from East to West. At the end of the run (on the West Coast), instead folding the curtains neatly, they were just quickly dropped into bags or hampers, to save time on the strike. The third version is that *East Coasting* a drop simply involves lowering a curtain/ drop "feet first" in to a bag or hamper. Whatever the case,

West Coasting involves 1. stagehands gathering the drop in their arms as it is lowered, then tying the furled drop to the batten for storage, or 2. tying the drop up like a snake with tie lines as soon as it is removed and placing it in a canvas bag. *West or East Coasting* a drop is a great way of insuring the drop or curtain will be full of wrinkles the next time it is re-hung; this is not so much a problem with scrims.

Summary

In this chapter, we learned that stage curtains can serve both as a scenic element for a production as well as provide masking for scenery, scene changes and equipment. There are many types and styles of *act curtains* too, namely the *Brail, Contour, Tableau* and *Draw* and *Guillotine*. These are usually made from a colored fabric and can be ornately decorated to match the style and theme of the venue. Other curtain types examined were the *Kabuki* and *Roller Drop*. These curtains were shown to be of use when there is little or no fly space. Also, *Teasers, tormentors, borders, legs* and *tabs* were used to hide the backstage areas from audience view. Lastly, we discussed the basic track hardware for both straight and curved curtain systems and why it is important for the Technical Director and Designer to know how these components are assembled and rigged.

Chapter 5:
Concert Shells

Introduction

Many performance facilities today are multi-purpose/multi-use facilities. These venues not only serve to support theatre productions, but serve as lecture and concert halls as well. In order to produce an optimal and focused sound quality to the audience and performers, acoustical shells are a necessary part of the function of these performance spaces. The theatre rigger needs understand how these shells are rigged for these events and removed when not required. We will begin by examining the general layout of the acoustical shell and then move on to how they are constructed and rigged.

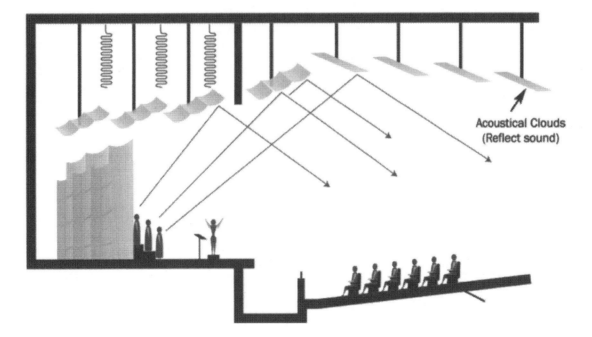

Acoustical Clouds
(Reflect sound)

The Layout
Acoustical shells are basically comprised of two components: wall towers and ceiling clouds. Towers are free standing ground units that wrap around the sides and rear of the performance area forming a "U" shape. They are designed to focus sound outwards toward the audience. Ceiling clouds, on the other hand, prevent sound from escaping into the fly space and, like the towers, focus sound outwards.

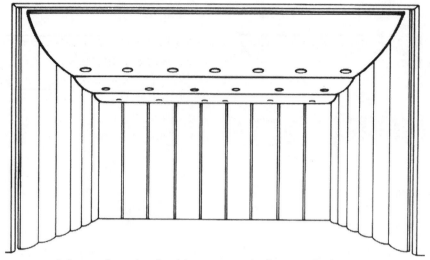

A front elevation looking at a typical acoustical set up.
-graphics courtesy of Wenger Corp.

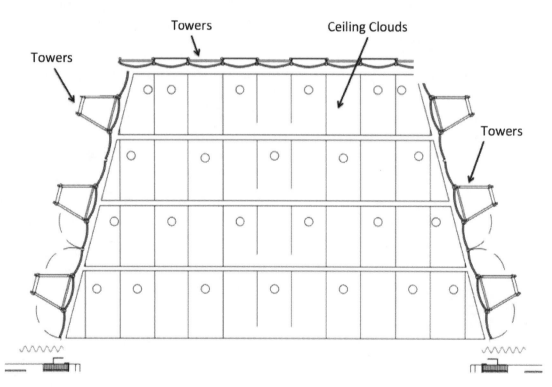

A Floor Plan of the stage showing the position of the side and rear wall towers and ceiling clouds.
-graphics courtesy of Wenger Corp.

Whereas, the towers are stored backstage and can be rolled into position, the clouds must be rigged and suspended from the theatre counterweight system. A lot will depend on the fly space that is available in the facility. The sectional drawing below shows one such layout in a performance venue with a fly space. Each cloud is stored in its upright position. Note the relationship of the clouds to each of the lines sets.

94

Cloud Positioning

The minimum spacing between pipe battens in a counterweighted theatre is 6 inches. When designing a multi-purpose venue, however, the theatre consultant will want to insure that the distance between battens can accommodate the 14 inches needed for the storage of the clouds, when rotated to the "closed" position. The illustration below shows a series of four cloud units (with installed ceiling lights) in the raised and lowered position. It also dimensions the space needed for each cloud. This means that the typical spacing between battens in these type of venues is 8 inches so that there is enough room for the cloud. Care still needs to be taken when raising and lowering the outside battens so the trim chains or liftlines don't scratch the finished surface of the clouds.

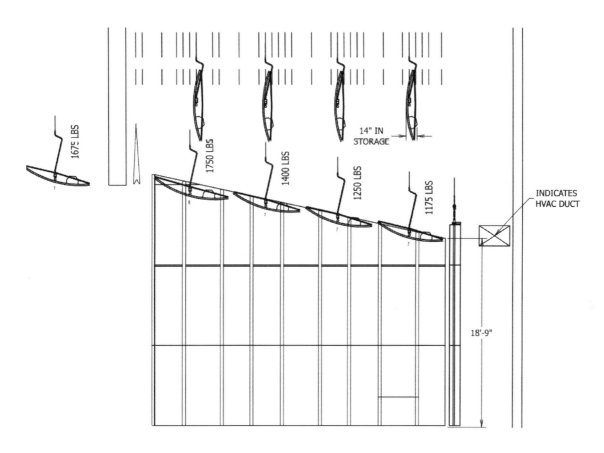

This sectional view shows the position of both the towers and ceiling clouds.

-graphics courtesy of the Wenger Corp.

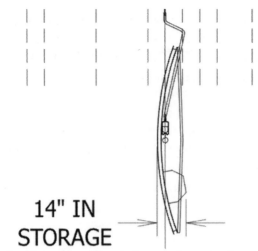

14" IN STORAGE

A close up for the ceiling cloud shown above in the stored position.

-graphics courtesy of the Wenger Corp.

Linesets

Ceiling clouds, depending on their width and depth, can be very heavy. Depending on their weight and their travel distance, one tall arbor or two normal height arbors might be needed in order to hold enough counterweight to balance the weight of the ceiling clouds. Because of their weight, most manually operated ceiling clouds at difficult to move. At times, a motorized assist hoist might be used to help raise and lower ceiling clouds.

The ceiling clouds will need to attach to pipe battens. Because the load distribution of the clouds may need to be spread evenly across the batten, truss battens may be used instead of single pipe battens. The reasons for this were discussed earlier in Chapter 1. The theatre consultant and structural engineer will decide what is best.

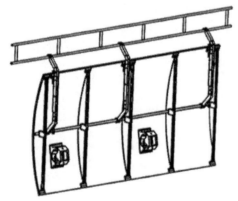

A typical ceiling cloud attached to a truss batten.

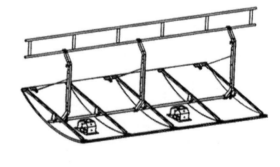

A ceiling cloud in its deployed position.

-graphics courtesy of the Wenger Corp.

Towers and tower storage

The next consideration is to the storage of the tower units. Towers MUST be stored either onstage in a *compact* area, or away from the stage area altogether. There are many styles and designs that are manufactured for any venue and any situation; some towers store in the upright position, while others can fold in half and be rolled through doorways into storage closets. The illustration below shows two styles of tower designs and how they can be stacked together for compact storage. Again, a theatre consultant will best decide what works best for your facility.

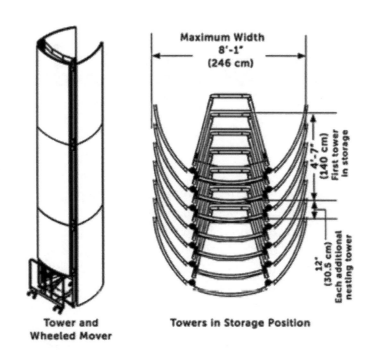

Towers in storage position.

-graphics courtesy of the Wenger Corp.

Section View of Unfolded Tower

Top View of Folded Tower

Section View of Folded Tower

Other tower designs allow for the towers to be folded and removed from the stage through doorways

-graphics courtesy of the Wenger Corp.

Chapter 6:
Fire Safety Curtains

Introduction

On December 30, 1903, fire broke out in the fly space of the newly constructed Iroquois Theatre in downtown Chicago proving to be the single deadliest theatre and building fire in United States history[1]. The known death toll reached 602. The cause; sparks from an arc-lite ignited a muslin drop. Despite efforts on the part of a stagehand to douse the flames, the fire spread quickly to the flammable scenery in the fly loft. A blocked fire curtain, smoke doors that were nailed shut, lack of a sprinkler system, locked exits and the lack of an emergency evacuation plan all contributed to the high death toll. Later inspection revealed the fire curtain was composed of an asbestos coated canvas material, which was destroyed in the fire! Yet, this theatre was deemed "completely fireproof" by Fireproof Magazine! Fire codes and sprinkler systems were in existence at the time, but public officials turned a blind eye as theatre owners rushed to turn a profit on the partially completed building.

As what happens in so many tragedies, it takes a great loss of life before public outcry forces officials to react. The aftermath of this tragedy was no exception. The same officials that had failed to enforce local fire codes were soon to enacted *new* legislation requiring fire code *enforcement* in public buildings. These regulations were soon to become the model for the rest of the country. Crash bars, for example, on exit doors and those ubiquitous "EXIT" signs now mark the path to safety. All of these improvements are a result of this legislation. Other regulations such as the composition of fire curtains, smoke doors, and flame retardant scenery soon followed.

Fire codes and safety equipment existed long before the Iroquois Theatre disaster. The first American Building Codes, relating to fire, date as far back as 1631, when John Winthrop, Governor of Boston, outlawed the building of chimneys next to thatched roofs. In 1648, the governor of New Amsterdam (New York) appointed four fire marshals whose responsibility it was to inspect chimneys. Their power even went as far as to issue fines. Other advances in fire safety occurred in 1872 when Phillip Pratt of Abington, MA, invented the first automatic sprinkler system for use in the fabric industry. The fire safety curtain itself dates as far back as 1794 with its introduction at the Theatre Royal in London. But, despite these advances in fire protection equipment and technology, not every building made use of them nor did officials always enforce their use. Such was the case with the Iroquois Theatre disaster. Today, there are a number of national and international organizations that govern or influence fire safety in our theatres.

[1]The Iroquois Theatre fire was not the worst theatre fire in recorded history. The Ring Theatre fire in Vienna, Austria occurred in 1881 with the loss of between 620-850 lives.

The stage of the Iroquois Theatre looking from the balcony

- International Building Code (IBC)
- The Uniform Building Code (UBC)
- Building Officials and Code Administrators code (BOCA)
- The Standard Building Code (SBC)
- American National Standards Institute (ANSI)

Of these, the International Building Code or IBC provides the greatest influence on local fire codes and regulations. Enforcement is left to local agencies.

The Fire Safety Curtain
Theatre buildings of the past were considered to be two separate buildings; an auditorium and stage building attached to a stage with a common proscenium opening. The fire safety curtain was originally designed to seal off the two buildings, but today, the idea of a stage area and an auditorium as being two separate buildings is a thing of the past. With the creation of the modern day Performing Arts Center with adjoining spaces such as rehearsal rooms, storage areas, scene shops and dressing rooms, the idea of complete separation is not as possible as in the past[2]. The fire safety curtain is essentially designed to protect the audience from the stage area in the case of fire and smoke and allow them *sufficient time for a safe and orderly egress.* Fire safety curtains must work in *conjunction with other building life and fire safety systems,* and be able to *reduce the transmission of radiant heat, block debris,* as well as *contribute to the control of smoke and gas movement[3].* In addition, ANSI E1.22 - 2009 11.12 requires that all fire safety curtains be in the closed position when the stage is not in use. This chapter will examine the three most common types of fire safety curtains used in the theatre; the Manual Straight-Lift, the Brail and the Motorized. We will also discuss the maintenance and operation of both the *balanced* and *over-balanced* systems. Before we begin, let's look at fire curtain basics in general.

[2]Conner, William, Burning Issues in Fire Curtain Regulation, ESTA Protocol, March 2001.
[3]Editor's note, ANSI E1.22 - 2009 is currently under review by the working group of the ANSI Standards Committee, PLASA.

Safety Requirements

As noted earlier, the International Building Code has become the established framework for all local municipal building codes in the U.S. The IBC establishes the minimum requirements for proscenium openings with heights of 50 feet or more. These are summarized from the IBC 2006, Section 410, Stages and Platforms.

- ***410.3.4 Proscenium wall.*** *Where the stage height is greater than 50 feet (15 240 mm), all portions of the stage shall be completely separated from the seating area by a proscenium wall with not less than a 2-hour fire-resistance rating extending continuously from the foundation to the roof.*

- ***410.3.5 Proscenium curtain.*** *Where a proscenium wall is required to have a fire-resistance rating, the stage opening shall be provided with a fire curtain of approved material or an approved water curtain complying* **with Section 903.3.1.1. The fire curtain shall be designed and installed to** *intercept hot gases, flames and smoke and to prevent a glow from a severe fire on the stage from showing on the auditorium side for a period of 20 minutes. The closing of the fire curtain from the full open position shall be accomplished in less than 30 seconds, with the last 8 feet (2438 mm) of travel requiring 5 or more seconds for full closure.*

- ***410.3.5.1 Activation.*** *The curtain shall be activated by rate-of-rise heat detection installed in accordance with Section 907.10 operating at a rate of temperature rise of 15 to 20°F per minute (8 to 11°C per minute), and by an auxiliary manual control.*

- ***410.3.5.2 Fire test.*** *A sample curtain with a minimum of two vertical seams shall be subjected to the standard fire test specified in ASTM E 119 for a period of 30 minutes. The curtain shall overlap the furnace edges by an amount that is appropriate to seal the top and sides. The curtain shall have a bottom pocket containing a minimum of 4 pounds per linear foot (5.9 kg/m) of batten. The exposed surface of the curtain shall not glow, and flame or smoke shall not penetrate the curtain during the test period. Unexposed surface temperature and hose stream test requirements are not applicable to the proscenium fire safety curtain test.*

- ***410.3.5.3 Smoke test.*** *Curtain fabrics shall have a smoke-developed rating of 25 or less when tested in accordance with ASTM E 84.*

- ***410.3.5.4 Tests.*** *The completed proscenium curtain shall be subjected to operating tests prior to the issuance of a certificate of occupancy.*

- ***410.3.6 Scenery.*** *Combustible materials used in sets and scenery shall meet the fire propagation performance criteria I of NFPA 701, in accordance with Section 805 and the International Fire Code. Foam plastics and materials containing foam plastics shall comply with Section 2603 and the International Fire Code.*

- ***410.3.7 Stage ventilation.*** *Emergency ventilation shall be provided for stages larger than 1,000 square feet (93 m2) in floor area, or with a stage height greater than 50 feet (15 240 mm). Such ventilation shall comply with Section 410.3.7.1 or 410.3.7.2.*

- ***410.3.7.1 Roof vents.*** *Two or more vents constructed to open automatically by approved heat-activated devices and with an aggregate clear opening area of not less than 5 percent of the area of the stage shall be located near the center and above the highest part of the stage area. Supplemental means shall be provided for manual operation of the ventilator. Curbs shall be provided as required for skylights in Section 2610.2. Vents shall be labeled.*

- *[F] 410.3.7.2 Smoke control.* Smoke control in accordance with Section 909 shall be provided to maintain the smoke layer interface not less than 6 feet (1829 mm) above the highest level of the assembly seating or above the top of the proscenium opening where a proscenium wall is provided in compliance with Section 410.3.4.

Types of Fire Curtains

There are several different types of fire curtains that are in use today.

- *The Manual Straight Lift Fire Curtain* resides above the proscenium arch and is used in venues where the grid is twice the height of the proscenium arch plus 5 feet. Once released, it travels along guide cables that run inside smoke pockets sealing the stage. This type of curtain can be *over-balanced* whereby gravity lowers the curtain to the stage, or *balanced* where additional weight is added to the curtain allowing it to be lowered.
- *The Brail Curtain* resides above the proscenium arch and is used in venues where the space above the proscenium is less than or equal to the height of the proscenium opening. It is not counterweighted so it is curtain heavy. A governor is employed to regulate the speed of the curtain along with a manual or powered brail fire curtain winch.
- *Motorized Fire Curtain* are simply motorized versions of the Straight-Lift or Brail Fire Curtains. The fire curtain hoists can generally carry the entire weight of the fire curtain; no counterweights are necessary. When the fire curtain is deployed, gravity lowers the curtain while a governor regulates speed.
- *Rigid and Framed Fire Curtains* are similar to *Manual Straight Lift Curtains* but are much heavier. These curtains are specifically designed to meet the requirements of local fire codes and/or unusual spaces. Because of the weight, these curtains generally employ counterweights and use a *Traction Motor* as an assist.
- *Tripped Curtain-* Due to reliability problems, *Tripped Fire Curtains* are not recognized by current building codes. Venues with *Tripped Fire Curtains* are encouraged to replace them with more reliable *Brail Curtains.*

Fire Curtain Fabric

Historically, fire curtains were made from woven asbestos. However, due to the health hazards associated with asbestos, newer curtains are now constructed from a specialized silica based fabric called *Zetek*. Just because your fire curtain is made from asbestos doesn't mean you have to panic. Many of these older curtains are still in use today. Because the asbestos is "woven" and coated with a sealant, there is little chance of exposure to the asbestos unless the fabric is torn. If there are any concerns about the asbestos curtain in your facility, contact a qualified theatrical inspection company.

The Standing Parts of the system

- *Smoke Seals-* form a seal between the top edge of the closed fire curtain and the top edge of the proscenium arch.

Smoke seals are attached to the top of the proscenium forming a seal between the wall and fire curtain.
-photo courtesy of JR Clancy

- *Guide Pockets (formally smoke pockets)* consist of steel channels running from the stage floor up along the proscenium arch wall. They are located on each side of the proscenium forming a physical barrier between the auditorium and the stage. *Guide (smoke) pockets* are not intended to form a smoke seal, but rather they prevent material from falling from the stage area into the audience
- *Yield Pad-* is a soft pad that is built into the bottom edge of the fire curtain. When the curtain is in the closed position, it forms a smoke seal that runs along the stage floor
- *Cable Guides and Curtain Guides* – are steel cables that are located inside the *smoke pockets*. Running from the floor to the grid, they guide the vertical edges of fire curtain as it is lowered to the floor. *Curtain guides* are attached to the side edges of the fire curtain and run through the *cable guides*

Curtain guides are attached to the side edges of the fire curtain and run through the cable guides.
-photo courtesy of JR Clancy

- *Signage-* A conspicuously placed sign with instructions for the manual release of the curtain.

IN CASE OF FIRE PULL RED RING TO LOWER FIRE CURTAIN AUTOMATICALLY ←

The Operational Parts of the system

- **The Fire Curtain-** is a curtain made from a fireproof fabric that is counterbalanced by a counterweight arbor. In the event of a fire, the curtain is automatically released thereby sealing the stage from the auditorium.

- **Fire Line-** is an 1/8" steel cable that runs from the floor on one side of the proscenium, then crosses the top of the stored curtain area near the grid, then runs down the other side of the proscenium wall to the floor. Older curtains incorporated a hemp rope fire line that was called a *cut line.* These lines required a knife to be placed next to the line with a sign that stated, *"In case of fire, cut rope".* Unfortunately, these knifes would disappear or become so dull as to render them unusable. If your venue still uses these types of release lines, they should be replaced with the more modern alternative. The modern fire line contains temperature sensitive *fusible links* evenly spaced every 15 feet (minimum 4 links) along the sides and the top. In the event of a fire, the *fusible links* melt and the curtain is automatically lowered to the floor.

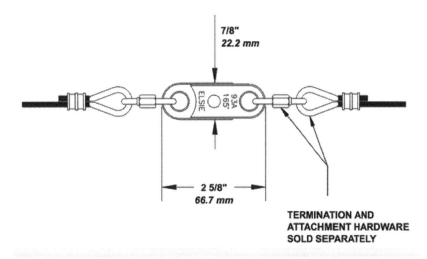

In the event of a fire, the fusible links melt and the curtain is automatically lowered to the floor.

-photo courtesy of JR Clancy

103

An *Electro Thermal Link* serves in much the same manner as the *fusible link* accept these connect the fire release lines to fire alarms or other electrical systems. The link releases as soon as electricity is applied and is re-settable.

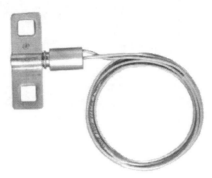

An electro-themal link works in conjunction with the building's fire detection systems
-photo courtesy of JR Clancy

- **Manual Releasing Devices -** can consist of a *latch release lever, ring and peg, pull* or *pin release.* These systems all require the curtain to be slightly heavier than the counterweight arbor. Should a *fusible link* melt, the release line will become slack and the ball will drop to the stage floor. The slack in the fire line will create slack in the *arbor release lever* thereby releasing the curtain. The *latch release lever, ring and pin* and *pull pin release* systems operate much the same way.

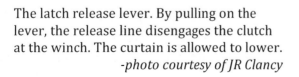

The latch release lever. By pulling on the lever, the release line disengages the clutch at the winch. The curtain is allowed to lower.
-photo courtesy of JR Clancy

Ring and Peg release with signage
-photo courtesy of H & H Specialties

Pull Pin release
-*photo courtesy of JR Clancy*

- **Electro-Mechanical Release** is a release device that works in conjunction with the building's fire alarm systems. It allows fire detection systems such as smoke detectors and fire alarm pull boxes to release the fire curtain when activated. The mechanism is attached to the *fire release line* and releases tension in the line allowing the fire curtain to close. The release mechanism may be attached to the *fire release line* at any point and can work with other manual fire release mechanisms.

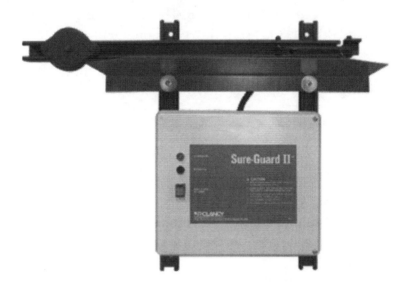

SureGuard II Release System by JR Clancy is one such example of an Electro-Mechanical Release
-*photo courtesy of JR Clancy*

- **Arbor Releases** - When the fire line goes slack, the arbor is released. There are several popular means for holding the arbor down until it is released: the *free end ball* and the *arbor lease leaver.*

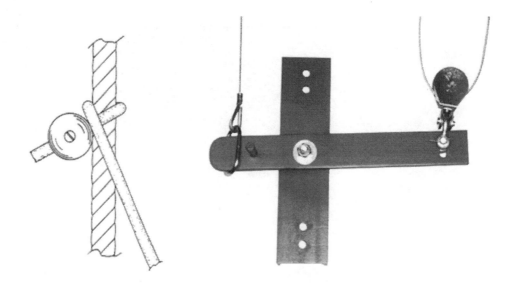

The free end ball release and the arbor release lever.

-photo courtesy of JR Clancy

- **The Free End Ball** is wrapped around the part of the purchase line that is attached to the bottom of the arbor, as shown about. This wrap is a type of prusiking knot called a fire knot that holds the arbor down. When the fire line goes slack, the free end ball falls, releasing the purchase line and the arbor. This is a very simple way to hold the arbor, but it is not always reliable – the fire knot does not always release when the fire line goes slack.

- **The Arbor Release Lever** is a more complex system than the free end ball, but more reliable. One end of a cable is connected to the bottom of the arbor and a ring on the other end is slid onto the end of the lever. Tension on the fire line keeps this lever horizontal. When the tension on the fire line is released, the arbor pulls the lever up, letting the ring slide of the end, completely releasing the arbor.

- **Round Weight Arbor Guide and Assembly** (of which there are several variations) is used to provide tension on the *fire release line*. When the releasing mechanism is pulled or a *fusible link* detaches, the *round weight arbor* drops and tension on the *fire release line* is eased. This mechanism is commonly used when a hoist is used to lift the fire safety curtain. When the fire line goes slack, this system takes tension off of the clutch level, causing the clutch to disengage and the fire safety curtain to fall.

Round Weight Arbor
016-8

Round Weight
016-9

Round Weight Arbor Guard
016-13

The Round Weight Arbor and assembly is used to provide tension on the Fire Release Line
-photos courtesy of JR Clancy

Deceleration Devices ANSI E1.22 – 2009 11.10 requires that the last 8 feet of travel take a minimum of 5 seconds. Slowing the curtain down so that it travels that last 8 feet is accomplished by several means

- *Dash pots* are used to dampen and control the last few feet of downward travel of manual fire safety curtains. A piston is regulated by the flow of hydraulic fluid slowing down the arbor.
- *Hydraulic Governors* are used to control the decent of motorized lift, including *Brail* (fold up) *Curtains.* When released, the curtain free falls by gravity to cover the proscenium opening. The descent of the curtain is controlled with an adjustable speed governor located inside the winch.

A hydraulic dashpot
-photo courtesy of JR Clancy

The Brail Winch with hydraulic governor
-*photo courtesy of JR Clancy*

Over-balance Devices

- **Over-balance Bar**
  In balanced systems, the counterweight arbor and fire curtain remain together *in balance* allowing the curtain to be raised and lowered manually without too much effort. In the event of a fire, a steel bar or weight is released down the center lift lines where it contacts the top of the fire curtain batten. This added weight makes the system curtain heavy and allows it to close.

- **Over-balance Arbor**
  In balanced systems, a separate counterweight arbor is released as tension on the *fire release line* goes slack. The weight of the *over-balance arbor* pulls up on the main arbor allowing the curtain to deploy.

Putting It All Together

Now that we have looked at the *standing* and *operational* parts of the *Fire Safety Curtain*, lets put all the parts together.

The Manual Straight-Lift Fire Curtain (unbalanced)

The *Straight Lift Fire Curtain* resides above the proscenium arch. Once released, it travels along *guide cables* that run inside *guide (smoke) pockets*. As discussed earlier, *guide (smoke) pockets* are located on the upstage sides of the proscenium walls. Note that these *Straight-Lift Fire Curtains* require a grid height of twice the proscenium opening plus a minimum of 5 feet. The curtain shown in the illustration below is intentionally left out of balance so that once released, gravity will allow the curtain to lower itself into position sealing the proscenium. In its open position, a fire release line that is attached to the arbor release restrains the curtain. *The fire release line* is comprised of 1/8" steel cable that contains a minimum of 4 fusible links distributed every 15 feet along the release line. In the event of a fire, any one of the fusible links will melt. The curtain will automatically be lowered into its closed position sealing the proscenium. Once released, either intentionally or unintentionally, the curtain must be reset.

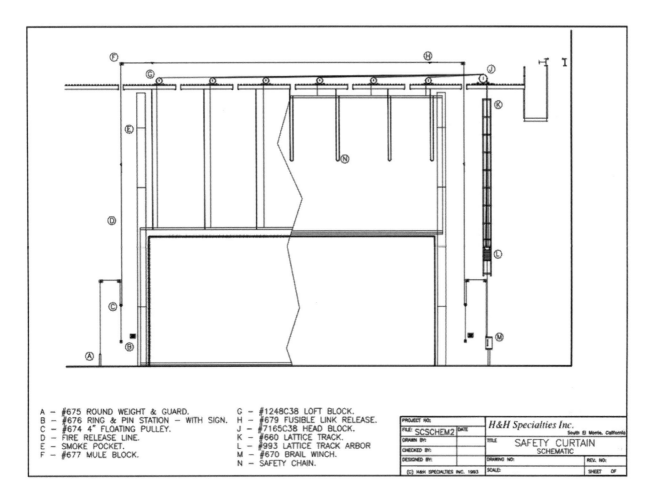

A – #675 ROUND WEIGHT & GUARD.
B – #676 RING & PIN STATION – WITH SIGN.
C – #674 4" FLOATING PULLEY.
D – FIRE RELEASE LINE.
E – SMOKE POCKET.
F – #677 MULE BLOCK.
G – #1248C38 LOFT BLOCK.
H – #679 FUSIBLE LINK RELEASE.
J – #7165C38 HEAD BLOCK.
K – #660 LATTICE TRACK.
L – #993 LATTICE TRACK ARBOR
M – #670 BRAIL WINCH.
N – SAFETY CHAIN.

PROJECT NO:
FILE: SCSCHEM2   DATE:
DRAWN BY:
CHECKED BY:
DESIGNED BY:
(C) H&H SPECIALTIES INC. 1993

H&H Specialties Inc.
South El Monte, California
TITLE   SAFETY CURTAIN
SCHEMATIC
DRAWING NO: REV. NO:
SCALE: SHEET   OF

The Manual Straight Lift Curtain (unbalanced) with Ring and Pin Release Station
- photo courtesy of H and H Specialties

The Manual Straight-Lift Fire Curtain (balanced) with the Over-balance Bar

The design of this *Straight Lift Fire Curtain* is similar to the curtain discussed above; the difference being that the system is kept *in-balance* just like a line set. Because the fire curtain remains *in-balance*, it will need additional weight to assist in its automatically being lowered into the floor. (See G in the diagram below). In the event of a fire, the *fusible links* melt allowing a steel bar to drop down the center lift lines to rest on the top of the fire curtain batten below. The problem with the over-balance bar system is that the curtain could fall too fast and not slow down the remaining 8 feet of travel. To solve this, the over-balance bar is often leashed to the grid so that it disengages the fire curtain batten the last 8 feet of travel. This allows the curtain's momentum to slow the curtain down as it comes to a complete stop sealing the floor. Lastly, just as with the un-balanced curtain discussed above, the curtain must be reset after it is released.

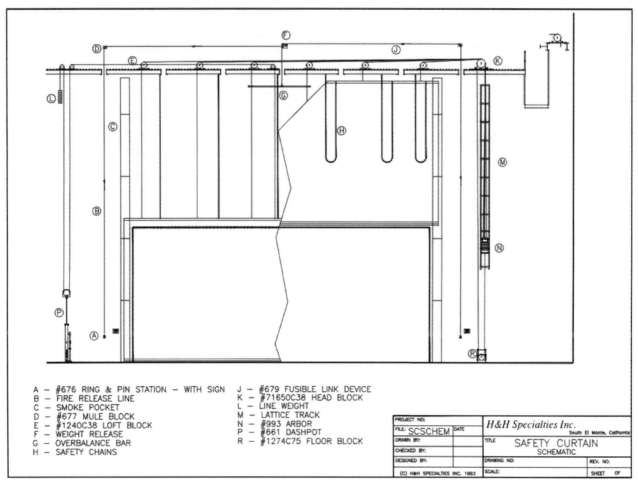

A — #676 RING & PIN STATION — WITH SIGN
B — FIRE RELEASE LINE
C — SMOKE POCKET
D — #677 MULE BLOCK
E — #1240C38 LOFT BLOCK
F — WEIGHT RELEASE
G — OVERBALANCE BAR
H — SAFETY CHAINS

J — #679 FUSIBLE LINK DEVICE
K — #71650C38 HEAD BLOCK
L — LINE WEIGHT
M — LATTICE TRACK
N — #993 ARBOR
P — #661 DASHPOT
R — #1274C75 FLOOR BLOCK

PROJECT NO:		H&H Specialties Inc.		
FILE: SCSCHEM	DATE		South El Monte, California	
DRAWN BY:		TITLE SAFETY CURTAIN		
CHECKED BY:		SCHEMATIC		
DESIGNED BY:		DRAWING NO:		REV. NO:
(C) H&H SPECIALTIES INC. 1993		SCALE:		SHEET OF

The Manual Straight Lift Curtain (balanced) with Over-balance bar

- photo courtesy of H and H Specialties

The Manual Straight-Lift Fire Curtain (balanced) with Lever Release and over-balance arbor

Again, this system is similar to the designs we have discussed previously. The system is in-balance and just like any in-balance system, it will need additional weight in order for the curtain to deploy. In this case, the addition weight comes from an over-balance arbor that provides lift on the main arbor. This arbor is attached to the main arbor by means of it own head block (designs may vary). When the *fusible links* melt or the *release lever* is pulled, the over-balance arbor drops providing lift on the main arbor. Note, that with this type of release system, the fire line will travel twice the distance of the fire curtain as the over-balance arbor falls. The line will need to be retrieved when resetting the system. Resetting simply involves pulling on the *fire line* and replacing it back into its release station. As this happens, the over-balance arbor will be raised back into its reset position. The fire curtain can then be returned to its stored position.

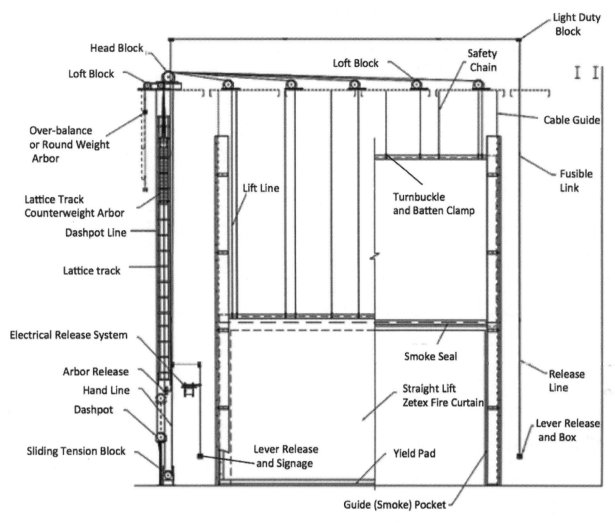

The Manual Straight Lift Curtain (balanced) with Lever Release and Over-balance arbor
- *photo courtesy of JR Clancy*

The Brail Fire Curtain Rigging System

The *Brail Curtain* is used in venues where the space above the proscenium is less than or equal to the height of the proscenium opening. Because it is NOT counterweighted, it is curtain heavy. A *hydraulic governor* is needed to regulate the speed of the curtain once it is deployed. A *brail fire curtain winch* (manual or electric) is used to raise and reset the curtain. Deployment is accomplished manually or by typical release devises discussed earlier or in the case of a fire, with the separation of the *fusible links*.

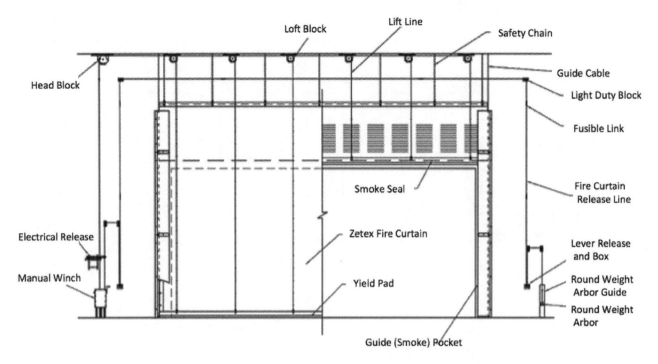

The Brail Fire Curtain with lever release and manual winch

- *photo courtesy of JR Clancy*

The Motorized Fire Curtain Rigging System

The *Motorized Fire Curtain* is simply a motorized version of the *Straight-Lift Fire Curtain*. Since the *line shaft winch* can carry the entire weight of the fire curtain, counterweights are generally not necessary.

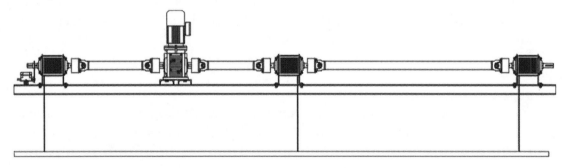

The Line Shaft Winch

- *photo courtesy of JR Clancy*

The operation of a motorized curtain is quite simple. The *line shaft winch* is located on the grid with each drum lining up with a lift line. The winch controls both the raising and lowering of the fire curtain. The *fire release line* controls the *line shaft winch* where it connects to the brake or clutch. If the *fire release line* goes slack, the brake or clutch is released and the curtain is lowered to the floor. A governor located at the motor regulates the speed.

Framed or Rigid Fire Curtains are the only types of *fire curtains* that may require the use of counterweights. In this case, *traction winches* may be used to assist in the raising and lowering of the curtain.

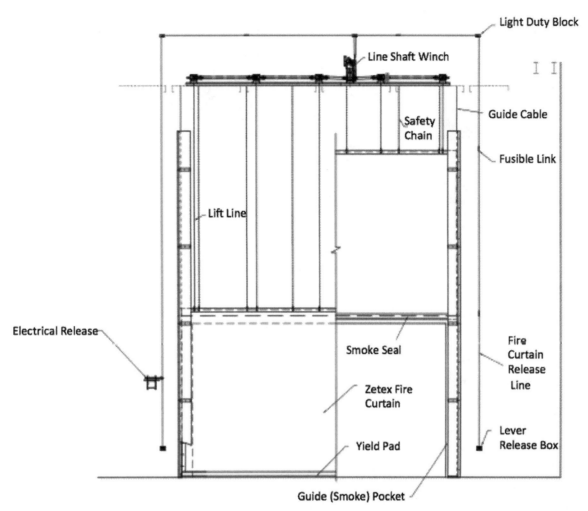

The Straight Lift Curtain with Lever Release and Line Shaft Winch
- *photo courtesy of JR Clancy*

Traction Winches are used to drive counterweighted *Framed or Rigid Fire Curtains*. The head block has "V" grooves that guide the lift line cables as the curtain is opened or closed during normal operation. However, during emergency operation, the *Fire Release Cable* is connected to the brake or clutch that disengages when the *Fire Line* goes slack. As the brake or clutch is released, the head block is allowed to freely rotate as the curtain is lowered into its closed position. A *hydraulic governor* controls the speed of the curtain while limit switches control travel.

A typical traction winch used to control Rigid Framed Fire Curtains
- *photo courtesy of JR Clancy*

Water Based Systems

There is still concern over the efficacy of fire curtains. In an article published in Protocol magazine, 2001, William Connor stated that was estimated that fewer than 25% of all fire curtains installed throughout the US would fail in the event of a fire[4]. As we discussed earlier, with the creation of the Performing Arts Center as a multi-use facility it is nearly impossible to completely seal off the stage in the event of a fire. He goes on to say,

> ... the concept of stage and auditorium as separable compartments is no longer valid. In the past theatres with stages were essentially two buildings with the proscenium wall in common and with little or no contiguous support space. Contrast that to modern era performing arts centers or even typical high schools where both the auditorium and stage are connected and surrounded by ancillary space. Also as a result of concerts in arenas, all forms of open stages, and even the common practice of building through the proscenium of a traditional theatre, the concept of separating the combustible scenery in a stage from auditorium is much less achievable than in the past

With these concerns, the idea of deluge and sprinkler systems seem to be a viable alternative to the more complex mechanics of the fire curtain. William Connor goes on to say,

> Modern stages and practically all new theatres are required to be [fixed with sprinklers]. The efficacy of modern sprinkler systems is better than 99%. In two theatres in the 1990s, there were fires involving substantial drapery and in both instances the fire was suppressed by the sprinkler system. (Significantly, in both cases the fire curtain did not operate.)

So what are the alternatives?

The two systems currently in use are the *Drencher* or *Deluge system* and the *Water Curtain*. The *Drencher* floods the stage with a large volume of water while the *Water Curtain* uses a fireproof fabric curtain that, once released, saturates the stage with water. However, both systems have their advantages and disadvantages that are noted below.

[4]Conner, William, <u>Burning Issues in Fire Curtain Regulation</u>, ESTA Protocol, March 2001

Water Drencher or Deluge System
This system basically creates a wall of water at the proscenium line preventing fire and smoke from entering the audience area. A large volume of water is stored above the stage. In the event of a fire, water cannons flood the stage area extinguishing any flames. As with most fire and smoke protection equipment today, the *Deluge* systems work in conjunction with fire detection equipment in the building. The *Deluge* system is a good choice for venues where there might be catwalks, scenery or other obstructions that protrude past the proscenium opening, but flooding and water damage has occurred frequently in venues where the system has been accidentally activated. Care needs to be taken in the building's design to insure that the water does not interact with electrical systems. Check with your theatre consultant and insurance carrier to see if this system is the right choice.

The Water Curtain is a slightly different means of sealing off the stage. The system is dependent on the use of a fireproof fabric curtain that is released at the proscenium line. Water flows from sprinkler heads mounted in front of the curtain, saturating it, thereby preventing sparks, smoke, and flammable material from crossing into the audience. However, care must be taken to insure that the curtain is not blocked by scenery or other obstructions. There is also the potential for flood damage should the system be accidentally triggered.

Maintenance and Inspection and Testing
Because *Deluge* and *Water Curtain* systems are integrated into the buildings fire activation and alarm systems, they will require annual inspection by a qualified person. Manual activation of the system during inspection can be performed without actually activating the water curtain. Whereas, ANSI E1.22-2009 standards do not cover *Deluge* systems, NFPA 15: *Standard for Water Spray Fixed Systems for Fire* -2015 does. It is best to check with your local fire regulations or theatre consultant.

Testing and Maintenance of Fire Safety Curtains
Fire Safety Curtains are required to be functional in the case of an emergency! Routine scheduled inspections and maintenance of *Fire Safety Curtains* are recommended by both NFPA (The National Fire Protection Association) and ANSI (American National Standards Institute) [5]. Two published standards cover *Fire Safety Curtains*. These are ANSI E1.22 – 2009, *Entertainment Technology*, PLASA and NFPA 80, *Standard for Fire Doors and Other Opening Protectives 2007 Edition, Chapter 20- Fabric Fire Safety Curtains*. Both of these documents are very specific on the frequency of *Fire Safety Curtain* testing and maintenance. Whereas, NFPA 80 and ANSI E1.22 do not cover the use, testing and maintenance of *Deluge* and *Water Curtains*, NFPA 15: *Standard for Water Spray Fixed Systems for Fire* -2015 does cover sprinkler systems. Both NFPA and ANSI standards that cover *Fire Safety Curtains* and *Water Based* systems are available on-line for download.

[5]The Occupational Safety and Health Administration regulations are law and SHALL be followed. NFPA and ANSI are self-regulating organizations that establish recommendations that SHOULD be followed. In the event of litigation, the courts will first refer to OSHA. If OSHA is not clear on the subject matter, then they will refer to any one or more of the self-regulating organizations. In short, NFPA and ANSI recommendations are just as good as law and SHOULD be followed.

To emphasize the pertinent parts of both standards:

NFPA 80, states,

- *20.7.1.1 The fire safety curtain assembly shall be closed at all times except when there is an event, rehearsal, or similar activity.*
- *20.7.1.3 Emergency operation shall be verified by the owner every 90 days.*
- *20.9.1 The rigging system shall be inspected annually.*
- *20.9.1.3 Retraining of the owner and staff shall be mandatory during each annual inspection.*

ANSI E1.22 – 2009 is more specific:

- ***12.3 Periodic User Testing*** *The emergency closing of the fire safety curtain system shall be tested at least once every 30 performances but not less than once every three months.*
- ***12.4 Annual Inspection*** ***12.4.1*** *A qualified person shall inspect the fire safety curtain system at least once a year.*
- ***12.4.2*** *Inspection shall include complete visual inspection of the curtain, rigging, and both the automatic and manual initiating and release devices.*
- ***12.4.3*** *Emergency manual closing shall be tested including testing each manual emergency release device at least once.*
- ***12.4.4*** *The log shall be reviewed by the qualified person.*
- ***12.4.5*** *The owner or the owner's designated representative shall be trained by a qualified person on the operation, maintenance, and testing requirements of the fire safety curtain system as a part of each annual inspection.*
- ***12.4.6*** *The authority having jurisdiction shall be notified of the time and place of the annual inspection.*

In addition, local codes may have more stringent requirements for the periodic inspection of your system as well as the replacement of parts. Consult with your local fire marshal for more specific information.

Some consideration for the testing of your *Fire Safety Curtain*:

- Treat the maintenance of your *Fire Safety Curtain* in the same manner as you would routinely test counterweight linesets or stage rigging components Check the NFPA or ANSI recommendations for the frequency of testing
- Most *Fire Safety Curtains* are integrated with other fire emergency systems such as fire alarms and smoke doors. Contact your building administrator if you need assistance in performing any of the following tests
- Visually inspect all components of the curtain before testing
- Insure that there is nothing that will block the curtain from deployment.
- Make sure that the release devices are not blocked or obscured from view (most are)
- Perform a complete raising and lowering test using either the automatic or manual release devices. Be sure to test each release line. (Note: if you testing the manual release lines, it is best to tie a tag line to it for retrieval. Do not test the system for the first time just before a performance. Give yourself at least three hours)
- When in the lowered position, inspect the curtain for wear and tear.
- As the curtain is being lowered, listen for any unusual noises. Areas to check are the Guide Lines, Loft and Head Blocks and any unusual noises in the winch systems

- Time the deployment. The curtain should close within 30 seconds with the last 5 to 10 feet of travel taking 5 seconds
- The curtain should not bounce when the yield pad lands on the deck
- Test the opening of the Smoke Doors
- Reset system and perform test again if necessary
- Maintain a log book of the test and each action performed
- Contact a *qualified* person or professional theatrical rigging company for yearly inspections or if you notice any problems during the test

Chapter 7:
The Rope Line System

Introduction

The *Rope Line System* is one of the oldest forms of counterweighted rigging around. Often called a *Hemp System*, the term gets it name from the fibrous rope used to operate the system[1]. The ancient Greeks used hemp rope with a device called the *machina* to raise and lower their scenic machinery. The most commonly known effect was the *deus ex machina* where an actor portraying a god would be lowered to the stage. Since the days of old sailing ships, hemp rigging has been used to hoist sails (running rigging) and stabilize masts (standing rigging). As soon as theatres had a need for movable scenery, it would only figure that sailors, who had a deep understanding of rigging systems, would carry over their knowledge into the theatre. Interestingly enough, sailors were brought in from seaport towns to raise and lower the huge *velarium* (or awning) over the coliseum in Rome, making them possibly the first arena riggers. It is believed they used a series of hemp rope rigging and pulleys along with the windless to achieve their task.

The *Rope Line System* of rigging specifically refers to a system of ropes, pulleys (blocks), and sandbags used to fly theatrical scenery and equipment in and out from the stage floor. As noted, it incorporates many of the old nautical rigging techniques from sailing traditions throughout the centuries. In contrast, the Manual *Counter Weight System*, which will be discussed in Chapter 8, raises and lowers stage scenery and equipment in a safer and much more controlled manner.

When we speak of hemp rigging, we refer to the manually operated block and tackle system or manually sandbagged system where a load needs to be raised and lowered. In this chapter, we will introduce you to the *Single Line* and *Multiple Line* set hemp systems, hardware and rope. Let's begin with an overview of the operating systems.

The Single Line Set System
The simplest system uses *a spot line*. The operating line runs from the pin rail over a head block to a loft block to the load. Originally made from a naturally fibrous rope called hemp, most operating lines today are made of a synthetic material.

---

[1]Manila, a type of hemp, was the most commonly used rope in the United States

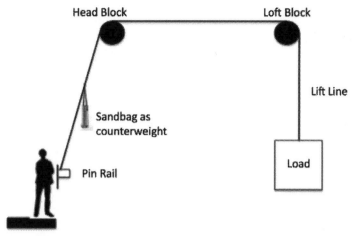

A single line (or spot line) system with no mechanical advantage. Note the use of a sandbag to aid in counterbalancing the load.

A single line system is made up of *a pin rail* (where you tie off the rope), a *head block*, a *loft block*, and a load. The rope itself consists of a load end (the place where the load is attached) and an operating end (the end that is hauled).

Multiple Line Set System

A more complex system utilizes multiple lift lines sets and multiple *loft blocks*. *Lift lines* can be as few as two, but generally around four. The *lift lines* run up from the batten to the loft blocks. From the *loft blocks* they run to the *head block*, which serves as a collector for the *lift lines*. A *trim clamp* can be attached to the *lift lines* as they run down from the *head block* enabling the operator to trim the lines and attach *sandbags* as counterweight. Again, the *pin rail* serves as a tie off point for the line set.

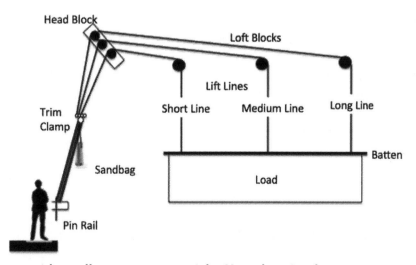

A multiple line system with sandbag as counterweight. Note the trim clamp serves as a collector point for the lift lines and allows for the attachment of a sandbag.

Hardware

Now that we have looked at the single line and multiple line systems, lets look at the specific hardware used in this system.

Loft Blocks, Head Blocks and Trim Clamps

In nautical terminology, a pulley is called a block. It consists of a sheave or grooved wheel that is strapped into a shell or frame allowing a rope to roll freely in the groove of the sheave. *Loft blocks* are essentially pulleys that are located in the fly loft of a theatre. They are attached to the theatre's grid structure allowing the *lift lines* to run down to a *batten* (or load). More details on *Head* and *Loft Blocks* will be discussed in Chapter 8.

Head Blocks, on the other hand, collect the *lift lines* from the *loft blocks*. The *lift lines* then pass down through the head block to a *trim clamp* and then to the pin rail. Essentially, there are two types of head blocks used in the rope line counterweight system; the newer single shaft head block and the older stacked head block. The former mounts all the sheaves together on a single ball bearing axle with four lift lines running off the sheaves. The latter head block stacks the sheaves separately and at an angle running in alignment with the resultant force. This older style head block dates from the 19th century with three sheaves mounted inside a steel shell. Three lift lines ran around the sheaves to the loft blocks and down to the batten.

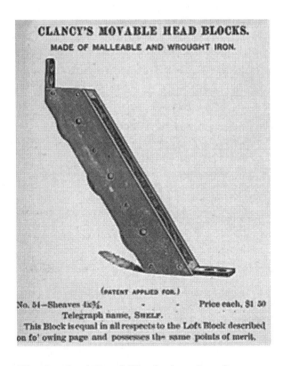

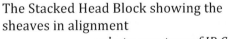

The Stacked Head Block showing the sheaves in alignment
-*photo courtesy of JR Clancy*

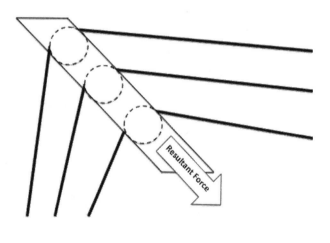

The angle of the Stacked Head Block is positioned in alignment with the resultant force

120

The newer single shaft hemp head blocks are equipped with ball bearings, something the older Stacked Head Blocks did not have.

-photo courtesy of J. Lillian Gray

The Rope Trim Clamp and Sandbag as counterweight

Many times, the loads suspended on the lift lines are too heavy to be operated by one stagehand. Then, sandbags can be attached to the lines as a means of counterbalancing the load. Two means of attaching the sandbag to the operating ends of the lift lines are the *rope trim clamp* and the *sunday*. The *rope trim* clamp is a device that holds the *lift lines* together and allows the operator to individually adjust the trim of the *lift lines*. A *sandbag(s)* can be attached to the lower ring of the trim clamp serving as a counterweight for the load. The sunday, on the other hand, is a much older means of attaching the sandbags to the lift lines. A looped rope or wire is tied with a Prussic knot on the operating ends of the lift lines. A sandbag can then be clipped to the sunday.

Rope trim clamp. The wing nuts on the sides allow for adjustments to the lift lines

-photo courtesy of Mutual Hardware

The sunday is a looped line tied onto a lift line with a Prussic knot. The sandbag would be clipped onto the loop. This method pre-dates the use of the rope trim clamps and is still in use today.

Sandbags serve as counterweights to the load that is placed on the batten. Note how the rope trim clamps are attached to the lift lines and the sandbags are attached to the trim clamps.

-photo courtesy of Frank Cortez

The author at the fly rail of the Paramount Theatre in Austin, TX. Note the two rails one above the other. The higher rail is for battens at low trim while the lower rail is for high trim. In addition, the sandbags are attached with sundays rather than trim clamps.

Wooden loft blocks were screwed into their position on the wooden grids of the 19th century. They were soon replaced with the newer, more durable, steel loft blocks. The photo right is from the JR Clancy catalogue.

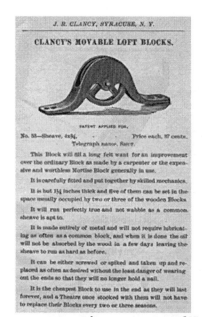

-photo courtesy of JR Clancy

122

The Pin Rail

The origins of the pin rail date as far back as the days of sailing ships, where sailors would tie off rigging lines to belaying pins located at the *rails* of the ship. The techniques and terminology carried over to the theatre as sailors became the first stagehands. Modern pin rails (often called fly rails) are made of steel rather than wood. They have either fixed or removable pins, made from either steel or hardwood such as ash or hickory.

The steel pin rail shown left and the belaying pin shown right.

-photo courtesy of Mutual Hardware

The Batten

Battens are linear pipes to which loads (scenery, lights or curtains) are attached. Originally made of wood, battens today are made from 21 foot Schedule 40 pipe that are joined together with a splice or pipe connector. The lift lines come down from the loft blocks above and are tied to the batten with a *clove hitch* followed by two *half hitches.* The fly system allows the batten to be vertically raised (flown out) into the fly space or lowered (flown in) to the deck. Parallel to the stage floor, they run stage right to stage left with the length of the batten being longer than the width of the proscenium opening. As a batten is raised to it's highest working position above the deck, it is at *high trim.*" Inversely, when it is lowered (4 to 5 feet off the floor), it is at *low trim.*

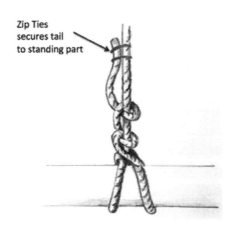

Tying off the lift lines to the pipe batten is done with a clove hitch
with two half hitches. The tail can be secured with a zip tie or wire tie.

Battens and lift lines

The older style head blocks had only three sheaves. Bridling off the lift lines became necessary to distribute the lift points evenly across the batten. Typically six bridle points would support the batten. The illustration to the right shows one of three bridled lift lines. The lift lines and bridle legs would have been eye spliced with a thimble. Shackles would have connected each line to a pear ring as shown in the detail below.

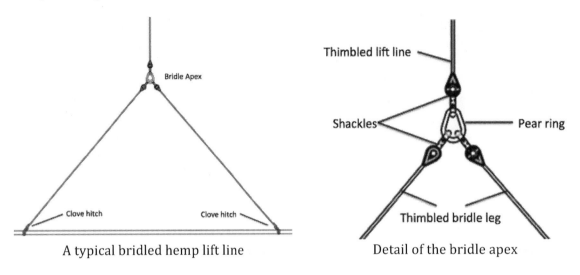

A typical bridled hemp lift line

Detail of the bridle apex

Tabs

Battens that run upstage to down stage are called tabs. These are usually located in the extreme off-stage areas where masking curtains are often tied. Because they run upstage to downstage, the direction of the lift lines may need to be re-directed by the use of *mule blocks*.

Loads

Loads can be attached to the battens in a myriad of different ways:

- Non traveling curtains such as borders and legs are tied on using a black string known as tie line
- Lighting instruments are hung using a lighting C-clamp (with safety cable in case the C-clamp should fail)
- Scenery can be attached with scenery chain or 1/8th inch steel cable

Opera Clamps (batten clamps –old school)

Opera clamps were primarily used in old hemp houses as a need to accomplish scene changes. In the 19th century, operas depended heavily on the use of painted drops for their scenic elements. Lift lines would be lowered to the stage and opera clamps would then be attached with a *bowline* (knot). *The opera clamps* would grab a wooden batten to which the top of a drop was permanently attached. The drop could then be flown. To change a drop, a line set would be brought in and the drop would be lowered into the arms of waiting stagehands. Using tie line, the stagehands would tie the furled drop onto the wooden batten. Next, the furled drop would be lifted and the batten released from the *opera clamps*. Stagehands would hang the drop on the backstage wall and get the next drop. The process would be reversed as the new drop was hung and then lifted into the fly space. Drops could also be folded in half (if necessary) by securing the bottom of the drop to the clamp- a process known as *"tripping the drop"*. This was a great way to fly out scenery with limited fly space. Another technique was to shorten a tall drop by rolling the top of the drop and batten, and then securing the rolled batten in the clamps.

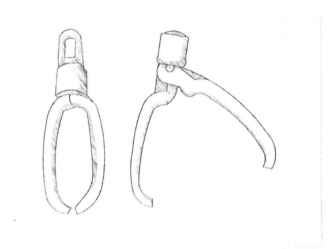

The opera clamp. Tension on the clamp was released as the batten was lifted allowing the cam to be rotated up and the jaws to release

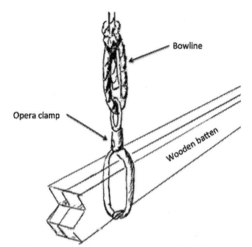

The opera clamp is secured with a bowline.

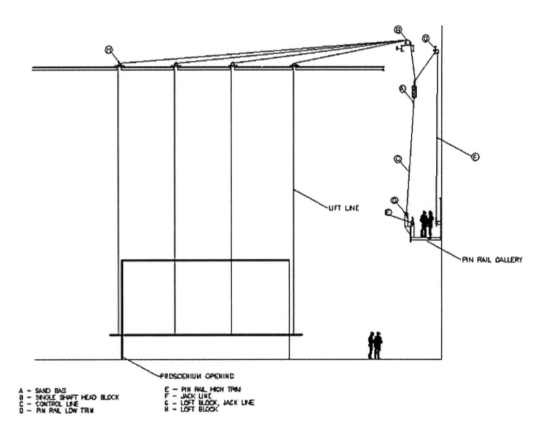

The Rope Line (Hemp) System at low trim. If the batten is hung with *opera clamps*, the scenic drop can be removed off the clamps and replaced with a new drop

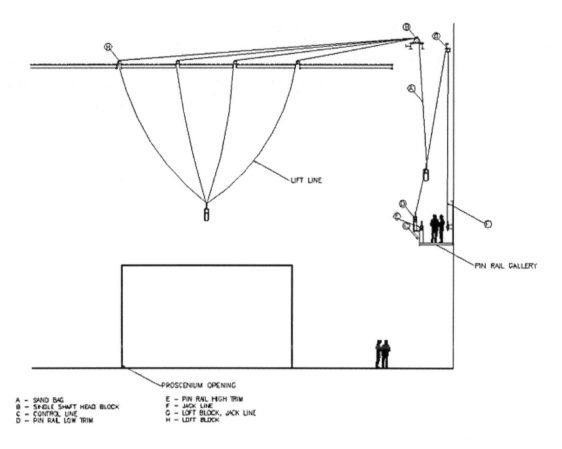

A – SAND BAG
B – SINGLE SHAFT HEAD BLOCK
C – CONTROL LINE
D – PIN RAIL LOW TRIM

E – PIN RAIL HIGH TRIM
F – JACK LINE
G – LOFT BLOCK, JACK LINE
H – LOFT BLOCK

PROSCENIUM OPENING

PIN RAIL GALLERY

LIFT LINE

If not in use, the line sets can be flown out with a sandbag as counterweight so they are not lost

Mule Blocks

Mule Blocks (sometimes called *Spider Blocks*) are blocks that change the direction of travel. They can also be used to divert the lift lines around obstructions.

Mule Blocks re-direct lift lines around obstructions

-photo courtesy of J. Lillian Gray

126

Spot blocks

Occasionally, individual lift lines need to be dropped from the grid or some other secure connection point. Spot blocks are blocks that are designed for temporary connection to the gridiron or any other secure structure. They can be loft blocks that can be positioned as needed or specially designed blocks that can be secured to a pipe batten.

Single sheave spot block that attaches to pipe.
        -photo courtesy of Sapsis Rigging, Inc.

Universal loft block that can serve as a spot block on the grid.
        -photo courtesy of JR Clancy

Snatch blocks

Snatch blocks, as discussed in Chapter 2, are temporary blocks that can be opened so the lift line can be directly inserted into the sheave without having to be threaded from the tail end of the rope. They are handy for hauling equipment to the grid, muleing lines or for use as an idler where a line needs to be lifted to prevent contact with other equipment.

Commercial snatch block

Rescue snatch block

Sandbags

Sandbags are heavy-duty canvas bags that, when filled with sand, provide counterweight to whatever load is attached to a batten. They come in a variety of sizes, ranging from 10, 25, 50 to 100 pounds. There are larger sizes available, but anything larger than 100 pounds can be unmanageable. They clip easily into a *sunday* or *hemp rope clamp*.

Sandbag attached to a rope trim clamp

Hemp round weight arbors

Round weight arbors are not commonly used. The arbor is permanently attached to the lift lines with a sunday. Adding or subtracting weights to the arbor can adjust the counterweight on the lineset.

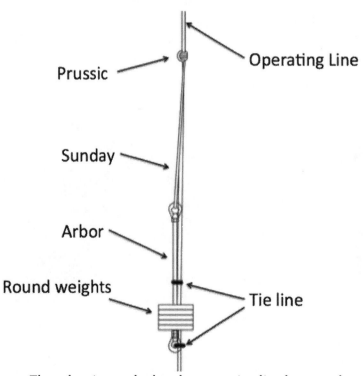

The arbor is attached to the operating line by a sunday

Operating the Rope Line System

Now that we have examined the hardware used in the Rope Line (Hemp) System, let's look at the operation and the techniques used. There are two types of Rope Line Systems; *unbalanced* and *balanced*. Both demand a great deal of care, knowledge, and experience when operating. The *unbalanced* system will require that the batten is slightly heavier than the counterweight so that the lineset will come in as needed. The balanced system maintains balance between the batten and the sandbags, but utilizes a secondary lineset call a jack line, that aids in the raising and lowering of the sandbag counterweight. Let's begin with the *unbalanced* system.

Unbalanced system

The *unbalanced* Rope Line System is slightly batten-heavy, so that the lineset can fly in. This demands an experienced and alert flyman (operator) as the system could run away from the operator if he is not careful.

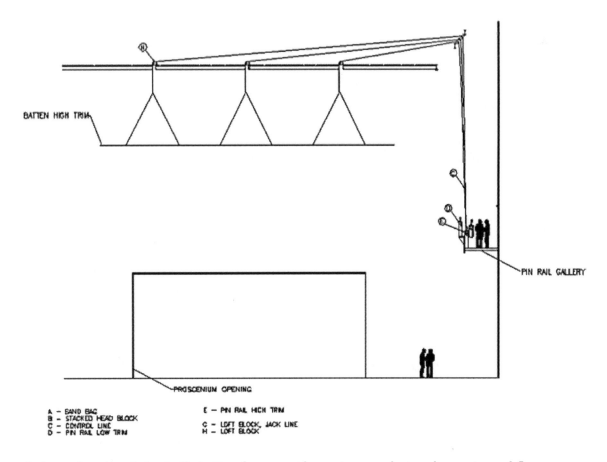

BATTEN HIGH TRIM

PIN RAIL GALLERY

PROSCENIUM OPENING

A — SAND BAG
B — STACKED HEAD BLOCK
C — CONTROL LINE
D — PIN RAIL LOW TRIM

E — PIN RAIL HIGH TRIM
G — LOFT BLOCK, JACK LINE
H — LOFT BLOCK

The unbalanced system is typically batten-heavy, and requires an alert and experienced flyman (operator).

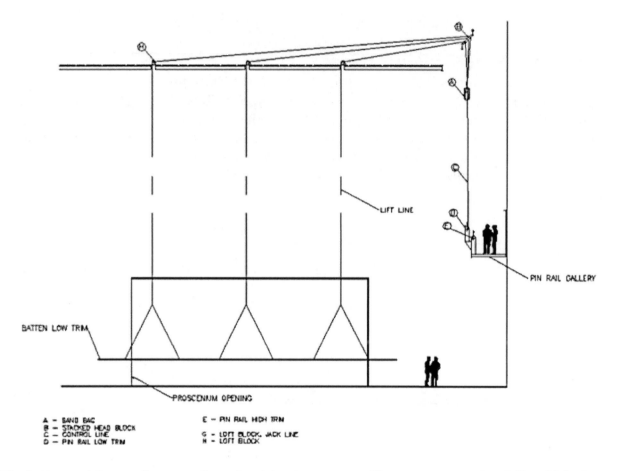

LIFT LINE

PIN RAIL GALLERY

BATTEN LOW TRIM

PROSCENIUM OPENING

A — SAND BAG
B — STACKED HEAD BLOCK
C — CONTROL LINE
D — PIN RAIL LOW TRIM

E — PIN RAIL HIGH TRIM

G — LOFT BLOCK, JACK LINE
H — LOFT BLOCK

If the batten and the sandbag are of equal weight, the system will not move unassisted. Should the batten be lighter than the sandbag, the sandbag will descend to the stage.

Balanced system and the Jack line

The *balanced* system uses a secondary rope called the *jack line*. The *jack line* is a separate line that runs over its own loft block at the grid. One end of the line attaches to the trim clamp at the sandbag; the other runs over the loft block at the grid and attaches to a pin rail at the wall of the fly gallery. Its purpose is to allow the flyman to lower the batten by pulling down on the *jack line*. Raising the batten can be done by easing the *jack line* and pulling down on the operating line. It is important to note that this system is relatively in-balance; that is, the load on the batten and the weight of the sandbag are equal. Without the jack line, the batten could only be raised, never lowered.

The illustration on the next page shows a *Rope Line System* utilizing a stacked head block with three lift lines running over the loft blocks to a batten. The batten is bridled, allowing for there to be six lift points across the batten instead of three. At the fly rail, there are two pin rails; one for high trim and the other for low trim. When the batten is at high trim, the operating lines are tied off at the lower rail. When at low trim, the operating lines are tied off to the upper rail. The pin rail for the *jack line* is located at the wall.

The fly gallery, showing the lift lines tied off to the right and jack lines tied off to the left.
-*photo courtesy of The Walnut Street Theatre, Philadelphia*

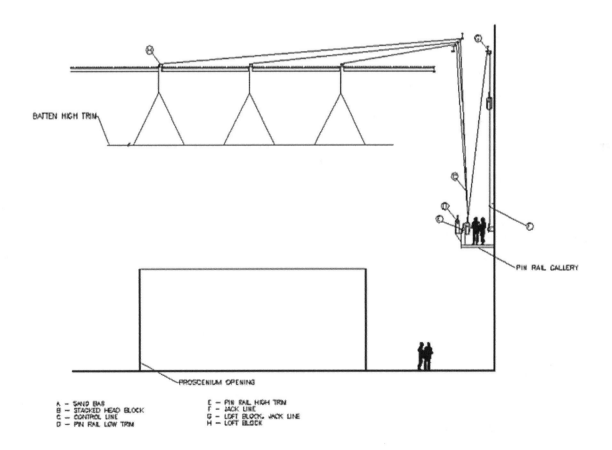

BATTEN HIGH TRIM

PIN RAIL GALLERY

PROSCENIUM OPENING

A – SAND BAG
B – STACKED HEAD BLOCK
C – CONTROL LINE
D – PIN RAIL LOW TRIM

E – PIN RAIL HIGH TRIM
F – JACK LINE
G – LOFT BLOCK, JACK LINE
H – LOFT BLOCK

The balanced Rope Line (Hemp) System at high trim tied to the low rail

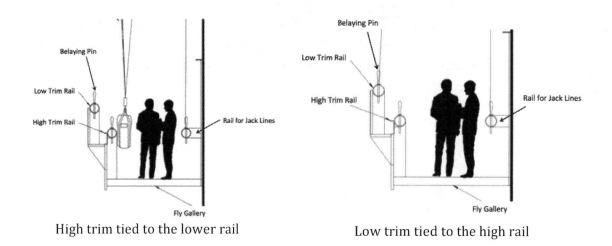

High trim tied to the lower rail   Low trim tied to the high rail

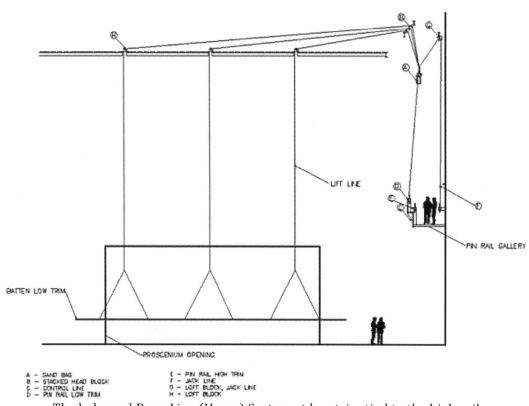

A — SAND BAG   E — PIN RAIL HIGH TRIM
B — STACKED HEAD BLOCK   F — JACK LINE
C — CONTROL LINE   G — LOFT BLOCK, JACK LINE
D — PIN RAIL LOW TRIM   H — LOFT BLOCK

The balanced Rope Line (Hemp) System at low trim tied to the high rail

In the illustration above, the batten is shown at its lowest position. Low trim can be established anywhere below high trim. A scenic drop, for example, that is flow from its high trim position will be tied off to its low trim position once the bottom of the drop is touching the floor. During a performance, the operating line is untied from its high trim position and simply allowed to fly in to its pre-determined low trim position. Note the position of the jack line and where it is tied off at its own rail position on the opposite wall. Because there is a balance in the load on the batten and the sandbag, the *jack line* serves to pull the batten out to its high trim position.

Setting up a Lineset on the Rope Line System

If you have never worked on a Rope Line System, the process of loading and unloading counterweight may seem confusing. Indeed, because of how this system works it often takes many steps to setup a lineset on a Rope Line System for a production.

The first two steps in setting up a lineset for use in a production first, trim/level the batten, and then to lower and load the scenery or lights on a batten. In actual practice, flying scenery is often more complicated that flying lights. The reason for this will become evident as it is explained.

You may have noticed in many of the illustrations above that there typically is no specific bridge/galley for loading on a Rope Line System. Instead, counterweight is loaded at the pin rail gallery. You also may have noticed in these illustrations that the the pin rail gallery is half way between the stage and the grid. These facts about the Rope Line System affect nearly everything about how the system is set up and used, so please keep this in mind as we proceed.

Trimming the batten

Trimming or leveling the batten can be done by adjusting each individual lift line before the load is placed on the batten. Once loaded, the distribution of the loads on each lift line will vary. Trying to adjust the trim of each lift line in the *sunday* or *trim* clamp can be extremely difficult, once there is a load on the batten, so make sure it is level before the batten is loaded. Once the batten is loaded, check the feel of how the load is being carried on the lift line by pulling on each line above the *trim clamp*.

It is important to make sure the load is distributed as evenly as possible across the batten. Point loads should be positioned at or close to a lift line so as to avoid over-stressing the batten. Attaching sandbags to operating end of the lineset may require several stagehands to assist in hauling the line and attaching the weight. Individual lift lines may shift in the sunday or trim clamp due to the change in load distribution on the lift lines. Make sure these are secured tight and trimmed.

Loading the batten and counterweight

Because a Rope Line System is typically operated from a pin rail gallery that is half way between the stage and the grid, the batten travel is limited to that distance, without have to "re-weight" the lineset.

If you are using a batten as an electric, it possible to partially load the batten, haul/muscle it out (to a height that is slightly higher that the batten will need to be at its high trim point), add counterweight (sandbags or arbors), lower it back in, partially load the batten again, and repeat the process until the batten is completely loaded. Now, place the batten at its trim height and you are done.

Loading and counterweighting lightweight scenery can be a little more challenging, if it needs to fly out above sightlines during the production. Assuming you need to fly a lightweight drop, attach it to the batten and fly it to it "high trim." This may require technicians on the stage to help lift and them hold the lines as someone on the pin rail gallery attaches a second trim clew or Sunday, and then the counterweight. After this is done, the excess rope can be pulled up and dressed.

Loading and counterweight heavy scenery is the real challenge. If you are flying a heavy wall, stand the wall, if possible, and then load your counterweight. After the batten is loaded, breast the sandbag out over the pin rain so that they can be lowered to the stage and the scenic unit raised. Of course, once the sandbags are at the stage, you will have to reload the counterweight and the pin rail and remove the sandbags that are sitting on the floor. You then have the haul the sandbags from the floor back up to the pin rail gallery. Of course, a block and fall can be used to make this job easier.

Sometimes a block and fall can be used to help muscle heavy scenery up before the counterweight is added. But, no matter how you do it, flying a heavy load on a Rope Line System takes time and patience to do safely.

Tying a Sunday – the prussic and double fisherman's bend
So far, we have discussed the two methods by which sandbags (or arbors) are attached to the line sets; the hemp trim clamp and the sunday. Let's look at tying a sunday. To begin with, a sunday is made from either a piece of 1/8" wire rope or 5 to 6 mm Spectra rope that is formed into a loop 3 to 4 feet in length. Spectra rope is stronger than steel cable and can be purchased from any recreational climbing equipment company. Wire rope can be Nicopressed into forming the loop while the ends of a Spectra rope will need to be tied using the *double fisherman's bend* to form a loop.

Step One: Using a single strand of Spectra rope, form a loop that is approximately 3 to 4 feet in length. Tie one end of the rope around the other as shown

Step 2: Take the other end of the rope and tie it around the other end as shown

Step 3: Pull the ends together until they meet

A Double Fisherman's Bend is a strong knot that is difficult to untie. It forms the loop in making a sunday.

Once a 3 to 4 foot lop has been tied with the *double fisherman's bend*, it is tied onto the lift lines using the *prussic knot*. The hook of the sandbag is snapped into the loop.

Step One: Make a loop with a double fisherman's bend

Step Two: Wrap the loop end around the lift lines through the loop

Step Three: Wrap the loop end three more times

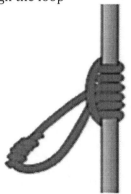

Step Four: Pull the loop end taunt and slide the knot end up or down the lift lines into desired position

Tying a sunday

Tying off to the Pin Rail

Tying off an operating line to a pin rail is a fairly easy task. The operating line, or lines, are *wrapped* around the pin in the same manner as shown below. This process of wrapping is known as *belaying* the rope or *tying off*. To belay (tie-off) a rope involves simply starting in the front of the rail and make two sets of figure 8 loops around the pin. The final loop is made by twisting the loop to the inside forming a half hitch. It is the half hitch that secures the line.

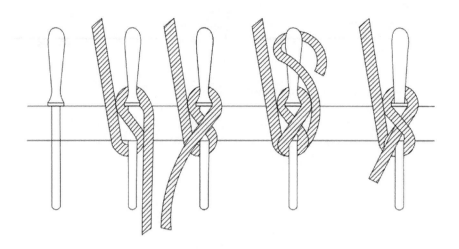

Releasing from the pin rail

Before releasing any line from the pin rail, get a feel for the weight that is attached operating lines. Grab the rope(s) above the belaying pin and pull it towards you. Look onstage at the batten that the lineset controls; it should rise up slightly as operating end of the line is pulled. If nothing moves and the rope remains taunt, then the batten maybe overloaded. If the rope pulls toward you and the batten can be raised slightly, then the load is manageable and can be operated safely. Always be sure to check a hemp line in this manner. Next, there are two methods for releasing a line from the pin rail. The first involves simply untying the line. This can be done with both the fixed and the loose pin rails. However, be careful as the load will be slightly batten-heavy and may require two flymen. The second involves releasing a line from the loose pin rail. Grab and hold the operating line in one hand while pulling up on the belaying pin with the other. The belayed line will be immediately released from the belay. This cannot be done if the lineset is too batten-heavy.

Laying out the lift lines.

As the batten is being prepared for lowering, it will be important to uncoil and layout the liftlines across a clear fly floor. This will insure that there are no knots in the lines before the lineset is released from the belaying pin. In preparation for bringing a lineset in to Low Trim— uncoil and dress the lines between the two tie-offs neatly across the floor. When the batten is lowered, watch where you step, lest you get tangled up in the running lines!

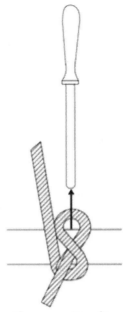

Pull up on the belaying pin while holding the operating line in the other hand. The belay is released.

Lowering a line set using resistance of the pin and rail

Using the resistance of the belaying pin, the lift line can be lowered smoothly into its low trim position. Loose pins will roll as the lines runs around the pin. Fixed pins will remain stationary.

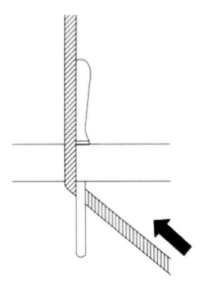

After the belay is unwrapped, ease off on the operating line using the resistance of the pin and rail to control the speed of the line.

Dressing the lines at the rail

Keeping the lines (ropes) organized and the fly floor cleared is crucial if the fly system is going to operate effectively. Most "old" pin rails are double pin rails (one high/one low) as described earlier. This facilitates not only high and low trim, but allows for properly dressing ropes. Once the operating lines are tied off to the belaying pin, the excess line must be coiled.

Many pin rails are actually double pin rails, one a couple of feet below the other. The addition pin rails give you extra room for hanging coiled ropes. Rope management is critical on rope line systems because tangled ropes can cause missed cues and even dangerous situations.

Forming a coil
To do this, grab the excess lines at the pin and begin making a coil about 3 feet in length, one arm's length. Once the lines are coiled, hold the coil in one hand and reach through the coil with the other. Grab the rope at the pin and twist the line twice while pulling the twist through the coil. The loop formed by the twist will go back over the pin securing the coil.

Trimming a batten
In most cases battens will have two trim positions: a high and a low trim (although occasionally, there may be mid-trim positions).

Unloading the Rope Line System
The danger of using both the balanced and unbalanced systems occurs during the loading and unloading process. When unloading, the batten is lowered to about 4 feet above the stage floor; at the same time the sandbag (weight) is raised to the grid. Unloading the batten without due caution at this point, can cause the system to become "out of balance" very quickly. Sandbags (or arbors) could come crashing in to the stage floor! The operation is minimalized with the use of jack lines, as the jack lines can support the sandbags and remain under control. But if the fly system does not have jack lines, the batten must be flown out first, so some sandbags (or sand) can be carefully removed. If the venue does not have a fly gallery, care will be needed, as the sandbags will be coming in to the floor. Always make sure the area around the fly floor is clear of scenery and unnecessary personnel. Once the batten is lowered back in, some of the load can be removed. Care must be taken to keep the system slightly batten heavy at all times. A *bull line* is often used by stagehands to keep an underweighted batten under control while weight is transferred. A *bull line* is a rope line that can be thrown over a batten while the batten is being loaded. This allows several hands to hold onto an underweighted batten until the batten has been loaded. **Remember, the loading/unloading process is a dangerous operation. Always let people know when a lineset is coming into the deck.**

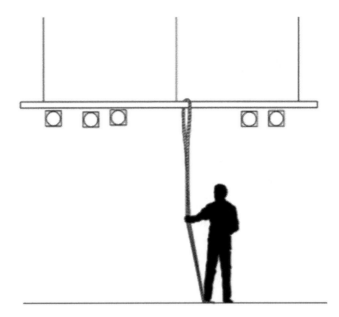

A *bull line* is often used by stagehands to keep an underweighted batten under control while weight is transferred.

Running a lineset during a production

Generally, most linesets will have a high trim and a low trim points, although it is possible for there to be mid-trim points too. First, tie-off the lines to establish your low trim height. If you have a bottom rail, the low trim is usually tied at this rail. When the batten is lowered from its high trim, it will automatically stop at this point since this is when it will run out of rope.

Now, raise the batten until you reach the high trim point. This is often the point when the sandbags are just above the pin rail and the scenic unit is above sight lines. If the sandbags do not need to come all the way down to the pin rail, you can mark this point on the lift line with a small sandbag or a bright marker of some kind.

Summary

While a Rope Line System is mechanically a very simple system, it is a very complicated system to operate. It is also easy to get batten out of level and dangerously out of weight. Rope management is extremely important. Tangled or knotted ropes can cause missed cues or even dangerous situations. At the same time, a spot line, a Rope Line System with a single line and no batten, can sometimes be the quickest and easiest way to fly a piece of scenery.

Understanding the Rope Line System will make you a better rigger because 1) it gives you tools for solving some common rigging problems, and 2) it helps you better understand the mechanical counterweight system that is commonly found in theatres.

Most modern theatres that have a mechanical counterweight system and walkable grids, also have at least one pin rail (and many times several). Pin rails are very inexpensive to install, yet they provide the means for installing short rope line set battens or spot lines in places where battens do not exist, making the theatre far more flexible.

Chapter 8:
The Manual Counterweight System

Introduction

So far, we have examined the equipment and rigging installations of the *Counterweight System* (Chapter 3) and the basic operation of the *The Rope Line System* (Chapter 7). This chapter will discuss the operation and loading of the *Manual Counterweight Systems*. Automated systems will be explained later in Chapter 12.

Early Counterweight Systems

First introduced in Austria in 1888, the *Counterweight System* was designed as a safer and easier alternative to the *Rope Line System* and before that, the windlass. You will recall that with the *Rope Line System*, the battens were slightly heavier than the sandbags using gravity assist. Even with the use of *jack lines*, the *"sandbag system"* often required two or more flyman to operate. The idea behind the *manual counter weighted system* was to employ the use of frames, called *arbors,* that would run in guides and hold lead or iron counterweights (called pigs after pig iron) to balance the weight of battens on stage. This would make it easier for one flyman to operate a lineset. Back then, the *counterweight systems* were of fairly low capacity. The arbors were made of wood and moved up and down along wire-guided tracks. Today, the *manual counterweight system* is made from steel and is the most commonly used system in auditoriums and performing arts centers today.

The Modern Lineset System
Introduction

The modern counterweighted system consists of components that work together to perform the task of raising and lowering heavy equipment in a fly space. It provides a simple mechanical means using cables, pulleys and weights to counterbalance a load thereby making it easy for one operator to manage several hundred pounds. Essentially, it is a counterbalanced lifting machine. The two types of *Manual Counterweight Systems* in use today are the *Single Purchase* and *Double Purchase Systems*. Let's begin with the *Single Purchase System*.

An early wooden counterweight arbor on a wire guided system.

The wooden arbor

The loading rail at the gallery. Linesets are marked so the flyman can more easily find the correct arbor to load.

Early head blocks showing the operating lines. Note the stacked head block at the top.

Wooden fixed floor block at the base of the lineset

An early wooden counterweight system

-photos courtesy of Frank Cortez

The Single Purchase Counterweight System

The *single purchase system* operates as a one to one ratio system. That is, for every one foot of batten travel upward (or downward), the arbor will descend (or rise) at a rate of one foot of travel. As scenery or equipment is added (or subtracted) from the batten, the corresponding amount of weight must be added (or subtracted) to the arbor. The idea is to keep both the batten and the arbor in equal weight at all times. This is what allows for the ease of operation by a single flyman. Should the load on the batten be heavier than the load on the arbor, we call this condition *"batten heavy"*. Inversely, if the load on the arbor is more than on the batten, we call this being *"arbor heavy"*. Either one of these conditions can put enough friction on the system to it makes it difficult for a flyman to operate. The illustration below shows a typical *single purchase counterweight system* and terminology.

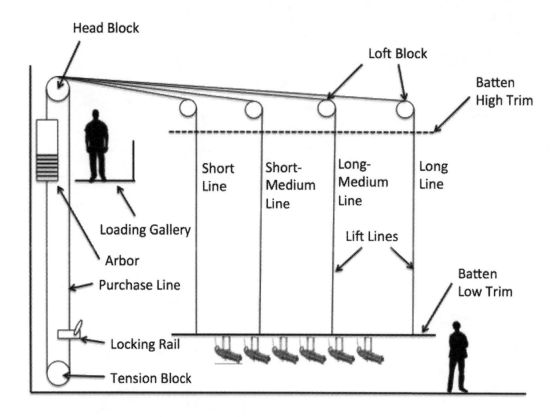

The illustration shows the parts of the *Single Purchase Counterweight System*. Note that the lift lines have names that are labeled furthest to shortest from the arbor.

The Double Purchase Counterweight System

The parts of the *Double Purchase Counterweight System* are going to be similar to those found with the *Single Purchase System*, the major differences being in the rigging of the arbor and the use of a mid-height fly gallery. The *Double Purchase Counterweight System* is used when there is an obstruction that needs to be avoided or limited floor space. The system is compound rigged; that is, one foot of arbor travel equals two feet of batten travel. In this arrangement the arbor will require two pounds of counterweight for every pound of load on the batten. The arbor will also need to be twice as long as the single purchase arbor in order to hold the extra weight. The illustration below shows a typical *double purchase counterweight system*.

142

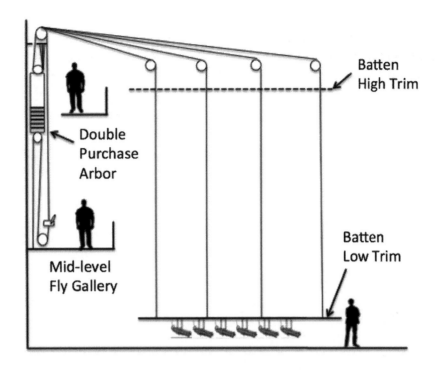

The *Double Purchase Counterweight System* is compound rigging; two feet of batten travel equals one foot of arbor travel. It is used when there is an obstruction that needs to be avoided or limited floor space. Note the mid-level fly gallery in the illustration above.

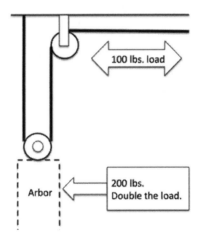

The basic principle behind the *Double Purchase System* was discussed in Chapter 2. The mechanical advantage of this system is 2:1.

In-Balance

Technically, the only time that the *single purchase counterweight system* is in *perfect* balance is when the arbor and the batten are at the same height or trim. This would be mid-point. With any other point of travel, the weight of the lift line cables can add weight proportionally to either the arbor end or batten side of the system. This may not seem like much to a theatre with a short fly loft, but to a theatre with an extremely tall fly space, it can be very noticeable to the operator. In this case, lift line compensators can be installed to overcome the weight differential. The *double purchase systems* does not need lift line compensators due to the short distance the arbor has to travel.

Out of Balance- The Runaway

Normally, the *hand lock* that is found at the *locking rail* is enough to secure small *out-of balance* conditions. *Hand locks* are NOT brakes and CANNOT support a load in excess of more than 50 pounds. As mentioned before, the *single purchase system* is only completely *in-balance* if the batten and the arbor are at the same elevation. The *hand lock* on the locking rail, MUST BE LOCKED AT ALL TIMES when not in use and the retaining ring should be in place over the hand lock. Arbors tend to drift if there is any variation in balance. Inexperienced flymen have been known to walk away from an un-locked purchase line only to have a slightly out-of balanced arbor begin to drift. When this happens, the lineset can begin to pick up momentum as the proportional weight of the lift lines adds to the overbalance. This condition can lead to a dangerous situation known as a *Runaway*! NEVER TRY TO STOP A RUNAWAY ARBOR! More of this will be discussed later in the chapter.

The Hand Lock

As mentioned previously, the hand lock (sometimes called a rope lock) can only secure a small amount of balanced loads - no more than around 50 pounds. It is NOT a brake! The lock consists of a handle, which controls pressure on cams inside the lock. The cams, in turn, squeeze the purchase line preventing slippage. The retaining ring should be secured around the handle when the lineset is not in use. This prevents the handle from accidently opening, disengaging the cams, and releasing the arbor. The illustrations below show a detail of the rope lock system. Note the *cam adjustment nut* that is located behind the lock. This *adjustment nut* allows for the distance between the cams to be changed so that the pressure of the cams can engage the rope when the lock is in the closed position. This should be checked before each operation of the lineset and as part of routine maintenance. Purchase lines, especially those made from hemp rope, can expand and contract with the humidity in the venue. This means the tension on the cams should be checked regularly.

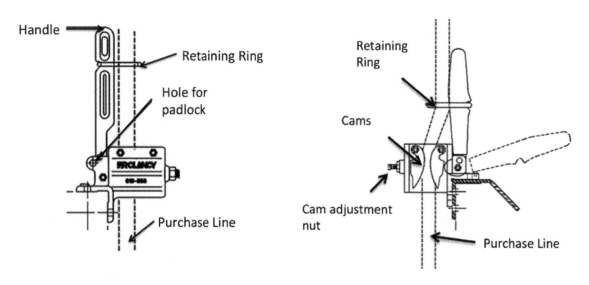

A typical Rope Lock as found at the locking rail. The purchase line runs through the cams of the lock and through the retaining ring. The retaining ring slips over the lock handle when the lineset is not in use. This prevents the handle from releasing should the handle fall.

Linesets showing the retaining rings correctly placed over the hand lock.

Loading and Unloading
The Single and Double Purchase Systems

The most dangerous process in working with the *Manual Counterweight System* is the loading and unloading process. During this time, heavy loads are being raised and lowered over the heads of people on deck. Only the most *experienced* stagehands should be involved with the loading and unloading of the arbors. Even so, experienced personnel can make mistakes and accidents can happen. You should always know the rigging system you are working with, and know your limitations. If there is something that you do not know about the rigging system you are working with, stop and seek out the proper advice. One thing you should remember; control of the counterweight system MUST be maintained at all times.

The Loading Process
The Lineset Schedule

The *Lineset Schedule* identifies all the battens in the venue and what type of equipment is flown on each pipe. If there is no equipment on a batten, it is left blank. Starting downstage and moving upward, linesets are numbered. Distance from the plaster line to each batten is also noted. Once you know the numbering and which battens are being used for what, you will need to calculate the weight of the load on each pipe. Curtain weight, for example, can be estimated by knowing the square footage of the drapery multiplied by the weight of the fabric per square foot.

Example: A border curtain is constructed of 25 oz. velour (unlined). It measures 50 feet wide x 6 feet tall.

50 x 6 = 300 square feet
300 x 25 oz = 7500 oz
With 16 ounces in a pound, we divide 7500 by 16
or
7500 / 16 = 468.75 pounds

This curtain weight should be added to the *Lineset Schedule* with the corresponding curtain. The same needs to be done with each leg, traveler curtain, scenic element, cyc and scrim. Electrics will need to be calculated based on the weight of each lighting instrument and cable run on the batten. Some technical directors will go as far as converting the load weight into the actual number of bricks to make things easy. A load chart for lighting instruments is included at the back of this book.

Knowing the weight of each batten on the lineset, will help determine the corresponding weight needed for the arbor. It will also help you determine if the lineset is overloaded. Don't guess. It is best to do your homework ahead of time and calculate the loads. Nothing is more a clue to an amateur status than coming to a load-in unprepared.

Pipe Weight

But what about pipe weight? Does this need to be included too? Generally, no. An empty batten already is loaded with a corresponding amount of pipe weight on the batten. This should always remain and should never be removed. Pipe weight bricks are usually painted in order to distinguish them from other bricks on the arbor. Once you know the load on each batten, its time to begin the loading process.

Loading with a Loading Gallery

The loading gallery is a catwalk system located at the grid. This allows loading access to the counterweight arbors once the batten is lowered to the deck. As the process begins it is important to maintain as much *silence* on stage as possible. Instructions will need to be called out to the loading gallery from the stage. *Silence* is necessary in order to hear the commands. *"I need 14 bricks on lineset 15. Let me know when you are complete"*, is a typical call out from the *head flyman* to the *loader*. *"Strip lineset 23 to pipe weight"*, is another, or *"Lineset 5, coming in!"*, is a third. All these commands are intent on maintaining safety onstage and accurate communication between the people at fly rail and the people on the ground. No weight should be added or subtracted from the arbor without direct instructions from the head flyman or technical director.

To begin:

1. Identify the batten on the lineset schedule that needs to be lowered to the floor. There should be a *flyman* at the locking rail and a *loader* at the loading gallery at the grid. These people should be fully trained in the operation and the process that is to take place. The *flyman's* job will be to raise and lower the arbor. The *loader* will be adding or subtracting weight on the arbor. Remember, with the *Double Purchase System* the weight ratio will be 2:1.
2. Before lowering the batten, the *flyman on deck* should always check to be sure that the batten is counterbalanced correctly to its corresponding pipe weight. Once this has been determined, the batten can be lowered to its *"low trim"* position. This is usually 4 feet above the floor. The corresponding arbor will now be up at the loading gallery.
3. Next, the *stage crew* can begin hanging the curtains and lighting equipment on the batten. The batten MUST be loaded first.

4. Once the batten is finished, the loading of the arbor can begin. Assuming you have pre-determined the weight of each batten, you can now call up to the loader and have the corresponding counterweight bricks (minus 15 to 20%) loaded on the arbor. Why 15 to 20% less? Never fully load the arbor until the counter balance between the batten and the arbor is checked. 15 to 20% less allows for a stopping point so that the balance can be determined. Some *flymen* will *"load it till it floats"*, which is to say, the arbor will be loaded until it begins to drift down. This can be a tricky operation, as it demands the full attention of the operator and the loader. The lock handle at the locking rail has to be released and left open so the arbor *can* drift. Once the system is *"in- balance"* and the batten at trim, the lock can be secured.

General Safety Rules:
- Remember: loading/ unloading is a dangerous process. During the loading, an un-balanced condition exists. As a rule, *counterweights should be the last thing loaded and the first thing removed.* Control of the system MUST be maintained at all times. The following rules should be observed:
  - Battens should be *loaded* first when at low trim. This keeps the weight at the ground. Once the batten is loaded, only then can the arbor be loaded.
  - When unloading a batten, the counterweights on the arbor (up at the loading gallery) are removed first and then the load on the batten can be removed. Again, this will keep the weight down on the ground level at all times.
- As the arbor is being loaded/ unloaded at the loading gallery, keep ALL personnel away from the area under the loading gallery. Rope off the area if necessary. Hard hats MUST be worn at all times. OSHA 1926.100(a) states that *"employees working in areas where there is a possible danger of head injury from impact, or from falling or flying objects, [ ], shall be protected by protective helmets"*.
- When loading/ unloading the arbors, the loader(s) should call out, *"Loading"* to alert on stage personnel that the loading/ unloading process has begun.
- The *loader* always should check with the *head flyman* or *technical director* on deck to make sure the stage is clear and that the loading/ unloading process can begin.

Safety at the Loading Gallery
Loading the arbor at the gallery demands the full attention of the loader. Sometimes, *two* loaders up at the gallery may be necessary to insure safety. Accidently dropping a 25-pound counterweight from an 80-foot gallery is out of the question. There is no room for errors. The *loaders* will need to select the correct sized bricks for the job. Bricks come in a number of

different sizes and are made from either cast iron, steel or lead. The standard thicknesses are 1 and 2 inches. Outside dimensions may vary depending on the manufacturer, but generally they come in 4 and 6-inch widths. Standard weights are generally 14, 22 and 28 pounds.

A counterweight brick

It will be important for the *loader*, *head flyman* and *technical director* to know the weight of the bricks in the venue. Bricks are usually stored on the floor of the loading gallery grating for easy access. The edges of the gallery will have *kick plates* that will rise as much as 6 inches from the floor grating. Bricks should never be stacked higher than the kick plate.

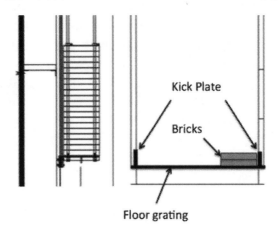

Bricks are stored and stacked on the floor of the loading gallery. They should never be stacked higher than the kick plate.

Calculating the Weight of a Steel Counterweight Brick

To calculate the weight of a counterweight brick, you need to know the number of cubic inches of material in the brick. We first calculate the total area of the brick based on the outside dimensions of the (its width, length and thickness). Next we calculate the area of the two slots, and subtract this area from the overall area we calculated first. Now that we know the area of the actual area of the material, we simply multiply this by the weight of the material, per cubic inch. Let's calculate the weight of the counterweight brick below.

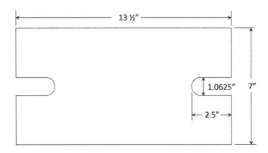

Begin by calculating the overall area of the brick. To do this we multiply the width by the length by the thickness. So,

$$7 \times 13.5 \times 1.25 = 118.125 \text{ cubic inches (ci)}$$

Now we need to calculate the area of the slots and subtract this amount from the overall area of the brick. Although the inside end of the slot is rounded, we can simplify our calculation be pretending that it is a rectangle. This shortcut will mean that our calculation is off slightly, but not enough to be stressed about. Let's use the formula:

$$Area = (Width\ of\ Slot \times Length\ of\ Slot \times Thichness\ of\ Brick) \times 2$$

148

So...

$$Area = (1.0625 \times 2.5 \times 1.25) \times 2$$
$$Area = 3.32 \times 2$$
$$Area = 6.64 \ ci$$

Next, subtract the slot area from the total brick area to the the area of the material.

Material area = 118.125 ci - 6.64 ci

Material area = 111.48 ci

Finally, multiply the Material area times Material Weight. Since steel weights 0.02836 pounds per cubic inch...

Brick weight = 111.48×0.2836

Brick weight = 31.6 pounds

Note: When I weighed a steel counterweight with these dimensions, it weighed 31.4 pounds, pretty close to our calculation. For simplicity sake, I would just call this weight 32 pounds to make it easy to keep track of when loading weight.

Loading the Arbor

When loading the arbor, the first thing the *loader* has to do is move the top *spreader plate(s)* so it (they are) is out of the way. A simple piece of tie line clove hitched to the arbor rod will do the job. *Spreader plates* are a complete annoyance to most flymen, but they do serve a purpose. Spaced in the arbor stack every 2-feet of brick height, *spreader plates* insure that the bricks stay in the stack in the event of a *runaway*. The last *spreader plate* locks the bricks in place by securing the retaining lock nuts. Store any unused *spreader plates* at the top of the stack. Never store unused spreader plates in the brick stack.

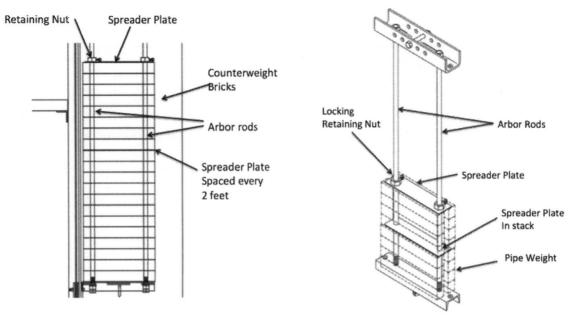

Spreader plates are located in the brick stack every two feet. The last spreader plate is secure with the last brick at the top by locking retaining nuts.

The Runaway

A *runaway* is essentially an out-of-balance arbor (or batten) that cannot be controlled by the operator. In either case, the *arbor heavy* lineset will slip through the rope lock whether the lock is engaged or not. (Remember, the rope lock does not serve as a brake and its holding power is limited to only around 50-pounds). The arbor will crash down on the wooden arbor stop splintering the wood and bending the steel stop bar. What happens next can be terrifying to the most seasoned *stagehand*. Without the spreader plates placed in the stack, the steel arbor rods splay outwards dumping the counterweight bricks on the stage floor. Now the out-of-balance situation is reversed as the load heavy batten comes crashing back into the deck. The lesson to be learned from all of this is to keep the spreader plates spaced every two feet in the arbor stack. This may not prevent a *runaway*, it will prevent the arbor rods from splaying out should one occur.

Continuing the Process

Once the *spreader plates* are secured by the clove hitch and the spreader plates are out of the way, the loading can begin. The *loader* picks up one brick at a time, tilting it enough so the offstage-notched end slips around the furthest arbor rod. While still tilted, the other notched end of the brick is slid over the closest arbor rod and the brick is lowered onto the stack. The process is repeated while ensuring a *spreader plate* is placed every two feet.

Unloading the Arbor

Essentially, the unloading process is the loading process in reverse with the same safety protocols in place as those discussed in the previous sections. The batten is lowered to the deck, and the weight on the *arbor is removed first*. Bricks are stripped down to pipe weight. Once the weight on the arbor is removed, the *loader* calls down to the *head flyman*, *"All clear"*. Only then can the load on the batten be removed.

150

Loading without a Loading Gallery

As mentioned earlier in the chapter, control of the counterweight system MUST be maintained at all times. The risks of a *runaway* arbor become *more and more of a possibility* due to the fact that the arbor is either over-weighted or under-weighted during this process. Again, proper training of the *flymen* and *loaders* is essential. If the procedures described are followed, these techniques will help you to maintain that control. Let's look at a few of the methods that can be used in this loading/ un-loading process. Each of these three methods will be discussed in depth.

1. Loading from the floor with a loading crew
2. Loading with a "bull winch" or capstan winch
3. Loading with a block and tackle.

Method 1: Loading from the floor with a Loading Crew

This method is the more commonly used technique, as it doesn't involve a lot of expensive equipment- it does depends on the shear "muscle" of a *loading crew*. Notice we used the term "*loading crew*" as it involves of two or three *loaders* positioned at the locking rail.

To begin with, the lineset is identified and the batten is brought into the stage as before. The *flyman (or loaders)* should check to be sure the batten is at pipe weight and *in-balance* before it is lowered. Once lowered, the *stage crew* can begin loading the batten- *but here is where the loading process gets a little tricky. Loaders* can generally (and safely) haul about 100-pounds dead weight. So, the *stage crew* should only *partially* load the batten to around 100-pounds. With the 100-pounds of weight on the batten and no weight on the arbor, the system is now *out-of-balance*. The arbor is up at the top stop batten. With the batten now loaded, the arbor has to be muscled down to the rail so that it can be weighted with bricks. This is why the 100-pound load limit works best.

Temporarily Securing the Arbor

So, once the arbor has been hauled down to the deck, the next problem is securing the arbor so it doesn't drift out while it is being loaded. There are several ways to do this. One way is to have one *loader* hold the arbor while the other two load the weights, or a better method involves using a snub line.

The Snub Line

The illustrations below show how the snub line is tied off to the purchase line at the rail. The snub line is a rope attached to the purchase line of an over weighted system using the friction knot. It can also be tied to both the up and down lines together before it is tied off to the locking rail. The snub line will temporarily hold until the proper weight is restored and the system is in trim.

The snub line is then tied off to the rail with a spliced eye or bowline then to the up line with a friction knot.

Another option is to tie off the snub line with an eye splice or bowline and then to both the up and down lines with a friction knot.

Tying a snub line will be discussed in detail in Chapter 9.

Dogging

Another technique that is frequently done involves grabbing both sides of the purchase lines and twisting them both together until friction in the line can hold the arbor in place. This process is called *dogging*. Some *loaders* use a steel bar to aid in the twisting. Once the arbor is loaded, the twist can be slowly released and the balance between the arbor and batten checked. But a word of caution is in order. *Dogging* can eventually damage the metal plates on the shoes of the tension block. If the shoes get damaged, then the tension block will lose its ability to 'float' and will have to be replaced. We show the *dogging* process only because it is frequently done as a "quick" means to secure the hand line when a *snub line* is not readily available. The biggest cause of damage is the over-tightening of the hand line by the flyman. It is *best* to use a *snub line.*

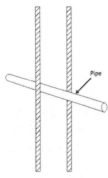

Step 1:
Place a ½" pipe between the two purchase lines

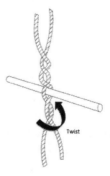

Step 2:
Twist the hand line using the pipe for leverage

Dogging the hang line is not recommended. We show it because many flymen do this use this technique usually because a snub line in not always available at the rail. It is a quick solution to the problem, but potentially damages the shoes on the tension block.

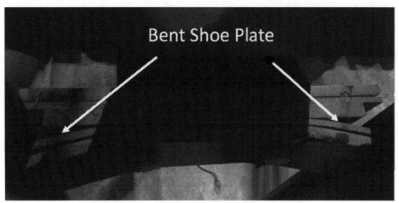

Bent shoe plates caused by dogging

Continuing the Process

Once the balance is assured, the *loaders* then add additional weight to the arbor to be *hauled up*. Again as before, there should be no more than around 100- pounds or what the *loaders* can safely handle. The arbor in now muscled *up* to the top arbor stop while the batten is lowered to the stage. Another friction twist is placed in the purchase line to hold the arbor in place while the batten is loaded. Again, the *stage crew* adds another 100-pounds to the batten and the process is repeated.

Reversing the Process- The Load Out

The load out simply involves reversing the process. The balanced batten is raised to high trim so 100-pounds brick weight can be removed from the arbor. The batten is then carefully lowered back to the deck and a corresponding amount of equipment weight is removed. The process is repeated until the batten is returned to pipe weight.

Method 2: Loading with a "Bull" Capstan Winch (Donkey Winch)

If your theatre is lucky enough to own a *bull* or *capstan winch*, this can make the process a little easier and faster as the arbor can literally be "bullied" down to the floor with the winch. A *capstan winch* is a marine winch that has been adopted for use on the stage. It consists of a motorized capstan drum or "winch" that turns at a slower rate of speed than the actual motor. The *capstan winch* MUST be secured to a load rated attachment point under the locking rail due to the extreme forces involved[1]. A *"bull line"* is attached to the bottom of the arbor and runs through a load rated pulley mounted to a load rated anchor point under the arbor. The *bull line* then runs from the pulley over to the capstan drum. As the empty batten is lowered, the loosened *bull line* simply follows the arbor up. Once the batten is lowered, it can be loaded. When ready to be raised, the *flyman* takes three wraps around the capstan drum of the winch and takes up the slack in the *bull line*. By a steady and continuous pull on the drum, the arbor is *winched* down to the floor where it can be counterweighted by the loaders. A *capstan winch* is a very handy piece of equipment. But like any tool, it requires special training in its use and safe operation. Dangers can occur if the *bull line* is not cleated (tied off) properly or if there are insufficient wraps around the drum... just to name a few.

The "Bull" or Capstan Winch can be a useful piece of stage equipment, but requires special training in its operation

Reversing the Process - The Load Out

Again, the load out involves reversing the process described above. The balanced batten is raised to its high trim position so that the *bull line* can be attached to the base of the arbor and the rope end wrapped around the capstan winch drum. Partial weight is removed from the arbor. The load heavy batten is at high trim. By carefully easing tension on the wraps of the capstan drum or reversing the motor, the operator can ease the batten back into low trim. Partial weight is removed from the batten until balance in the system is achieved. Next, the balanced arbor is brought back into the floor and the process is repeated until the arbor is at pipe weight. Remember- *control is everything*. An additional *bull line* attached to the batten may allow stagehands at the batten to help the *loaders* in the process. (see the section on Advanced Techniques at the end of the chapter).

Method 3: The Block and Fall Method

The last method we will discuss involves the use of a *Block and Fall* to haul the arbor down to the deck. This method is similar to the *Capstan Winch Method* as the winch is simply replaced by a *Block and Fall*. The major concerns are that 1) the *Block and Fall* is long enough to reach from the floor to the venue ceiling and 2) be strong enough to handle the loads place on it. The attachment point at the floor of the locking rail needs to be load rated just as we saw with the *Capstan Winch* setup.

The *Block and Fall Method* gives the *loaders* a mechanical advantage that we discussed in Chapter 2. Because operating any *fall line* can be difficult work, we also want to give the *loaders* the same load consideration that we saw in the first method; that is, load only enough weight on the batten that can safely be managed at the *falls*. They will be able to tell the *stage crew* how much weight they can safely handle. As soon as the arbor has been hauled to the floor and the hand lock is engaged, the *Block and Fall* can hold the arbor in position. The *loaders* can now begin their process of loading weights. The process is repeated until the batten is loaded.

[1]The attachment point on the floor must be able to support the forces placed on it by the fully loaded arbor. It is recommended that a qualified engineer be consulted to insure floor points are within recommended load limits.

Reversing the Process- The Load Out
The load out is again similar to what we discussed with *Capstan Winch*. The balanced batten is raised to its high trim position so that the *Block and Fall* can be attached to the base of the arbor and to the floor anchor point. Partial weight is removed from the arbor. The Block and Fall carefully lowers the loaded batten to the floor. Again, partial weight is removed from the batten. Once in balance the arbor is brought back into the floor and the process is repeated.

Show Operation

Operating the Lineset System during a Production
Once the arbors have been loaded, the battens can be set to their *trim* positions for the show and the trims marked out on the purchase lines. *Trim* is the term that indicates the proper height of the flown scenery, curtains or electrics. *Trim* heights are based in part on the sightlines taken off the section plan. Border curtain trim is usually measured from the bottom hem of the curtain to the floor while electrics are measured from the batten height to the floor. Flown drops will find their *high trim* position based on the bottom edge being out of sightlines; the *low trim* will be when the drop is lowered to the floor.

Spiking
There are several methods for marking (spiking) trim heights on the purchase lines- one uses colored spike tape, the other uses ribbon or strips of duvetyn. We recommend the later. Spike tape may be quick and easy to use for the fly operator, but there is the possibility that the tape can slide off the mark during the show-to-show operation. It also can leave behind a tape residue on the rope, which is not easy to remove. Colored ribbon or strips of duvetyn work best, as they cannot come undone and are easy to remove at the end of production.

Take a blunt screwdriver with the ribbon fixed to the end and push the end of the screwdriver between the strands of the purchase line. Once the ribbon is through, hold on to the ribbon while removing the screwdriver. Un-double the ribbon and pull it partially through the strand. Wrap the ribbon around the purchase line and tie with a knot.

Setting the Trim Marks on the Handle
The most common method for setting trim marks is to place the trim mark so the top of the tape falls at the top of the locking handle. For drops and scenic units, there will need to be two marks per lineset; one for high trim and the other for low trim. When setting trim, bring the drop into the floor. Lock it off. Place the spike ribbon so that it falls even with the top of the lock. Some flyman prefer to use colored ribbons to differentiate between high and low trims. Next, pull the drop out to high trim, lock it off and repeat the process.

Operating a Lineset
Operating a lineset requires a bit a skill and practice. What you don't want to over-shoot the trim marks in either direction. This is known as *over-hauling*. Nothing is more of a demonstration of

155

"amateur status" than to bring a curtain or drop into low trim and have the bottom hem gather in bunches only to raise back up again to low trim. When raising a drop (or any pipe for that matter), never "grid" the batten. Gridding a batten is that awful "clang" you hear up in the fly space as the batten reaches it limits and smacks the upper stop batten. It's also noisy during a production.

There are several techniques for operating a lineset. The important things to remember is always wear gloves and always control the arbor momentum with the up-line. Without gloves, you risk rope burns and hemp splinters. Without the control of the up-line, you will be fighting arbor momentum as it approaches the trim marks. Always slow an incoming drop with the back line and an outgoing drop with the front. You will retain complete control of the arbor mass without jumping tension blocks and without slamming the arbor against the upper or lower wooden stop battens. You will maintain 100% control.

Some other key points to consider:
- Before releasing the hand lock, always grab both the up and down lines together. This will keep the lineset from creeping in before the lock is released.
- When flying out, some scenic pieces may be heavy and will require the operator to overcome inertia to get the lineset moving.
- It is much easier to pull down on a rope than pull up.

During a show or rehearsal, remember:
- to check your cue sheets to verify which lineset you will be using and when. Linesets should be clearly labeled at the rail and visible in the dim glow of the index lights.
- that timing is everything. Practice as needed to get your timing correct.
- during a performance, the flyman cannot call out warnings to people on the stage. This is why rehearsals are important and alertness in required at all times.

Advanced Techniques

During loading process there will be times when the system will be out-of-balance for a short time period of time and the purchase line will need to be secured by the process we called *dogging.* Traveler curtains for example may be properly weighted when flown, but quickly become arbor heavy as the weight of the curtain is lowered to the floor. The purchase line will need to be dogged in order to keep the arbor from moving. Let's look at some other methods for tying off the arbor and controlling the loads in an out-of-balance situation.

The Bull Line
Essentially, a *bull line* is a stout, large diameter rope. We first saw the use of a *bull line* with the *capstan winch.* In that case, the *bull line* was attached to the bottom of the arbor and ran to the winch. When used with a batten, the *bull line* is thrown over the batten and doubled. (see illustration below). Usually 1-inch diameter works best as it gives the stagehands better grip. The line allows a stagehand to manhandle the batten with their weight while the arbor is being unloaded and flown out. The over-load should be no more than 100-pounds or the bull line may

become unmanageable. Standing on the rope as it lies on the floor will better help hold the rope steady. Since the bull line is thrown over the batten, always make sure the line is long enough to reach the high trim batten position.

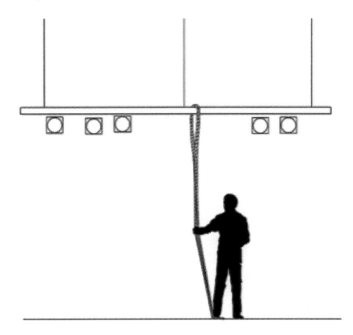

The bull line can be used to counterbalance an out-of-weight batten. It is looped over the batten rather than tied to it. Standing on the bull line can help with the control.

Uncle Buddy (Rope Loc)

The Uncle Buddy or Rope Loc is a device that was first introduced by *Buddy*, a Seattle stagehand; thus its name. It attaches to both lines of the purchase, rocks back and secures the line by hooking on to the lower outside line. It serves as a brake by temporarily holding the purchase lines in place until the arbor is in balance with the batten.

The Uncle Buddy or Rope Loc.

Haven Locks and Rope Grabs

Rope Grabs and Haven Locks are devises that can be easily secured to purchase lines. Once attached to the line, they will need to be secured to the locking rail with shackles and a roundsling. Whereas the Rope Grab is for rope only, the Haven Lock comes manufactured for either filament rope or wire rope. Both are expensive to purchase, but worth the investment.

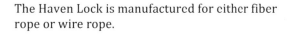

The Haven Lock is manufactured for either fiber rope or wire rope.

Rope Grab
-photo courtesy of Miller

Knuckle Busters

Knuckle Busters are used when the flymen are generally inexperience and the exact positioning or trim of a drop is crucial. It is essentially a small clamp that is placed on the purchase line at the low trim mark and is too large to fit through the hand lock. Once the low trim hits the knuckle buster at the low trim mark, the purchase line will go no further. Unfortunately, if there is too much momentum in the arbor, the drop will overhaul the tension block and over-run the drop.

A Knuckle Buster

-photo courtesy of Mutual Hardware

Marrying Pipe Battens

If the load on one batten exceeds the capacity of the arbor, the batten can be married to a second free batten next to it. The second batten is attached to the first one by attaching cheeseboughs or chains at the lift line points. DO NOT USE LIGHTING SAFETY CABLES! The two battens will work as one with two arbors balancing the load. This is often done with electrics. When marrying

158

battens, do not fly the battens out to the extreme high trim as the new direction of the lift lines can create fleet angles that exceed 1.5 degree and create wear on the loft block sheaves.

Arbors that are too Low to Load

There are times when the counterweight bricks are too low to be able to reach from the loading platform. If this is the case, dummy counterweight bricks can be manufactured to serve as "filler bricks." These "filler bricks" are made from blue foam that is sandwiched between ¼" plywood. The dummy bricks are stacked on top of the pipe weight bricks. Standard steel counterweights bricks can easily be stacked within reach from the loading platform. Blue foam can take a tremendous amount of weight without being crushed.

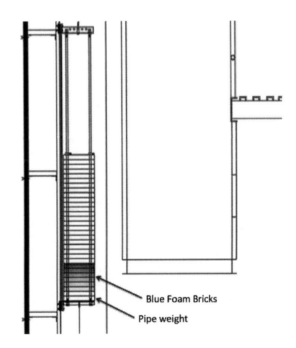

Blue foam "dummy bricks" are stacked on top of pipe weight bringing the loading of standard bricks within reach of the loader.

Summary

This chapter focused on the operation of the manual counterweight system. We learned the basics of loading and unloading the *Single Purchase* and *Double Purchase Systems* as well as some tricks stagehands and riggers use to control the system. The important lesson to be learned in this chapter is to be *in control of the system at all times.*

Chapter 9:
Rope, Knots and Terminations

Introduction

There are literally thousands of different knots. Most are divided into one of three categories: loops, hitches or bends. All knots, no matter of the category hold due to friction. The friction is created by the parts of the rope making contact with other parts of the rope as they twist around each other to form the knot.

Since using rope is an essential part of being a rigger, understanding the basic knots and how to tie them correctly is essential to theatre rigging. While you do not have to know how to tie every knot, it is good to know how to tie several knots in each category. The more knots you know how to tie, the better the chances of choosing the best knot for the job. Every knot has its pros and cons - some are eazy to tie, some are easy to untie, some are more secure than others, and choosing the best knot for the job is important.

There are many excellent books on knots and it is a good idea to get one and learn to tie them properly. A good internet resource for learning knots is Animated Knots by Grog: http://www.animatedknots.com. There are also apps for mobile devices that can help you learn to tie knots.

This chapter has some good information on knots and how to tie some of the most common knots used by theatre technicians.

Parts of rope
A rope is technically called a line and is divided into parts.

- *The working end* or *tail* is the end of the rope that is used to actually tie the knot. The working end can also be referred to as the tag or tail.
- Making a U shape section to the rope forms *a bight*. Most knots begin by forming a bight.

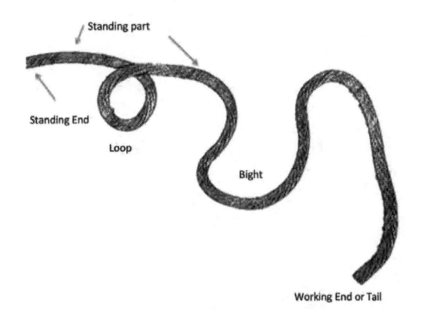

- Putting a twist in *the bight* forms the loop. This twist will form either an overhand loop or an underhand loop. An overhand loop is when the working end of the rope lies over the top of the *standing part*.
- *The standing part* is the length of rope that lies between the *working end* and the *standing end.*
- *The standing end* (or bitter end) is the opposite of the working end or tail of the rope.

Knot Efficiency

No knot is 100% efficient (will hold 100% of the breaking strength of the rope). The bending of the rope creates friction that reduces the strength of rope. The tighter the bends, the more the efficiency is reduced. The least efficient knot is an overhand knot, which is only 50% efficient. Most knots are between 60% and 75% efficient. Since there is really so little difference in the efficiency of most knots, it is not something that I think technicians should be overly concerned with. Generally, keeping the number 60% in the back of your mind will do.

There are literally thousands of different knots, but most falling into the one of the follows three types:

1. **Hitch** *is u*sed to attach a rope to something like a pipe batten, cleat, belaying pin and cable bundle. Types of knots include the *clove hitch, cleat hitch, Prussic* and the *trucker's hitch*

2. **Loops** consist of any type of knot that creates a closed loop for attachment. Types of knots include the *bowline, alpine butterfly loop, hangman's noose, figure 8.*
3. **Bend:** Joins two ropes together. Examples include the *sheet bend, alpine butterfly bend, Carrick bend, figure 8 bend, sheet bend* and *square knot*

Every knot has its strengths and weaknesses, which is why it is important to know more than one knot of each type. One of our favorite knot books is *The Book of Knots (how to tie 200 practical knots)* by Geoffrey Budworth and Jason Dalton. This book not only shows you how to tie knots, but it also rates each knot as to strength, security, ease of tying and ease of untying. These ratings, along with other information about each knot, can help you chose the best knot for particular needs. An important note about *The Book of Knots*: Some books sellers may tell you that this book is "Out of Print." It is not. Barnes and Noble publish this book and they can print copies when they need them.

Most Important Knots to Know

We will start with the most crucial knots to theatre rigging; the *Bowline, Clove Hitch, Half Hitch, Figure Eight, Figure Eight Loop, Alpine Butterfly and Choker*. These are knots you should know how to tie well. We will then move on to some others.

The Bowline

The *Bowline* is the most basic knot to the theatre rigger.   To tie a *Bowline*, make an overhand loop in your left hand making sure that the standing part of the rope is under the loop. Grab the tail with the right hand, come up under and though the loop. Next, take the tail around the back of the standing part, come around and go back through the loop. To tighten, pull both the standing part and the tail.

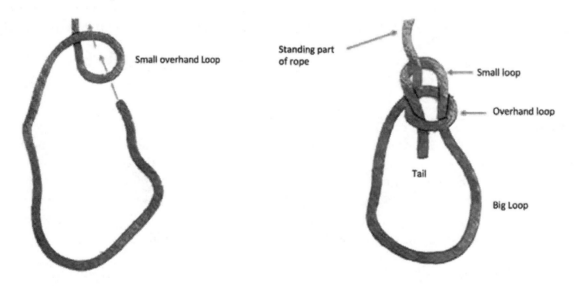

The bowline with the tail tied to the inside. This is the correct way to tie a bowline.

The tail should be tied to the inside of the loop. If the tail is tied to the outside, the knot can capsize by rolling over a beam suddenly releasing the load. The illustration below shows the bowline with the tail to the outside.

The Bowline tied with the tail to the outside. This should be avoided as the knot can capsize and come undone if rolled over an I-beam.

Clove Hitch and Half Hitch

The *Clove Hitch* is another essential hitch. It is a knot that is able to tighten itself around pipes and cable bundles. A simple all purpose hitch, the "clove", as it customarily called, is easy to tie and untie. It is a good binding knot, but as any hitch knot, it should be used with caution because it can slip or come undone if constant pressure is not maintained on the line. That is why two half hitches are often tied when finishing a *Clove Hitch* as it keeps the hitch from loosening when there is no pressure.

The Clove Hitch

Take the tail of the rope and wrap it around the pipe once making an X. Wrap the rope again, this time insert the tail under the X.

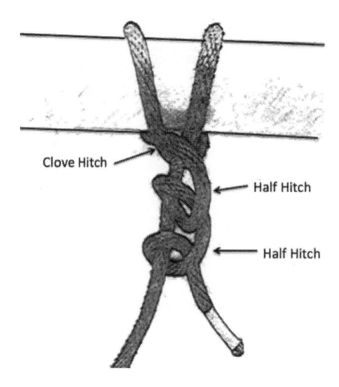

The Clove Hitch with two Half Hitches

Lastly, take the tail and insert it around and thru the standing part of the rope for the *Half Hitch*. Two Half Hitches secure and complete the knot.

The Figure 8

The *Figure Eight* knot is tied at the end of a rope that is running through a pulley (block). Its purpose is to keep the rope from accidently running through the sheave and un-reeving itself. An easy knot to learn, the *Figure Eight* takes the shape of the number 8.

The Figure 8

The Figure Eight (or Flemish) Loop

The *Figure Eight Loop* is a loop formed on a bight. It allows for a loop to be tied to a ring or a carabineer. It is reasonably easy to remember, tie, and check as it takes the form of the Figure Eight that we tied above. It is also an extremely secure loop knot.

Start by making a bight in the standing part.

Next, run the bight under the standing part.

The bight is run through the loop at the base making the number 8.

The completed Figure Eight loop

Alpine Butterfly

The *Alpine Butterfly Loop* is also known as the *Lineman's Knot*. It is an excellent, mid-line rigging knot as it forms a fixed loop in the middle of the rope without needing to have access to the ends. This is made on the bight. The mid-line loop makes it convenient for multi-directional loading, attaching carabineers and anchorages.

Step 1: Wrap rope around hand.

Step 2: Cross the tail end across palm.

Step 3: Take top loop and pull below crossed tail.

Step 4: Pull loop under wraps and pull through.

The finished Alpine Butterfly Loop

The Choker Hitch

The *Choker Hitch* is a self-tightening knot that is formed on a bight. It is used in wrapping roundslings around truss and securing rope around battens.

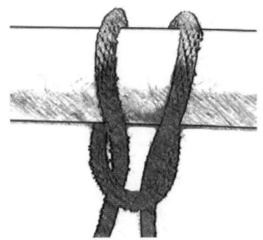

The choker hitch

Additional Knots to Know

The next series of knots are not as frequently used by the theatre rigger as the first seven, but they are certainly useful to have in your repertoire.

The Trucker's Hitch

The *Trucker's Hitch* is considered a "lashing or tie down" knot. It is very useful to "temporarily" lash down equipment when ratchet straps are not immediately available. This is not to say that the *Trucker's Hitch* should take the place of ratchet straps. It should not. The knot is limited to the breaking strength of the rope and D:d ratios on the loops. It should only be used to "temporarily" lash down equipment in a pinch. As you will see, the knot forms a very crude block and tackle with a 3:1 ratio. Tying a *Trucker's Hitch* is can be done in several steps. Let's assume we are securing a load to a palette cart. The standing end of the rope is secured to the opposite end of the cart with a bowline. The working end of the rope is thrown over to the opposite side of the load.

Step 1: Mid-way up this opposite side, make a *slip knot* in the rope (shown left). (The *Alpine Butterfly Loop* can be used too).

Step 1: The slipknot is the loop formed midway in the rope

Step 2. Run the Tail through an attachment point at the bottom of the palette and thread the tail through the loop formed midway in the rope.

Step 3. Pulling on the working end of the rope will tighten the line with a 3:1 ratio..

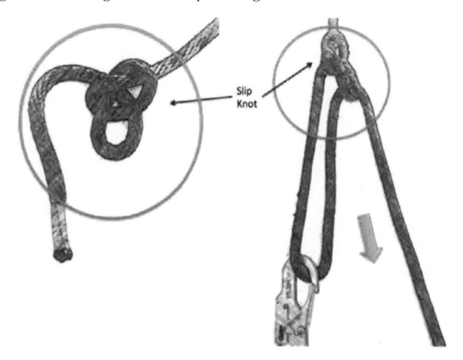

Step 2: The Tail runs through the loop formed midway in the rope.
Step 3: Pulling on the working end of the rope will tighten down the load with a 3:1 ratio.

Step 4: Once tension on the load is complete, secure the *Trucker's Hitch* with two *Half Hitches*

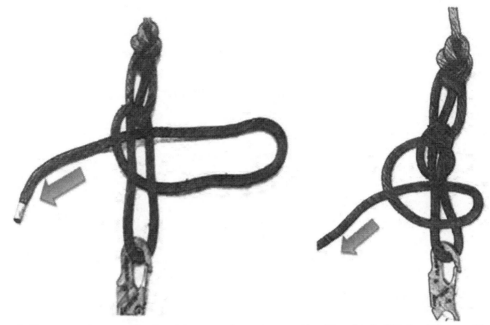

Step 4: Once tension on the load is complete, secure the *Trucker's Hitch* with two *Half Hitches*.

The finished Trucker's Hitch

Carrick Bend

The Carrick Bend is used for joining two larger diameter lines that cannot be easily tied with other knots. While it is easy to tie, it is not always easy to remember. Unlike many bends, it is easy to untie and it will not jam closed after taking on heavy loads.

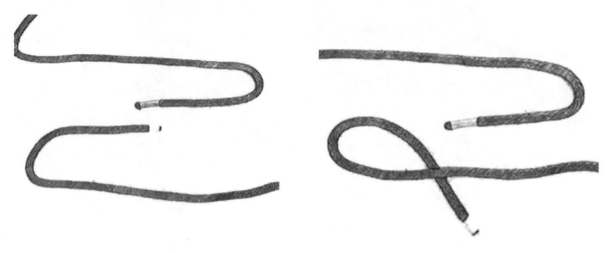

Step 1: Form the two lines in a bight; an upper rope and a lower rope.

Step 2: Next, form a loop in the lower line as shown. The tail should be laying under the standing part.

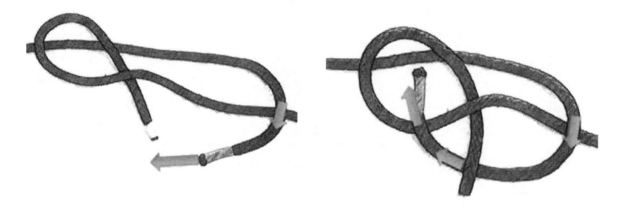

Step 3: The tail of the upper line will run over the standing part of the lower line.

Step 4: Next, the tail of the upper line will run under the tail of the lower line and over the loop.

Step 6: The tail of the upper line will run under the standing part of the lower line and back up over the loop. The end result will look like a pretzel with both ends pointing away from you.

Step 7: Next, tighten the knot a bit @ being sure to still leave a good amount of tail. Pull the two standing ends to cause the knot to "turn on itself" and tighten.

Note: Some people tie this knot with the tails opposite each other (as shown here) while other tie it with the tails (next to each other). Because this knot is symmetrical, the knot holds equally no matter which way the tails point.

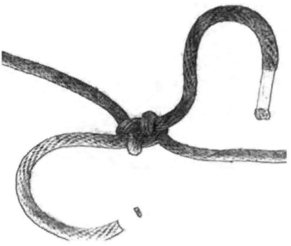

The finished Carrack Bend

The Overhand Knot

The *Overhand Knot* is a very secure, permanent knot that is often hard to untie. It is often tied at the end of a rope to keep the ends from unraveling until they can be properly whipped or lashed at a later time.

The Overhand Knot

The Double Sheet bend

The sheet bend is another knot that joins two ropes together. This knot is effective in binding two ropes together when each rope is of a different diameter.

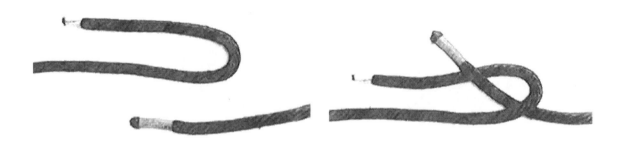

Step1: Shape the upper line into a bight.

Step 2: The tail of the second line runs under and through the bight.

Step 3: The tail will run up and under the standing part and tail of the first line.

Step 4: Pull the tail through leaving enough tail to finish the knot.

Step 5: The tail will pull through the loop forming a half hitch. If you stop here, you have a *single sheet bend*.

Step 6: Next, pass the tail back under the standing parts and thread under and through the half hitch.

The finished double sheet bend.

The Prussik

Prussik was an Austrian Climber who introduced this wrap/hitch back in the 1930's. It is a great friction knot that allows one rope to be secured to another so that it will not slide. If it is choked around another rope or multi-cable, it is extremely secure; if it is loosen, it will slide up or down the rope it is fastened to. In theatre applications, the *prussik* is often used as a "sunday" to tie off the purchase line of a counterweight system or to choke a cable bundle for strain relief.

The *Prussik* is a good all-around friction knot

The Bowline on a Bight

The Bowline on a Bight makes two loops in the middle of the standing part of a rope. You do not need to thread the tail like we did in the *Bowline.* This knot also makes a convenient seat when a bo'sun's chair is unavailable.

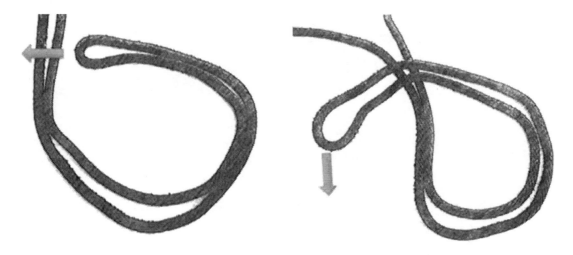

Step 1: Form the standing part of the line into a bight.

Step 2: Make an overhand loop with the bight.

Step 3: The tail end of the bight will cross towards the loop.

Step 4: The tail end of the bight will enter the loop from the underside.

Step 5: Divide the tail of the bight so that it will cross under the loop of the bowline.

Step 6: Pull the loop of the bight up and over the standing part of the rope.

Step 7: The loop of the bight is pulled up while tension is taken up on the bowline loop. This tightens the knot.

The completed bowline on a bight.

Theatre Rigger's Rope
Rope Type
The question most often asked by riggers is, *"what type of rope is best to purchase?"* Most riggers use a 5/8" solid braid multifilament polypropylene or polyester line as a general hauling line. For a *bull line*, you will want something closer to 1-inch diameter. Regardless, you want a rope that is extremely flexible and easy to handle. A 5/8" to 1" diameter rope is easy to pull and hold onto. What you DO NOT want to use is a rope from the recreational climbing industry. Its application is for just that: ascending or descending. It is too stiff and its 3/8" diameter is too small to handle.

Recommendations are:
1. *Spectrum Show Braid.* This is a double-braided rope constructed of a core of filament polyester with a filament polyester sleeve. It offers low stretch and very good wear characteristics.

2. *Solid braid multifilament polypropylene.* This solid braid polypropylene is more economical than polyester. It uses much smaller fibers compared to other polypropylene ropes, which give it a softer feel. The fibers do tend to pick if they catch on small abrasions.

Spectrum Show Braid　　　　　Solid Braid Multifilament Polypropylene

Coiling a rope

Learning how to coil a rope properly will help keep twists and knots out of the rigging line and allow it to play back out evenly when needed. Riggers will NEVER coil a rope around their elbow, as this does not allow the rope to lie evenly in the coils. Nothing can be more frustrating, or a demonstration of amateur status, than to lower down a rigging line only to have knots and twists show up in your line. When a rope is coiled, it must spin one turn in order for it to lie evenly. Coiling around the arm does not allow the rope to twist. The result is a rope that develops twists that form a figure 8 in the coil that remain when rope is uncoiled.

Never coil a rope around your arm. It puts twists in the line that remain.

Proper coiling will keep the line free of kinks and twists. Start by holding the tail end of the rope in one hand and pulling the standing end of the rope out a comfortable distance with the other. Form a loop allowing the coil to form naturally while twisting the rope one turn with your fingers. The rope must make one turn for every loop in the coil. The coil formed will be around two feet in diameter with no twists. If the rope is extremely long or heavy, use the same technique by laying the rope out on the floor (Note: the same method is used to coil lighting or audio cable). If there is an extreme amount of kinks and twists, you may need to stretch the rope out on the floor its entire length before coiling.

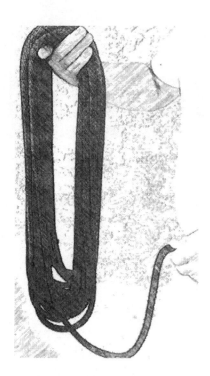

Hold the tail end in one hand while forming a loop with the other.

Finishing and Stowing

Form a loop allowing the coil to form naturally while twisting the rope one turn with your fingers. Finishing the coil is done so that the loops formed will not become tangled while the rope is being stored or transported. There are basically two methods for finishing the coil.

- *Gasket Coil (Butterfly Coil)*: The first method is preferred when the rope is to be stored (stowed) for a period of time. It secures the coils firmly by wrapping the entire line with a perpendicular wrap. Once the coil is made, leave around four feet of line for the wrap. While still holding the coil in one hand, wrap the entire coil with the excess three feet. Forming a loop with the last sixteen inches, pull the loop through and over the entire coil. Wrap the entire coil with the extra three feet of tail. Forming a loop with the last sixteen inches, pull the loop through the inside of the coil and over the top. The finished line ready to be stowed.

- *Rigger's Method (The Alpine Coil):* The rigger's method, *or alpine coil* (as it is better known), allows for the coil to be carried over the shoulder, leaving the hands free for climbing. Start by coiling the rope as described above. Again, leave about four feet of tail for the wrap. Next, form a bight in the in the tail end close to the coils. Wrap the remaining rope around the bight working the wrap forward. Tuck the tail into the bight and pull the bight closed.

Form a bight in the in the working end close to the coils. Wrap the remaining rope around the bight working the wrap forward. Tuck the tail into the bight and pull the bight closed.

The finished *Riggers Coil*

Rope Maintenance

Polyester and polypropylene rope are very resilient to use (and misuse) and will last for many years. Still, proper care should be taken to avoid contact with chemicals, UV radiation and sharp corners and edges. After use, coil the rope, as described above, being careful to remove all kinks, knots and twists in the line. Check the rope before each use for abrasion and wear. The ends should be checked for unraveling. Basically, your rigging line should be stowed so that it is ready for use when needed.

Throwing the Rope

Before throwing a rope, it must be properly coiled or flaked to prevent tangling when it is deployed. If using a coiled or flaked rope, it can remain at your feet or on the I-beam. If the rope is lying across beams, make sure that there will be enough slack in the line to throw. From the coil or slack, make several small coils in the throwing hand based on the throwing distance. Hold the excess rope in the other hand. The rope maybe thrown overhand or underhand, but the throw should be as smooth as possible keeping the throwing arm as straight as possible. Look slightly above your target. Aim for that spot. Throw the rope up and out making sure the throw is as smooth as possible. Just before the rope is released, yell out the warning *"rope"* to make sure other riggers are aware of the action.

Tying the Snub Line

There are several methods for tying a snub line at the rail. All of these involve the use of a friction knot of some kind. The method described below is one such method. The photos and descriptions below are courtesy of *David Vick, IATSE, Local 274 and Scott C. Parker, IATSE, Local 8.* They can be viewed by going to:

http://hstech.org/how-to-s/how-to-tech/rigging/methods-how-tos-instructions-etc/714-holding-a-flyrail-handline-in-place112

The snub is tied with 5'-6' lengths of 1/4"-5/16" line, with an eye either tied or spliced in one end. A good rope to use can be purchased from New England Ropes' Sta-Set for overall wear resistance and breaking strength. It is recommended that six to eight of these lines be pre-measured and made up ahead of time so that they are readily available at the rail when needed.

Eyes splices are preferred to knotted ones, because they're stronger and don't weaken the line. You can buy lines pre-spliced, or get a splicing fid & learn to do it yourself; it's actually quite simple.

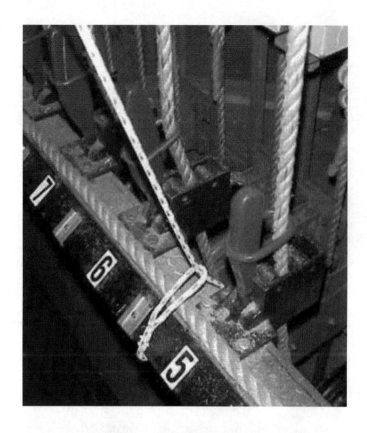

Step One: Begin by choking the line around the rail, with the working part of the line coming up from behind & through the eye.

Step Two: Take a turn around both counterweight lines with the snub line, passing it underneath itself as it comes back around - as if you were beginning a clove hitch.

Step 3: Laying the line "on top of" the first wrap, take another wrap. Be sure to pass the second wrap underneath the line coming up from the rail as before. Pull up on the working end to wedge it firmly under the line coming up.

Step 4: Continue taking wraps in the same fashion, pulling tightly as you go. The finished snub should have 4-5 full turns, or approx. the same height in turns as the width of both ropes that you're snubbing. This is the main working part of the snub.

Step 5: Once the turns are tight & secure, tie off the end of the line above the snub wrapping with a clove hitch. This doesn't contribute to the snub's working friction much; it's primarily to keep the end from dropping below the wraps, which would cause them to undo themselves. By keeping the end up & tight, the snub remains secure indefinitely.

The finished snub line.

Knots in wire rope

Tying knots in wire rope is not as common of a practice in theatre rigging as tying knots in fiber rope. However, because theatre rigging commonly uses wire rope, we want to include some popular knots/splices and can be easily made with wire rope (particularly, the 7x19 construction wire rope known commonly as "aircraft cable.")

Because wire rope is stiffer than fiber ropes, not all knots work well in wire rope, just as many knots do not work well in very slick ropes and fishing lines. However, many knots can be used in wire rope. One advantage of wire rope is its strength – it is very strong compared to most fiber ropes. For this reason wire rope has many uses in the theatre.

In this section, we will give the name, knot type, efficiency, common use for each knot, as well as notes about the knot and its use. We will also describe how each knot is tied. No tools, other than a cable cutter, are needed for making these terminations.

Knowing how to tie these knots can make certain rigging tasks much faster and easier.

Knot Name: Flemish Eye
Knot Type: Loop
Efficiency: Up to 90%
Common Uses: Anywhere an eye is needed in a wire rope
Notes: The most common knot/splice for making an eye is a Flemish Eye (aka Farmer's Eye, Molly Hogan Eye, or a Canadian Eye). Unlike traditional splices, this splice involves re-twisting the strands of the cable instead of tucking them. There are several slight variations of this splice, but we will cover the variation that my tests have proven to be the strongest (up to 90% efficiency rating in some tests – making it even stronger than using cable clips).

Step 1
Untwist the strands dividing them into two groups: one with three outer strands and the other with three outer strands plus the core strand.   Give yourself plenty of leads to work with.

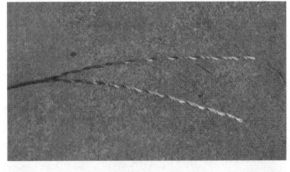

Step 2
Cross the two sets of strands and begin twisting them back together to form the eye. Each set of strands should twist around the other at least three times.

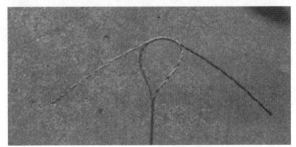

Step 3
Keep twisting until the eye is completely formed.

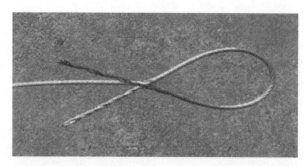

Step 4
Finish the eye by using electrical tape to secure the tail to the leading part of the cable to prevent it from getting "caught" on things when in use. Some manuals show a cable clip being used to clamp the tail to the leading part of the cable, but now we are using real "hardware."

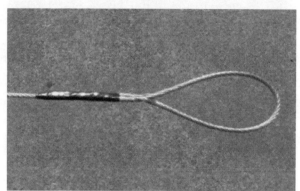

Knot Name: Circus Hitch
Knot Type: Hitch
Efficiency: 60%
Common Uses: Terminating a cable to beam or pipe
Notes: The Circus Hitch (aka a Carney Knot) is probably the best-known cable knot. This hitch is great for guying cables because it can be tied with tension on the line. This is an extremely secure hitch that will not loosen, even when there is slack in the line.

Step 1
Tie a typical clove hitch around the pipe with your cable. You can use the clove hitch as a means to put significant tension on the leading part of the cable, if desired. Leave yourself plenty of tail with which to create the stopper portion of the hitch.

Step 2
Tightly wrap the tail, at least four wraps, down the leading part of the line.

Step 3
Bend the cable 180 degrees and tightly wrap back down the lead line (over the top of your previous wraps) toward the pipe. Then feed the end of the cable tail into the small opening between the lead part and the tail directly at the clove hitch, and pull tight.

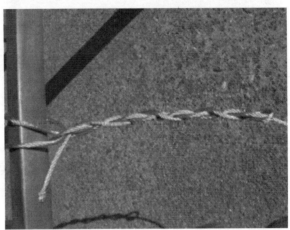

Knot Name: General Purpose Knot
Knot Type: Loop
Efficiency: 60%
Common Uses: Terminating a cable to beam or pipe
Notes: The General Purpose Knot (not a very original name) is another knot that works very well for tying a cable to a beam or pipe. Although it is not as strong or as secure as the Circus Hitch, the General Purpose Knot is extremely fast and easy tie. It should also be noted that like a Sheet Bend, which will be covered later, this knot is loose and springy until tension is placed on the cable.

Step 1
Tie an overhand knot in the cable (we will call this twist of the cable the "first wrap").

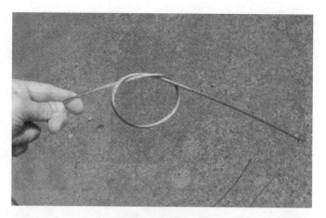

Step 2
Pass the working end around whatever you are attaching it to and then bring it back through the loop that you created when you made the overhand knot. Be sure that it is threaded through the loop in the proper direction.

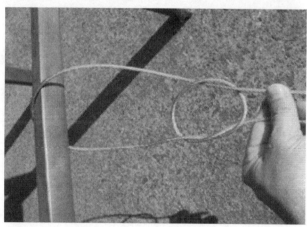

Step 3
Thread the end through the loop a second time (opposite the first twist).

Step 4
Thread the end through the loop a third time, making another wrap next to the first wrap.

When a load is placed on the line, the knot will tighten.

Knot Name: Simple End Splice
Knot Type: Bend / Splice
Efficiency: ?
Common Uses: A Simple End Splice (the name we have given this splice because we have never heard it called a specific name) is similar in some ways to a Flemish Eye splice – the strands are untwisted and then re-twisted to form the splice. This is not an especially strong splice, but it is quick and easy, and keeps the cable the same diameter so that the splice can pass easily over a sheave. This is a great splice to use when you need to replace a cable because you can use the old cable to pull the new one through the sheaves.

<u>Step 1</u>
Untwist the strands of one cable (at least 100 times the diameter of the cable) dividing each into two groups: one with three outer strands and the other with three outer strands plus the core strand. Cut off the bundle with three stands and re-twist the end back in place.

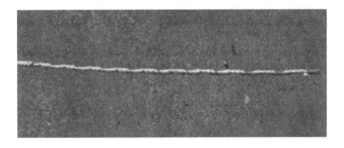

<u>Step 2</u>
Untwist the strands of the second cable, dividing each into two groups: one with three outer strands and the other with three outer strands plus the core strand. Untwist this bundle a couple of inches longer than you did for the first cable. Cut-off the bundle with the four strands and re-twist the strands back into place.

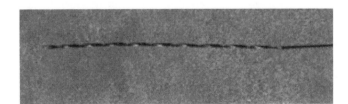

Step 3
Twist the two bundles of strands together to make a single cable.

Step 4
Cut these "tail strands" to the proper length and twist into place.

Step 5
Use electrical tape at the ends of the splice to prevent the wire from fraying-out and catching. Keep the tape as smooth as possible (on small diameter cable run the tape down the cable rather than wrapping the cable).

Knot Name: Double Sheet Bend (aka Double Cat's Paw knot)
Knot Type: Bend
Efficiency: 60%
Common Uses: For a stronger attachment than the simple end splice, a Double Sheet Bend (aka Double Cat's Paw knot) is generally a good knot. When first tied, this knot is rather loose, and it can take several hundred pounds of force to tighten it completely, but when tight, it will hold quite well.

We should also note that there is a different knot for rope that also goes by the name Double Cat's Paw, so do not be confused if you see this name.

This knot can also eliminate the need for an expensive Kline Haven Tool, used to pull wire rope.

Step 1
Bend one cable to form a bight.

190

Step 2

Insert the working end of the second cable up through the bight, wrap around the back of the bight, and then over the top of the bight, making certain that it passes under itself. Note: A Single Sheet Bend, as seen at the end of this step, is a "good" knot, but not as secure as a Double Sheet Bend.

Step 3

To make this a Double Sheet Bend, (continuing in the same direction) pass the working end around the back of the bight a second time, and again over the top of the bight, making certain that it passes under the standing part again. Then pull tight.

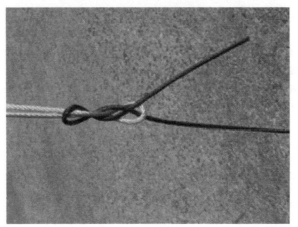

Summary

Learning to tie knots takes lots of practice. However, a theatre rigger who cannot tie secure knots is not really much of a rigger. This is an essential skill for riggers, and one that you will be glad you have.

Let us leave you with one additional website for information on type knots – http://springknollpress.com/knots/index.html

This site has three downloadable PowerPoint presentations that teach how to tie 10 knots that will be useful to theatre technicians.

Chapter 10:

Rigging Hardware

Introduction

In Chapter 3, we discussed Stage Equipment and Rigging Installations and in Chapter 9, we discussed wire rope. What we did not discuss was the hardware that is used to fasten this equipment together or any of the other miscellaneous hardware used in theatre rigging. Working Load Limits (WLL) and Design Factors are just as important to keep in mind when working with theatre hardware, as it is with theatre equipment. Keeping this in mind, let's take a look at some of the hardware used in theatre rigging.

Typical Hardware
We noted in Chapter 3 that all hardware does not have the same *Design Factor*. Repeated below is some of the common *Design Factors* that we discussed in Chapter 3.

- Synthetic Slings: 5:1
- Wire rope slings: 5:1
- Stage rigging (counterweight rigging system, including the wire rope): 8:1
- Shackles: 6:1
- Fiber ropes: 7:1 to 12:1
- Chain (except grade 43): 4:1
- Grade 43 chain: 3:1
- Ratchet straps: 3:1
- Turnbuckles: 5:1
- Most Sailing hardware (including stainless steel shackles): 2:1

Other Design Factors related to hardware are:

- Bolts: 5:1
- Verilocks: 5:1
- Quick Links 5:1
- Wire rope clips 5:1

Bolts
Most theatrical scenery is held together by bolts fastened with nuts. Essentially, as a nut is tightened along the threads, the shaft of the bolt stretches as it is put under tension and the

192

material compresses. The nuts are made of a slightly softer metal then the bolt allowing it to both deform and engage the bolt threads. Bolts are torqued (tightened) to a force that is generally greater than the compressive forces place on the material being tightened. If the density of the bolt were to be the same density of the material, the threads would strip and/or the head would be wrenched off. Thus, bolts are "graded" based on the hardness of their steel. The most common grades are Grade 2, Grade 5 and Grade 8. The chart below describes each of these grades.

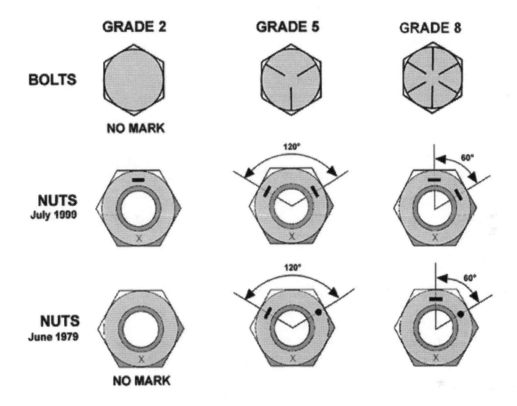

The higher the grade, the stronger the bolt, but also the more brittle. Grade 5 or higher is recommended for rigging applications.

Shackles

Shackles are commonly used in arena rigging for connecting slings to other slings or connecting slings to the hooks on a chain hoist. Before we get into how shackles are used, look at the figure below to understand the two body shapes for shackles and the three types of pins.

Anchor Shackle   **Chain Shackle**

Anchor shackles, aka Bow shackles, are the most common type shackle used in arena rigging because the "bell shaped" allows this type of shackle to be used as a "collector ring" so that multiple lines, can be connected at a single point. Chain shackles, aka D shackles, cannot be used as collector rings - the loads must always be aligned with the centerline of the shackle. This makes them less useful for arena rigging.

Round Pin Anchor   Round Pin Chain   Screw Pin Anchor   Screw Pin Chain   Bolt-Type Anchor   Bolt-Type Chain

Shackles pins can be "round pins" - that use a cotter pin to hold them into place, "screw pins" - where a threaded end screws into a threaded "ear" on the shackle's body, or a bolt - that uses a captive nut to keep it in place. Arena rigging is done almost exclusively with Screw Pin Anchor Shackles.

Multiple lines (bridle legs) are commonly connected to another piece of steel with an anchor shackle at the bridle's apex, as shown below.

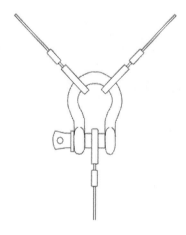

This is allowed, within limits. The Crosby Group says...

SHACKLES, RINGS, LINKS AND MASTER LINKS CAN BE USED AS A COLLECTOR RING. DO NOT EXCEED AN INCLUDED ANGLE OF 120 DEGREES ON ANY COLLECTOR RING (60 DEGREES EITHER SIDE).

It should be noted that users are not limited to the number of legs that can be connected to a connector ring (including a shackle) as long as rule above is followed, and the load on the shackle is "reasonably centered." Below is an image showing an example of off center loading of a shackle. (Note: off centering of the load is ONLY permitting on screw pin and bolt type shackles, NEVER on round pin shackles).

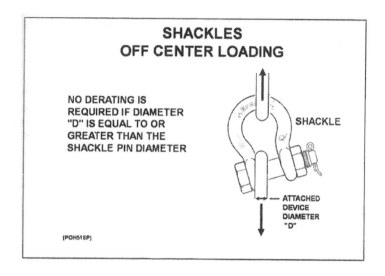

Related to off center loading, Crosby states...

IF THE ATTACHING LINKS' DIAMETER ARE EQUAL TO OR LARGER THAN THE SHACKLE PIN DIAMETER, NO REDUCTION OF THE WLL IS REQUIRED, REGARDLESS OF THE LOCATION ON THE PIN.

and

IF THE LOAD IS NOT CENTERED ON THE SHACKLE PIN AND THE ATTACHING LINK IS SMALLER THAN THE SHACKLE PIN DIAMETER, THE WLL SHOULD BE REDUCED 15 DUE TO THE RESULTING ANGULAR LOADING.

Another situation that sometimes arises with shackles is "side loading." When a rigger says that a shackle is "side loaded," he means that the load on the shackle is on opposites sides of the shackle and none of the load is on the pin of the shackle, as in the illustration below.

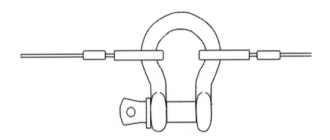

But, this is not what shackle manufacturers mean when they use the term "side loaded." According to *The Crosby Group Product Application Seminar Workbook (ASME/OSHA BASED), Edition 7A,* Crosby would define this as an Incorrect Shackle Alignment" and say that it is not allowed. See below.

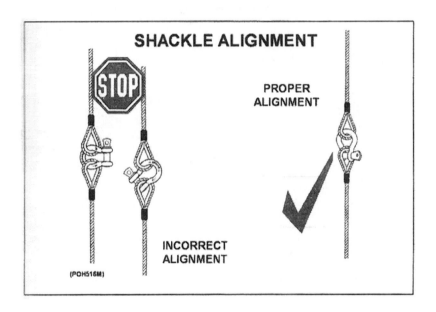

Shackles should be inspected for wear before being installed.

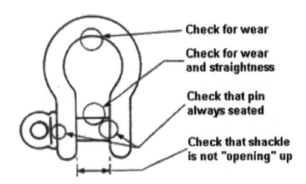

1. Inspect the body of the shackle for excess wear. Wear of 10% or more of the original diameter is where the shackle needs to be replaced.
2. Inspect the shackle body for bending. A bent shackle often indicates excessive side-loading.
3. Inspect the shackle eye and pin holes for stretching or elongation.
4. Inspect the shackle pin for distortion, surface blemishes, wear and fractures.
5. Inspect the seating of the pin.

General Notes on Shackles

- Shackles should always be larger than the cable size
- Pin should only be finger tight
- Mouse shackles on long term or permanent installs
- Different manufacturers have different ratings
- Shackle does not care if it's pin up or pin down
- Back off pin 1/8-1/4 turn
- If a shackle is very hard to open it might have been overloaded

Quick Links

Quick links are made from zinc plated steel rod and are threaded at one end and have a nut on the other. The quick link is often used to secure scenery chain and is only intended to be loaded along the axis. When used, the nut must be drawn all the way down with no threads exposed. They are not intended for overhead lifting.

Oval Quick Link

Pear Quick Link

Cable Grips (Grip Locks or Verilocks)

Cable Grips enable the quick adjustment of wire rope cable when leveling scenery or lightweight objects. They are a one-step, adjustable suspension devise that is often used in the Convention Center industry as they reduced the time necessary for installation and leveling. When depressing the plunger, they glide smoothly up and down the wire rope cable. When the plunger is released, the three-ball mechanism inside engages the cable.

Cable Grips come in a variety of sizes depending on the wire rope used, but generally do not exceed a load rating more than 250-pounds. As in any hardware, it is important NOT to exceed the WLL. Manufactured with a Design Factor of 5, Cable Grips are intended for use on *static loads only* and should not be used for overhead lifting. As in any hardware, the Design Factor should be changed to 10 when suspended over the heads of people or performers.

Once the scenery is level, the dead end of the cable should be threaded through the scenery attachment hardware and looped back up to the live end of the cable where the dead end can be fixed with wire rope clips. This provides redundancy should the hardware fail.

Slings

Round slings are generally used to wrap truss, although they often find their way into the theatre in some form of lifting applications. They are soft, non-abrasive, and do not damage the aluminum chords when used properly. There are many different types of slings on the market, each are designed for a specific purpose. In this chapter, we will discuss two basic types of round slings. These are synthetic core and wire rope core. Both consist of an endless core loop that is covered with a protective, synthetic fabric jacket. Note: Round slings are sometimes called "Spansets". It should be noted that "Spanset" is a brand name, like "BandAid" and not the correct name of the product.

photo courtesy of TomCat Truss

Synthetic core slings are made from 100 polyester strands. These strands are looped around forming a continuous core of strands. The core is then covered with a synthetic fabric sleeve that serves to hold the strands together and to protect them from wear. A tag is then sewn onto the sleeve containing the basic product information about the sling. OSHA regulations require the tag to be in place and the information legible. If this tag is missing or the writing is illegible, do not use the round sling.

Wire rope core slings, called GAC Flex or Steel-Flex, are made from steel Galvanized Aircraft Cable that is wound in an endless configuration forming an Independent Wire Rope Core (IWRC). They are then covered with a double-wall polyester jacket. A velcro tag may be opened allowing the inspection of the wire rope core. Wire rope core slings tend to be less flexible than polyester core slings, but have greater strength and are resistant to heat damage.

photo courtesy of LiftAll, LiftLIt® Manufacturing Company, Inc.

Color-coding identifies the sling and its load rating in various configurations. It's the commercial industry that uses colored slings that are color coded according to load capacity.

Color Code		Approx. Body Diameter	Approx. Weight/Foot	Rated Capacity in Pounds					Minimum Length
				Vertical	Choker	Basket	60°	45°	
Purple		0.60"	0.20 LB	2,600	2,100	5,200	4,500	3,700	3'
Green		0.80"	0.30 LB	5,300	4,200	10,600	9,200	7,500	3'
Yellow		1.00"	0.50 LB	8,400	6,700	16,800	14,500	11,900	3'
Tan		1.20"	0.60 LB	10,600	8,500	21,200	18,400	15,000	3'
Red		1.30"	0.75 LB	13,200	10,600	26,400	22,900	18,700	3'
White		1.40"	0.90 LB	16,800	13,400	33,600	29,100	23,800	6'
Blue		1.75"	1.15 LB	21,200	17,000	42,400	36,700	30,000	6'
Orange		2.00"	1.30 LB	25,000	20,000	50,000	43,300	35,400	6'
Orange		2.25"	1.50 LB	31,000	24,800	62,000	53,700	43,800	6'
Black		2.50"	2.00 LB	40,000	32,000	80,000	69,300	56,600	6'
Black		3.00"	2.50 LB	53,000	42,400	106,000	91,800	74,900	7'
Black		3.25"	3.50 LB	66,000	52,800	132,000	114,300	93,300	7'
Black		3.75"	4.00 LB	90,000	72,000	180,000	155,900	127,300	7'
Black		4.00"	4.50 LB	100,000	80,000	200,000	173,200	141,400	7'

Load Capacity Charts for Round Slings

-photo courtesy of CoreSlings.com

It is only in the entertainment industry that we find the sling jackets colored black. The load data on the attached chart is for a *specific* brand of round sling so be sure you are using the correct manufacturer's data chart. It shows the Working Load Limits (or WLL) that are assigned to the various sling colors. You can see that there are a variety of "black colored" slings with their corresponding load ratings. Always be sure to check the load rating data found on the sling tag. Note: that the load capacities change as the sling is used in a vertical, choker, basket and angled configurations. These configurations are also printed on the tag for convenience. Working Load Limits will be discussed further at the end of this chapter.

Inspection
OSHA 1910.184 covers the safe use and inspection of round slings. Specifically, OSHA 1910.184(d) states,

> *Each day before being used, the sling and all fastenings and attachments shall be inspected for damage or defects by a competent person designated by the employer. Additional inspections shall be performed during sling use, where service conditions warrant. Damaged or defective slings shall be immediately removed from service.*

Thing to look for are:

• Heat/ chemical damage
• Abrasion/wear/hard, stiff or crunchy to the touch
• Knots
• Frayed jacket/ open exposed core
• Cuts in the jacket
• Damaged/ illegible or missing tags

Measuring a round sling. To correctly measure the length of a sling, stretch out the sling and measure from the inside edge of the sling to its opposite inside edge. Slings generally come in lengths of 1.5-feet to 8-feet.

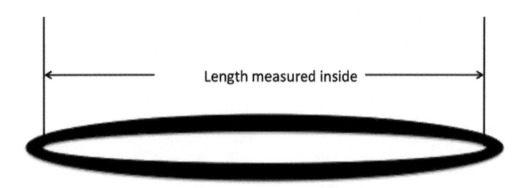

Length measured inside

Measuring a Round Sling

Compression Sleeves

Swaging is the process of forming an eye in the end of a wire rope using a compression sleeve (called Nicopress) and a swaging tool. Originally patented by the National Telephone Supply Company, a properly swaged Nicopress sleeve will form a termination equal to the breaking strength of the wire rope; that is, 100% efficiency.

A Nicopress Sleeve

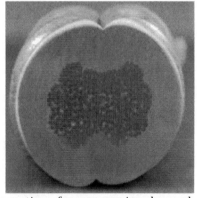

A cross section of a compression sleeve showing the compressive force that is exerted on the wire rope strands.

A swaging tool is used to apply the appropriate amount of compressing force to the sleeve when swaging. There are several companies that make swaging tools; Nicopress which is made by the National Telephone Supply Company, and LocoLoc which is made by The Loos Company. Both are highly reliable and conform to industry standards. Both companies also manufacture a Go-No-Go tool that is unique to their product and must be used to test the efficiency of the swages made.

A swaging tool

A Go-No-Go is used to check the crimps made to the compression sleeve.

How to Make a Proper Termination

In making any swaged termination, follow these simple rules:

1. Always use the correct size compression sleeve for the correct size wire rope
2. Always extend the wire rope past the sleeve
3. Always make sure that the sleeve is not tight against the thimble so it does not deform the thimble when it is compressed
4. Always use the correct size notch in the compressing tool for the size sleeve you are using
5. Use the correct number of compressions for the size sleeve you are using. Follow the manufacturer's recommendations
6. Make sure you compress the sleeve in the proper order
7. Always check your compressions with the same Go-No-Go tool as the compression tool you are using

Nicopress copper sleeve using ¼" wire rope

Loos copper sleeve using ¼" wire rope

3 2 1

1 2 3

3 1 2

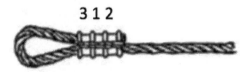

Correct order of swaging

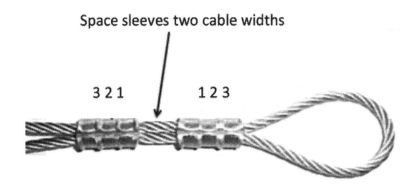

Space sleeves two cable widths

3 2 1   1 2 3

The correct order for swaging two sleeves

Note: Nicopress sleeves for ¼" wire rope uses three compressions, while the Loos sleeve will use four compressions.

Each manufacturer has compression charts for use with their sleeves (See the Reference Data located in the Appendix 2). Be sure to consult the charts to match the number of crimps required for the gauge wire rope you are using.

Hydraulically swaged sleeves
Hydraulically swaged sleeves use a single compression dye that compresses the entire sleeve. There are several hand held tools and bench mounted tools that can do this. Each use a specific sized dye for use with the correct size swage.

Copper vs Aluminum
The debate often centers on whether to use copper compression sleeves or aluminum. The problem with aluminum sleeves is that aluminum is soft causing the sleeve to slip especially under a shock load. Many industries have banned them altogether because they are not manufactured to any kind of standards. DO NOT USE ALUMINUM COMPRESSION SLEEVES. It is best to stay with copper.

Wire Rope Clips
Wire rope clips are generally used in the field to make an eye on the end of a wire rope when swaging is not possible. Properly installed wire rope clips will only offer 80% efficiency of the

wire rope's WLL (90% for 1" to 3.5" sizes). Before we begin looking at how wire rope clips are attached to wire rope cable, let's look at the parts of the clip.

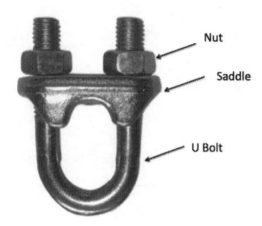

Think of a saddle. The wire rope clip basically forms a saddle with the U Bolt forming the Girth. You may have heard of the expression, *"Never saddle a dead horse."* Well, that expression relates to the correct method for attaching the clips. When a wire rope is formed around a thimble, the "live end" of the cable is the cable that continues on the length of the wire rope. The "dead end" is the terminated end.

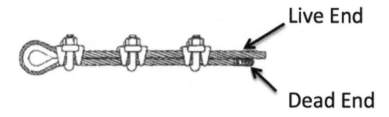

The correct method for attaching the clips has the saddle resting on the "live end" of the line with the "girth" or U Bolt strapping under the "dead end."

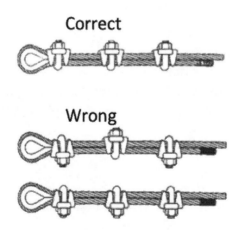

There are a few methods of attaching wire rope clips to the wire rope. The preferred method is shown below.

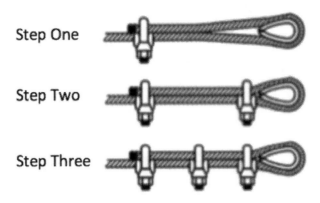

Wire rope clips should not be reused, as they may not torque properly on the second application.

Wire rope clips are made from either zinc plated, stainless, or galvanized steel. Like any other hardware, they should be marked with a PIC or Product Identification Code for traceability with the size forged into the saddle. They should meet or exceed all requirements of ASME B30.26.

Inspection
Before use, wire rope clips should be visually inspected for damage, corrosion, wear, and cracks. Make sure that the correct size clip is being used for the correct gauge wire rope.

Turnbuckles
Turnbuckles are an excellent means to adjusting the tension on wire rope cables such as lift lines. Considerations when using turnbuckles are:

- They should be manufactured of forged steel and meet the requirements of ASME B30.26
- When used a part of a permanent installation, they should be moused or secured with lock (jam) nuts to prevent rotation of the body of the turnbuckle.
- Turnbuckles are designed to be used in a straight in-line pull only.

Several types are shown below.

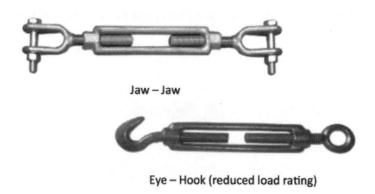

Jaw – Jaw

Eye – Hook (reduced load rating)

Eye - Eye

Lock nuts are permitted as a means to lock the rotation of a turnbuckle if the nuts are properly torqued to the manufacturer's specifications. Mousing with either a plastic cable tie or wire is also an acceptable means of insuring that the body of the turnbuckle will not rotate.

A Eye –Eye Turnbuckle with A jam nut

A properly "moused" turnbuckle

Load rating data for turnbuckles can be found in Appendix 2.

Chain

Chain has a variety of very practical uses around the stage. But even experienced professionals have difficulty in matching the correct grade of chain with the correct application. This section will discuss the various grades of chain and what constitutes "overhead lifting." A more detailed explanation on chain and overhead lifting will be covered in the Appendix 3.

In Chapter 1 we discussed the differences between static and running rigging. Let's go over this again:

> **Standing rigging** is rigging that does not move- it is *static*. It is attached at both ends. Essentially, it is rigging that is used to hold something in place. Guy-wires are a good example of standing rigging. But remember, all static rigging will eventually become dynamic as they take up the force loads they were asked to support.

> **Running rigging**, on the other hand, is rigging that moves through a pulley. It becomes dynamic as it moves to overcomes inertia. Lift lines on battens can be said to be static as long as they are not in motion. As soon as the batten is raised or lowered (running through a loft or head block), they become dynamic.

Simply put, when referring to overhead lifting we are referring to *running rigging*: ie. rigging that moves through a cog or wheel. It's that simple. Liftlines that run through a head or loft block are *running rigging* and MUST be rated for overhead lifting. Chains running through a cog are *running rigging* and MUST be rated for the same. It does not mean something *attached* to the chain or wire rope has to be rated for overhead lifting. It simply means that the suspended object MUST be able to withstand the dynamic loads placed on it (*static*). Battens, for example, are attached to liftlines. They are NOT running rigging, but rather, they are attached to liftlines that are, and they WILL take on the dynamic forces of that system. Suspended scenery does not have to be rated for overhead lifting because it does not run over a cog or a wheel, but the chain or cable that *flies* it DOES if it moves. Got it?

The Grading of Chain

Grade refers to the tensile strength of the metal and is expressed in Newtons (or approximately 0.224805 lb) per square millimeter. Grading is used by manufacturers to indicate the ultimate breaking strength of chain, ie: the higher the grade number, the greater the breaking strength. Carbon and alloy metals are infused in chain to increase its hardness and tensile strength. (We will discuss this shortly). Tensile strength is calculated by multiplying the grade times the total area of two cross sections of a chain's link.

Example:
If the sum area of two cross sections equal 160mm, then

160mm x 800 grade = 128,000 Newtons ultimate breaking strength.
128,000 Newtons x .224805 lb = 28,775.04 pounds ultimate breaking strength
or
128,000 Newtons / 1000 = 128 kiloNewtons

Tensile Strength

So, what is *tensile strength*? This is an important term to understand in our discussion on chain. Essentially, tensile strength refers to:

The ability of a material to resist a force that tends to pull it apart. It is usually expressed as the measure of the largest force that can be applied in this way before the material breaks apart.

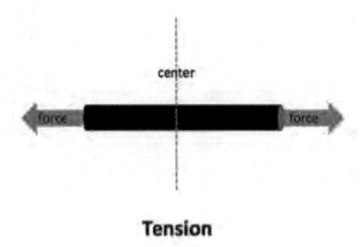

Tension

The amount of carbon content infused into steel will essentially strengthen and harden the metal. But strengthening the steel comes at a loss. With the increase in carbon content, the steel loses its *ductility or ability to flex.* Alloy metals are blended into the steel to bring back some of the ductility that was lost by the infusion of carbon.

A chain's grade refers the tensile strength of the metal. The numbers refer to one tenth of the actual grade class. For example, if the grade stated is 70, then the actual grade class is 700. If it is 80, then the grade class is 800. Many times, the markings are simply abbreviated as 7 or 8 to simplify the identification markings.

The National Association of Chain Manufactures produces the following chart below. It shows the graining system for chain and its recommended use.

Grade 100 Alloy Chain	Premium quality, highest strength alloy chain, heat treated, used in a variety of sling and tie down applications. For overhead lifting applications, only Alloy Chain should be used.
Grade 80 Alloy Chain	Premium quality, high strength alloy chain, heat treated, used in a variety of sling and tie down applications. For overhead lifting applications, only Alloy Chain should be used.
Grade 70 Transport Chain	A high quality, high strength carbon steel chain used for load securement. **Not to be used in overhead lifting.**
Grade 43 High Test Chain	A carbon steel chain widely used in industry, construction, agricultural and lumbering operations. **Not to be used in overhead lifting.**
Grade 30 Proof Coil Chain	General purpose, carbon steel chain. Used in a wide range of applications. **Not to be used in overhead lifting.**
Machine Chain	Short pitch straight link or twist link, general utility chain made of carbon steel. **Not to be used in overhead lifting.**
Coil Chain	Long pitch straight link or twist link, general utility chain made of carbon steel. **Not to be used in overhead lifting.**
Passing Link Chain	Short, wide link chain which resists kinking or tangling, made of carbon steel. **Not to be used in overhead lifting.**
Stainless Steel Chain	A corrosion-resistant chain manufactured from stainless steel, used in food processing, chemical, marine, and high temperature environments.

Chain Markings of Alloy Chain

All alloy chain must have identification markings. OSHA 1910.184(e)(1) states,

Alloy steel chain slings shall have permanently affixed durable identification stating size, grade, rated capacity, and reach.

Stamped markings on G80 chain

Stamped markings on G100 chain tag

Testing

OSHA's 1910.184(e)(4) requires a non-destructive tension test or all manufacturers that verifies the construction and workmanship of a sling or chain. This testing is referred to as Proof Testing.

The employer shall ensure that before use, each new, repaired, or reconditioned alloy steel chain sling, including all welded components in the sling assembly, shall be proof tested by the sling manufacturer or equivalent entity, in accordance with paragraph 5.2 of the American Society of Testing and Materials Specification A391-65, which is incorporated by reference as specified in Sec. 1910.6 (ANSI G61.1-1968). The employer shall retain a certificate of the proof test and shall make it available for examination.

Federal law requires that all welded assemblies used for overhead lifting MUST be proof tested to twice the Working Load Limit.

WARNING: Do not use chain that does not have a load rating! Chain products are engineered for specific applications. Dog chain, for example, is intended just for that purpose: to tie up your dog. It is not to be used for rigging.

Shock loads on Chain

The steel in an alloy chain has a modulus of elasticity of 30,000,000 psi, so it has even less elasticity than wire rope and therefore, potentially greater shock loads. This is why the shock load on the beam supporting a load being lifted by a 16 fpm chain hoist can be 20 to 50 percent greater than the load being lifted, simply due to the starting and stopping of the hoist. A 64 fpm chain hoist can create a shock load that is 200 percent greater than the load being lifted, by starting and **stopping** the hoist.

According to Phil Braymen, Engineering Manager at Laclede Chain Manufacturing Company, "... the chain industry does not test, certify or condone shock loading" of chain. The NACM (National Association of Chain Manufacturers) states, "Manufacturers do not accept any liability for injury or damage which may result from dynamic or static loads in excess of the working load limit."

To help understand how static loads affect chain, I ran several tensile tests using 1/4" Grade 30 proof coil chain. At its working load limit, 25 percent of its breaking strength, this chain stretches only about one half of one percent of its length. At approximately 60 percent of the breaking strength of chain, the yield point of the steel, the chain stretches approximately 1 percent of its length. However, when the force on the mild steel chain reaches the yield point, two things happen. First, the shape of the links begins to deform, causing the links to get narrower and longer. Then, the metal enters its "plastic stage," where the metal stretches significantly under slight increases in force. During this stage, the growing tension on the chain slows dramatically as the deforming and elongating chain absorbs the energy. The tension grows even slower as the tension surpasses 90 percent of the breaking strength of the chain. In the final 40 percent of the breaking strength of the chain, the stretch of the chain is approximately 7.5 times greater than in the first 60 percent. This nearly constant changing of the rate of stretch under different amounts of force makes accurately calculating shock loads on chain, using a mathematical equation, a near impossibility.

Note: While the tests described above were done with Grade 30 proof coil chain, this grade of chain is not recommended for overhead lifting. Even the major manufacturers of counterweight rigging systems now use alloy chain for trim chains on linesets. The description above is only intended to demonstrate the behavior of chain under an extreme load.

The bottom line is that shock loads on chain can be quite high and can very easily exceed the working load limit of the chain, especially given the low design factor used for chain. Shock loading chain should be avoided whenever possible.

Grade 63 Chain
Many have expressed concern over the manufacture and use of Grade 63 chain since it IS an alloy grade, but falls below grade 70, which is a Transport Grade chain. I discussed this with Greg Waits, the Product Standards & Service Manager at Columbus McKinnon.
His response and documentation are as follows:

"Concerning the question about over-head lifting, grade 63 is an alloy steel chain that may be used for over-head lifts. However, it really doesn't make sense to use G63 chain (because of reduced working load limit) unless the sling is being used in heat up to about 850° F.

Also, other materials may be used such as CM's bundling chain (a grade 30 product) as long as they meet the provisions of the appropriate specifications.

To help clarify this, I quote a couple sources:
OSHA's 29 CFR, 1910.184(e)(5) "Sling use. Alloy steel chain slings shall not be used with loads in excess of the rated capacities prescribed in Table N-184-1. Slings not included in this table shall be used only in accordance with the manufacturer's recommendations."

My understanding is that this clause is commonly interpreted to mean OSHA would approve for O/H lifting a non-alloy sling that the manufacturer recommended, for example for a particular application. In the case of G30 bundling chains, they are typically used in acids or hot dip galvanizing operations since the lower carbon steel is much less affected by acids than alloy steel. I believe OSHA tends to default to requirements of industry standards, so...

Another quote:
ASME B30.9-2006 section 9-1.2.3 Other Materials and Components
"Chain or components other than those listed in paras. 9-1.2.1 and 9-1.2.2 (i.e., alloy) may be employed. When such materials are employed, the sling manufacturer or a qualified person shall provide specific data. These slings shall comply with all other requirements of this Chapter."

OSHA's interpretation follows in the attached (albeit dated) two memorandums:

Standard Interpretations

05/12/1983 - Evaluation of variance application requesting the use of proof coil and high test chain slings under certain procedures.

◄ Standard Interpretations - Table of Contents

● **Standard Number:**   1910.184(e)

May 12, 1983

MEMORANDUM FOR:	JAMES J. CONCANNON Director Office of Variance Determination
THRU:	DONALD A. SHAY Director Office of Compliance Programming
FROM:	JOHN K. BARTO Chief Division of Occupational Safety Programming
SUBJECT:	Evaluation of Variance Application #1686, which Contains Eastern Airlines Request to Allow the Continued Use of the Proof Coil and High Test Chain Slings Under Certain Procedures

The use of other than alloy steel chain is not prohibited specifically in 29 CFR 1910.184, but only alloy steel chain is recommended by chain manufacturers for overhead hoisting. Proof coil and high test chain is used for purposes where failure of the chain would not endanger human life or result in serious damage to property or equipment. Proof coil and high test chains should only be used in accordance with the manufacturer's recommendations.

◄ Standard Interpretations - Table of Contents

Contact Us | Freedom of Information Act | Customer Survey
Privacy and Security Statement | Disclaimers

Standard Interpretations
05/18/1978 - Only alloy steel chain is recommended by chain manufacturers for overhead hoisting.

Standard Interpretations - Table of Contents

- **Standard Number:** 1910.184

MAY 18, 1978

Mr. Merle E. Broich
Safety Coordinator
Owatonna Tool Company
Owatonna, Minnesota 55060

Dear Mr. Broich:

This is in response to your letter dated April 24, 1978, regarding interpretations of standards for chain slings in 29 CFR 1910.184.

The Occupational Safety and Health Administration General Industry Standards specifically address alloy steel chain slings used in the movement of material by hoisting machinery. The use of other than alloy steel chain is not prohibited specifically in 29 CFR 1910.184, but only alloy steel chain is recommended by chain manufacturers for overhead hoisting. A copy of the American Society for testing and materials A 391-65 (Reapproved 1970) standard specification for alloy steel chain has been enclosed to properly describe alloy steel chain.

I hope this information will be helpful to you. If I may be of any further assistance, please feel free to contact me.

Sincerely,

John K. Barto, Chief
Division of Occupational
Safety Programming

Enclosure

Standard Interpretations - Table of Contents

OSHA and the Path of Responsibility

When it comes to rigging, rigging inspections, and rigging failures, there IS a path of responsibly when it comes to rigging safety. **OSHA regulations ARE law!** They must be followed. ASME, ANSI, NACM, et al., are simply self-regulating organizations. They are not law. However, their standards will hold up in a court of law.

The pecking order is:

1. *OSHA. OSHA's CFR (code of federal regulation or ASME which is voluntary regulations that OSHA WILL BORROW FROM AND CHARGE YOU WITH THE MOST SEVERE OF THE TWO REGULATIONS. (ASME builds codes and works with OSHA hand and glove to develop federal and state regulations and codes).*
2. *ASME, ANSI or NACM, et al. Voluntary organizations. Of the three, ASME has gotten down to the nuts and bolts of safety issues and code development. ANSI generally takes a backseat behind manufacturer's recommendations.*
3. *Manufacture's Recommendations*
4. *Industry Standards*

Summary

There are lots of different types of hardware used in theatrical rigging and lots of rules and regulations the MUST be followed when it comes to rigging safely. While some of this material has been covered in this chapter, other hardware is covered in Chapter 22 – Rigging Scenery to Fly.

Chapter 11:
Grids

Introduction

There are many different sizes of theatres and types of stage configurations. Some of these theatre may be large venues that hold several thousand audience member, while other might be small studio theatres. No matter the size and configuration of the space, the rigger's job involves hanging things (scenery, lights, speakers and other things) above the stage and house.

Sometimes the rigger's job involves things that move – can fly "in" and "out," while at other times these elements are merely suspended (dead-hung) above the ground. In both cases there needs to be some structure to which the rigging is attached. Sometimes this structure is simply pipes or I-beams, while at others, there is some type of walkable structure above the stage. Most of the structures discussed in this chapter are non-movable, except for rolling battens. These structures, to which rigging is attached, is the subject of this chapter.

Non-walkable structures
I-beams
When engineers talk about loads on a structure, they often refer to the "load path," that traces the load from its source, through the structure of the building and back to the earth. The structural skeleton of most large buildings is mostly composed mostly of I-beams, although beams of other shapes (T, C and L) are also found. Horizontal I-beams are typically used in theatres to support other structures, such as catwalks and grids, they can also directly support stage rigging equipment (underhung loft block are made to clamp to I-beams). And the spacing of these I-beams is often critical to the placement of the things they support.

I-beams in a theatre can support things that are permanently attached to them, temporarily attached to them or trolleys that roll long their bottom flange. I-beams are very strong and the many devices specifically made to work with them make them highly useful for riggers.

Pipe Grids
Pipe grids are commonly found in studio theatres and mainly used for holding lighting instruments (which is why they are sometimes referred to as "lighting grids"). They can also be used for hanging scenery, speakers, etc.

Pipe grids are made of 1-1/2" schedule 40 black pipe, the same a pipe battens, and are suspended from the structure of the building. The spacing of the pipes that make up the grid can vary, but are typically on 4 feet to 6 feet centers. The intersections of the pipes that make the grid are joined by *grid cross connector clamps.* The pipes themselves are joined with a *pipe splice sleeve*, which makes the assembly of the pipe grid easier for the installers.

Any like a standard pipe batten, pipe grids should be supported every 10 feet – 12 feet. Pipe grids are typically accessed by ladders or lifts from the floor below.

Grid cross connector clamp

A pipe splice sleeve. These sleeves are typical for pipe grid assembly. They are not customarily used on theatre battens as the hex nuts may loosen with time. Not so with a pipe grid.

A typical pipe grid

Rolling Battens

Rolling battens are a unique solution for creating flexible hanging positions in studio theatres. While a pipe grid is fixed structure, each suspend point on a rolling batten, similar to standard pipe battens on a counterweight system, is attached to a trolley that run on a track (typically an I-beam). These battens can be rolled horizontally about in the theatre to position them in different locations. The number of rolling battens can vary, but it is fairly easy to add battens, it needed. Also, battens can be single battens or truss battens, if the span between the suspension points is more than 12 feet.

216

One variation of rolling battens is to add a swivel between the trolley and the batten clamp. Now the battens can be positioned at different angles in the theatre. By using pipes of different lengths, and almost infinite variety of configurations can be achieved.

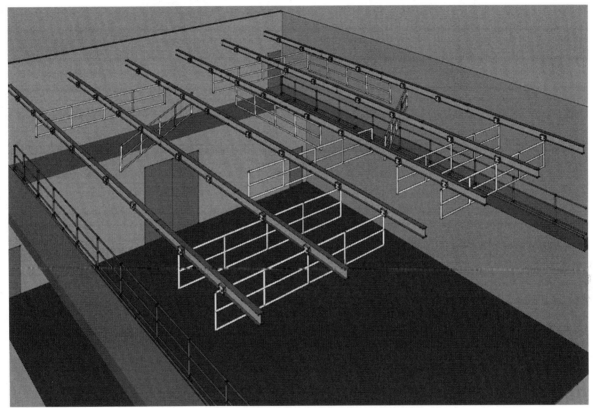
Model showing various positions for rolling battens

Walkable structures
Gridirons
The most common material for gridirons above a stage is 3" C channel. Typically arranged on 6" centers, running upstage/downstage, this type of grid is very stable and versatile. Some theatre's have overhung loft blocks, which mount to the large C channels that make the loft block wells, as well as to the grid itself; while other theatre may have underhung loft blocks, where the grid is virtually empty. In these spaces, blocks, for spot lines, can be easily mounted at almost any location on the grid using J-bolts, that hook to the flange of the steel. Gridirons can cover the entire stage area or only directly over the acting area, not over the wings.

Alternatives to a channel steel grid is welded steel bar grating and aluminum press-locked bar grating (sometimes referred to as "subway grating"). These types of grid floors are not as strong as channel steel grids. While they are usually strong enough for many rigging purposes, they are not suitable for hanging chain hoists from to lift heavy objects.

11-W-2
Cross Rods 2" C/C

19-AP-4 (Aluminum)
Cross Rods 4" C/C

Catwalks

Catwalks are found in many, if not most, theatres. They are used as both access ways and work platforms. Technicians routinely use catwalks to hang and focus lighting instruments on front-of-house lighting positions. While catwalks are commonly used in studio theatres as lighting positions, some proscenium theatres also use catwalks as lighting positions over the stage.

Catwalks not only make good lighting positions, but they can also provide access rigging points, or even be rigging points for speakers, scenery or other items that need to be hung over the stage or the audience.

Tension Wire Grids

An excellent choice for studio and thrust theatres, a tension wire grid consists of pre-stressed modular frames with 1/8" woven galvanized aircraft cable. These panels create a nearly visually transparent grid floor above the theatre, on which technicians can work without fear of falling and through which lights can shine.

SkyDeck tension wire grid

You can rig loads of several hundred pounds directly to a tension wire grid, if there is a plate at least one square foot in area pressing down on the wire mesh, or individual panels can be removed to allow scenery or performers to be flown through the grid.

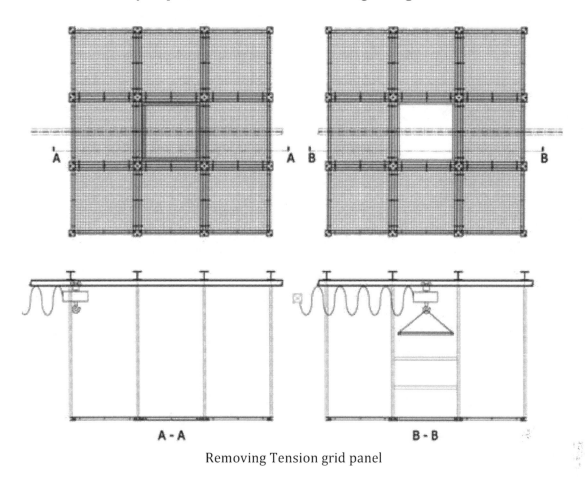

A - A   B - B

Removing Tension grid panel

Summary

A theatre is a type of factory which produces a product – theatrical productions. And since each production has different needs, theatres need to be as flexible as possible to allow many options– an important point for architects and theatre consultants to remember when designing a new theatre space. It can sometimes take a fair amount of creativity to be able to suspend something exactly where it is needed in a theatre, and riggers often have to make use of whatever structure is available.

The primary intended use of the space and the budget are critical factors in determining that structures will be available for rigging. As seen above, there are many choices when it comes to designing a rigging structure. Each decision will ultimately create opportunities and limitations for the directors and designers, and the actors and technicians who must realize these productions.

Chapter 12: Automated Rigging Systems

Introduction

The world of automated/motorized stage rigging systems seems to be changing almost daily. Today, there are many options available for automating theatrical rigging; all have the ability to manage a wide range of loading conditions with just the push of a button. Systems can be manually controlled, or computerized, so that rigging cues are run, much the same way lighting cues are run.

While the initial cost of motorized rigging systems is higher than that of counterweight rigging systems, motorized rigging systems can reduce the construct cost of a new facility by: reducing the amount of structural steel required, allowing for lower ceilings, eliminate arbor pits, and deletion of the wing space required for the counterweight rigging. There could also be a reduction in labor cost since motorized rigging systems do not require counterweight to be added and removed from arbors each time the load a batten changes. This results in faster setup and strikes and reduces labor required. Also, a single operator can run all of the rigging cues, saving even more money on labor costs. And, because the hard physical work of rigging has been removed, technicians with physical disabilities can operate the rigging system. Automated rigging also has the advantage of being accurate and reliable.

Most importantly, motorized rigging is safer because you eliminate the danger of falling counterweight and runaway linesets.

And speaking of safety, many of today's automated rigging systems feature an array of safety features including: weight detectors, slack line sensors, position detectors, dual brakes and multiple limit switches. These features are designed to ensure that the hoist is doing what you want it to do and nothing else.

This chapter will explore the two basic types of automated systems: the *Motor Assist Fly System* and the *Dead Haul* flying system. We will also examine some of the equipment available and how it operates. As always, please consult with a qualified theatre consultant or engineer to see what system is best suited to your facility.

Variable Speed vs. Fixed Speed Hoists

Fixed Speed hoists are often used to raise and lower *very* heavy loads such as curtains, acoustical panels, lighting pipes, and speaker arrays. These speeds are constant and set according to the load being lifted. In general: the heavier the load, the slower the speed. Electrics are set to a speed around 20 fpm, while heavy acoustical panels are set to around 3 fpm. Fixed speed hoists are also less expensive than variable speed hoists.

Variable Speed hoists are used when battens need to fly in and out quickly during scene changes. The less heavy scenery, for example, may need to move in and out quickly at speeds of up to 100 fpm, yet slow down to speeds of less than 1 fpm before coming to a complete stop. These hoists are ideal when scenery has to change before an audience. JR Clancy states,

> *Top speeds are dictated by three main considerations:*
>
> 1. *The heights of the proscenium and fly loft tower. The speed of the hoist determines how quickly scenery can be moved into or out of the audience's view.*
> 2. *The user's requirements: A venue with a wide variety of users or production types may want to provide the maximum versatility given by higher speed hoists.*
> 3. *Cost – higher maximum speeds generally come at an increased price.*

They go onto say,

> *"As a guide, scenery sets in college or regional theatres typically run at up to 120 or 180 fpm. Major performing arts centers and opera houses may have speeds of up to 240 fpm, while some of the newest international opera houses are using hoists with speeds of up to 360 fpm. Main curtain hoists have been built to operate at even higher speeds".*

Even faster hoists are available. For example: Clancy's Titan High Performance Hoist is available in various in 20 fpm, 240 fpm, 360 fpm, 600 fpm and 725 fpm speeds. While load capacities range from 1,000 pounds to 3,300 pounds.

Variable speed hoists require solid state vector drives rated for hoisting duty, with the reliability and safety features necessary for use in a theatrical environment. Dynamic braking systems are also generally required on high-speed units. These factors make variable speed hoists costlier than fixed speed hoists.

The Motor Assist Fly System

Motor Assist Fly Systems look very similar to your manual counterweight system; there are loft blocks, head blocks, and arbors. The major difference is seen at the operating (locking) rail. A drum winch is mounted on the floor where the tension block is normally located. The purchase line is replaced with a steel double leaf chain along with a steel/urethane rope that permits the use of a standard head block. What is noticeable is that the lock at the locking rail is no longer necessary. Instead, the lock is replaced with an operating (control) station. The arbor is pre-loaded with a fixed set of counterweights. The motor simply raises and lowers the batten eliminating the need to constantly load and readjust the counterweights. With fixed weights in the arbor, typically around 25 fpm, these hoists are able to handle loads ranging from 0 to 2000-pounds.

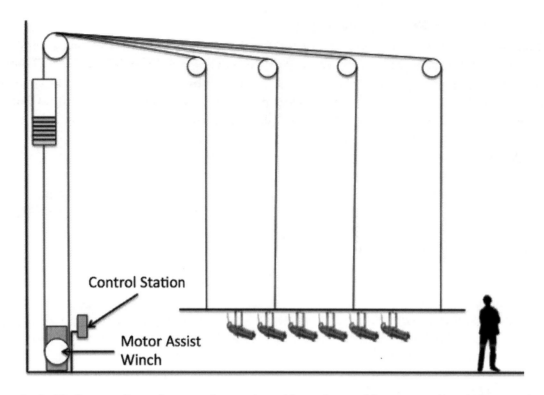

Control Station

Motor Assist
Winch

The Motor Assist Fly System allows the easy of operation without the need for constantly re-balancing the arbor.

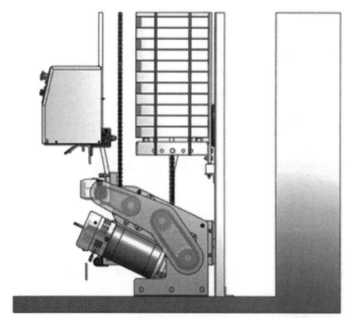

The PowerAssist ® automated winch mounts easily under the arbor.
-photo courtesy of JR Clancy

Utilizing the space of two manual linesets mounted on 6" centers, the Motor *Assist System* is often used for raising and lowering heavy loads such as electrics, acoustical ceilings and shells, as well as large, traveler curtains.

Advantages

The *Motor Assist* is often used in theatres when most of the linesets are manually operated counterweight rigging systems, but when additional assistance is needed to raise and lower particularly linesets with especially heavy loads, like acoustical ceilings and electrics. A single acoustical ceiling piece can weight over two thousand pounds. Anyone who have moved these knows how difficult they can be to move in and out. Also, moving lights, which are becoming commonplace in theatrical productions can make electrics extremely heavy and difficult to move manually.

Motor Assist systems typically use fixed speed motors. Also, because the lineset is counterweighted, the motors do not need to be as large as with Dead Haul systems. These facts help made Motor Assist system very affordable.

Controls

The basic control station for must motor assist systems consists of a simple push button control box located at either the rail or another pre-determined location. A simple, push button control station with reversing starter replaces your rope lock. Or, a system, like J.R Clancy's SureTarget^{TM} system, that lets the operator program four preset target positions, or their SceneControl 100 and 500 automation consoles which consoles allow users to write cues for a complete production. Many control stations are typically equipped with key operated switches to prevent unauthorized use.

PowerAssist® hoists, by J.R Clancy, is a good example of a motor assist rigging system.

The PowerAssist ® automated winch showing the push button control station
-photo courtesy of JR Clancy

Dead Haul Systems

Unlike Motor Assisted rigging systems, Dead Haul systems completely replace the counterweight rigging and therefore must lift the entire load that is flown on each batten. There are many variety of Dead Haul rigging systems. Some must be mount directly above the stage, while others allow the winch to be mounted either above the stage or in an offstage location, and some have the winch located on the batten.

Let's take a look at some of these systems.

The Multi-Line Winch System

A multi-line winch system utilizes a winch with multiple cables (lift lines) connected to one large drum. The cables run up to a multi-sheaved headblock, and then to loft blocks, like you would find in a standard mechanical counterweight system.

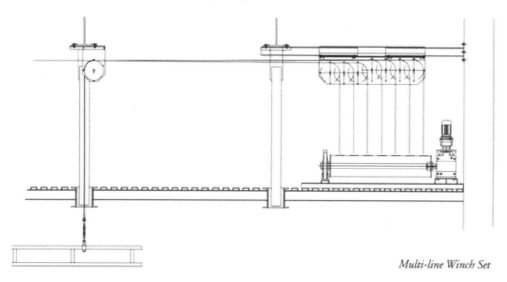

Multi-line Winch Set

Pile Up (Yo-yo) Hoists

When the headroom between the hoist and the headblock is limited, a hoist with a yo-yo drum might be required in order to prevent fleet angle issues. This is a very compact hoist that can fit into tight spaces.

Line Shaft Systems

Line shaft hoists are some of the oldest and most reliable automated rigging systems. These systems consist of a motor, a drive shaft and a series of cable drums mounted along the shaft. The motor can be mounted at one end of the shaft or anywhere along it. The system can be mounted on a traditional gridiron or underhung from I-beams.

Unlike mechanical counterweight systems, there are no headblocks or loft blocks, the lift cables run directly from the drums to the battens.

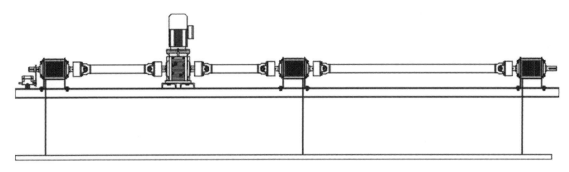

The Line Shaft Winch

- photo courtesy of JR Clancy

Self-Climbing Hoists

I-Wiess's Vialift is an example of a self-climbing hoist. This system incorporates the hoist and batten into a unit – the lift cables attach to anchor point at the ceiling, making it a good choice for spaces with low ceiling heights. A 5-ton machine self-locking screw jack with a traveling nut gives this hoist the ability to lift 500 pounds, in addition to its own weight, with an 8:1 design factor. While this is not a powerhouse lifting rig, it has a couple of unique features. One is the availability to purchase it with an optional electrical raceway with 12- 20A lighting circuits - which allows it to function as a lighting position.

This hoist can climb its four 1/8" diameter cables up to 40 feet, at a speed of 20 feet per minute.; and the batten can be up to 34 feet in length. The hoist can be run from a wall-mounted control station, or via DMX and/or Ethernet.

High performance Zero Fleet Angle Hoist

This type of hoist has become very popular and most stage rigging manufacturers make at least one model of this type hoist. J.R Clany's Titan host, and ETC's Prodigy P1 and Vortek Classic, are examples of this type of hoist.

These hoists are extremely versatile. They can be easily mounted either horizontally or vertically on in a wide variety of location in the theatre. This type of hoist is excellent for non-standard layouts.

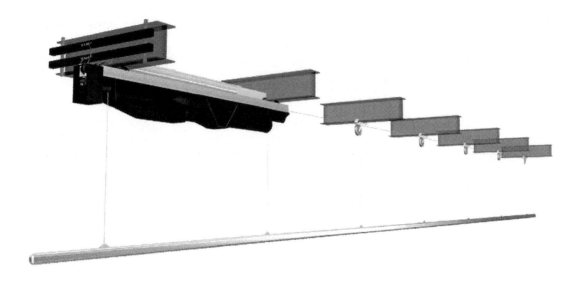

Rigging Controls

For fixed speed hoists, the simplest controls system is a manual station with up and down push buttons. These systems should be push-to-run controls - meaning that if the operator takes his/her finger of the button, the winch stops. These systems should have an emergency (E-stop) that kills the power to the winch, not just the controls. A key operated lockout is also a good idea.

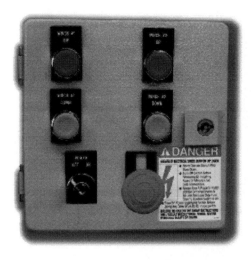

A three phase reversing starter is used to control fixed speed winches. The motor is reversed by switching the phases of the power from ABC to CBA.

A speed pot or joystick can be the user interface to a variable speed drive required for variable speed winches. These drives need to be setup so that torque is created by the motor before the brake is released, and that the brake is engaged before torque is completely removed.

Early winches used DC motors and drives, but improvement in AC drives has resulted in this being the current standard. Flux vector drives, with an encoder mounted on the motor shaft allowing it to precisely monitor rotation speed, allow these systems to run smoothly at any speed. These are popular in high performance systems.

While PLC based controller are used in simple automated flying systems, supplicated rigging control panels that have the ability to control speed, time and position of many winches at the same time. Some theatres are moving toward point hoists, where there is a separate winch for each point. This is the rigging equivalent of dimmer-per-circuit. The controller can precisely control and synchronize the movement of these winches. They can also be used to create 3D performer flying effects. Some such systems allow the operator to see a 3D representation of the effect on a monitor as the cue is being written.

Part III:
Arena Rigging Hardware and Techniques

Chapter 13:
Truss and Hoist Rigging

Introduction

No one ever wants <u>LESS</u>. This statement might sum up rigging over the last hundred years. A hundred years ago, flying scenery consisted mostly of canvas drops. They were lightweight and easy to move. Lighting was mostly strip lights. As time progressed, we flew a lot of wood-framed flats, which were heavier than canvas drops, but manageable. Lights also got heavier and we got a lot more of them. Today, big musicals use LOTS of heavy, three-dimensional set pieces that can weight thousands, or even tens of thousands of pounds. And, a theatrical production might use 500-700 moving lights that weigh over 100-pounds each, plus hundreds of conventional lights.

Large touring productions, with lots of scenery and effects, often need more space than is available, so they fly entire control platforms with computers, consoles and personnel for running the show. Spotlights and operators were also routinely flown, as were huge speaker clusters. The limitations of the permanent rigging in theatres could no longer meet their needs; so many productions simply suspended their own rigging from the gridirons. Much of this rigging was borrowed from arena rigging, which was designed for touring.

Because stage productions continue to get larger and more complex, many of the same principles of arena rigging, especially the mechanics (physics/math), can be used to solve many theatrical-rigging problems. It is not uncommon to see helicopters, cars, huge video walls, and entire houses flown for stage productions.

At the same time, many theatres use aluminum box truss and chain hoists as lighting positions, both over the stage and the house. What was once "arena rigging" is permanent rigging in many theatres.

For these reasons, it is important that theatre riggers also have a good understanding of the basics of arena rigging equipment and techniques. This unit attempts to provide this information.

Truss
Let's begin by discussing the various types of aluminum truss and truss components. We will also be looking at truss orientation, installation and inspection. To begin, ANSI E1.2 2012 covers all the design, manufacture, inspection, and use of aluminum trusses, structural components and towers. This chapter will follow these ANSI guidelines and recommendations. ANSI guidelines

related to the entertainment industry are available for free download at:
http://tsp.plasa.org/tsp/documents/index.html

Parts of a Truss and Truss Terminology
Truss comes in a variety of shapes and sizes. However, the terminology remains basically the same. To start, lets look at the basic parts of an I-beam for comparison. An I-beam consists of a top flange, a bottom flange, and a web. The top and bottom flanges are the flat part at the top and bottom of the beam. They directly correspond to the top and bottom chords on the truss. Their function is to maintain the stability of the web. The chords of the truss do the same thing; they maintain the stability of the diagonals/spreaders.

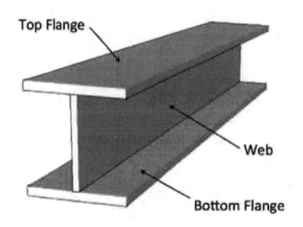

Top Flange

Web

Bottom Flange

Parts of an I-Beam

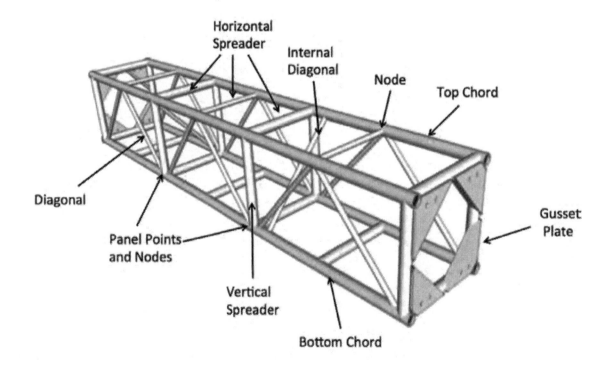

Horizontal Spreader

Internal Diagonal

Node

Top Chord

Diagonal

Panel Points and Nodes

Vertical Spreader

Bottom Chord

Gusset Plate

The web of the I-beam is the vertical member that supports the top and bottom flanges. It is similar to the diagonal and vertical supports of the truss. The web's function is to spread the applied forces to the flanges. The truss diagonals perform a similar function in that they transfer the vertical forces horizontally to the chords. There always will be *tension* and *compression* in about 50% of all of the truss members.

Truss Orientation

The design of box truss typically has the horizontal cross members on the two top and bottom faces. The diagonal and vertical members are typically on the other two side faces. *Truss orientation* needs to be such that the diagonals form a continuous pattern usually forming the letter **A**. Truss load data is only valid if the truss is oriented in the manner.

Some riggers may argue that orientation on general box truss doesn't matter. All that is important is to insure that the diagonals are on the sides and form the same letter pattern between sections. This may be true on some general box truss, but if you examine the horizontal spreaders on the top chord of some truss, you will note that some struts are narrow while some are wide. Because truss is used to hang equipment from the lower cords and spreaders, it is best to keep the truss in the letter **A** orientation.

Truss hung on its side may seem structurally sound, however, hanging a truss in this manner would change the load characteristics considerably. Manufacturers would not stand by their product if the truss should fail.

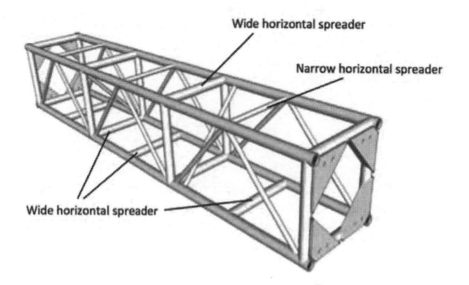

Wide horizontal spreader

Narrow horizontal spreader

Wide horizontal spreader

Truss configured correctly. If there is any doubt about orientation, check with the manufacturer.

Panel Points and Nodes

Panel-Points-and-Nodes form the point where the diagonal, vertical and horizontal spreaders are welded to the chords. Structurally, they are the strongest point on the truss to apply a vertical force. They allow for the vertical force to be distributed horizontally from diagonal to diagonal.

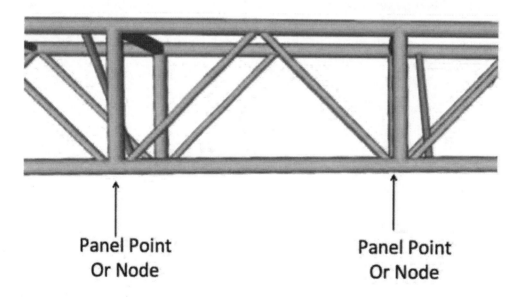

**Panel Point
Or Node**

**Panel Point
Or Node**

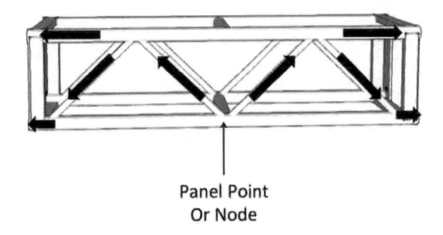

Panel Point
Or Node

Some of the Forces that are distributed on a truss

When loads are applied at a panel point, the forces are distributed horizontally from diagonal to diagonal.

When applying a force at the panel point, forces on the structure needs to be kept *in compression*. The *internal-diagonals* are not that integral to the structure of the truss. If present, they help to maintain the form of the truss during construction. *Connecting-points* are where one truss is joined to another. These points are considered to be strong connections, however some manufacturers may recommend not hanging a substantial load at these junctures. Again, it's always best to check with the manufacturer.

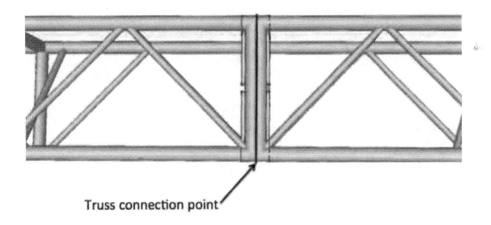

Truss connection point

Terms:
Before we begin examining truss loading, lets become familiar with some terminology.

- **Allowable load:** maximum static equivalent load that can be safely imposed on truss/tower in addition to the self-weight.
- **Competent person** (OSHA definition)"Competent person" means one who is capable of identifying existing and predictable hazards in the surroundings or working conditions, which are unsanitary, hazardous, or dangerous to employees, and who has authorization to take prompt corrective measures to eliminate them.

- **Compression**: when forces on an object are pressed together toward the center of the object. Compression is best on panel points.

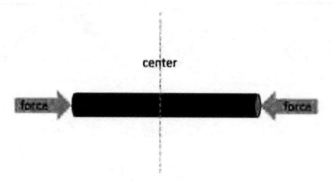

Compression

- **CPL (center point load)**: a concentrated load that is applied at the mid-span of a beam.
- **Deflection:** the degree or angle to which a structural element is displaced under a load.

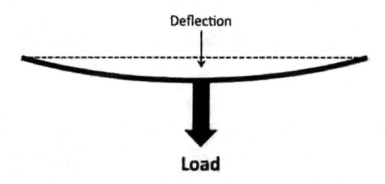

- **Dynamic loading:** forces caused by the acceleration or deceleration of an object.
- **Panel point (node):** The point of intersection where the spreaders (stretchers) and diagonals meet a chord.
- **Point load:** a load, which is localized to a specific location on a beam.
- **Qualified person** (OSHA definition) "Qualified" means one who, by possession of a recognized degree, certificate, or professional standing, or who by extensive knowledge, training and experience, has successfully demonstrated his ability to solve or resolve problems relating to the subject matter, the work, or the project.
- **Shear:** arises from a force that is applied perpendicularly to the material cross section on which it acts.

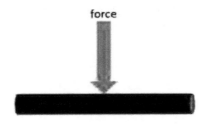

Shear

- **Span:** the distance between the supporting points.
- **Tension:** when the forces on the object stretch or pull away from the center.

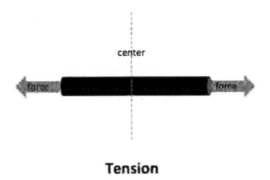

Tension

- **Torque:** a measurement of how much force acting on an object which causes the object to rotate. The object rotates about an axis. We call this axis the pivot point.

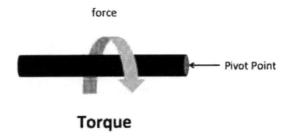

Torque

- **UDL (uniform distributed load):** a load that is evenly spread over the length of a beam.

Working with truss requires a familiarity with all of these terms. It also requires a working knowledge of the size and make of the truss and a familiarity with the manufacturer and engineer's limitations of the particular truss you are working with.

Truss Loading Data Charts

Manufacturers provide truss loading data charts that give detailed information relative to the truss type, truss span, and load type. Manufactures provide load data charts for every type of truss they manufacture. These charts are available on their website and should be referred to when loading their truss. The chart below is for a Tomcat 20.5 x 20.5 plated truss. Note the chart shows the number of sections and span for each section to the left and the Maximum Allowable Uniform Loads and the Maximum Allowable Point Loads (center point loads (CPL), third point loads (TPL) and quarter point loads (QPL) at the top.

Example: a 30 ft. span of 20.5 x 20.5 plated box truss will allow a maximum of 4,260 pounds for a *Uniform-Distributed-Load-(UDL)*. Deflection will be 1.25 inches. The *Maximum-Allowable-Point-Load* for a *Center-Point-Load (CPL)*-on the same 30-ft span will be 1,927 pounds with a deflection of 0.92 inches.

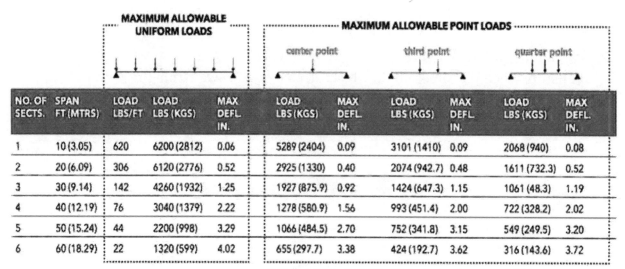

NO. OF SECTS.	SPAN FT (MTRS)	LOAD LBS/FT	LOAD LBS (KGS)	MAX DEFL. IN.	LOAD LBS (KGS)	MAX DEFL. IN.	LOAD LBS (KGS)	MAX DEFL. IN.	LOAD LBS (KGS)	MAX DEFL. IN.
1	10 (3.05)	620	6200 (2812)	0.06	5289 (2404)	0.09	3101 (1410)	0.09	2068 (940)	0.08
2	20 (6.09)	306	6120 (2776)	0.52	2925 (1330)	0.40	2074 (942.7)	0.48	1611 (732.3)	0.52
3	30 (9.14)	142	4260 (1932)	1.25	1927 (875.9)	0.92	1424 (647.3)	1.15	1061 (48.3)	1.19
4	40 (12.19)	76	3040 (1379)	2.22	1278 (580.9)	1.56	993 (451.4)	2.00	722 (328.2)	2.02
5	50 (15.24)	44	2200 (998)	3.29	1066 (484.5)	2.70	752 (341.8)	3.15	549 (249.5)	3.20
6	60 (18.29)	22	1320 (599)	4.02	655 (297.7)	3.38	424 (192.7)	3.62	316 (143.6)	3.72

5/8" diameter Grade 8 Bolts with standard washers through 3/8" gusset plates

-chart courtesy of Tomcat Truss

Again, it is very important to consult these charts when working with any truss. These charts are NOT interchangeable between manufacturers. Failure to comply with Load Data Charts may result in death or serious injury.

Two good "general" rules of thumb you may want to remember are:
1. If the total weight you plan to place on the truss (no matter the location of the hanging point or points) is less than half of the total UDL for your span, you will not be overstressing the truss
2. The total weight to be placed on the cantilevered truss must be less than the allowable CPL for a span 4 times the length of the cantilever.

Truss Connections
There are two basic connections for truss sections. These are bolted (plated) and spigoted (with eggs and fork). The strength of these connections are based on the load data for each type and size of truss. The strongest of these connections is the spigoted, but each connection is suitable for the size and type of truss.

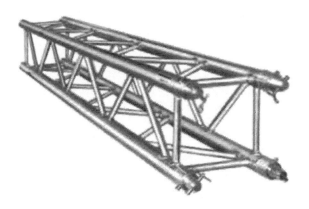

Spigoted Truss with eggs or nipples

Bolted Truss

Spigoted Forked Truss

-photos-courtesy of James Thomas Engineering

Bolted Truss uses four grade 8 truss bolts with washers and nuts. These are attached at the gusset plates. Grade 8 bolts are stronger than the more conventional grade 5 bolt and are identified by the six radial lines at the bolt head. They are made from carbon alloy steel, which allows for greater *torque* strength in the bolt threads. Grade 8 nuts are used along with high alloy washers. When attaching these bolts to the end plates, a truss bolt socket and ratchet is used to snug the bolts. Snug them as you would lug nuts on the rim of a tire. Do not over tighten and, most importantly, do not use an impact driver.

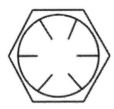

Grade 8 truss bolt markings.

Grade 8 truss bolt.

-photo courtesy of Tom Cat

239

Spigoted Truss has steel nipples (sometimes called eggs) that are inserted at one side of the truss chords. When the truss sections are in alignment, the spigots mate and are secured with a hitch pin and clip. Do not force the eggs into place. They should fit easily. Spigoted Truss using forks have steel male and female forks that mate at each end of the truss chords. When the truss sections are in alignment, the forks mate and are secured with hitch pins and clips.

Towers and Truss Components

As concerts began making the transition from indoor venues to outdoor spaces, there arose a need for supporting the horizontal truss structures from the ground. Truss manufacturers started beefing up their horizontal truss so that it could support loads vertically. This set up became known as *ground-supported-truss.* Floating sleeve blocks were created as a means of connecting the horizontal truss to the vertical towers while enabling the truss to be raised and lowered by chain hoists. The sleeve blocks surround the towers enabling the truss to slide up and down. Head blocks with sheaves mounted inside allowed the chain to run from the hoist over the head block to the horizontal truss.

Rarely do we find ground supported truss in a theatre venue, simply because there is a grid or counterweight system to rig from. However, if there is not, or the ceiling structure cannot support the weight, the ground-supported structure may be the only option.

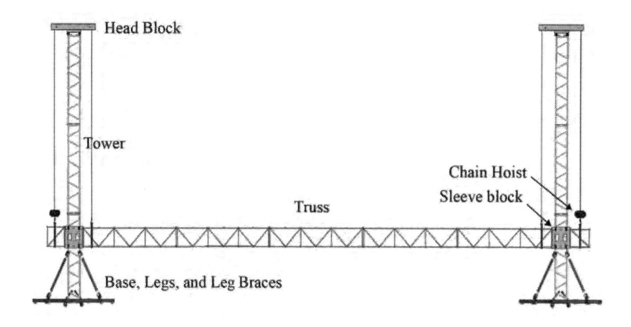

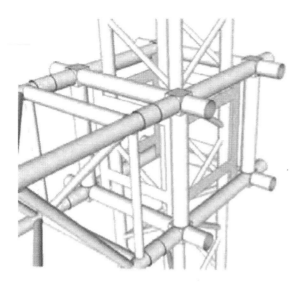

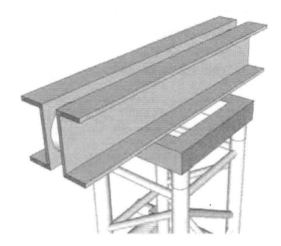

Close up of a sleeve block. The design may vary depending on the type of truss being used.

Close up of an aluminum head block. Note the chain sheaves at the top.

The future of the design and manufacture of truss will always be based on the demands of the industry. As production demands change, so will truss design. Today, the most important factors are span, loading, lifting, ease of assembly, and transport. Customer demand is based on:

- the length of truss needed for the job
- the amount of weight that will be used on the truss
- points on the truss needed to lift the truss into position
- speed and ease of assembly
- transportation costs to and from venues

Most manufactures have multiple designs, both lightweight and heavyweight, for a wide variety of customer needs. Truss catalogues are a great resource for available truss and truss products.
A few catalogs that are available online are:

James Thomas Engineering
http://jthomaseng.com/pdffiles/Product 20Range 202014_merged.pdf
TomCat Truss
http://www.tomcatglobal.com/Tomcat/media/tomcat/Catalogue/TOMCATUCATU (pdf).pdf?ext=.pdf
Tyler Truss
http://www.tylertruss.com

The reference to truss and truss types discussed here are based on the James Thomas Engineering Catalogue, but you should note that there are many other reputable truss manufacturers. While many types of truss are manufactured for the concert industry, the basic truss types we will be using in a theatre venue will be the ladder truss and the box truss.

Truss Types

Ladder-Truss is a two dimensional version of box truss. It is strong when placed in the vertical position as shown, but weak when placed on its side. This truss is great where there is little space on each side of the truss as it fits well into narrow width spaces. Due to its strong design, *ladder truss* is often used for lighting battens and acoustical panels.

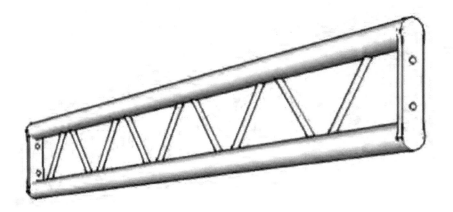

Ladder Truss is often used as lighting battens and to support acoustical panels.

General Purpose Box Truss is the most popular truss used in theatre venues today. It is easy to assemble and can accommodate many different lighting rigs, PA systems, and video walls. They come in a variety of sizes (a few are shown below) and can be used in both indoor and outdoor venues.

12"x 12" Box Truss   18"x 12" Box Truss

Other Truss Types Triangle truss must be oriented so the apex is at the top. The hinged portion of a bi-fold truss must be kept toward the top as well. Flipping it over significantly reduces it load capacity.

242

Triangle   Tri fold

Inspection

ANSI E1.2 U 2012 covers the design, engineering, manufacturing, loading and inspection of aluminum truss in the entertainment industry. It recommends that a *qualified-person* perform periodic inspections at least once a year and that the owner keep inspection records on file for each truss component. This does not mean that truss inspection should be limited to just the owner and to once a year. A *competent person* has the responsibility to perform a visual inspection before each use. The following is a partial list of items that need to be visually inspected prior to use:

❑ Truss geometry. Check for twisting or bending of the truss or tower units

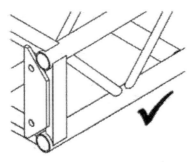

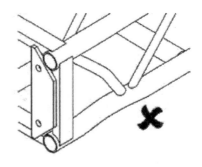

❑ Unusual bending in the truss chords.
❑ Camber, dents, abrasion or wear in the cords, diagonals or spreaders

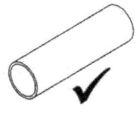

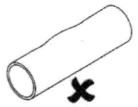

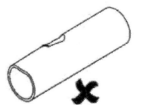

❑ Missing diagonals or connecting plates (if used)

243

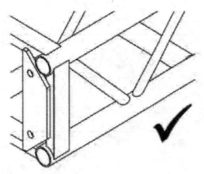 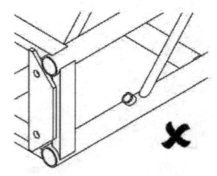

- ❏ Deformation, corrosion, or excessive wear around the truss bolt holes or pinholes.
- ❏ Proper grade fasteners. Check for wear and corrosion
- ❏ Check for cracks and abrasions around the welds

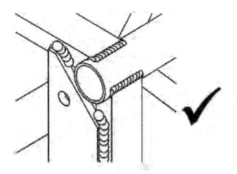 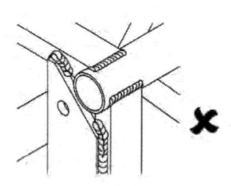

If any of these problems are noted, then the truss must be labeled DO NOT USE and removed from service until a *qualified-person* can perform a more complete inspection or make repairs to the system. For a free copy of this and other ANSI recommendations for the entertainment industry, please visit:

http://tsp.plasa.org/tsp/documents/published_docs.php

Hanging the Truss

Now that we have had the opportunity to look at truss, lets discuss some of the methods used in hanging. We already have discussed proper truss orientation and the importance of panel points. There are several methods used to wrap a truss with round slings. The important points to remember when wrapping truss are:

1. Always keep the panel points in compression
2. Load the truss evenly so as to avoid rotation
3. Wrap the chords evenly so as to avoid rotation and support the chords
4. Never wrap the sling on a splice or a fitting

Wrapping the truss with round slings. There are three *basic* methods for wrapping the truss. There are many others, but these are the most common. What method you use will be determined by the diameter of the truss (size), sling length, and trim.

Choking the lower chords using two slings is often chosen for larger diameter truss. Two 3 to 6-foot slings form a choker hitch on the lower chords. Note the choker faces to the outside. Wrapping to the inside may affect stability especially if the truss is loaded unevenly. The upper chords can be wrapped if necessary to reduce the length of the sling and shorten headroom or they can run to the outside of the upper chord joining at the shackle.

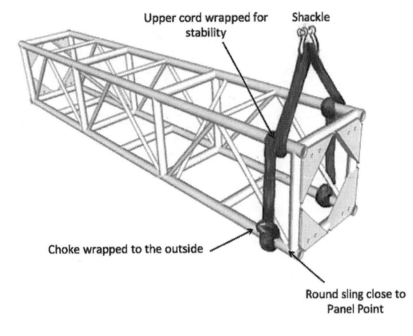

Upper cord wrapped for stability

Shackle

Choke wrapped to the outside

Round sling close to Panel Point

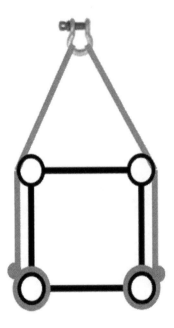

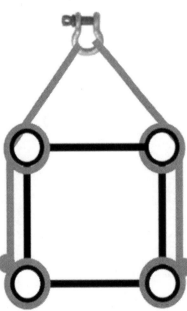

Section View- Upper chords un-wrapped   Section View- Upper chords wrapped

245

Wrapping the entire panel point with one sling is often done with smaller truss and a longer 8-foot sling. The sling is run under the bottom chords, wrapped one turn, run on the outside, wraps the upper chords, before meeting to join at the shackle. The upper chords can be wrapped if necessary to reduce the length of the sling and shorten headroom or they can run to the outside of the upper chord joining at the shackle.

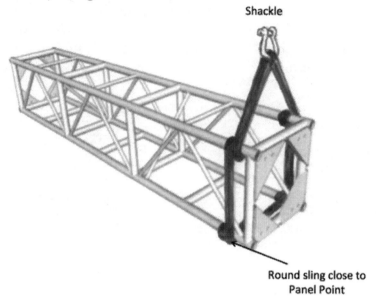

The X wrap is another very stable wrap that is used around the panel point of a truss. The illustration below shows two round slings that are used to hang the truss. Each sling is choked to the lower chords and then crosses each other to the upper chords. At this point they can either wrap the upper chords (as shown) or they can just run around the outside of the top chord to the shackle. Wrapping the upper chord is optional, but it is often done to shorten the length of the round sling and add additional stability.

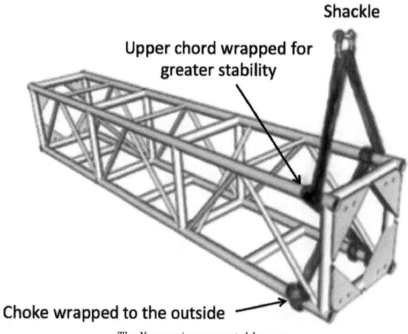

The X wrap is a very stable wrap

The illustrations below show variations of an X wrap using both single and double round slings.

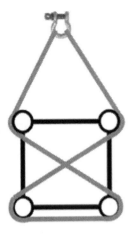

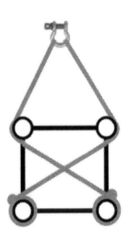

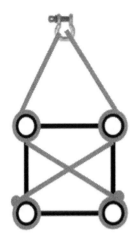

Single round sling

Two round slings with no wrap at the upper chords

Two round slings with wrap at the upper chords

Section Views

The last wrap we will discuss is to be used when there is very little headroom between the hoist and the ceiling. This is typical when hanging truss in ballrooms and convention centers. In this situation, only the lower chords are wrapped using 2-short or 1-medium length round slings. This enables the hoist to be positioned down into the truss minimizing headroom distance. As with grapples, hanging a truss in this manner requires a certain amount of care. When hanging equipment and cables on the truss, the rigger must insure that the load on the truss is evenly balanced. With the round slings connected only to the bottom chords, the *Center of Gravity* at the shackle is very low and the truss can become *out of balance* very easily.

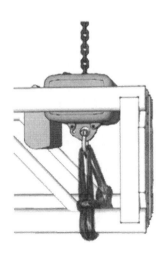

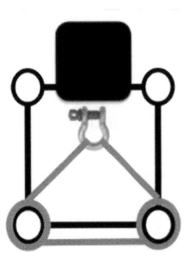

Bridle Angle at the Shackle. The bridle angle at the shackle should be no more than 90 degrees. A higher angle puts too much stress on the sling and upper chords.

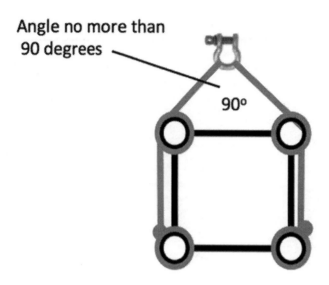

Angle no more than
90 degrees

90°

Tag Location. Round sling tags provide manufacturer's information about the make-up and load rating of the round sling.

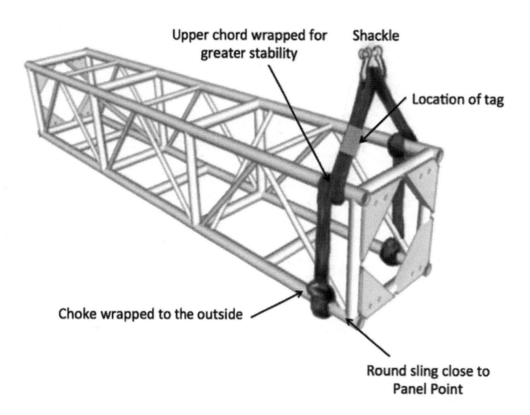

Upper chord wrapped for greater stability

Shackle

Location of tag

Choke wrapped to the outside

Round sling close to Panel Point

On steel core or Steel Flex slings, the tags are attached with velcro at the juncture where the sleeve is stitched. The velcro can be opened if requested by the Fire Marshall allowing inspection of the core. Polyester core slings have the label stitched on. Too often stagehands will correctly wrap the chords of a truss only to incorrectly wrap the tags around the chords or shackle.

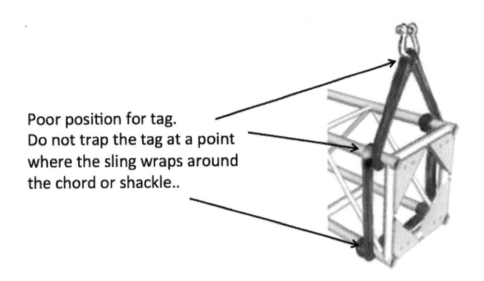

Poor position for tag.
Do not trap the tag at a point
where the sling wraps around
the chord or shackle..

Slings should be wrapped so the tag is positioned on a "straight run", usually at the top- just below where the shackle attaches so it's out of audience view. This allows inspection of the tag if required, but it also prevents the information on the tag from being worn off. OSHA does NOT have a regulation for the *placement* of slings on truss. They do, however, have a regulation that requires the tag of a lifting sling to be legible. ASME (American Society of Mechanical Engineers) B30.9Q2010 Rigging Practices also states not to have the cover splice located within the choke when using round slings. If the information on the label is not legible then you cannot use the sling. If you place the label inside the choke or wrap, the writing on the tag will eventually wear off.

Safeties Steel safeties are run from the hoist hook through the truss to the other hoist hooks or from the truss to an I-beam. They are used as a back-up should there be a failure of the synthetic round slings due to excessive heat or fire. Steel Flex was created due to concerns over the synthetic slings. The Steel-Flex sling does not usually require a back-up safety based on heat related issues. In the United States the decision to use a safety back up for a Steel-Flex sling is determined by the venue or the Fire Marshal. However, redundancy is always a good thing in the event of some unforeseen disaster.

Chain Hoists
Chain Hoists are a staple of the entertainment industry. They are the "muscle" for the lifting overhead truss systems off the ground and into position.

They are used to hang and secure such things as lighting equipment, speaker arrays, video walls and projection equipment. Like so many other tools and equipment borrowed from other industries, the electric chain hoist found its way into entertainment rigging to satisfy a need- to hoist lighting, sound and video equipment into the air. In the early days of arena rigging, up-riggers had to haul up both the chain and the hoist to a position on the I-beams. Considering the amount of weight the up-rigger had to haul, this became "out of fashion" very quickly. The chain hoist was soon modified to run inverted so that up-riggers only had to haul up the chain and the bridle legs. Now, the hoist is connected directly to the truss round slings by means of a shackle. Essentially, a chain hoist *is* an electric motor that climbs a chain while pulling a load.

One Ton hoists attached to a section of box truss. Note how the round slings are wrapped at the panel point.

Chain Hoist capacities range from 1/8 Ton to 3 Ton. However, the most common capacities used in the entertainment industry are 1/4 Ton, 1/2 Ton, 1-Ton and 2-Ton.

Attaching the chain bags to the hoist. When attaching the bag hooks to the chain hoist, the hooks need to be placed facing out. This avoids the links of the chain from snagging the points of the hook. Always check to be sure you are using the correct size bag for the correct length of chain. Nothing can be more embarrassing and dangerous than to have a hoist nearing its trim height and hear,

" chink.....chink...chink..chink. chink.chink.chink.chink!"

as the excess chain brings all of the remaining chain crashing to the stage floor. Make sure you are using the correct size bag for the correct length of chain.

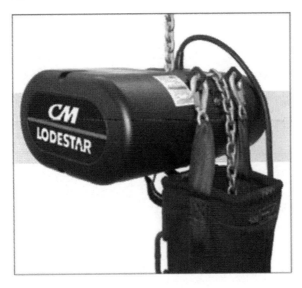

Note the bag hooks point to the outside.
-photo courtesy of Mountain Productions

Summary

In this chapter, we discussed the various types of aluminum truss and truss components and chain hoists. The comparison between an I-beam and a truss showed us that the top and bottom flanges of an I-beam directly correspond to the top and bottom chords on a truss and that the chords maintain the stability of the diagonals and spreaders similar to the web of an I-beam. We learned that a truss, when under load, is always in a state of either tension or compression. *The-panel-points* and *nodes* are the strongest point on the truss to apply a vertical force. They allow for the vertical force to be distributed horizontally from diagonal to diagonal. To aid in the loading of various truss types, manufacturers provide us with truss loading data charts that give detailed information relative to the truss type, truss span, and load type. They provide load data charts for every type of truss they manufacture. These charts are available on their website and should be referred to when loading their truss. In addition, there are two basic connections for truss sections, *bolted-(or-plated)* and *spigoted*. The strength of these connections are based on the load data for each type and size of truss.

As concerts began making the transition from indoor venues to outdoor spaces, there arose a need for supporting the horizontal truss structures from the ground. Truss manufacturers started beefing up their horizontal truss so that it could support loads vertically. This set up became known as *ground-supported-truss.*

Lastly, we learned the importance of truss inspection. ANSI E1.2 - 2012 covers the design, engineering, manufacturing, loading and inspection of aluminum truss in the entertainment industry. It recommends that a *qualified-person* perform periodic inspections at least once a year and that the owner keep inspection records on file for each truss component. A *competent-person-*has the responsibility to perform a visual inspection before each use.

Chapter 14:
Two-point Bridles

Introduction

A bridle can have two, three or more legs, but by far, the most common type of bridle is a two-legged bridles. Bridles are commonly used to position a load at a point where there is no immediate support, which is why they are so commonly used in arenas, where support beams are often spaced, 20 to 40 feet apart. Bridles can also be used reduce the load on a single point, by spreading it over several points.

Because many techniques that are most often associated with arena rigging are also used in theatrical rigging, we will occasionally reference theatrical rigging through this unit, beginning here. In Chapter 7, we discussed how bridles can be used to reduce the span distance between lift lines on a batten, thereby making the batten more rigid. We can also use a bridle to suspend a heavy load at specific point on a batten. For example: supposed you wanted to hang a 400-pound point load on a standard pipe batten, and that location is in the center of the span between the lift line. As we discussed in Chapter 7, the weakest point on a batten is in the center of the span between the lift line, and the result of placing a 400-pound load at this point would most like result in a bent batten. However, you could use a bridle where the anchor points were at two of the lift lines and the apex of the bridle was centered between then. Problem solved.

In this chapter we will look at some of the math used to calculate the length of two-legged bridles, as well as the tension on the legs. For a more in-depth look at bridle math, read *Rigging Math Made Simple, 3rd Edition* by Delbert L. Hall.

Calculating the Length of Bridle Legs
In order to put the apex of the bridle at a specific point, the lengths of the two bridle legs must be specific lengths. In order to compute the length of each leg, we will need to know a) how low the bridle's apex (bridle point) is below the anchor point for that leg of the bridle (vertical distance), and b) how far the apex is away from the anchor point for that leg of the bridle in a horizontal distance. This gives you a Horizontal (H1 and H2) and Vertical (V1 and V2) distances for each leg. See drawing below.

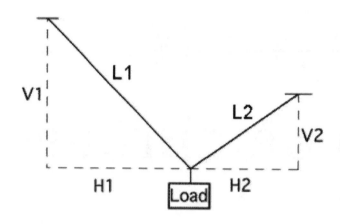

Note: I find that many rigging math problems are easier to understand and solve if I begin by making a diagram of the problem.

We can compute the length of L (the hypotenuse of the right triangle) by using the Pythagorean Theorem $A^2 + B^2 = C^2$, only we will use $V^2 + H^2 = L^2$, converted into the equation $L = \sqrt{H^2 + V^2}$.

Example: Calculate the lengths of L1 and L2 where, V1 = 10', H1 = 4', V2 = 6, and H2 = 3'.

L1 = SQRT $(10^2 + 4^2)$

L1 = SQRT $(100 + 16)$

L1 = SQRT (116)

L1 = 10.77 feet

L2 = SQRT $(6^2 + 3^2)$

L2 = SQRT $(36 + 9)$

L2 = SQRT (45)

L2 = 6.7 feet

Tension on Bridle Legs Overview

The span between the anchor points for each leg and the height of the bridle's apex determines the bridle's *bridle angle* (the angle between the two bridle legs). This angle is very important in determining the tension on the legs. Let's begin by looking at a broad view of this topic.

In the bridle below, the legs are nearly vertical (the slight angle is used here in order to make both legs visible). If both legs were absolutely vertical, 100% of the load would be in a vertical direction and the weight being suspended would be equally divided between the two legs. And since the anchor points are directly above the load, there would be no load/force in the horizontal direction. Therefore, if the load being suspended weighs 100 pounds, the tension on each bridle leg would be 50 pounds.

The anchor points on the bridle below are farther apart. Once again, the combined vertical force on the anchor points must equal the weight of the suspended load. But, because the load is NOT directly below either anchor point, there is also a horizontal force on the anchor points. Because of the combined horizontal and vertical forces on the anchor points, the combined tensions on the two legs is greater than the weight of the load.

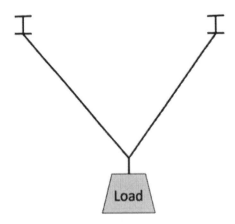

The table below shows how the tension on each leg increases as the ratio of the horizontal and vertical distances gets greater and the bridle becomes flatter. These tensions assume a 100-pound load.

Angle from Vertical	Bridle Tension on each leg (lb)	Horizontal Tension on each leg (lb)
30	58	29
45	70	50
60	100	87
80	288	284
89	2,865	2,865
89.5	28,648	28,648

So, it is important to realize that the closer the legs are to vertical, the less tension on the bridle legs. Conversely, the flatter the legs (closer to horizontal), the greater the tension on the legs. With a little practice, by knowing the load being supported and estimating the angle of the legs, you can make a reasonably close estimate of the tension on the legs.

Tension on Bridle Legs

However, now that you know how to compute the lengths of the bridle legs, you can compute the load on each leg by simply knowing the Horizontal and Vertical distances of the apex from the two anchor points.

To compute the tension on the two bridles, we use the equations:

$$Tension\ on\ L1 = Load\ \times\ \frac{L1 \times H2}{(V1 \times H2) + (V2 \times H1)}$$

$$Tension\ on\ L2 = Load\ \times\ \frac{L2 \times H1}{(V1 \times H2) + (V2 \times H1)}$$

Before you start screaming, "I can't remember all of that!" relax and take a deep breath. I will soon teach you a trick that will make it fairly easy to remember. But before we get to that, draw a diagram like the one below.

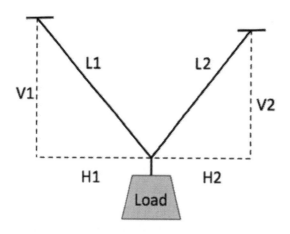

Now, add the following values to your diagram:

L1 = 5′	L2 = 6.7′
V1 = 4′	V2 = 3′
H1 = 3′	H2 = 6′
Load = 500 lb	

This will help you to be able to quickly find the values that you need.

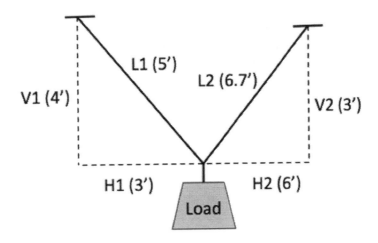

Below is the equation for finding the tension on Leg 1, but I have made the first part of the equation **BOLD**, and I have added an arrow to the diagram so that you can visualize which two numbers are multiplied.

$$\text{Tension on L1} = \text{Load} \times \frac{\mathbf{L1 \times H2}}{(V1 \times H2) + (V2 \times H1)}$$

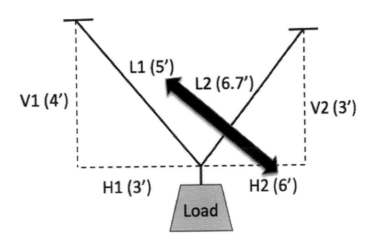

Since you want to find the tension on L1, the "trick" is to begin by multiplying L1 (high) by the "low" side of Leg 2 (which is H2). If you wanted to find the tension on L2, you would multiply L2 (high) by the "low" side of the L1 triangle, which would be H1. Got it? So plugging in these variables in our equation we get:

$$\text{Tension on L1} = \text{Load} \times \frac{\mathbf{5 \times 6}}{(V1 \times H2) + (V2 \times H1)}$$

$$\text{Tension on L1} = \text{Load} \times \frac{\mathbf{30}}{(V1 \times H2) + (V2 \times H1)}$$

Next, we want to figure out what we divide this number by. This is actually very easy to remember. We just need to remember that we multiply V on one side by H on the other, and add the two numbers together. You can also remember that you always multiply one "high" side and one "low" side, if that helps you. So, let's look at the first pair of numbers for this section of the equation:

$$\text{Tension on L1} = \text{Load} \times \frac{30}{(\textbf{4} \times \textbf{6}) + (\text{V2} \times \text{H1})}$$

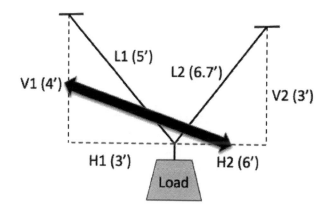

And now the second pair of numbers:

$$\text{Tension on L1} = \text{Load} \times \frac{30}{(\textbf{4} \times \textbf{6}) + (\textbf{3} \times \textbf{3})}$$

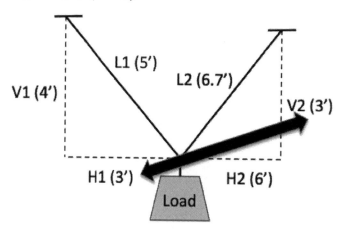

Again, one "high" side and one "low" side. So, now finish solving the equations.

$$\text{Tension on L1} = \text{Load} \times \frac{30}{(4 \times 6) + (3 \times 3)}$$

258

Tension on L1 = Load $\times \dfrac{30}{24 + 9}$

Tension on L1 = Load $\times \dfrac{30}{33}$

Tension on L1 = Load $\times .909$

Finally, we just plug in the Load and multiply.

Tension on L1 = **500** $\times .909$

Tension on L1 = 454.5 lb

Let's now calculate the tension on Leg 2.

Tension on L2 = Load $\times \dfrac{L2 \times H1}{(V1 \times H2) + (V2 \times H1)}$

Again, we multiply the part that we are trying to find the tension on (now, L2) by the "low" number on the other side of the diagram. Substituting the values we get:

Tension on L2 = Load $\times \dfrac{\mathbf{6.7 \times 3}}{(V1 \times H2) + (V2 \times H1)}$

Tension on L2 = Load $\times \dfrac{\mathbf{20.1}}{(V1 \times H2) + (V2 \times H1)}$

Did you notice that bottom part of this equation is exactly the same as the equation for finding the tension on Leg 1? Because they are the same, we do not have to re-calculate those numbers. We can plug-in the results from our first equation (33) and we have:

Tension on L2 = Load $\times \dfrac{20.1}{33}$

Tension on L2 = Load $\times .609$

Tension on L2 = 500 $\times .609$

Tension on L2 = 304.5 lb

Knowing bridle math can help ensure that you do not to overload your anchor points and create unsafe situations.

Summary

Bridles are extremely useful for solving many rigging problems, both in arena (truss) rigging, and in theatrical rigging. The next several chapters deal with different ways to suspend a load

Chapter 15:

Suspending a Beam from Two Vertical Legs

Introduction

Many math problems that you find on a rigging exam show a horizontal truss/beam supported by two vertical legs/lift lines, each at the end of the truss/beam. The reason for this is simple, this type of problem can be solved very easily and very accurately. When the legs are not vertical, calculating the tension on the leg requires additional steps; and if there are more than two legs, our calculations will only get us to a close estimate of the tension on the legs. Both of these topics are covered in future chapters, but now, let's deal with calculating the tension on two vertical legs supporting a load.

The diagram below is an example of a single point load on a beam.

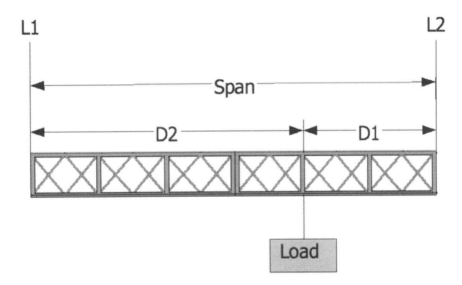

The equations for calculating these tensions are:

$$Tension\ on\ L1 = \frac{Load \times D1}{Span}$$

and

$$\text{Tension on } L2 = \frac{Load \times D2}{Span}$$

or

$$\text{Tension on } L2 = Load - L1$$

Note: You can also think of it as L1 = Load x (D1/Span) and L2 = Load x (D2/Span) and if that is easier for you to remember.

The trick I use to remember the method of solving this problem is to remember that to find the tension on one leg, you begin by multiply the Load by the distance of the Load to the OPPOSITE leg. Then you divide the result by the Span. Therefore, to calculate the tension on Leg 1, we need to know the distance of the Loads from L2, which I am calling D1. Do not get hung-up on the terms D1 and D2; instead, understand what they represent.

Let's work a problem to see how this works.

If the Span between the legs is 20 feet, the distance from the Load to L2 (D1) is 5 feet and the distance from the Load to L1 (D2) is 15 feet (note: D1 + D2 must equal Span), and the Load 1 is 200 lb, what is the tension on L1 and L2?

$$\text{Tension on } L1 = \frac{Load \times D1}{Span}$$

$$\text{Tension on } L1 = \frac{200 \times 5}{20}$$

$$\text{Tension on } L1 = \frac{1000}{20}$$

Tension on L1 = 50 lb

$$\text{Tension on } L2 = \frac{Load \times D2}{Span}$$

$$\text{Tension on } L2 = \frac{200 \times 15}{20}$$

$$\text{Tension on } L2 = \frac{3000}{20}$$

Tension on L2 = 150 lb

We might not always be given D1 and D2. In fact, we can solve this problem if we know either D1 or D2, since the Span = D1 + D2.

Uniformly Distributed Load

In the problem above we worked with a single point load. If there are two or more loads, one way to calculated the tension on the legs is to calculate each load separately, then add. A more efficient way to do this is to determine if you have a uniformly distributed load (UDL), and if so, you can calculate multiple loads as one. Let's looks at some examples.

Let's start with something simple - look again at the problem we just solved.

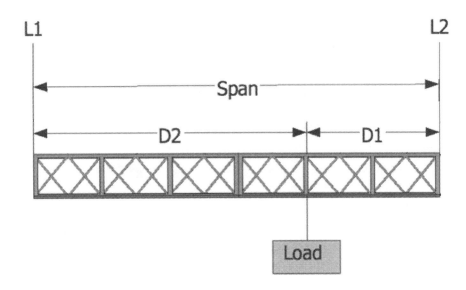

When we solved this problem we totally ignored the weight of the truss itself. Of course, it is not weightless, so we need to calculate it. Let's assume it weights 100 pounds. How much of that weight is on L1 and how much is on L2?

The truss is a UDL because each segment of the truss weights exactly the same as every other segment of the truss. When we have a UDL, we next need to determine where the "center" of the UDL is located. It this case, it is at the center of the Span (10 feet from each leg). So, to calculate the new tension on L1, we could use the same equation we used above and say that we a 100-pound load located at 10 feet from L2. This would work fine, but since the load is at the cent of the Span, half of the 100 pounds (50 pounds) will be support by L1 the the other half (50 pounds) will be supported by on L2. So, we can just add 50 pounds to each of the loads we calculated earlier to get the new tensions.

Now, look at the drawing below.

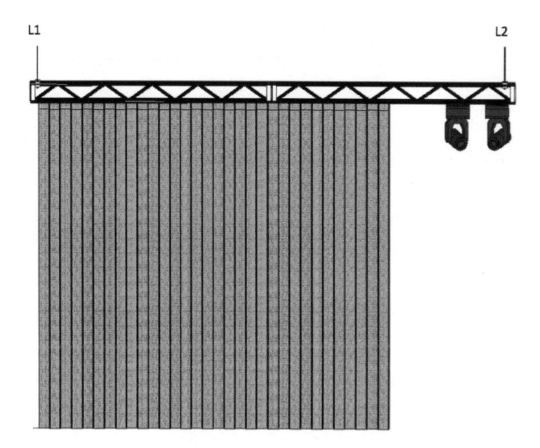

Assuming that the Span = 20 feet, the Truss weighs 6 lb per ft, the two moving light weigh 75 lb each and are positioned 17 ft and 19 ft respectively from point L1, and the curtain measures 15 and wide x 15' tall and weighs 170 lb, what is the tension on L1 and L2?

Do we have a UDL? Actually, three of them. let me explain.

The first on is easy to see - the truss. It spans the entire Span and weighs 120 pounds (6 x 20). That means that:

Tension on L1 = 60 pounds

Tension on L2 = 60 pounds

The second UDL is the curtain - since each foot of a curtain weights exactly the same as every other foot of curtain. Now, we need to find the center of this load. Since one end starts at L1 and its length is 15 feet, the center of the curtain is 7.5 feet from L1. We can use this measurement to calculate the tension it puts on L2.

Tension on L2 = (7.5 x 170) / 20

Tension on L2 = 1,275 / 20

Tension on L2 = 63.75 pounds

and

264

Tension on L1 = 170 - 63.75

Tension on L1 = 106.25 pounds

The third UDL is the two moving lights. Since they weight the same (75 pounds each) we can consider them as a UDL. And since one is 17 feet for L1 and the other is 19 feet from L1, their center is 18 feet from L1 (or 2 feet from L2, if you prefer). Their combined weight is 150 pounds.

Plugging these numbers into our equations we get...

Tension on L1 = (2 x 150) / 20

Tension on L1 = 300 / 20

Tension on L1 = 15 pounds

and

Tension on L2 = 150 - 15

Tension on L1 = 145 pounds

Our final step is to total the amounts:

Total Tension on L1 = 60 + 106.25 + 15 = **181.25 pounds**

Total Tension on L2 = 60 + 63.75 + 145 = **258.75 pounds**

Cantilevered Loads

The last type of problem we will look at in this chapter is a cantilevered load. Look at the problem below. Oh, and one thing about this problem, like the very first problem in this chapter, we will assume that the truss weights nothing. While we know this is not really true, it will simplify the problem a bit and let us concentrate on the real issue - the cantilevered end.

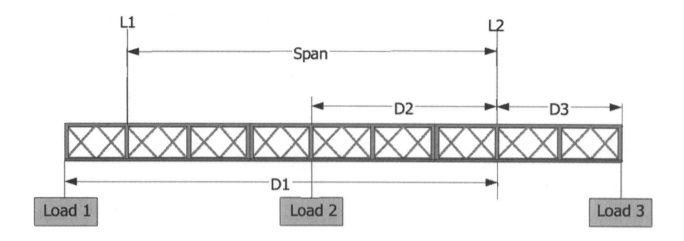

Actually, in this problem, there are two cantilevered loads, one on each end of the truss.

The equations for solving this problem are:

$$Tension\ on\ L1 = \frac{(Load\ 1 \times D1) + (Load\ 2 \times D2) - (Load\ 3 \times D3)}{Span}$$

Tension on L2 = (Load1 + Load 2 + Load3) – L1

There are two things that might look odd about the equation for calculating the tension on L1. First, we have combined calculating three tension from three loads into one long equation. Do not fret over this. Just like the UDL problems in the section on UDLs, you can break this into multiple, simple problems and combine the tensions. Second, we have never used a subtraction ("-") operation before, and you are probably wondering "why do it now?" Because we have a cantilevered end, you need to think of this rig as a teeter-totter or a lever, where the fulcrum is at the point where the Leg attaches to the truss. When we are computing L1, the fulcrum is where L2 attaches to the truss. If Loads 1 and 2 did not exist, the L1 end of the truss would pivot up (at the point where L2 attached to the truss) because Load 3 would not have anything counterbalancing it on the other side (and the L1 cable, chain, or round sling would not provide any resistance).

This should tell you that the cantilevered load on the outside of L2 puts a positive force on L2 but a negative force on L1. (Remember: downward forces are "positive" and upward forces are "negative"). Because this is true, we need to include this negative force when we calculate the load on L1. When all of the loads were between the two Legs, you only had positive forces, so all of the forces were "added." Since we now have a negative force, we need to "subtract" it. That is why we have "– (Load 3 x D3)" in this equation.

One more thing to remember before we work a problem - remember, when we calculate the forces on L1, ALL of our distance measurements are made from L2. And because Load 1 is "outside" of L1, D1 will be greater than the Span. This may seem odd, but it is true. So, using the diagram above...

If the Span is 30 feet, Load 1 is 200 lb, D1 is 35 feet, Load 2 is 150 lb, D2 is 15 feet, Load 3 is 100 lb, and D3 is 10 feet, what is the tension on L1 and L2?

$$\text{Tension on L1} = \frac{(\text{Load 1} \times \text{D1}) + (\text{Load 2} \times \text{D2}) - (\text{Load 3} \times \text{D3})}{\text{Span}}$$

$$\text{Tension on L1} = \frac{(200 \times 35) + (150 \times 15) - (100 \times 10)}{30}$$

$$\text{Tension on L1} = \frac{7,000 + 2,250 - 1,000}{30}$$

$$\text{Tension on L1} = \frac{8,250}{30}$$

Tension on L1 = 275 lb

Tension on L2 = (Load1 + Load 2 + Load3) – L1

Tension on L2= (200 + 150 + 100) - 275

Tension on L2= 450 - 275

Tension on L2 = 175 lb

Summary

In this chapter we dealt with calculating the tension of a beam that is supported by two vertical legs. This "beam" could be a pipe batten, a wooden beam or an aluminum truss. Whether this beam is permanently installed or just installed for a single show, it is important to understand the load on each leg.

Chapter 16:
Angled Legs and Horizontal Breastlines

Angled Legs Supporting a Beam

Ideally, you would like all of the legs supporting a beam to be vertical and we learned earlier that we can use bridles to position points. However, what if a bridle is not practical? Let's look at what happens when the leg is not vertical.

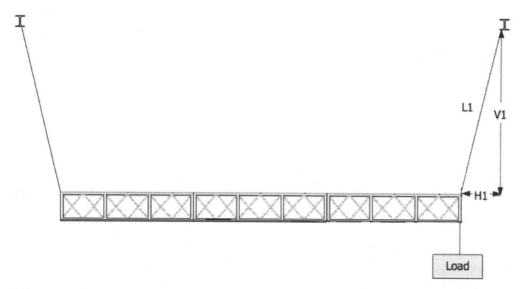

If the hanging point were directly above the load, then the tension on this leg would be equal to the Load (assuming the truss weighed nothing). But since the Load is not directly below the hanging point, the tension on the Leg will be greater than the load. So what is the tension on the Leg? The equation to solve this problem is:

$$Tension\ on\ L1 = Load \times \frac{L1}{V1}$$

Before we solve this problem let's realize that it is pretty unusual to have a single load on the end of a truss/beam, as shown above. In reality, this Load actually represents the vertical force on the end of the beam, as we calculated it in Chapter 14. We first have to know the vertical force at this leg before we can calculate the tension on leg.

The way I remember this formula is that the tension on L1 is always greater than the vertical weight of the downward force at the point where the leg attached to the beam (in this case, the Load), so the Load must be multiplied by a number that is greater than 1. Since the length of L1 (the hypotenuse of the right triangle) is always greater than the vertical distance (V1), dividing L1 by V1 will always give you a number that is greater than 1. Then, multiply the Load by this multiplying factor. Let's work through an example.

If H1 = 4', V1 =10', and the Load = 400 lb, what is the tension on L1?

The first thing we need to do is to compute the length of L1 using the Pythagorean Theorem.

$$L1 = \text{SQRT } (10^2 + 4^2)$$

$$L1 = 10.77 \text{ feet}$$

Now we put this length into the equation above and get:

$$\text{Tension on L1} = \text{Load} \times \frac{10.77}{10}$$

$$\text{Tension on L1} = 400 \times 1.077$$

Tension on Leg L1 = 430.8 lb

As you see, the fact that the leg is not vertical caused the tension to increase. The greater the angle, the larger the increase.

Horizontal Breastline

A breastline is a unique type of bridle leg. It is a rope or cable that runs horizontally and is used to swing/breast a hanging object out from directly beneath its suspension point(s). For example, you might breast an electric upstage or downstage in order to keep another piece of scenery away from the lighting instruments. Because this line (or lines) runs horizontally, it is not lifting the load, just pulling it out of alignment. Since there is no vertical force on a breastline, the tension on it tends to be rather low. To compute the tension on a breastline, we use this simple equation:

$$Horizontal\ Force = Load \times \frac{H1}{V1}$$

This equation is somewhat similar to the one that was used above finding the tension on an angled leg - we calculate a multiplying factor, them multiply the Load times this number.

Below is a diagram of this breastline configuration.

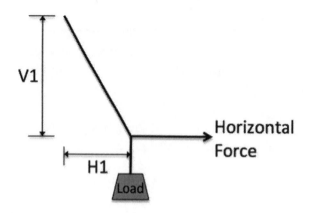

Let's work an example.

Calculate the horizontal force on a breastline where V1 is 30', H1 is 2', and the Load = 700 pounds.

So, plugging the numbers into our equation, we get:

$$\text{Horizontal Force} = \text{Load} \times \frac{2}{30}$$

$$\text{Horizontal Force} = \text{Load} \times 0.0666$$

$$\text{Horizontal Force} = 700 \times 0.0666$$

Horizontal Force = 46.62 lb

As you can see, compared to the weight, 700 pounds, it does not take a lot of force to breast this load 2 feet.

When you breast a load out of its normal hanging position, the supporting line becomes an angled leg and we use the same equation that we discussed at the beginning of this chapter

$$Tension\ on\ L1 = Load \times \frac{L1}{V1}$$

to calculate the tension on the supporting line.

Part IV:
What Every Rigger Should Know

Chapter 17:
Rigging Inspections

Introduction

Any rigging system that moves is subject to wear. Sheaves wear against shafts, lift lines wear against head and loft blocks, mule blocks, head, loft blocks, idlers, operating lines wear with loading. Time, temperature and humidity along with the frequency all play a part in the wear and tear on a rigging system. With the increased awareness towards theatre rigging safety, inspections are becoming more and more commonplace in the industry. This chapter will examine preventative maintenance, routine inspections, frequency of routine inspections and then move onto the conduct of formal rigging inspections by *qualified* professionals. We will follow with examples from rigging inspection reports.

Preventative Maintenance and Routine Inspections

Preventative maintenance plays an important role in the development of any routine inspection program and can be performed by any *competent*[1] technician.

This not only allows for a *safe* working environment, but aids in the creation of scheduled routine maintenance procedures. Considerations to preventative maintenance should include, but are not limited to the following:

1) Obtain loading diagrams (if possible) from the theatre consultant or engineer that planned your facility. This will help in your understanding of the capabilities and capacities of the space and its systems.

2) Instinctively "know" your rigging system(s). Having a "sense for" and "feel of" the rigging system(s) in your theatre facility will help you determine if something is *wrong*. Every time a system is used, ask yourself, is the system difficult to operate? Is there friction anywhere in the system? Are there any "grinding" noises? Is there slack in the system that should not be there?" These questions will help identify potential problems before they occur.

---

[1] OSHA defines a *competent* person as "one who is capable of identifying existing and predictable hazards in the surroundings or working conditions which are unsanitary, hazardous or dangerous to employees, and who has authorization to take prompt corrective measures to eliminate them."

3) Know the proper operating procedures for the equipment you are using. If in doubt, contact the manufacturer. Before using any system, ask the following, "are the loads balanced and distributed evenly? Are the locking mechanisms adjusted accordingly? Are brakes functioning? Are spreader plates properly spaced every 2 feet within the arbor stacks? Are the locking collars secured on top of the last plate in the counterweight stack? Is there any fouled rigging?

4) Schedule periodic training and equipment review sessions for all personnel (including yourself) using the equipment. Know their (your) experience, abilities and limitations. Train your staff to visually inspect the rigging system(s) before each use.

5) Schedule periodic inspections of your rigging system(s). Check for any wear, abrasions or deterioration of rope, cables, and pulleys.

6) Schedule periodic rigging inspections by an outside professional theatre rigging company or ETCP certified professional based on frequency of use.

Create a checklist for **General Preventative Maintenance** that is relevant for your facility. The following checklist can serve as a guideline for creating one specific to your venue.

- Fire extinguishers. Make sure inspection labels are current
- First Aid kits. Make sure contents are current
- Check all exits signs. Make sure they are lit and not blocked
- Check for blocked fire exits, doors and walkways
- Check for storage areas for blocked egress
- Make sure all equipment has safety warnings posted as necessary
- Check that there is adequate work light on stage, fly rail & grid especially when the stage in not in use
- Open pit and trap areas must be roped off with reflective tape
- Inspect lighting cables for damage or wear
- Inspect lighting equipment for damage and safety cables
- Inspect and run all linesets for movement and wear
- Inspect operating lines for movement and wear
- Check for fouled linesets and rigging lines
- Check to insure cams on locking rail are adjusted and functional and rings are in place
- Inspect pinrail and belaying pins
- Insure all linesets are clearly labeled
- Insure that spreader plates are spaced evenly (every 2 feet) within the counterweight brick stack and the locking collars are secured
- Ensure that fly operators have full visibility of stage and moving objects
- Check that counterweight bricks are stored safety and are not higher than kick plate on loading platform
- Check for any rigging obstructions
- Remove unused temporary rigging such as floating blocks
- Run and inspect all curtains & tracks for movement
- Inspect any acoustical shells, raceways and permanent items on battens
- Inspect the fire curtain. Is it working? Make sure scenery, cables or obstructions do not block the fire curtain from being lowered to the stage floor
- Check that all flame proofing certificates are current and on file
- Insure that all scenery is flame proofed

274

Frequency of routine inspections

The frequency of your routine inspections will vary depending upon loading conditions and on how often the system(s) is used. It is important to remember- *always visually inspect rigging or rigging system(s) before each use.* Your stage crew can easily perform a visual inspection as part of their pre-show checklist duties and report any problems to the technical director. Other, more specific routine inspections can be performed by *competent* personnel on a quarterly, semi-annually or annually basis. Again, the frequency of inspections will depend on loading, usage, location and parameters specific to your facility. Any *complicated* rigging system(s) may require contacting a *qualified*[2] theatre-rigging professional for further evaluation. The chart below can serve as a guideline for conducting routine inspections.

Equipment Item	Heavy Use	Moderate Use	Light Use
Hemp lift lines and system	Quarterly	Semi-annually	Semi-annually
Head blocks, loft blocks, idlers, arbors, tension blocks, track guides and shoes	Annually	Annually	Bi-annually
Cable lift lines and battens	Annually	Annually	Bi-annually
Purchase lines and rope locks	Quarterly	Semi-annually	Semi-annually
Automated winches	Quarterly	Semi-annually	Semi-annually

*Note: the fire curtain should be checked periodically as part of these routine inspections. Please consult your local fire regulations.

Maintaining Records

Maintaining inspection records are crucial for insurance purposes and OSHA requirements. More importantly, records are also useful in tracking problems allowing for follow up inspections if any future problems are detected. Records can also be useful in tracking the life of equipment and making replacement recommendations as needed.

Preparing for the Formal Rigging Inspection

Whereas competent personnel can conduct routine-rigging inspections and maintenance, a qualified outside rigging firm or ETCP certified technician should periodically conduct more comprehensive rigging inspections. Providing as much information about your facility will assist them in performing a thorough evaluation of your space. Most rigging inspection companies have general information forms that guide you through the process. But if not, the following checklist will aid you in collecting the appropriate pre-inspection information.

---

[2] OSHA defines a *qualified* person as one whom, "by possession of a recognized degree, certificate, or professional standing, or who by extensive knowledge, training and experience, has successfully demonstrated his ability to solve or resolve problems relating to the subject matter, the work, or the project."

Maintenance and Inspection Records
1. List the date of your last formal rigging inspection including the inspection report and who conducted the inspection
2. Note any corrections made based on rigging report recommendations including the theatre consulting firm
3. Dates of routine maintenance and informal rigging inspections including notes on maintenance work performed

Basic facility information (attach ground plans and sectionals if available)
1. Type of venue (proscenium, arena, thrust, black box, other)
2. Rigging manufacturer
3. Year rigging system was installed
4. Dimensions (plaster line to back wall, proscenium opening (both width and height). Dimensions of thrust or arena stage or performance area
5. Distance from stage floor to grid or structural steel
6. Grid construction (steel, wood, or cable)
7. Accessibility to grid
8. Number of working linesets
9. Number of deadhung pipes
10. Length of battens

Specific facility information- rigging system
1. Type of rigging system - counterweighted or rope-line (sandbag)
2. Type of wall attachment - J or T-Bar or Wire Guided
3. Single Purchase or Double Purchase
4. Operating Line material (manila, polyester, etc)
5. Over or under hung head blocks
6. Over or under hung loft blocks
7. Number of mule blocks
8. Idlers on loft block or sag bars
9. Number or manually operated winches

Automated systems
1. Number of *drum winches* in venue
2. Number of *zero fleet winches* in venue
3. Number of *counterweight assist* in venue
4. Number of *FOH climbing hoists*
5. Year(s) installed
6. List what they support
7. Number of cables or chains used in winch or hoist systems
8. Accessibility
9. Location
10. Travel distance
11. Is *counterweight assist winches* chain driven or cable driven
12. Location of control(s)

Fire Curtain
1. Fire curtain type- Straight Lift or Brail Lift
2. Year installed
3. Manual or motorized
4. Material or fabric
5. Last time released/ maintained

The Rigging Inspection Report
The rigging inspection report is intended to make recommendations based on observations made by a qualified ETCP stage technician/ professional. The ETCP professional is NOT a licensed engineer, so the inspection will in no way presume or make recommendations regarding the structural integrity of the building. The report is simply based on observations made of those accessible rigging areas and components. Inspection results are submitted only for your consideration and action. These should be broken down into:

- System Overview
- Definitions of Recommendations
- The Detailed Report
- Miscellaneous
- Report Summary and Recommendations
- Glossary of Terms

System Overview
Based upon the pre-inspection evaluation, the inspector should begin the inspection report with a venue and system overview. Should any further action be needed, this overview will assist theatre consultants and engineers with a general information on your facility.

Definitions of Recommendations
The inspection report needs to explain any and all recommendations that will be used in the report. These definitions will range from those items that need you to take immediate action (because they pose an immediate danger to life, limb and property) to those items that are acceptable. Understanding these definitions will aid you in taking action with respect to the safety of your facility.

The following are commonly used terms:

Decommission
To take a component out of service because it is in a state of damage or disrepair that could potentially cause grave bodily harm or even death

Replace
When a component is in a state of damage or disrepair. The component is not an immediate danger of failure but has effectively ended its service life

Repair

When a component is in a state of damage or disrepair that can be serviced onsite to allow it to function properly & safely

Hazard

A dangerous condition that could cause bodily harm or even death at any time

Acceptable

When a component is in a good, operating condition and that there is no apparent sign of there being any threat to those using the system

The Inspection

Introduction

Inspection details specifically show each and every area of the theatre venue examined. Examination areas include, but are not limited to:

- Beam Port Lighting Positions (inspect mountings if necessary)
- Box Boom Positions (inspect mountings if necessary)
- Balcony Rail Position (inspect mountings if necessary)
- Catwalks
- Life line attachments (if any)
- Rigging systems (both hemp and counterweight)
    - Lofts Blocks (including idlers)
    - Mule Blocks
    - Head blocks
    - Tension Blocks
    - Grid
    - Pin Rail- wooden or steel
    - Locking Rail- are the line set numbered? Are the cams worn? adjustment screws bent?
    - Operating lines- condition? Last replaced?
    - Jack Lines
    - Lift lines
    - Sag bars (if any)
    - Arbors and lift line attachment points
    - Shoes
    - Battens and lift line attachment points
    - T or J Track, Wire Guides and attachment points
    - Fleet angles
    - D:d Ratios
    - Truss and Chain Hoists (if any) plus attachment points
    - Fire Curtain (Manual or Motorized)
    - Release mechanisms
    - Dash pots

The Fire Curtain

Typically, rigging inspections begin downstage and work their way upstage.

Beginning with the fire curtain, the release mechanisms are first checked to insure that nothing blocks the travel of the fire curtain itself. This is a common problem in most theatre venues as fire curtains tend to be ignored by technical directors and theatre managers (see the chapter on Fire Curtain regulations). The fire curtain is next released to determine if it is functioning properly. It should drop to the deck completely *sealing* the proscenium opening. If the fire curtain does **not** move, then the inspector will check for:

- Fire curtain release issues
- Release intentionally disabled
- Jammed fire line
- Too much counterweight on arbor

If the curtain only comes partially into the deck, or if it crashes hard into the floor, then the problem is most likely with the dashpot. It could need replacement or adjustment. Once these issues have been resolved, then the fire curtain is reset and the test is performed again to insure the curtain is working properly. If the fire curtain still fails to perform properly, then recommendations for more major repair considerations may be in order.

With the curtain in its lowered position, the face of the fabric is inspected for tears, wear, and other damages. While working on the floor, deceleration devises (like dashpots), manual release stations and re-settable thermal releases will be checked for functionality. The attachment points in the smoke pockets will also be examined for wear or damage. On the gridiron the inspection will continue by checking the function of all loft blocks, pulleys, over-balance bars (if any) and release lines. Cables and fusible links will be checked for wear and corrosion while release lines will be checked for wear and possible rot. The same tests are performed if the fire curtain is automated.

The Linesets

Once inspection of the fire curtain has been completed, examination of the linesets begins. Most rigging inspection companies will ask that you remove everything from battens that is reasonable to remove (mostly curtains, scenery, lights, etc.) Typically, large and heavy items, such as traveller curtains, steel frames movie screens and orchestra shells are not removed. Starting with the furthest downstage lineset, each batten is lowered to working height, or as close to the deck as possible. As the battens are lowered, each operating line (rope) and rope lock are checked for wear, tear and damage. In addition, the shoes on the tension pulley are examined for wear and proper operation. Lastly, the wooden crash bar is inspected for any indication of an arbor crash. While each batten is lowered, the arbor is checked for smooth operation. If the arbor does not move smoothly, it needs to be determined why. Grinding sounds or unusual noises may indicate a friction issue. Adjustments to the rope lock and tension block can be made at this time.

When the batten is "in", the following items are checked:

- Is the batten bent?
- Are there protective end-caps on the ends of the batten?
- Are the battens numbered?
- Are batten splices properly made?

- Are the trim chains properly sized and properly made?
- Are the nuts on the batten clamps tight?

In addition,
- The nuts on every cable clip is checked for tightness and every swaging sleeve is checked with a "go-no go" gauge
- Turnbuckles are checked for cotter pins, or mousing
- All attachment points of the electric raceway are checked including multi-cable attachment points
- If the batten has a traveller curtain on it, then the mechanics of the track are tested and visually inspected, as well as the curtain itself

If the batten cannot be brought to working height, a personnel lift may be needed to complete this inspection.

After the batten has been inspected, the batten is "gridded" and all parts of the arbor are inspected for damage, maintenance problems, or non-compliance to modern rigging standards. The guide system (J-Track) for each arbor is thoroughly inspected for alignment and every wall-mounting bracket is checked at its attachment point. Bolts securing the locking rail to the deck or walls of the theatre are also examined. This process is continued for every lineset.

The Grid
Moving up to the gridiron, the inspection continues with the loading bridge.
- Is there a kick plate to prevent counterweighs from being kicked/pulled off of the bridge?
- Are the counterweights spread evenly across the bridge or stacked in a single pile?
- Are the linesets numbered?
- Is a fall arrest harness necessary for technicians to safely load counterweight?
- Any signs of a runaway arbor?

On the gridiron itself, each of the head blocks, loft blocks and idlers are checked for alignment, placement and security. Starting downstage and working up, the fleet angles of each lift line is checked as it runs from the head blocks to each loft block. A technician on the deck will raise and lower each batten numerous times. Each lift line will be examined for wear and other issues. Noise or grinding might indicate a bad bearing or a friction/rubbing problem. If the theatre has sag bars, these will be checked for wear and alignment.

Smoke Doors
Finally, if the stage has smoke doors above the stage, each of the doors will be checked to insure that they open and close properly. Each of the cables and mechanisms of these doors are checked for operation. Also, if there is any spot-line rigging, it is also inspected at this time.

Inspecting automated systems and winches
Inspecting automated systems usually occurs with each lineset. The same inspection considerations must be taken for any lift line cables and batten attachments, but the automated battens do not necessarily have to be stripped prior to inspection. As each manual line set is run

in and out, the same can be done with any counterweight assisted winches, zero fleet winches or drum winches. The actual inspection of the winch motor components such as brakes, drums, bearings, pillow blocks, gear boxes and lubrication can occur separately or as each lineset is inspected. If the winch is hydraulic, the fluid levels are checked along with filters and hose connections. Controls are inspected for operation including emergency E stop functions. The same inspection criteria is done for any FOH electric chain hoists, including limit switch operation.

Typically, motorized drum hoists are the most widely used in theatrical applications. The drum is long enough to accommodate all of the lift lines required for a particular lineset. With helically grooved drums, the lift lines wrap neatly within the grooves in a single layer and prevent damage to the lift line cables. When inspecting the drum on any winch type, careful examination is made to any wear or fray on the cables.

Photos are helpful

Detailed photos of problematic areas help to clarify those areas that need specific attention. The following illustrations are excerpts from various rigging inspections. They show how rigging problems might be highlighted in an inspection report.

Example- Rigging Inspection 1

The curtain track on line set 2 is hung with two pieces of scenery chain. The large rings of the chain are inserted one through the other allowing one ring to slip through the other. It is recommended that this be *replaced immediately* with appropriately spaced batten clamps, turnbuckles and chain.

Two non-load bearing scenery chains connected to each other through the O rings. This is dangerous as the load could pull the O ring through the other. These must be replaced immediately.

Example – Rigging Inspection 2

Found attached to the SL Catwalk was a shackle rigged in the following manner (see Figure 8). Fortunately, this arrangement was supporting no load, but it was evident that it had supported a load in the past. Wire rope should never be rigged in this manner as it would cause an unsafe D:d ratio on the wire rope and the pin of the lower shackle could potentially rotate. Proper rigging would simply involve inserting the thimble directly into the pin of the upper shackle thereby removing the choke. It is recommended that the entire wire rope and shackles be *replaced and re-rigged.* It is also recommended that any new shackles be moused to remove any possibility of pin rotation.

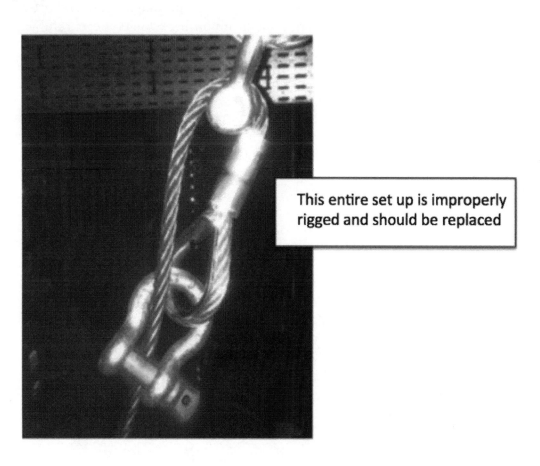

This entire set up is improperly rigged and should be replaced

Example - Rigging Inspection 3

Recent plumbing activities to the fire sprinkler system by outside contractors have left a great deal of "trash" around the grid area. These present an immediate danger and should be remedied before any further activity takes place on the stage below. Plywood pieces, used to support ladders, have been left scattered across the grid leaving the possibility of these pieces falling through to the stage below. The images below also shows a steel counterweight left out on the grid and dangerous plywood pieces as well as copper conduit pipe. This should be removed and returned to the loading platform immediately.

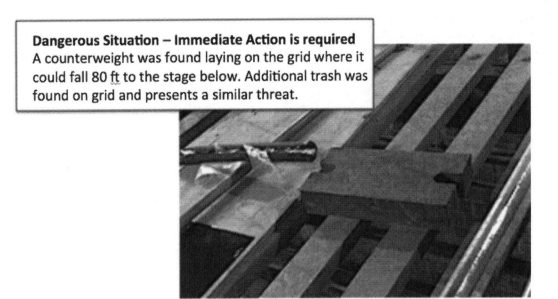

Dangerous Situation – Immediate Action is required
A counterweight was found laying on the grid where it could fall 80 ft to the stage below. Additional trash was found on grid and presents a similar threat.

Dangerous Situation- Immediate Action is required
Trash from apparent construction work was left on the grid. The copper conduit pipe along with plywood scraps can fall through the steel channel to the stage below.

Report Summary and Recommendations

The rigging inspection report should conclude by summarizing the finding from the body of the inspection along with recommendations. A typical inspection reports might summarize as follows:

Base on a careful examination, it is determined that the rigging system in the _____ theatre is in poor condition. Observations of dead hung batten positions show that these connections were made using either jack chain or non-load bearing hardware. It is recommended that these connections be replaced immediately and that no other equipment or curtains be hung on these pipes until corrective action is taken.

Additionally,

Recommendations made in this report are based on observations that could be viewed, and the assumption that other connections were made in a similar manner. As noted in this report, there are some rigging issues that should be dealt with immediately, and a several potential bigger issues that should be addressed as soon as possible. A structural engineer should be consulted in all matters of renovation and execution. Ideally, a theatre consultant, working in conjunction with a structural engineer, would best provide solutions to many of the problems presented in this report. They would also be able to best address the needs of the user to those of the performance space. The following is a summary of recommendations to the existing system.

Glossary of Terms

A Glossary of Terms should be included at the end of the report. This may seem trivial to most theatre technicians, but is helpful to explain terms to those not familiar with stage and rigging terminology. See Appendix 1.

References

Lastly, a reference section should be included at the end of the report. References may refer to OSHA, ANSI, NACM, or ASME standards or recommendations in case there are any questions that maybe raised by the report. It is best to head off any questions before they are raised.

Choosing a Rigging Inspecting Company

Selecting a rigging inspection company is not difficult. The best place to begin is with USITT or PLASA. Either organization will be able to help you find a reputable, certified rigging inspection firm in your area. The cost of a rigging inspection may vary depending upon the size and scope of your venue, but most rigging inspections run $800 to $1300. Hotel and travel expenses may also need to be considered. If your school is having financial difficulty with inspection costs, USITT has created a *Rigging Inspection Initiative* that can help defray inspection expenses for qualifying secondary schools. This *Rigging Safety Initiative* is made through a generous gift from Founding Sponsor J.R. Clancy, and allows secondary educational facilities to apply for a grant to be used towards a rigging system safety inspection in their performance spaces. Contact USITT to see if you qualify.

Once you have found a reputable company or companies, here are some pointers on what you should expect and what you should ask for.

1. *Ask for* a written formal proposal and quote. If the inspection is being summited for the purpose of bids, your school or organization's administration will require this anyway. This proposal should include costs and what the inspection will include. The list of included items was discussed earlier in this chapter. It should not just be limited to your theatre's rigging, but should also include beam ports positions, box booms, catwalks and any other area over the stage and audience.
2. *What you should expect* is a detailed, written evaluation of your venue's rigging and related overhead theatre spaces. It will advise you, make recommendations and prioritize

safety corrections and concerns that you will need to address. Remember, most rigging inspectors are NOT engineers; they are however, by OSHA definition, *qualified* persons.

3. *Ask* if the report will give you solutions to any of the problems discovered. Most do. *Ask* if they the solutions will include a quote for the cost of repair.

4. *Ask* how long the inspection will take and how long the report will be. Most inspections will take the good part of a morning for a small venue to several days for a large performing arts facility. Written reports may take a week up to several weeks.

5. Ask for examples of previous inspection reports as well as references. This will give you an example of what you can expect.

Remember, accidents don't just happen; they are caused by the series of events that led up to the failure. The best solution to preventing accidents is to not let the failure to happen in the first place. In this chapter, we examined how simple routine maintenance and inspections should be carried out on a monthly, weekly, and even daily basis. It doesn't have to cost you a fortune to *routinely* inspect your rigging systems, *but a failure will!* On-staff personnel can easily perform maintenance and inspection tasks by simply following the monthly inspection checklists outlined earlier in this chapter. We also stressed the importance of rigging inspections by certified theatre rigging professionals and how they can insure that your rigging systems remain in a safe and operational condition for years to come. After all, gravity IS our friend.

Chapter 18:
Fall Protection

Introduction

Falls can occur in any occupational setting. They can occur with such simple acts as walking up or down stairs, to walking out on I-beams in an arena, to focusing lights from an A-frame ladder. In 2013, the Bureau of Labor Statistics reported that 828 fatalities occurred in in the construction industry. Of these, 302 resulted from falls making this the leading cause of death in the industry. Sadly, these statistics have remained fairly constant over the last several years, fluctuating only by a few percentage points.

In this chapter, we will discuss fall prevention, the ability to recognize fall hazards, the requirements of fall protection, and differences between fall restraint and fall arrest. In addition, we will examine PFAS (or Personal Fall Arrest System) equipment, rescue plans, and the process for creating a safe working environment. It will be important to remember as we go through this chapter, that no, one, single, fall scenario or situation is ever the same. Every fall situation is going to be different and will require its own Fall Protection Plan. Let us first begin by examining what happens during a fall.

The Anatomy of a Fall
A fall begins usually with a loss of balance is followed by a misplaced center of gravity. Loss of balance begins when there is an interruption to otherwise steady and controlled movement. Misplaced center of gravity happens when there is an internal loss of bearings. As soon as we experience a loss in balance, our brain tries to compensate by redirecting the body's center of gravity. If the brain is successful, then normal activity resumes. If it is not, then the brain goes into immediate "damage control" by assessing the situation to minimalize the impending damage to follow. Most people think that they can react to the initial stages of falling by immediately reacting as soon as a "loss of balance" is experienced.

Guess Again!
It takes a person about 1/3rd of a second for a person to become aware that they are falling and another 1/3rd of a second to react to the fall. In that 1/3rd of a second, the body has already free fallen 18 inches. In 2/3rd of a second approximately 7 feet of free fall has occurred. In 8/10th of a

second, the brain is now able to respond to the fall, but the body has now travelled approximately 10 feet.

Forces

A 215-pound worker falling 6 feet can generate a fall force of as much as 2,795 pounds on the body. At 10 feet, these forces can be as high as 4,515 pounds. Without a proper deceleration harness, these forces can cause serious injury and even death. With proper fall protection, these forces at 10 feet are reduced to 829 pounds[1]. This why OSHA limits the forces on the body to no more than 1,800 pounds with an arresting harness and a free fall distance to no more than 6 feet. The diagram below illustrates the distances that would be experience during and after a fall.

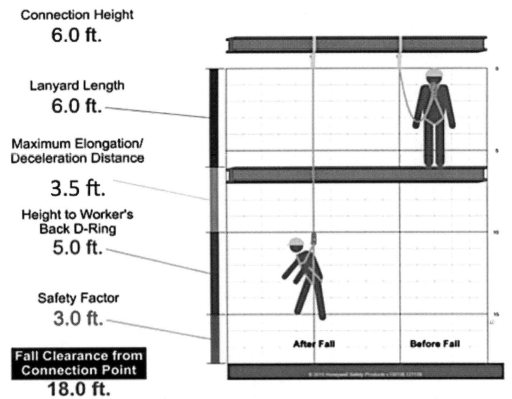

Note that the anchor point is 6 feet above the worker. The length of the lanyard is 6 feet. OSHA allows for only 6 feet of free fall, so it is best to keep the anchor point as high as possible[2]. If a worker were to fall, then the he would only fall the length of the arresting lanyard plus an additional 3.5 feet, which is the maximum deployment of the shock absorber. Add in the average height of the worker 6 feet plus a 3 feet safety factor that accounts for any elongation of the system, then the distance from the anchor point that accounts for any elongation of the system, then the distance from anchor point can be as much as 18 feet. This is why it is very important to make sure of your distance from the anchor point to the ground as well as any obstructions in between. A fall arresting system is useless if you hit the ground or any obstruction somewhere within that 18 feet. Suspension trauma and fall arrest solutions to this problem will be explored later in this chapter.

1 The formula for shock loads is Force = Weight x ((Free Fall Dist. / Stopping Dist.)+1)
2 In the entertainment industry, this anchor point may be only waist high, as we will see with Horizontal Life Lines.

Fall Protection (fall arrest and fall restraint) begins with Fall Prevention

Fall Protection begins with Fall Prevention. The working environment cannot be deemed safe unless fall protection is incorporated into every aspect of the work place. Prevention begins with planning and planning begins with an analysis of all the potential fall hazards that can place workers at risk. Once these hazards have been identified, then a Fall Prevention Plan can be put into effect.

The important thing to remember is, don't feel overwhelmed about creating a Fall Prevention Plan. There are plenty of resources available to assist and on-line templates are available. OSHA (The Occupational Safety and Health Administration) and CCOHA (Canadian Centre for Occupational Health and Safety) are two such resources. ANSI (American National Standards Institute) publishes standards relating directly to the entertainment industry. In addition, Fall Prevention classes can also be found through such organizations as PLASA and USITT. They can be contacted directly for additional information and class schedules. Information is also available at the end of this chapter.

A plan should include, but is not limited to:
- The identification of potential fall hazards
- What type of fall protection is required for the specific job?
  - Hand railings or guard rails
  - Fall Restraint
  - Fall Arrest
  - others
- The training of employees on recognition of safety hazards associated with the working environment
- The training of employees on the safe use of fall protection equipment
- What to do in the case of an emergency. The Emergency Action Plan

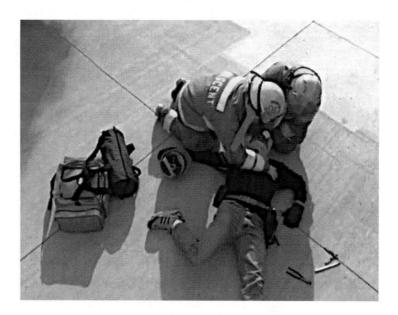

An Emergency Action Plan is an important part of Fall Prevention
– photo courtesy of Miller-Honeywell

Fall Protection is the end result of Fall Prevention

Essentially, *Fall Protection* is a system that will prevent a person from falling to a lower level. It is a series of steps taken to control or eliminate the possibility of an accidental fall. It can be as simple as placing handrails along stairs, or a railing along the edge of a platform. At times, however, hand railings or guardrails are not enough and workers need to access areas that are extremely close to fall areas. In these cases, more protective equipment is required. A "leash" or tether worn with a Body Belt is one means of providing protection. It allows a worker to approach a fall area, but will not allow the worker to fall to a lower level. This is known as *Work Positioning* or *Fall Restraint*. *Fall Arrest*, on the other hand, is a system that will "arrest" a person in mid-fall and prevents them from serious injury or death. A full Body Harness worn with a shock-absorbing lanyard is one such method; another is Body Harness worn with the Self-Retracting Life Line (or SRL). In any case, *Fall Restraint* and *Fall Arrest* are the end products of a comprehensive Fall Prevention Plan.

The Requirements for Fall Protection – Understanding the Regulations

The Entertainment Industry is considered to be general industry and is covered under OSHA regulations 29 CRF, 1910 and 1926. OSHA regulations are not specific to the entertainment industry like ANSI recommendations. You may have noted the use of the words "regulation" vs. "recommendation." The difference between ANSI and OSHA is that ANSI recommendations are created by specific industries (such as the Entertainment Industry) and are considered to be "self-regulatory." ANSI recommendations are simply that - recommendations. OSHA regulations, on the other hand, are "law" and enforceable. Whereas ANSI recommendations may not be enforceable like OSHA's, failure to abide by ANSI recommendations have resulted is stiff penalties and fines in court.

Paraphrasing the regulations

Here are some key points that are paraphrased for convenience. Please consult the OSHA website listed in the back of this chapter for the exact phrasing.

1. *Fall Protection* must be provided when workers are at:
   - 4 feet – general industry
   - 6 feet – construction
2. *The Fall Arrest* system must -
   - limit the maximum force on a person to 1,800 (8 kN) pounds when used with a body harness.
   - be rigged so that an employee cannot free fall more than 6 feet.
   - bring an employee to a complete stop and limit the employee's maximum deceleration distance to 3.5 feet.
   - utilize an *Anchorage Point* for attachment of a *Personal Fall Arrest System* (PFAS). The Anchorage Point must be capable of supporting at least 5,000 pounds (22.2 kN) per person attached. It also must be independent of supporting any other structure or equipment.

3. The *Fall Restraint* system
   - must limit the maximum force on a person to 900 pounds (4 kN) when used with a Body Belt.
   - allows for the use of Body Belts as part of a Fall Restraint system. They are not acceptable for use as a Fall Arrest system.
4. Training
   - Before fall equipment is used, employees must be trained in the safe use of the equipment and the PFAS.
5. Workplace safety
   - The Employer is responsible for safety in the work place. They are also responsible for providing the necessary equipment and training to keep employees safe.
6. Competent Person
   - An OSHA "competent person" is defined as "one who is capable of identifying existing and predictable hazards in the surroundings or working conditions which are unsanitary, hazardous, or dangerous to employees, and who has authorization to take prompt corrective measures to eliminate them".
7. Qualified Person
   - A qualified person is one who, by possession of a recognized degree, certificate, or professional standing, or who by extensive knowledge, training and experience, has successfully demonstrated his ability to solve or resolve problems relating to the subject matter, the work, or the project.

Knowing the ABCs of fall protection

Knowing your ABCs is an easy way to remember the parts of a fall arrest system.
These consist of:
- The Anchor Point
- The Body Harness
- The Connecting Device

A- Anchor Point

There are many different types of anchorage points- all vary on the needs of that particular industry. The types of anchorage points discussed in this chapter will relate specifically to the entertainment industry. Essentially, an anchorage point is a means of attachment for a *Personal Fall Arrest System*- specifically, the connecting device. The Fall Arrest Anchorage Point must be capable of supporting at least 5,000 pounds (22.2 kN) per attached worker. If two workers are to be connected, then the load capacity of the anchorage point must be doubled. The anchorage point must also be independent of supporting any other structure or equipment. The Fall Restraint Anchor point must support at least 1,000 lb. per employee attached.

Permanent Anchorages

The first type of permanent anchorage points are Horizontal Life-Lines or HLL often found rigged on arena I-beams. Riggers working at height on the I-Beams will be attached to permanently installed HLL. This type of lifeline allows the worker to easily move horizontally across the beams.

Riggers attach a steel basket around an I-beam. Note their shock-absorbing lanyard is connected to a horizontal lifeline overhead similar to the one shown below.
– *Photo courtesy of Ben Kilmer*

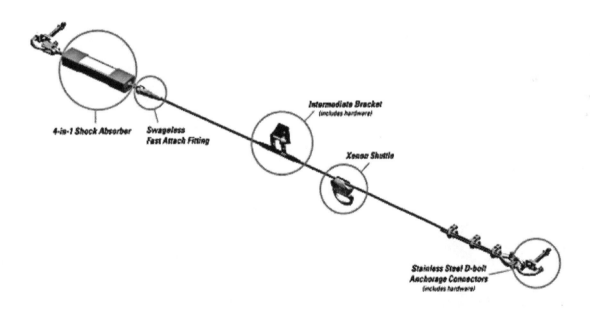

4-in-1 Shock Absorber Swageless Fast Attach Fitting

Intermediate Bracket
(includes hardware)

Xenon Shuttle

Stainless Steel D-bolt
Anchorage Connectors
(includes hardware)

This illustration shows an HLL that in intended for permanent installation.
– *Photo courtesy of Miller-Honeywell*

Other permanent anchorage points are fixed such as the one shown to the below left. However, as you can see, it does not allow the worker as much horizontal mobility as does the permanent HLL. The anchorage point to the right allows for greater flexibility of movement.

This photo shows a permanently mounted D-ring attachment bolted to the bottom flange of an I-beam.

– photo courtesy of Miller-Honeywell

The beam trolley allows for an anchorage point to be made where more flexibility of movement is required.

–photo courtesy of Sapsis Rigging Inc.

Temporary Anchorages

Other types of anchorage points are those that are temporary. Beam clamps allow for an attachment point to be made directly to an I-beam. They are flexible enough to allow an anchorage point to be made wherever one is needed. Unfortunately, they also do not allow for a great deal of horizontal movement.

A Beam Clamp attachment point. Note the worker's connecting device runs from the dorsal ring of his harness to the anchorage point.

–photo courtesy of Miller-Honeywell

The Double Ring Tie-off Strap is a simple strap that can be choked around an I-beam providing a similar anchorage point.

–photo courtesy of Miller-Honeywell

292

The Guardian Beamer 2000 and 3000 are lightweight and adjustable anchor points that can move along with the rigger. Many riggers use these as anchor point while installing permanent anchorages and life lines as they are quick to attach to the flange of the beam.

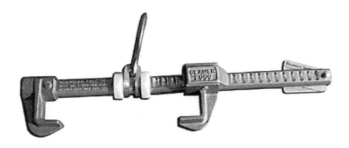

The Beamer 2000, a lightweight, adjustable and portable anchor point.

-photo courtesy of Guardian

At times riggers will need to access truss while it is trimmed to its final height.
Follow spot operators too will need to climb into their follow spot chairs from wire rope ladders suspended from the truss to the floor. Once up, they must walk along the truss cords to their spot positions. Horizontal Life Lines provide the necessary anchorage points. Similar to the permanent Horizontal Life Line, portable HLLs run along the truss from end to end. Pear rings at the chain hoist hook support the life line as it runs down to connect at a strap at the truss ends.[3] They are rated for one or two persons. Please note that all horizontal life line connectors must be have a legible tag stating that the product meets ANSI Z359.1-2007 standards for Personal Fall Protection Systems. If the tag is missing or illegible, don't use it!

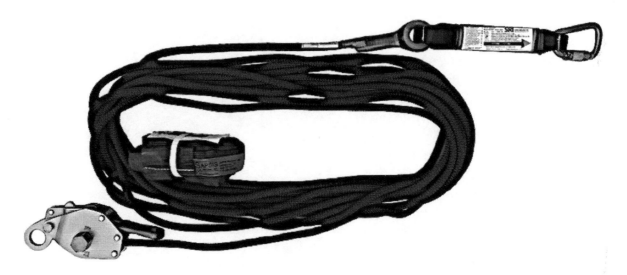

The ProPlus Temporary Horizontal Life Line system is ideal for touring shows and venues where the truss location changes from show to show. It is designed to be used by 1 or 2 technicians at a time.

–photo courtesy of Sapsis Rigging, Inc.

[3]See the new ANSI E1.39 – 2015 standard regarding the Selection and Use of Personal Fall Arrest Systems on Portable Structures Used in the Entertainment Industry

The *Self Retractable Life Line* or SRL is viable alternative to the shock-absorbing lanyard. It is generally used when working on ladders, truss, truss towers or when the fall distance is less than 18 feet. The worker connects his harness directly to the life line. Any sudden vertical fall force will activate the SRL mechanism within 6" and decelerate the worker to within 2 feet, locking- similar to that of a seat belt engaging. While a 6-foot shock-absorbing lanyard will allow for six feet of free-fall clearance, the SRL limits free falls to 2 feet. With this shorter distance, the *Self-Retracting Lifeline* can be used with a much shorter distance to the ground. A word of caution! Always know the equipment you are working with. Always read the accompanying manuals. The big danger with SRLs is the possibility of "swing falls," that is, walking horizontally out on a beam or truss, falling, then swinging horizontally into an obstruction. In addition, the WLL of most SRLs is 310 pounds, (this includes all clothing, tools and gear). Check the label for WLL information. Again, just like Horizontal Life Lines, all Self Retracting Life Lines MUST have a tag or legible label stating that the product meets ANSI Z359.1-2007 standards for Personal Fall Protection Systems. If it doesn't have a legible tag, don't use it!

-photo courtesy of Sapsis Rigging, Inc.

Fall protection is required for vertical ladders without cages over 24 feet. The Climbing Safety Sleeve is designed to be use in this situation. The worker can ascend or descend the ladder while the sleeve simply slides along the pre-rigged rope. If a slip or fall occurs, a locking mechanism engages limiting the fall to a few inches and reducing the possibility of serious injury. Whereas, no fall protection is necessary for portable ladders, the worker must maintain three points of contact with the ladder at all times.

- photo courtesy of Sapsis Rigging, Inc.

B- Body Harness and Body Belt

Both the Body Harness and the Body Belt are acceptable means of fall protection, but remember, the two are NOT interchangeable. The *Body Harness* is worn as part of a *Fall Arrest System*, whereas the *Body Belt* is only worn for *Fall Restraint* or positioning. According to OSHA, the maximum forces on a person wearing a Body Harness are limited to 1,800 (8 kN) pounds. The maximum forces on a person wearing a Body Belt are 900 pounds (4 kN).

The full Body Harness. Note the Dorsal Ring at the top of the back.
–photo courtesy of Miller-Honeywell

The Full Body Harness consists shoulder straps, straps that wrap between the legs and a Dorsal Ring attachment point. It is usually secured at the chest or waist by interlocking buckles. The Dorsal Ring attachment point should rest squarely between the shoulder blades. Harnesses must be sized for the worker and be snug, not tight to the body. In addition, workers wearing a Full Body Harness must weigh more than 130 pounds. and less than 300 pounds (310 is the limit with tools). Inspection needs to be performed before each use and annually by a competent person. They should never be modified. In the event of a fall, they should be taken out of service immediately and destroyed. When inspecting a harness before use, begin with the belts and the rings. Bend the straps in a U shape, checking for worn or frayed edges, pulled or broken stitching, cuts and chemical damage to the webbing. Check the Dorsal Ring for any distortion or wear to the metal. Check the padding for wear or break through from sharp objects. Examine carefully the buckles and rivets for any distortion and wear. Remember, this is your life you are protecting. Don't take chances. If you find any wear or suspected damage to the harness, don't wear it. Take it to a competent person for further examination and inspection.

Body belts come in single or double D-ring and are used for Fall Restraint and Positioning only. They basically, put the worker on a short leash allowing freedom of the hands for work. If a person can fall over the edge, then a PFAS must be used. Body Belts are not to be used as a Fall Arrest Harness. A person who uses a body belt as a personal fall arrest system is exposing himself to such hazards such as falling out of the belt and serious internal injuries. Inspection and maintenance of the body belt is the same as noted for the Fall Arrest Harness- inspection before each use and yearly inspection by a competent person.

–photo courtesy of Miller-Honeywell

C- Connecting Devise

A connecting devise is a lanyard or leash usually made up of rope, wire rope, or strap that connects the harnessed worker to a deceleration device, lifeline, or anchor point. In the case of Body Belts, this can be as simple as a rope or adjustable strap. With a Personal Fall Arrest System, a deceleration device will be needed. The most common type of deceleration device used in the entertainment industry is the "rip-stitch" lanyard and the Self Retracting Lifeline. Both serve to dissipate the tremendous energy of a fall arrest and limit the energy imposed on a worker during a fall arrest.

Visual inspection should be performed before each use. Examine the lanyard from one end to the other, slowly rotating the lanyard while inspecting for chaffing, worn or frayed edges. Special attention needs to be at the splice or stitched ends and the shock-absorbing pack. Do not open the pack- simply inspect for wearing or tears. Examine the area where the pack is sewn to the D-Ring. Hardware should be checked for bent or twisted jaws. Have a competent person inspect the lanyard once a year.

Suspension Trauma

Suspension trauma or orthostatic hypotension (shock) is an effect, which occurs when the human body is held in vertical suspension due to the force of gravity and a lack of movement. The effects can begin in as little as 2 or 3 minutes. Venous pooling occurs in the legs due to gravity and can quickly lead to unconsciousness and even death. It is crucial that a rescue begin immediately! No one should ever use a PFAS without an Emergency Action Plan in place. If you do not have a plan, do not put yourself at risk.

The Emergency Action Plan

The Emergency Action Plan is exactly what it says it is; a plan that can be acted on when a person has fallen from height. OSHA requires that employers provide the "prompt rescue of employees in the event of a fall or shall assure that employees are able to rescue themselves." The following are considerations are necessary to any EAP:

- Insure that workers are able to rescue themselves or, if not, have available the equipment necessary to rescue suspended workers immediately.
- Train workers in the effects of suspension trauma. If they have fallen, they should be taught to pump their legs to avoid the effects of venous pooling
- Realized that suspended workers are in danger of the effects of suspension trauma within minutes and that these effects are life threatening
- Have immediate access to rescue equipment in the vicinity of the job site so that the EAP can be put into effect
- Train all workers in the use of fall rescue equipment

The first reaction to any fall is to call 911 and, in the case of a fall, it is important to do so. However, the EMS does not have the equipment necessary to rescue workers at height. Their response would be to call the fire department. It may take as long as 20 or 30 minutes for the EMS and a fire department squad to arrive on site, and an additional 10 minutes for them to get the necessary equipment in place to begin the rescue- by then, the fallen worker maybe dead. In addition, workers in the entertainment industry are at heights that maybe beyond the limits of fire department rescue equipment, so a rescue from the ground maybe next to impossible. This is why it is so important for a rescue plan to be in place so that rescue can begin immediately.

Once the worker is rescued, it is important to maintain the ABCs - Airway, Breathing, and Circulation and lay the person in a reclined position. However, there is growing controversy over a condition known as "reflow syndrome" in suspension trauma victims. According to the Journal of Emergency Medical Services[4], placing a victim in a supine position allows venous blood to rush to the heart and cause "reflow syndrome." "Venous blood that has pooled in the legs suddenly reaches the heart with immediate ventricular fibrillation, rupture and infarct of the heart, and lethal damage to the liver, kidneys and brain." They maintain that the injured worker needs to be kept in a semi-reclining position (usually a 30 degree recline) and monitored for the effects of suspension trauma. Do not loosen the harness around the legs as this may aggravate the "reflow" condition. If the worker is unconscious, then be sure to keep air passages open. Lastly, make sure the worker is fully evaluated by an Emergency Medical Professional.

---

[4]The Journal of Emergency Medical Services http://www.jems.com/articles/print/volume-34/issue-8/patient-care/dangerous-suspension-understan.html

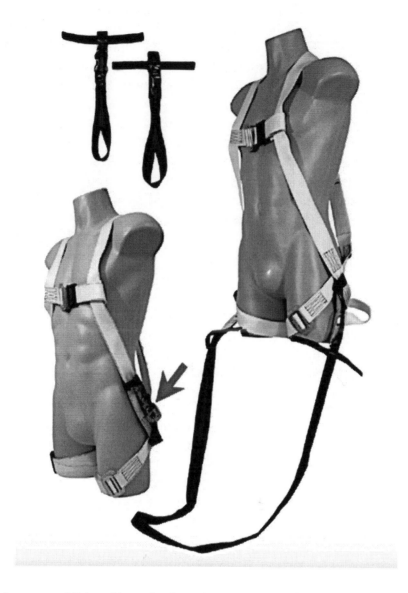

Suspension straps help to reestablish and keep the flow of blood in the legs while suspended. In the event of a fall, the worker can release the straps and step into a loop thus relieving constriction on the legs.

-photo courtesy of Sapsis Rigging, Inc.

The Pro-Plus Rescue System. *-photo courtesy of Sapsis Rigging, Inc.*

Aerial Work Platforms

In addition to climbing I-beams and scaffold, arena workers also must access rigging points from otherwise inaccessible positions. This is where the Scissor Lift and the Articulating Aerial Boom Lift come in handy. A personal fall arrest system (PFAS) is required whenever you are working in an Articulating and/or telescoping boom and bucket truck. They are not required for scissor lifts as the bucket is enclosed and only moves in a vertical position. When operating any aerial work platform, consult the operator's manual for any and all safety requirements. As of January 1, 1998, OSHA's fall protection rule requires the use of a full body harness for fall arrest in place of a body belt when working from an aerial work platform. Manufacturers also require that operators must wear a full body harness and lanyard that is attached to the designated anchorage point when using an articulating boom or bucket.

Some OSHA highlights regarding aerial lifts are:
- Tying off to an adjacent pole, structure, or equipment while working from an aerial lift shall **not** be permitted.
- Employees shall always stand firmly on the floor of the basket, and shall not sit or climb

on the edge of the basket or use planks, ladders, or other devices for a work position.

- A full body harness shall be worn and a lanyard attached to an anchor point on the boom or in the basket when working from an aerial lift.
- The brakes shall be set and when outriggers are used, they shall be positioned on pads or a solid surface. Wheel chocks shall be installed before using an aerial lift on an incline provided they can be safely installed.
- An aerial lift truck shall not be moved when the boom is elevated in a working position with men in the basket, except for equipment, which is specifically designed for this type of operation.

The important thing to remember in all of this is: OSHA requires the use of full body harnesses as fall protection on all aerial and articulating booms. Even though the basket of an articulating boom is enclosed, the arm is subject to extreme fluctuations of movement when moving over regular and irregular surfaces. The potential exists to catapult the worker from the basket, flailing him to and fro. Wearing a Fall Arrest Harness with a 6-foot. Arresting Lanyard could be disastrous should the worker be ejected from the basket. For the same reason, moving an articulating boom truck while the arm is articulated is against OSHA regulations and manufactures guidelines. Always be alert to potential fall hazards when operating an aerial lift.

Summary

Remember these important key points:
- Fall Protection begins with Fall Prevention. The working environment cannot be deemed safe unless fall protection is incorporated into every aspect of the work place. Prevention begins with planning and planning begins with an analysis of all the potential fall hazards that can place workers at risk. Once these hazards have been identified, then a Fall Prevention Plan can be put into effect.
- A plan should include but is not limited to:
  - The identification of potential fall hazards
  - What type of fall protection is required for the specific job
  - Hand railings or guard rails
  - Fall Restraint
  - Fall Arrest
  - The training of employees on recognition of safety hazards associated with the working environment
  - The training of employees on the safe use of fall protection equipment
  - What to do in the case of an emergency
  - The Emergency Action Plan

Chapter 19:
Ladders and Lifts

Introduction

Working at heights is a necessary in most theatres. Whether you are hanging lights, painting, doing carpentry work and rigging, at some point you will need to work of a ladder or lift. Because working at heights puts you in greater danger of being injured, it is important know how to use these tools safety. This is the purpose of this chapter.

In the first section of this chapter, we will discuss the many different types of portable ladders and rules for using them safely. Since scaffolding is commonly used in many theatres for working at heights, the second section will look at these tools. Finally, the third section, we will look at several types of aerial lifts.

Portable Ladders

Ladder safety is critical. More than 160,000 people are injured, with more than 300 deaths, each year due to unsafe use of ladders.

There are many factors that must be taken into consideration when choosing a portable ladder. The first is the environment.

Portable ladders are made from one of three basic materials: wood, fiberglass or metal (aluminum). Fiberglass ladders are the best choice if you are working around electricity, since fiberglass does not conduct electricity. If you are not working around electricity, then an aluminum ladder might be the best choice, since aluminum is the lightest material, making them the easiest to move. Wooden ladders are the least expensive.

The next consideration is the Duty Rating of the ladder. This rating indicates the maximum load that the ladder is designed to hold (your weight plus and tools or supplies that will be supported by the ladder). Below is a table showing the five categories of duty ratings.

Type	Capacity
IAA (Special Duty)	375 pounds
IA (Extra Heavy Duty)	300 pounds
I (Heavy Duty)	250 pounds
II (Medium Duty)	225 pounds
III (Light Duty)	200 pounds

Note: The height of the ladder is <u>not</u> a factor in determining its load capacity.

All ladders should be inspected before use to ensure that they are not damaged and that the rungs and rails are free of dirt or slippery substances. NEVER use a ladder that is damaged. All ladders, except wooden ladders, have rubber shoes that must be fully in contact with the floor. Also, most ladders are designed to only hold a single person. Never put two people on a ladder unless the ladder was specifically design to hold two people.

Falls from portable ladders are one of the leading causes of occupational fatalities and injuries; and over-reaching is the leading cause of ladder accidents. Below are some general rules for ladder use:

- Read and follow all labels/markings on the ladder.
- Avoid electrical hazards! – Look for overhead power lines before handling a ladder. Avoid using a metal ladder near power lines or exposed energized electrical equipment.
- Always inspect the ladder prior to using it. If the ladder is damaged, it must be removed from service and tagged until repaired or discarded.
- Always maintain a 3-point (two hands and a foot, or two feet and a hand) contact on the ladder when climbing. Keep your body near the middle of the step and always face the ladder while climbing (see diagram).
- Only use ladders and appropriate accessories (ladder levelers, jacks or hooks) for their designed purposes.
- Wear clean slip-resistant shoes when climbing or working on a ladder.
- Ladders must be free of any slippery material on the rungs, steps or feet.
- Do not use a self-supporting ladder (e.g., step ladder) as a single ladder or in a partially closed position.
- Do not use ladder if you are tired, dizzy or prone to losing your balance.
- Do not use ladders in high winds or storms.
- Only one person at a time is permitted on a ladder unless the ladder is specifically designed for more than one climber (such as a Trestle Ladder).
- Ladders must not be placed in front of closed doors that can open toward the ladder. The door must be blocked open, locked, or guarded.
- Do not use the top step/rung of a ladder as a step/rung unless it was designed for that purpose.
- Use a ladder only on a stable and level surface, unless it has been secured (top or bottom) to prevent displacement.

- Do not place a ladder on boxes, barrels or other unstable bases to obtain additional height.
- Do not move or shift a ladder while a person or equipment is on the ladder.
- An extension or straight ladder used to access an elevated surface must extend at least 3 feet above the point of support. Do not stand on the three top rungs of a straight, single or extension ladder.
- The proper angle for setting up a ladder is to place its base a quarter of the working length of the ladder from the wall or other vertical surface (see diagram).
- A ladder placed in any location where it can be displaced by other work activities must be secured to prevent displacement or a barricade must be erected to keep traffic away from the ladder.
- Be sure that all locks on an extension ladder are properly engaged.
- Do not exceed the maximum load rating of a ladder. Be aware of the ladder's load rating and of the weight it is supporting, including the weight of any tools or equipment.
- Do not use a ladder that is too tall or too short for your needs.

Ladder Varieties
There are numerous varieties of portable ladders: single ladders, extension ladders, step ladder, trestle ladders and articulated ladders.

Single (straight) and extension ladders are intended to be leaned against a wall of other sturdy support. One of the biggest mistakes made, when using these types of ladders, is not having the ladder at the proper angle. The feet of the ladder should be one foot away from the wall, for every four feet of height (where the ladder makes contact with the wall), approximately 75 degrees. If these ladders are used to provide access to a platform above the floor, the top of the ladder should extend three feet beyond the platform height, but the platform height (where the ladder makes contact) is used for calculating the distance that the feet are away from the platform.

Single Ladder   Extension Ladder

Step and trestle ladders are probably the most common types of ladders found in theatres. These ladders are intended to be be freestanding and should not be leaned against a wall for support. They should only be used on level surfaces that are free of clutter. All four feet of the ladder should sit on the ground. Never step on the top step or top cap of a step ladder, and do not sit on or straddle the top cap.

When a step ladder is carrier by one person, the front end should be slightly higher than the back end.

Step Ladder   Trestle Ladder

IMPORTANT: Many theatres build ladder dollies on which they mount trestle ladders. This allows them to quickly roll the ladder to locations and greatly reduces the time to do certain tasks, like focusing light. These dollies are a violation of OSHA standards and have resulted in serious injuries and death. DO NOT PUT A LADDER ON WHEELS UNLESS THEY ARE DESIGNED BY THE LADDER'S MANUFACTURER.

Ladder on Dolly

If you need a rolling ladder, some manufactures make casters for some step ladders. These casters are typically spring-loaded so that the position of the ladder automatically "locks" when a person steps onto the ladder.

Another option is mobile ladders. These fixed height ladders made of steel, aluminum or fiberglass. These ladders may be made of either aluminum or fiberglass. They have locking systems to hold the ladder in place when a person is on them. Unlike regular step ladders, these ladders only require the user to have two points of contact with the ladder, making it possible for the user to work with both hands while on the ladder. Also, many of these ladders also permit the user to face away from the ladder when descending, making descending much faster.

Mobile Ladder

Articulated ladders has locking hinges that allow it to set up in multiple configurations. These hinges need to be kept lubricated and inspected before each use to insure that they are working properly.

Articulated Ladder

The American Ladder Institute's offers an online Ladder Safety Training program (http://www.laddersafetytraining.org). This site allows safety supervisor to track the training and completion of modules by workers/trainees. This is a tremendous resource for ladder safety training and contain much more information on ladder safety that what is in this chapter.

Scaffolding

Scaffolding is occasionally used in theatres to create work platforms for stagehands, including riggers, to work, to support equipment or both. There are many different types of scaffold, and this chapter will not not discuss them specifically. Also, aerial lifts, discussed in the next section of this chapter, are also considered work platforms and therefore will be mentioned in regard to specific OSHA standards discussed below.

OSHA's brochure *A Guide to Scaffold Use in the Construction Industry* discusses OSHA requirements for the use of scaffolding by using them to answer key questions that a user might have about their use. Below are excerpts from this document that apply most to the use of scaffolding in a theatre.

What are the highlights of the scaffolding standard?

• Fall protection or fall arrest systems—Each employee more than 10 feet above a lower level shall be protected from falls by guardrails or a fall arrest system, except those on single-point and two-point adjustable suspension scaffolds. Each employee on a single-point and two-point adjustable suspended scaffold shall be protected by both a personal fall arrest system and a guardrail. 1926.451(g)(1)

• Guardrail height—The height of the toprail for scaffolds manufactured and placed in service after January 1, 2000 must be between 38 inches (0.9 meters) and 45 inches (1.2 meters). 1926.451(g)(4)(ii)

• Crossbracing—When the crosspoint of crossbracing is used as a toprail, it must be between 38 inches (0.97 m) and 48 inches (1.3 meters) above the work platform. 1926.451(g)(4)(xv)

• Midrails— Midrails must be installed approximately halfway between the toprail and the platform surface. When a crosspoint of crossbracing is used as a midrail, it must be between 20 inches (0.5 meters) and 30 inches (0.8 m) above the work platform. 1926.451(g)(4)

• Footings—Support scaffold footings shall be level and capable of supporting the loaded scaffold. The legs, poles, frames, and uprights shall bear on base plates and mud sills. 1926.451(c)(2)

• Platforms—Supported scaffold platforms shall be fully planked or decked. 1926.451(b)

• Guying ties, and braces—Supported scaffolds with a height-to-base of more than 4:1 shall be restrained from tipping by guying, tying, bracing, or the equivalent. 1926.451(c)(1)

• Capacity—Scaffolds and scaffold components must support at least 4 times the maximum intended load. Suspension scaffold rigging must at least 6 times the intended load. 1926.451(a)(1) and (3)

• Training—Employers must train each employee who works on a scaffold on the hazards and the procedures to control the hazards. 1926.454

• Inspections—Before each work shift and after any occurrence that could affect the structural integrity, a competent person must inspect the scaffold and scaffold components for visible defects. 1926.451(f)(3)

• Erecting and Dismantling—When erecting and dismantling supported scaffolds, a competent person must determine the feasibility of providing a safe means of access and fall protection for these operations. 1926.451(e)(9) & (g)(2)

When is a competent person required for scaffolding?

OSHA's scaffolding standard defines a competent person as "one who is capable of identifying existing and predictable hazards in the surroundings or working conditions, which are unsanitary, hazardous to employees, and who has authorization to take prompt corrective measures to eliminate them."

The standard requires a competent person to perform the following duties under these circumstances:

• In General:
- To select and direct employees who erect, dismantle, move, or alter scaffolds. 1926.451(f)(7)
- To determine if it is safe for employees to work on or from a scaffold during storms or high winds and to ensure that a personal fall arrest system or wind screens protect these employees. (Note: Windscreens should not be used unless the scaffold is secured against the anticipated wind forces imposed.) 1926.451(f)(12)

• For Training:
- To train employees involved in erecting, disassembling, moving, operating, repairing, maintaining, or inspecting scaffolds to recognize associated work hazards. 1926.454(b)

• For Inspections:
- To inspect scaffolds and scaffold components for visible defects before each work shift and after any occurrence which could affect the structural integrity and to authorize prompt corrective actions. 1926.451(f)(3)
- To inspect ropes on suspended scaffolds prior to each workshift and after every occurrence which could affect the structural integrity and to authorize prompt corrective actions. 1926.451(d)(10)
- To inspect manila or plastic (or other synthetic) rope being used for toprails or midrails. 1926.451(g)(4)(xiv)

- For Suspension Scaffolds:
    - -To evaluate direct connections to support the load. 1926.451 (d)(3)(i)
    - -To evaluate the need to secure two-point and multi-point scaffolds to prevent swaying. 1926.451(d)(18)

- For Erectors and Dismantlers:
    - - To determine the feasibility and safety of providing fall protection and access. 1926.451(e)(9) and 1926.451(g)(2)
    - - To train erectors and dismantlers (effective September 2, 1997) to recognize associated work hazards. 1926.454(b)

- For Scaffold Components:
    - - To determine if a scaffold will be structurally sound when intermixing components from different manufacturers. 1926.451(b)(10)
    - - To determine if galvanic action has affected the capacity when using components of dissimilar metals. 1926.451(b)(11)

When is a qualified person required for scaffolding?

The standard defines a qualified person as "one who—by possession of a recognized degree, certificate, or professional standing, or who by extensive knowledge, training, and experience— has successfully demonstrated his/her ability to solve or resolve problems related to the subject matter, the work, or the project."

The qualified person must perform the following duties in these circumstances:

- In General:
    - - To design and load scaffolds in accordance with that design. 1926.451(a)(6)

- For Training:
    - - To train employees working on the scaffolds to recognize the associated hazards and understand procedures to control or minimize those hazards. 1926.454(a)

- For Suspension Scaffolds:
    - - To design the rigging for single-point adjustable suspension scaffolds. 1926.452(o)(2)(i)

    - - To design platforms on two-point adjustable suspension types that are less than 36 inches (0.9 m) wide to prevent instability. 1926.452(p)(1)
    - -To make swaged attachments or spliced eyes on wire suspension ropes. 1926.451(d)(11)

- For Components and Design:
    - - To design scaffold components construction in accordance with the design. 1926.451(a)(6)

What other standards apply to scaffolds?

29 CFR contains other standards that apply to construction work such as the responsibility to initiate and maintain programs (1926.29(b)(1)); exposures to dusts and chemicals (1926.33, .55, .59, .62, and.1101); hand and power tools (1926.300 - .307); electrical (1926.300 - .449); personal fall arrest systems (1926.502); and ladders (1926.1050 - .1060).

Are there requirements for work on platforms cluttered with debris?

The standard prohibits work on platforms cluttered with debris. 1926.451(f)(13)

How wide does the work area need to be on scaffolding?

Each scaffold platform and walkway must be at least 18 inches (46 centimeters) wide. When the work area is less than 18 inches (46 centimeters) wide, guardrails and/or personal fall arrest systems must be used. 1926.451(b)(2)

Are guardrails required on all open sides of scaffolding?

The standard requires employers to protect each employee on a scaffold more than 10 feet (3.1 m) above a lower level from falling to that lower level. 1926.451(g)(1)

To ensure adequate protection, install guardrails along all open sides and ends before releasing the scaffold for use by employees, other than the erection and dismantling crews. 1926.451(g)(4)

Guardrails are not required, however,
• When the front end of all platforms are less than 14 inches (36 centimeters) from the face of the work; 1926.451(b)(3)

• When outrigger scaffolds are 3 inches (8 centimeters) or less from the front edge; 1926.451(b)(3)(l)

• When employees are plastering and lathing 18 inches (46 centimeters) or less from the front edge. 1926.451(b)(3)(ii)

What materials are unacceptable for guardrails?

Steel or plastic banding must not be used as a toprail or a midrail. 1926.451(g)(4)(xiii)

What are supported scaffolds?

Supported scaffolds are platforms supported by legs, outrigger beams, brackets, poles, uprights, posts, frames, or similar rigid support. 1926.451(b)

The structural members, poles, legs, posts, frames, and uprights, must be plumb and braced to prevent swaying and displacement. 1926.451(c)(3)

Do employees working on supported scaffolds need to be trained?

All employees must be trained by a qualified person to recognize the hazards associated with the type of scaffold being used and how to control or minimize those hazards. The training must include fall hazards, falling object hazards, electrical hazards, proper use of the scaffold, and handling of materials. 1926.454(a)

When do supported scaffolds need to be restrained from tipping?

Supported scaffolds with a height to base width ratio of more than 4:1 must be restrained by guying, tying, bracing, or an equivalent means.1926.451(c)(1)

How can one prevent supported scaffolding from tipping?

Either the manufacturers' recommendation or the following placements must be used for guys, ties, and braces:

• Install guys, ties, or braces at the closest horizontal member to the 4:1 height and repeat vertically with the top restraint no further than the 4:1 height from the top.

• Vertically—every 20 feet (6.1 meters) or less for scaffolds less than three feet (0.91 meters) wide; every 26 feet (7.9 meters) or less for scaffolds more than three feet (0.91 meters) wide.

• Horizontally—at each end; at intervals not to exceed 30 feet (9.1 meters) from one end. 1926.451(c)(1)

What are the footing and foundation requirements for supported scaffolds?

Supported scaffolds' poles, legs, posts, frames, and uprights must bear on base plates and mud sills, or other adequate firm foundation. 1926.451(c)(2)(i) and (ii)

What materials can be used to increase the working level height of employees on supported scaffolds?

Stilts may be used on a large area scaffold. When a guardrail system is used, the guardrail height must be increased in height equal to the height of the stilts.
The manufacturer must approve any alterations to the stilts. 1926.452(v)

Note: A large area scaffold consists of a pole, tube and coupler systems, or a fabricated frame scaffold erected over substantially the entire work area. 1926.451(b)

What are the requirements for access to scaffolds?

310

Employers must provide access when the scaffold platforms are more than 2 feet (0.6 meters) above or below a point of access. 1926.451(e)(1)

Direct access is acceptable when the scaffold is not more than 14 inches (36 centimeters) horizontally and not more than 24 inches (61centimeters) vertically from the other surfaces. 1926.451(e)(8)

The standard prohibits the use of crossbraces as a means of access. 1926.451(e)(1)

What types of access can be used?

Several types of access are permitted:
• Ladders, such as portable, hook-on, attachable, and stairway 1926.451 (e)(2),
• Stair towers 1926.451(e)(4),
• Ramps and walkways 1926.451(e)(5),
• Integral prefabricated frames (1926.451(e)(6).

What are the access requirements for employees erecting and dismantling supported scaffolds?

Employees erecting and dismantling supported scaffolding must have a safe means of access provided when a competent person has determined the feasibility and analyzed the site conditions. 1926.451(e)

Does the standard prohibit any types of scaffolds?

Shore and lean-to scaffolds are strictly prohibited. 1926.451(f)(2)

Also, employees are prohibited from working on scaffolds covered with snow, ice, or other slippery materials, except to remove these substances. 1926.451(f)(8)

What is fall protection?

Fall protection includes guardrail systems and personal fall arrest systems. Guardrail systems are explained below in another question. Personal fall arrest systems include harnesses, components of the harness/belt such as Dee-rings, and snap hooks, lifelines, and anchorage point. 1926.451(g)(3)

Vertical or horizontal lifelines may be used. 1926.451(g)(3)(ii) through (iv)

Lifelines must be independent of support lines and suspension ropes and not attached to the same anchorage point as the support or suspension ropes. 1926.451(g)(3)(iii) and (iv)

What are the fall protection requirements for all scaffolds?

Employers must provide fall protection for each employee on a scaffold more than 10 feet (3.1meters) above a lower level. 1926.451(g)(1)

A competent person must determine the feasibility and safety of providing fall protection for employees erecting or dismantling supported scaffolds. 1926.451(g)(2)

How will I know what kind of fall protection to provide for a specific-type of scaffold?

The chart on the below illustrates the type of fall protection required for specific scaffolds.

Type of Scaffold	Fall Protection Required
Aerial lifts	Personal fall arrest system
Boatswains' chair	Personal fall arrest system
Catenary scaffold	Personal fall arrest system
Crawling board (chicken ladder)	Personal fall arrest system, or a guardrail system, or by a 3/4 inch (1.9 cm) diameter grabline or equivalent handhold securely fastened beside each crawling board
Float scaffold	Personal fall arrest system
Ladder jack scaffold	Personal fall arrest system
Needle beam scaffold	Personal fall arrest system
Self-contained adjustable scaffold when supported by ropes	Both a personal fall arrest system and a guardrail system
Single-point and Scaffolds	Both a personal fall two-point suspension arrest system and a guardrail system
Supported scaffold	Personal fall arrest system or guardrail system
All other scaffolds	Personal fall arrest system or guardrail systems that not specified above meet the required criteria

When can personal fall arrest systems be used when working on scaffolding and aerial lifts?

Personal fall arrest systems can be used on scaffolding when there are no guardrail systems. 1926.451(g)(1)(vii)

Use fall arrest systems when working from the following types of scaffolding: boatswains' chair, catenary, float, needle beam, ladder, and pump jack.
1926.451(g)(1)

Use fall arrest systems also when working from the boom/basket of an aerial lift.
1926.453(b)(2)(v)

When are both fall arrest and guardrail systems required?

Each employee on a self-contained adjustable scaffold shall be protected by a guardrail system (with minimum 200 pound toprail capacity) when the platform is supported by the frame structure, and by both a personal fall arrest system and a guardrail system (with minimum 200 pound toprail capacity) when the platform is supported by ropes. 1926.451(g)(1)(iv)

What protections from overhead falling objects do the standards require?

To protect employees from falling hand tools, debris, and other small objects, install toeboards, screens, guardrail systems, debris nets, catch platforms, canopy structures, or barricades. In addition, employees must wear hard hats. 1926.451(h)(1) & (2) and (3)

What are the training standards for employees who work on scaffolds?

All employees who work on a scaffold must be trained by a person qualified to recognize the hazards associated with the type of scaffold used and to understand the procedures to control and minimize those hazards. 1926.454(a)

What are the training standards for employees who work, erect, dismantle, move, operate, repair, maintain, or inspect scaffolds?

A competent person must train all employees who erect, disassemble, move, operate, repair, maintain, or inspect scaffolds. Training must cover the nature of the hazards, the correct procedures for erecting, disassembling, moving, operating, repairing, inspecting, and maintaining the type of scaffold in use. 1926.454(b)

Other recommended training topics include erection and dismantling, planning, personal protective equipment, access, guys and braces, and parts inspection.
Appendix D

What are the retraining requirements for employees working on scaffolds?

The standard requires retraining when (1) no employee training has taken place for the worksite changes, scaffold changes, or falling object protection changes; or (2) where the employer believes the employee lacks the necessary skill, understanding, or proficiency to work safely. 1926.454(c)

Aerial Lifts

Aerial lifts are vehicle-mounted (rolling) device used to elevate personnel. There are three basic types of aerial lifts/platforms:

- Manual vertical aerial platforms
- Powered vertical aerial platforms
- Boom supported aerial platforms

These lifts may go by other names, such as personnel lifts, Genie lifts, scissor lifts, Condor lifts, aerial towers, man lifts, cherry picker, etc., and be made by a variety of different manufacturers. All aerial lifts come with an operator's manual. It is the responsibility of the operator to read and understand this manual, and all decals and warning labels, before operating the lift.

Before operating any lift, the operator should do a "pre-operation inspection" of the lift to ensure that it is in proper working condition. NEVER operate a lift if any component is defective. Remove the lift from service and mark the lift with a lockout tag until it has been repaired.

The most common type of aerial lift found in theatres is a vertical aerial platform/ personnel lift. These are typically rolling motorized lift towers, made for lifting one person. These lifts may or may not have outriggers, depending on their design. Lifts without outriggers have floor locks that should be engages, to prevent the lift from moving, whenever it is in use. These lifts should not be moved/rolled, when the platform/basket is raised.

Vertical aerial lifts should only be used on a level surface. Most lifts of this type have a bubble level on the base of the lift so that the operator can check to see that the lift is level, before the platform/basket is raised. Some lifts will not operate if the lift is not level or if the outriggers are not properly installed.

JLG Push Around Vertical Mast Lift

Before using any ladder or lift, a pre-operation inspection should be performed to ensure that the tool is not damaged and is is perfect operating condition.

The following is a typical checklist for vertical lifts:

- Wheels
- Battery and charger
- Bubble level
- Floor locks, outriggers, stabilizers and other structures
- Operating and emergency controls
- Personal protective devices
- Missing or unreadable placards, warnings, or operational, instructional and control markings
- Mechanical fasteners and locking pins
- Cables and pulleys
- Electrical cables
- Loose or missing parts
- Guardrail system

Before you operate any lift, check your work environment:

- Do not operate if the lift is not level
- Clear the floor of any clutter, and wet/slick places
- Know where all electrical hazards are located and stay clear of them
- Know where all overhead obstacles are located
- Weather conditions (wind, rain, snow)

Operational procedures

- Always use three points of contact when mounting the lift
- Wear clean, heavy-soled shoes with good support
- Secure gates and chain before operating
- Only stand on the floor of the lift - NEVER stand on rails or toeboard
- Never operate a lift if you are dizzy or impaired in any way
- Never overreach from the lift
- Do not use the lift as a crane
- Do not put ladders or scaffolds on a lift
- Wear a safety belt or harness and tie-off to the attachment point in the lift, if provided). Never tie off to an adjourning structure
- Never climb out of a lift platform when it is raised
- Never exceed the load rating of the lift and distribute the load evenly
- Do not move the lift when the platform is raised, unless the lift is designed for this operation.

Scissor lifts are drivable vertical lift platforms that are sometimes used by riggers. Like the vertical lifts described above, the platform is directly above the base, although many scissor lifts allow a portion of the platform to slide-out and cantilever a short distance from the base. These lifts have much higher load capacities than mast type vertical lifts and can hold two people. They are also much heavier and cannot be used on some stages, especially ones with trap doors. These can be electrically powered or engine powered.

JLG Scissor Lift

Boom lifts can be drivable, like scissor lifts, or trailer mounted, intended to be used from a stationary position. The boom can either be a telescoping boom lift or articulating. Boom lifts have two major advantages over vertical aerial lifts: 1) typically allow workers to get higher (many have working height of over 60 feet), and 2) the platform can extend away from the base so that workers can get to positions not possible with a vertical lift. The drivable boom lifts are typically extremely heavy, whereas to trailer mounted boom lifts are not, which makes them a good choice for some theatre work (although they limited in height to under 55 feet).

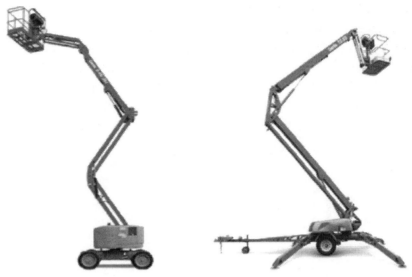

Drivable   Trailer Mounted
      Genie Articulated Boom Lifts

Chapter 20:
Training and Certification

Introduction

A good philosophy to have is that "you are always a student." There is always more to learn, so it is important that you keep reading, studying and taking workshops throughout your career. Working with other experienced technicians is another good way to acquire new knowledge or skills. You never know when someone is going to teach a new technique or provide you with information that you make you a better technician.

In this chapter, we will look at a few places where you learn more about working in the theatre. We will also discuss some certifications that you might want to consider in order to show your qualifications.

Conferences

There are several national and regional theatre conferences in the United States that offer high quality sessions on technical theatre. Here are a few.

United States Institute for Theatre Technology (USITT)

The United States Institute for Theatre Technology, Inc. (USITT) mission is to connect performing arts design and technology communities to ensure a vibrant dialog among practitioners, educators, and students. It's annual conference offers many programs on a wide range of theatre topics. It's Stage Expo has exhibits by hundreds production related vendors.

Live Design (LDI)

LDI offers comprehensive professional training opportunities in the industry, during a full-week of sessions that range from in-depth hands-on courses, to technical updates and panels in a traditional classroom setting; you'll find the best trainers and masters in lighting, projection, rigging, electrics, and software, sharing their expertise. LDI offers both short sessions and multi-day long workshops on many theatre-related topics. It also has a large exhibition of production related vendors.

North American Theatre Engineering and Architecture Conference (NATEAC)
"It is the mission of the North American Theater Engineering and Architecture Conference (NATEAC) to promote communication between the architects, engineers, consultants, and manufacturers responsible for designing and building new theaters and renovating existing facilities in North America. It is also our goal to promote a higher level of interaction between these professionals and the end users of their facilities."

Southeastern Theatre Conference (SETC)
SETC is the largest regional theatre conference in the United States. While most of the sessions are more performer related, there are some good design/tech sessions as well.

Workshops

ETCP Recognized Rigging Training Programs

Rigging (http://etcp.esta.org/cert_recognized/training_programs/rigging_list.htm)
Columbus-McKinnon - Entertainment Technology
JR Clancy
Electronic Theatre Controls (ETC)
Gravitec Systems Inc.
Harrington Hoists and Cranes
Mountain Productions
Tait - Navigator Automation Systems
National Production Services
Building Services, LLC
Safer Venue and Flyhouse
Stage Rigging
Tomcat
Total Structures

Electrical (http://etcp.esta.org/cert_recognized/training_programs/electrical_list.htm)
Academy of Production Technology
Electronic Theatre Controls (ETC)
Harrington Hoists and Cranes
Tait - Navigator Automation Systems
Phillips Strand Lighting
Vari-Lite

Other Workshops
The Stagecraft Institute of Las Vegas - (htttp://stagecraftinstitute.com)

Newsletters

The free newsletters below provide good information on theatrical topics.

The Flywire (http://www.eepurl/T7gMf)
Aerial rigging newsletter by Delbert Hall.

netHEADS! (http://www.sapsis-rigging.com/netHEADS.html)
The newsletter of Sapsis Rigging, Inc.

Certifications

Entertainment Services and Technology Association's (ESTA)
Entertainment Technician Certification Program (ETCP)
These certifications can be obtained by taking either an online exam or a paper exam.

Rigging - Arena: encompasses rigging that employs chain hoists and truss systems to temporarily suspend objects from overhead structures in any environment. ETCP recognizes that these methods and hardware are used throughout the entertainment industry in arenas, convention and trade show spaces and in theatrical venues. However, the principles, practices, and components are consistent and similar in all applications and are different from those used in traditional theatrical spaces.

Rigging - Theatre: encompasses rigging that employs the use of counterweighted systems, mechanical systems and hydraulic systems, usually, but not always, permanently installed in facilities for the use of theatre technicians in the execution of their rigging responsibilities.

Entertainment Electrician: encompasses knowledge and skill related to electrical work, as well as liability issues, the health and safety of workers and audiences, and compliance with the electrical and other laws of the local area, including laws requiring performance by Qualified Personnel in the entertainment industry.

Power Distribution: encompasses knowledge and skill sets surrounding the assembly, use, and disassembly of power distribution systems for a wide variety of entertainment venues and markets. These include the corporate, trade show, outdoor event, theatrical, and motion picture/television segments of the industry. The development of the program has been fully funded by sponsorships.

The United States Institute for Theatre Technology's (USITT)
Essential Skills for Entertainment Technicians (eSET): a proficiency program for entry-level technicians. Technicians must first pass a Terms & Safety Test (which must be taken before taken online before taking one of the practical exams). Practical eSET exams in Lighting & Electrics, Rigging, and Costuming are currently being offered at the USITT's annual conference. Future exams in Audio, Scenery, Projection, and Wigs & Makeup are in the planning stage. USITT sells an eSET mobile app to help technicians prepare for the Terms and Safety Test.

Occupational Safety and Health Administration's (OSHA)

OSHA-10 (Construction) A 10-hour course that covers topics valuable to construction-related work such as Fall Protection, Personal Protective Equipment, Scaffolding, OSHA Inspection Procedures and more. Offered online.

OSHA-10 (General Industry) A 10-hour course that covers topics related to general industry work such as Personal Protective Equipment, Flammable and Combustible Liquids, Machine Guarding, Lockout Tagout Procedures and more. Offered online.

OSHA-10 (Entertainment) A 10-hour course that overs OSHA policies, procedures, and standards, as well as general industry safety and health principles. Topics include scope and application of the OSHA general industry standards as related to the Entertainment Industry. Special emphasis is placed on those areas that are the most hazardous, using OSHA standards as a guide. In-person training offered at several major conferences.

OSHA-30 (Construction Industry Outreach Training) A 30-hour comprehensive safety program designed for anyone involved in the construction industry. Specifically devised for safety directors, foremen, and field supervisors; the program provides complete information on OSHA compliance issues. Offered online and in-person.

Aerial Lift Certification Typically, a one-hour training session that teaches OSHA guidelines for proper use of aerial platforms and personnel lifts. Offer online and at many aerial lift rental locations.

Other Certifications

RigStar (http://rigstar.com)
In-person arena rigging training and certification.

Part V:
Rigging Problems

Chapter 21:
Rigging Scenery to Fly

This chapter looks at a number of rigging problems that a technician might face when mounting a production, and how they might be solved. Needless to say, there are multiple ways to solve every rigging problem, but here are some of our favorites.

Theatrical rigging hardware for hanging flats
Before we begin discussing how to hang a flat from a batten, let's look at some of the theatrical hanging hardware designed for this purpose.

<u>Trim Chain - Snap and Ring</u>

Used to connect the pipe batten and hanging iron to the flat. Height can be varied by removing or doubling up on chain links

Size: 24" 30" or 36" lengths

<u>Hanging Iron (non rated)</u>

Attaches to stile of flat
Size: 7 1/2"X 1"X 3/16"

Hanging Iron (rated)

Attaches to stile of flat.
WLL: 1,500 pounds

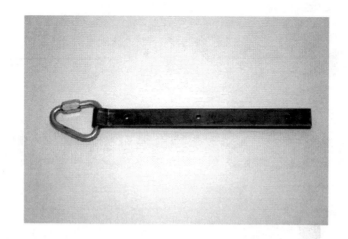

Bottom hanging iron

Designed to be used on the
lower rail of flats when
scenery is to be above
ground
Size: 6"X 1"X 3/16"

Dee Ring Plate and Welded Dee Ring

Dee Ring size: 1/4" steel
wire X 2" I.D.
Plate size: 3"X 3/4"

Ceiling Plate w/o Ring

Used to fasten the lines to
a heavy or large canvas
flat which is to be used as
a ceiling. Does not have a
ring attached
Size: 2 1/2"X 7"

Ceiling Plate w/ Ring

Used on the down stage side of ceilings and provides the best method of fastening the flat. Ring attached
Size: 2 1/2"X 7"

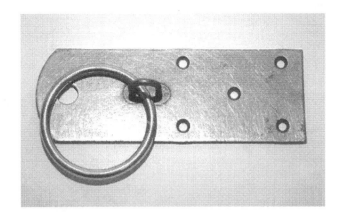

Hanging flats with wire rope

There are many ways to rig a flat to be suspended or flown. Some are good way and others are not. There is a big difference between suspending a flat and flying it. Suspending it, or dead-hanging it so that is does not fall down, does not present the same safety issues as rigging it to fly in and out. In this section we will give a brief overview of thing to do and not to do.

If a flat is merely being suspended, it is acceptable to hang it from its top, either the top rail or near the top of the stiles, because the cables are not actually supporting the weight of the flat. However, if you want to fly it, the flat needs to be supported from either the bottom rail, so that the flat is in compression, or with a rated hanger iron that is through-bolted to the rails of the flat (not attached with wood screws). Hardware can also be welded to steel framed flats.

To keep the flats has vertical as possible, we recommend that holes be drill vertically through the top rail and the toggles, and the cables (sometimes called *tail downs*) pass through them. These cables need turnbuckles to allow you to level the flat and ensure that equal tension is on each cable.

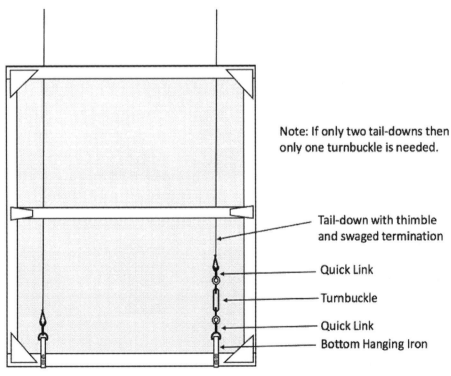

Note: If only two tail-downs then only one turnbuckle is needed.

Tail-down with thimble and swaged termination

Quick Link

Turnbuckle

Quick Link
Bottom Hanging Iron

Scenery Bumpers

Scenery Bumpers can be placed near the off-stage ends of batten, especially electrics, to divert gently push battens away, in order to prevent scenery from catching on lights or curtains as battens are moved in and out.

Keeping battens from twisting

Lighting instruments must sometimes be "out-hung" (hung so that the yoke is parallel to the stage floor) in order to be at the desires position. If all, or most, the instruments are hung on the same side of the batten, this can cause the battens to rotate.

A Pipe Stiffener is used by attaching the pipe clamp to a batten pipe while tying the loop to the cable supporting the batten. One pipe stiffener is place near each lift line. This prevents the batten pipe from rotating with its supports due to torques created by equipment mounted to the batten.

Supporting batten extensions

Battens do not always extend as far into the wings as is needed. When this is the situation, batten extensions are often used. Since pipe battens are typically made from 1.5" ID schedule 40 steel pipe, 1" ID schedule 80 pipe, which has an OD of 1.32", fits well inside of the pipe batten to make an extension. Schedule 80 pipe has a thicker wall which gives it extra strength and helps compensate for the smaller size of the pipe. Also, a welded ring on the end of the extension prevents it from being pushed deep into the pipe batten and also provides an attachment point for guy wires.

Many rigging installers will drill holes near the ends of the batten and tack-weld machine nuts over the holes. These nuts then allow a thumb screw or hex bolts to be used to "lock" the extension in place.

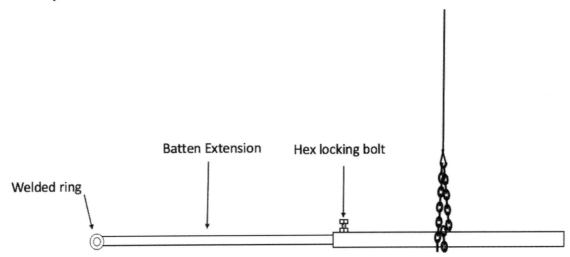

If extended several feet, a batten extension with a heavy load on it can droop at the unsupported end, causing whatever is hung on them not to hang level. It this section we will look at three ways to support batten extensions.

Bridling

Dead-hanging the end of the batten extension is not a great method if the batten need to fly "in" and "out" during the production. When you have this need, one solution is to rig a bridle that helps support the cantilevered end of the batten. Using a strong, low-stretch cord, about 1/4" in diameter, tie a *rolling hitch,* or similar prusiking knot, around the lift line that is nearest the end of the batten. You can get this type of cord from most outdoor outfitters like REI. This knot should be at the center of your cord. Next, securely tie one end of the cord onto the batten, about 3 feet onstage of lift line, using clove hitch (back it up with two half hitches). Next, tie the other end of the cord around the batten extension until, with a clove hitch and half-hitches. Finally, adjust the rolling hitch, if necessary, and slide it up the lift line as much as possible so that both bridle legs are very taut. These legs should both be around 45 degrees to the lift line.

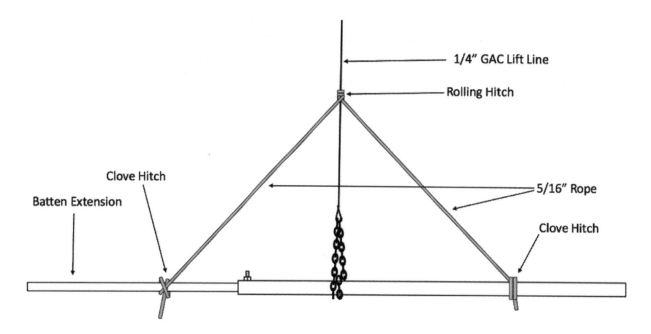

Bridle tied to lift line on counterweight system
(Half-hitches not shown)

Adding and addition lift line

Another solution for this problem is to add an additional lift line. This is not as difficult as it sounds. Because these lines typically do not have to hold a lot of weight, 1/8" GAC will usually work well.

Begin by mounting the pulley, at the grid, above of batten extension. This could be a loft block mounted to your grid, or a cable pulley hung from the beams above the grid. Next, hang a cable pulley from a sling placed around the offstage beam that supports the head blocks. Run one end of a cable through the pulley at the head block and attach it to the Head of the arbor, where the other cables are attached. The other end goes over the pulley above the batten extension and drops to the floor. Finally, pull the cable taut and attach it to the batten extension. A Circus Hitch, discussed in Chapter 9, is a quick and easy way to attached this cable to the batten extension. It should be noted that most electrics have an additional lift line – to support the electrical cable.

Dealing with "out of weight" situations

Typically, whatever you have on a batten stays there, so that once the arbor is weighted for the load, it does not change. However, there may be times when something needs to be added or removed from a batten during the show, and when that occurs, you can be faced with a tricky and potentially dangerous "out of weight" situation. Below are two possible ways to deal with such a situation.

Substitute weights

A *substitute weight* is a weight that takes the place of the weight of a load that has been removed from a batten - thus keeping the lineset in balance. Let's look at a situation when this solution might be employed.

The scenic designer for a production wants a large wall, weighing 300 pounds, to "fly in" for a scene. In the next scene, the scenic designer wants the entire set, including this wall, to rotate 180 degrees on the revolve built into the show's deck. Assuming that you have devised a way to stabilize the wall when it revolves, how are you going to deal with this wall being attached to the batten? You are probably not. You need to disconnect it from the batten so that it can spin with the revolve.

There are lots of ways to deal with the disconnecting of the wall from the batten, but we are only going to concern ourselves with the loss of the weight of the scenery from the batten when it is disconnected. In this case a substitute weight (or weights) is one solution to this problem. Look at the diagram below.

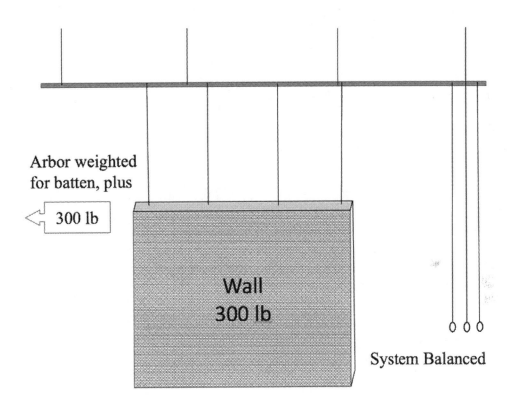

This diagram shows the walls hanging from cables connected to the batten. If the wall weight 300 pounds, then 300 pounds of counterweight is added to the arbor so that the system is in weight. The system is balanced, so the wall can fly in or out as needed.

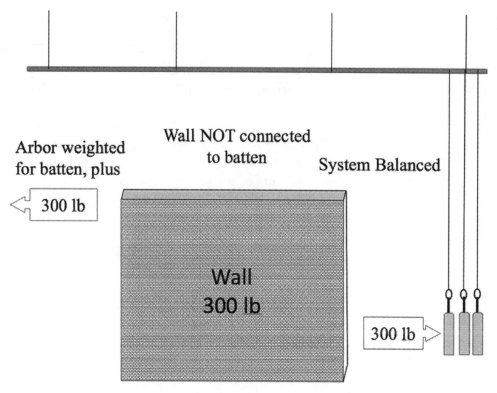

Note: All of the counterweight does not need to be on the same end of the batten.

When the wall is lowered to the stage, 300 pounds of substitute weight (sandbags) are lifted and connected to the substitute weight cables. Now the batten can be lowered a bit further taking tension off of the cables that were suspending the wall (which is now sitting on the deck) because the 300 pounds of substitute weight is taking the place of the weight of the wall. The cables that were supporting the wall can now be disconnected from the top of the wall and the batten flown out, as shown below.

Now that the wall is not connected to the batten, the wall is free to turn with the revolve in the next scene. Problem solved.

The Carpet Hoist System
The substitute weight system described above is an easy system to set up and operate, but depending on the amount of weight needing to be substituted, this system can require several stagehands to perform the switch. A system that can be operated by a single technician is a carpet hoist system. However, unlike the substitute weight system described above, which requires only a single lineset, a carpet hoist system requires two linesets that are adjacent to each other: one will hold the scenery and the other will hold the weight. Please note, great care must be taken when setting up a carpet hoist.

To solve the same problem as described above, the first step in creating a carpet host is to make two "catcher bars" that must be securely attach to the top of the arbor of the adjacent lineset to which the wall will be attached. These bars must be long enough to "catch" on the bottom of the adjacent arbor, the one that will hold the 300 pounds of substitute weight.

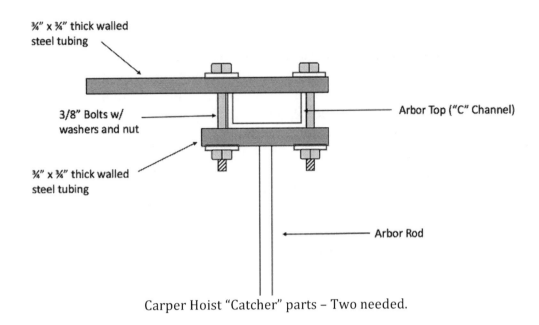

¾" x ¾" thick walled steel tubing

3/8" Bolts w/ washers and nut

¾" x ¾" thick walled steel tubing

Arbor Top ("C" Channel)

Arbor Rod

Carper Hoist "Catcher" parts – Two needed.

Now, fly the empty "weight batten" in. This flies the arbor "out." Lock this arbor with and uncle Bubby or a snub line (as described in Chapter 9), then load 300 pounds of counterweight onto this arbor. Note: this lineset is now 300 pounds out of weight.

Next, fly "in" the batten that will eventually hold the wall until it is higher than wall, attach the cables that will eventually be attached to the top of the wall, and then fly it out until it is higher than the height of the all.

Stand the wall and attach it to the supporting cables, then fly the batten out until there is tension on the cable. Adjust until the load is evenly distributed on the cables. At this point, you cannot lift the wall because there is not enough weight on the arbor, but that will soon change.

Now, throw several bull lines over the batten on the lineset with the 300 pounds of counterweight. Using these bull lines the help you control the arbor, release the Uncle Buddy or sub line and slowing lower the arbor until it rest on the "catchers." This then transfers that 300 pound of weight to the arbor supporting the wall – creating a balanced load. When you want to move the wall, BOTH arbors must move.

When the wall is brought to the deck, during the production, the purchase line of the weight batten MUST be secured using an Uncle Buddy and a snub line BEFORE the wall is detached from its support cables. After the cable are released, the batten that was supporting the wall can be flow "out." Since this arbor has always been at pipe weight, it is in balance. However, the "weight" lineset is out of balance and the arbor is being supported by the purchase line and the snub line or Uncle Buddy.

Once setup, a carpet hoist takes fewer stagehands to operate, but with practice, it works very well.

The Draw Bridge Problem

Twice in my career as a scenic designer, I have designed sets for *The Man of La Mancha*. Both of these productions have included drawbridges. The unique problem with rigging a drawbridge is the fact that the tension on the lift lines changes as the drawbridge is raised and lowered. While there is the temptation to use a winch and not worry about it, understanding how the placement of a critical pulley can change the load and what the loads are and can help make running this effect much easier when using the "old school" method of operation. In this lesson, we will look at how to calculate the tension on the line supporting the drawbridge.

The drawbridge for our production might look something like the one in the diagram below.

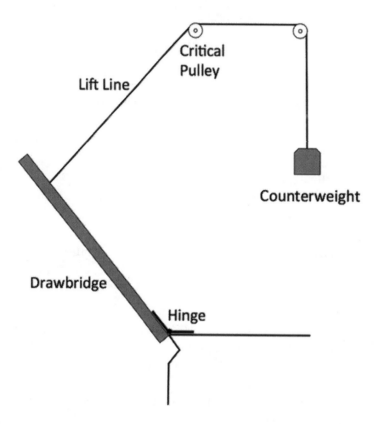

A lift line (actually two lines, but since we want to calculate the total tension on the line we need to treat it as a single line), is connected to the drawbridge and will lift it. The first pulley that the line runs through is the "critical pulley" because its position is a determining factor in the angle of the line, which then helps determine the tension on the lift line.

When the drawbridge is "up" (closed), there is no tension on the lift line - the entire weight of the drawbridge rests in the hinge. But as the drawbridge lowers (opens), the load on the lift line slowly increases.

To calculate the tension on the lift line, we need to know:
W - Weight of the drawbridge
COG - Distance from the hinge to the center of gravity of the drawbridge
D2L - Distance from the hinge to the point on the drawbridge where the lift line is attached

334

DA - Angle of the drawbridge (0 = horizontal, 90 = vertical; a negative angle means that the top of the drawbridge is lower than the hinge)

LA - The inside angle between the drawbridge to lift line

To calculate the inside angle between the drawbridge and the lift line (LA) we must know the position of the "critical pulley" in relationship to the point where the lift line attaches to the drawbridge. We need to know "H" - the horizontal offset distance and "V" - the vertical offset distance, of this pulley. All of these variables are shown in the drawing below.

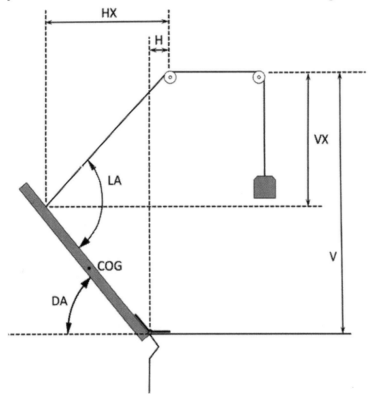

Let's begin by describing the specifics of the drawbridge rig. In this example, the drawbridge will be 10 feet long and completely symmetrical. This puts its COG at 5 feet from the hinge. (Note: If the drawbridge were not symmetrical - for example, if it were wider on one end, then we would have to calculate where the COG is located.) Let's place the lift line(s) 8 feet from the hinge(s). Next, let's put the top center of the "critical pulley" 5 feet offstage of the hinge, and 25 feet above the hinge.

Now, let's calculate the tension on the line when the drawbridge is raised to 20 degrees above horizontal. So...

W = 300 pounds
COG = 5 feet
D2L = 8 feet
V = 25 feet
H = 5 feet
DA = 20 degrees
LA = ? (this is the first thing we need to calculate)

To calculate the Line Angle (LA), we will use the equation:

$$LA = 20 + ATAN\left(\frac{VX}{HX}\right)$$

where,

$$VX = V - ((SIN(DA)) \times D2L)$$
and

$$HX = H + ((COS(DA)) \times D2L)$$

In order to calculate LA, we need to add two angles: the angle of the drawbridge (DA) and the angle from a horizontal reference line that is at the height of the point where the lift line attaches to the door to the line itself. Since we already know DA, we need to calculate this second angle; but to do this, we need to know two things: the horizontal distance from the point where the lift line attached to the drawbridge to the critical pulley (HX), and vertical distance from the the point where the lift line attached to the drawbridge to the critical pulley (VX).

To find these distances we use simple trigonometry.

So, plugging in the numbers we find that,

$$VX = 25 - ((SIN(20)) \times 8)$$
$$VX = 25 - (0.3420 \times 8)$$
$$VX = 25 - 2.73616$$
$$VX = 22.2638$$
and

$$HX = 5 + ((COS(20)) \times 8)$$
$$HX = 5 + (0.9396 \times 8)$$
$$HX = 5 + 7.5175$$
$$HX = 12.5175$$

Now that we know these lengths, lets calculate the angle of the lift line.

$$LA = 20 + ATAN\left(\frac{22.2638}{12.5175}\right)$$
$$LA = 20 + ATAN(1.7786)$$

$$LA = 20 + 60.6537$$
$$LA = 80.65 \text{ degrees}$$

Now that we know the Line Angle, we can calculate the force needed to support the drawbridge at a 20-degree angle. To do this we use the equation:

$$Tension = (COG \times W \times COS(DA)) / (D2L \times SIN(LA))$$

Once again, this is basic trigonometry. Let's plug in the numbers and solve it.

$$Tension = (5 \times 300 \times COS(20)) / (8 \times SIN(80.65))$$

$$Tension = (1500 \times 0.9397) / (8 \times 0.9867)$$

$$Tension = 1409.9539 / 7.8937$$

$$\boldsymbol{Tension = 178.6\ pounds}$$

The following chart shows how this tension changes as you lift this drawbridge from -20 degrees to 90 degrees:

Drawbridge Angle	Angle of Lift Lines	Tension on Lift Lines
-20	46	246 pounds
0	63	211 pounds
20	81	179 pounds
45	106	138 pounds
60	124	112 pounds
75	143	80 pounds
90	164	0 pounds

Since it takes a lot of math to calculate all of the tensions above, this seems to me to be a situation that would benefit greatly from being done in an Excel spreadsheet - so I created one - Drawbridge.xlsx. You can find this spreadsheet in the download page on the Spring Knoll Press website. This spreadsheet will let you look at 10 different angles for any drawbridge setup. You can also change the location of "critical pulley" and compare the Line Angles and tensions, helping you select the best setup for your needs.

One more thing. Since there is very little weight on the lift line when the drawbridge is close to vertical, putting a jack line on the sandbag makes it possible to control the drawbridge better. Jack lines were discussed in Chapter 7 and look something like the one in the illustration below.

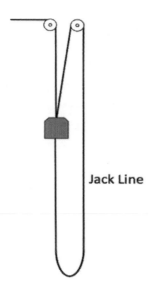

Jack Line

Trying and traveling scenery simultaneously

It is common to have scenery flying "in" and "out" during a production. And, it is not unusual to put scenery on a traveler track so that it can be moved across the stage. What is unusual, and a bit tricky, is to have scenery traveling across the stage while flying "in" or "out." The reason is simple, the way traveler tracks are typically rigged, the travel line that the operator uses to move the scenery would fly "out" along with the batten holding the travel track. In this section, we will look at two methods of rigging a traveler track where the travel line is always in reach of the operator, no matter where the batten and the track are.

It should be noted that each of these methods has its own advantages and disadvantages. The first method uses very little hardware and is easy to rig; but operation is tricky because the traveling and the flying of the scenery are not completely independent. The second method makes the operations of traveling and the flying the scenery independent, but this requires more hardware. Let's look at how to rig each.

Method 1.
Look at the illustration below. In this method, we only need one additional pulley from how we might normally rig a traveler track. This single pulley is rigged to the grid above the offstage end of the track. We do, of course, need a longer travel line.

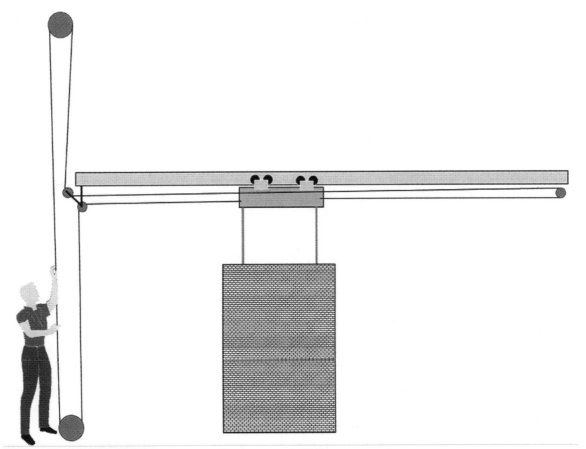

Batten and lift lines not shown

The trick to rigging this is that the live-end pulley must be at the very end of the track, and one part of the travel line will go down to the floor block on the stage, as normal, but the other part goes up and around the single pulley hung below the grid.

The operational issue with this rig is that when the track flies "in" or "out" the travel line must move at the same pace in order for the scenery NOT to move left or right. Practice is needed to control the movement of the scenery as desired.

Method 2.
This method is rigged so that it operates more like a traditional traveler track system, with both parts of the travel line coming down from the live-end pulley toward the stage. The big difference is that they both turn 180 degrees and go up, before passing around the (floating) tension pulley. A rope tied to the tension pulley runs up to a pulley hung below the grid and then back down, where it is tied to the batten supporting the track. This rope is taut and keeps tension on the travel line. Whichever direction the batten moves, our floating tension block moves in the opposite direction, at the same speed.

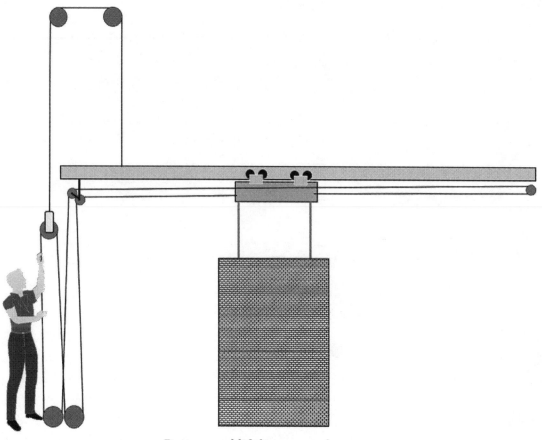

Batten and lift lines not shown

Since the floating tension pulley may want to spin, twisting the parts of the travel line, you can add guide cables, similar to the ones used on some counterweight arbors.

Because of how this system is rigged, it is easier of control the travel of the scenery on the track. The operator just has to adjust to the fact that the travel line moves as the scenery is flown "in" and "out."

Dead-hanging with Rabbit Ears

If your theatre has a walk-able grid, you could use a rope to dead-hang the end of the batten extension. One device that can simplify this process is a shop-built devise called Rabbit Ears. Each set of Rabbit Ears is made to hold one rope, so a single set of Rabbit Ears can be used to support a batten extension, or several sets can be used to support a entire batten. A set of Rabbit Ears, which has one fixed ear and one pivoting ear, can be placed on the grid at the desired location. A spot line is then passed through the hole in the top of the Rabbit Ears and dropped through the grid to the stage. After the rope is tied-off to the load, such as a batten extension, the slack in the rope is pulled up. When the rope is taut (or the load is at the desired height) the moveable rabbit ear, a cam with a handle, is closed until it puts enough pressure on the rope to capture it. The rope is then wrapped around the two ears in a figure-eight pattern, as you would do in tying-off a rope to a belaying pin on a pin rail. Finally, the excess rope is coiled and laid out of the way. The Rabbit Ears are not actually attached to the gridiron; the load on the rope holds the Rabbit Ears in place on the grid.

340

A set of Rabbit Ears

Because of the strength needs, the "ears" are constructed from ¾" seven-ply birch plywood. The ear housing is made from 2x6 pine, and the base can be made from any ¾" plywood. The base can be nearly any size or shape – 9"x12" is a typical size, with the ear housing centered. The base needs to be large enough to be stable when it sits on the grid. It is also a good idea to rest a foot on the base of the Rabbit Ears in order to keep the Rabbit Ears in place as the rope is pulled up.

The fixed ear is glued and secured into the ear housing by two 3/8" x 3-1/2" machine bolts (3" wood screws can be used instead of the bolts). Another 3/8" x 3-1/2" machine bolt is used for the axle of the pivoting ear. All bolts are countersunk to prevent the rope from catching on the bolts, and lock nuts are used on all bolts. Four 2-1/2" wood screws can be used to attach the base to the ear housing.

The two ear housing plates on the left and the two ears on the right

The greatest variations in Rabbit Ears are in the size and shape of the base and in the design of the cam on the pivoting ear. Off-setting the ears' housing on the base can make it possible to get the Rabbit Ears better positioned around obstructions on the grid, while the cam can have a smooth edge, a scored edge, or scalloped edge.

Note: The axle hole is drilled in the ear housing approximately 4-1/2" from the fixed Rabbit Ear, and approximately 2-5/8" above the base.

Rabbit Ears do not have a specific maximum load rating, and are intended for relatively low loads – whatever weight you can lift by pulling on the lifting line running through them.

A Vectorworks drawing of the Rabbit Ears can be downloaded from
http://springknollpress.com/downloads/RabbitEars.vwx

An AutoCad drawing of the Rabbit Ears can be downloaded from
http://springknollpress.com/downloads/RabbitEars.dwg

Chapter 22:
Rigging Aerial Effects in a Theatre

Introduction

Many theatrical productions not only occur on the stage, but also above them. Aerial effects, like those we associate with *Cirque du Soleil*, have become part of more traditional theatrical performances, as well is dance productions. And traditional performer flying effects, like those for *Peter Pan*, have also increased. This chapter will discuss what these types of effects have in common and several important aspects of their rigging.

Anytime a performer is suspended above the stage, whether by a harness or using their own physical strength, there is an increased risk of injury to the performer. Before you attempt any aerial effect, you must have the skills and the equipment to do it properly.

Overview

The fact is, there is no one correct way to rig an aerial effect. Sometimes an aerial apparatus is rigged to part of the physical structure of the theatre, such as the gridiron, and sometimes to a batten on a lineset. Sometimes the apparatus is stationary and sometimes it needs to moves. Some aerial rigs are very simple and some very complicated. The objective of this chapter is to provide you will some common information on how these effects can be rigged, not be an in-depth source on aerial rigging. So let's begin with some basics.

First, one basic difference between tradition theatrical rigging (scenery and lights) is that these object generally remain suspended throughout the production - and the load/tension on the rigging remains constant. This is not true with aerial effects - the performer seldom stays suspended above the stage for more than several minutes. Therefore, aerial rigging must deal with almost constantly changing tensions on the rig. Also, even though we use rigging to move scenery or lights in most theatrical productions, the movement is relatively slow and very controlled. By contrast, performers may move very quickly and in a wide array of directions. Plus, they may make very sudden stops, producing very high shock loads.

In the sections below, we will discuss these aspects of aerial rigging and some ways to dealing with them.

Guy Lines and Securing Points

A guy line is a fiber or wire rope that stabilizes a point by preventing it from moving (swinging or pivoting) laterally. Guy lines take relative little force compared to supporting lines. In some circumstances, guy lines can be quite long, so they are best made from a material with very little stretch, such as wire rope (guy wires on telephone poles are usually made of 1x19 wire rope, which is very stiff and has very little stretch).

Since aerial points usually swing in various directions at different times, they are almost always stabilized with more than one guy line (sometimes with three, but most often with four or more guy lines). When the force on the point is directly in-line with the direction that a line is running, nearly all of the force is on a single guy line. However, that is seldom the case. Often, two or more guy lines share the lateral force. Look at the drawing below.

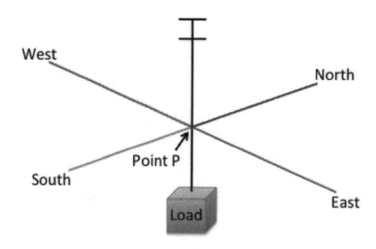

In this example, the point that we want to stabilize is where the four guy lines meet, Point P. The four anchor points are at the same height above the grounds as Point P and they are aligned with the compass heading for North, South, East and West. This is an ideal situation with all the points being on the same plane. If the Load swings North, then the guy line that runs South is put in tension and takes almost all of the force. The guy lines running East and West, try to take some of the force, but their angle is too great and they actually take very little of the force. The line running to the North is put in compression and takes absolutely no force.

But what if the direction of the swing is Northeast? In this case, the West and the South lines equally share the force, while the North and the East lines are put in compression and take none of the force. As the Load swings in different directions, the tension on the four lines change, but there is always tension on at least one line, except for the very brief moments when the Load is directly below Point P. In this example, as in many cases, the direction of the force on Point P is always horizontal (or so close to horizontal that the difference is mute).

Guy lines are typically not initially put under a great deal of tension, just enough to take the constructional stretch out of the line. The stiffer (less stretch in the) guy lines, the less movement in Point P. Special rigging plates, like Rock Exotia's Rockstar makes an excellent rigging point for Point P.

It should be remembered, the closer the direction of the force to the direction of the guy line, the better - zero degrees is the idea difference. However, you seldom have an "ideal" guying situation. This is where knowledge and skill come into play.

Below we will look at several guying problems and discuss how they might be solved.

In the drawing below there are three anchor point options (A, B and C) for a single guy line. Let's assume that there will be four guy lines terminating at Point P, but for now, let's only look at the options for one of the guy lines. Let's also assume that this rig is in a theatre and Points A and B are on the gridiron and Point C is at a catwalk that hangs below the grid.

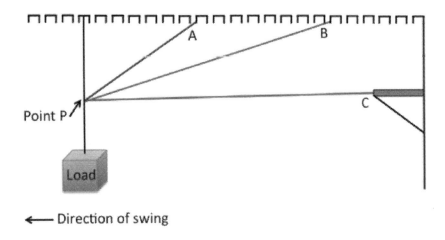

Which is the best place anchor point? The correct answer is C, because this anchor point makes the guy line closest to matching the direction of the force on Point P when the Load swings away from the anchor point.

Now, what if that catwalk was not there? What do you do? Well, the next best option shown is Point B, but are there other/better possibilities?

One of my cardinal rules is "There is never a perfect solution, you have to look at the pros and cons of each possible option and choose the best solution based on your needs and resources." So, let's look at other possible options?

Option 1: What if you have a catwalk, similar to the one in the drawing above, but it is lower than Point P? Once option is to use two guy lines to form a two-legged bridle. If the angle of each leg is the same degree from horizontal, then the direction of the force on Point P will be horizontal. See drawing below.

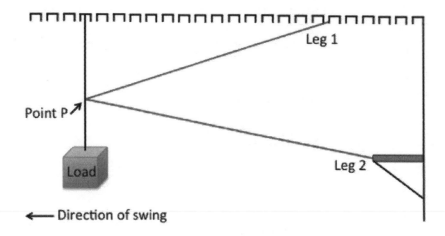

Leg 1

Point P ↗

Load

Leg 2

←— Direction of swing

Option 2: But what if there are no catwalks at all? Another option might be able to install an anchor in this wall at the same height as Point P. This might be a good solution if you can get to the height of Point P to install the anchor, have the materials/skills to install an anchor in the wall and are you allowed install an anchor in the wall.

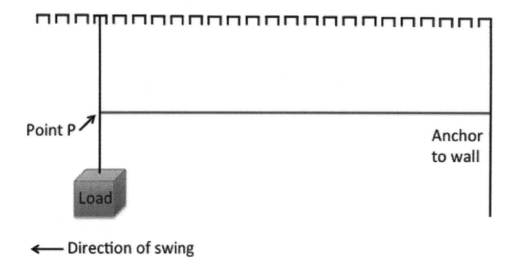

Point P ↗

Anchor to wall

Load

←— Direction of swing

Option 3: Now, let's look at a situation where there is no catwalk, and no way to put an anchor in the wall. Another option is called "bucking" and it allows you to run a guy line that is on the same plane as Point P, at least when it attaches to Point P by using a deflecting line coming off of the grid. See drawing below.

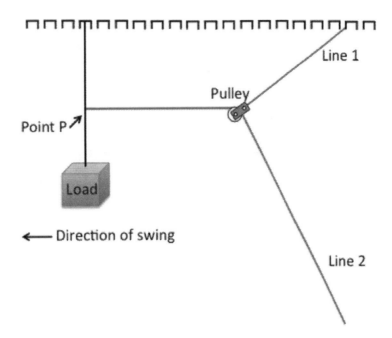

Point P↗

Load

←— Direction of swing

Pulley

Line 1

Line 2

Here we have two lines: a deflection line with a pulley, which hangs from the grid, and the guy line which attaches to Point P, passes through the pulley on the end of the deflecting line and then attached to an anchor point, usually on or near the deck. The length of the deflecting line is adjusted until the pulley is at the same height as Point P, and the guy line is pulling horizontally.

These are three options that allow you to have your guy line in the same direction as the force on Point P. However, there will be times when none of these options will work for you and you have to install a guy line that will not be in-line with the force. In these situations, you have to choose the best possible option, and understand its limitations - and try to deal with them in other ways.

In the section above we have been dealing with the height of the anchor points, now we need to deal with their placement around the stage. Some may be higher than Point P and other might be lower, but we will always try to get them at the same height as Point P, if possible.

Many stages have mechanical counterweight systems that move scenery and lights that are attached to horizontal pipes called battens. These battens run SL/SR across the stage and are often raised and lowered during the production. Rigging our guy lines so they do not interfere with the moving of these battens is another challenge that we must face.

One solution is to hang the aerial apparatus from a batten and then stabilize (guy) the batten. In essence, the entire batten becomes Point P. Below is a drawing showing how I typically try to arrange the guy lines to stabilizing a in a theatre.

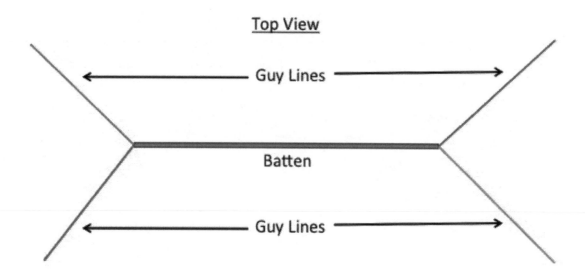

Top View

Guy Lines

Batten

Guy Lines

Like before, we want the height of the four anchors at the same height as Point P, our batten. Since we want to stabilize the batten from swinging in any direction, we probably want to use four guy lines, running North, South, East and West. To keep our guy lines out of the travel path of other battens, we guy from the ends of the batten, with the North and East lines on one end of the batten and the South and West ends on the other.

There are many ways to attach guy wire to battens or beams, but I typically use a circus hitch, as discussed in Chapter 9. This is a quick and easy solution, and because guy lines typically hold relatively small loads, their 60 percent efficiency rating is not an issue.

Now, let's look at a different, more complicated situation. What if we need the batten to travel up and down before and after the act, but we need it stabilized during the act? Obviously, having four semi-permanently anchored lines will not work, and the time it takes attach these lines to anchors points, and secure the arbor, during the show will probably take more time that will probably be deemed acceptable. Below is a drawing that shows a solution that I have used successfully to solve this problem. This can be a complicated setup to rig, so the description below provides only "general" information on how it is rigged and does not address some of the finer details.

This solution uses six guy lines, three on each end of the batten. Two on each end of the batten run up to the grid, at a 45 degree angle, one runs upstage to the grid and the other runs downstage to the grid. When the batten reaches its "low trim" these four cables get tight and stop the descending of the batten- defining its low-trim height. These lines will also help keep the batten from swinging upstage and downstage. The third line on the ends of each batten drops to the stage floor. These two lines will stabilize the SR/SL movement of the batten. The batten can be breasted to one side and the guy line on that end of the batten, which has be made a pre-determined length, quickly attaches to an anchor in the wings on that side of the stage. This line is parallel with the batten and the anchor should be as far offstage as possible so that the angle of the guy line is a flat as possible (it should be 45 degrees or less). After this guy line is connected to its anchor, the batten is swung back into plumb and the second hanging guy line is attached to an anchor point that is as far into the opposite wing as possible. This is the only guy line that is adjustable. I have used both ratchet straps and pulleys to quickly tighten this final guy line. When it is tightened, it pulls tension on all six guy lines, thereby stabilizing the entire rig.

The descriptions above provide information on just a few ways to stabilize a point in a theatre or studio. Because every space is different, the rigger must inspect the space and determine the best guying option.

Performer Flying Effects

Traditional performer flying effects for stage productions, such as *Peter Pan*, *Wizard of Oz* and *Mary Poppins* are a different type of aerial effect. In these productions, the desire is to create the illusion of flight. There are several companies that specialize in creating these types of effects and describing in detail how to create them is beyond the scope of this book. However, if you are considering doing a production with performer flying effects, it will be useful to have a basic understanding of how they are created and the requirements.

The two most common categories of flying systems are *pendulum flying systems* and *tracked flying systems*. There can be many variations of rigs within each of these categories - some are very simple and others are quite complex. Some systems use counterweight to make it easy to lift the performer, other use mechanical advantage, while some use a combination of these methods. Still other systems use high speed winches that are specifically designed for lifting people.

In most situations, parts of these systems, if not the majority of performer flaying systems, will be attached to a batten (if the theatre has a counterweight system). If the theatre does not have a counterweight system, then it may be suspended from the structure of the building. In both case, it is the maximum height that the system hangs above the stage is very important, and is often a major determining factor as to what specific type of rig is used.

If you need to suspend a rig from an I-beam, the simplest solution is to wrap the beam with a round sling. If the beam is against the ceiling, then you will need to use beam clamps.

A good general rule is that the higher the rig, the better (up to around 60 feet). This is particularly true for pendulum systems, since the height directly affects the distance that a performer can easily swing across the stage. When a theatre has less than 20 feet of height, pendulum swings must sometimes be augmented by a track. Also understand, pendulum swings not only occur on standard *pendulum systems,* but are also commonly done on *track systems,* as well.

Once a system is attached to a batten, the arbor is counterweighted to the weight of the rig, and the batten is flown to the desired height. The counterweight system is now "in balance." This will change when the performer is flown because the weight of the performer and the weight of the operator lifting the performer will be added to the batten. To keep the rope lock from slipping and the batten from coming "in" the arbor is secured at its present height by a cable, chain or ratchet strap. I like 2" ratchet straps with a breaking strength of 10K pounds. Remember, ratchet straps only have a 3:1 DF, so use big ones.

I typically pass the ratchet strap over the top of the arbor and then around the largest steel near the locking rail. Do not pass them around the idler/tension block for the purchase line, because these pulleys are not stationary.

Also, if the batten is not very close to the grid, guy cables are often used to keep the batten from swinging. This was described earlier in this chapter.

Many performer flying systems are designed so that that nothing needs to be secured to the stage floor. This helps facilitate the movement of performers and scenery on and off the stage. However, in some cases, it may be necessary to secure pulleys, or even a winch, to the stage floor.

If you need to create a performer flying effect for a production, it is strongly suggested that you hire a company that specializes in creating these effects. These companies have the proper equipment, including harnesses (fall protection and climbing harnesses are not intended for performer flying), to create the effects needed for stage productions. They also have skilled flying directors who know how to choreograph these effects.

Appendices:

Appendix 1:
Glossary

Reprinted courtesy of J.R. Clancy, Inc.

A

A-Guide	A-shaped aluminum members fixed in parallel rows for the purpose of guiding arbors or clews. They are intended for use on counterweighted systems employing compensating chains and in zones of high seismic activity. This is a Clancy product.
Acoustical Reflector Panel (Cloud)	A reflective panel hung in the auditorium, generally above the audience, that is used to direct sound into desired zones. Often decorative in nature.
Act Curtain	A curtain (sometimes designed for a specific show) that is opened to signal the beginning of a performance. The Front Curtain is often used for this purpose.
Acting Area	The stage area used by actors for performances.
Actuator	(1) Any mechanical or electrical control device (a push button) that initiates an action. (2) A screw jack or a hydraulic or pneumatic cylinder used to cause an action like opening a door.
ADA	The Americans with Disabilities Act. It requires access to public spaces by people with disabilities.
AIA	American Institute of Architects.
Altus™	Clancy Altus series rigging controllers hoists use industrial grade PLC computers, touch screen displays, and industrial grade operators that require an operator present at the console when any equipment is moving. Cues and presets can be created, modified, stored, and replayed. Targets, speeds, and positions are displayed.
ANSI	American National Standards Institute
Apron	The portion of stage that extends beyond the proscenium opening.
Apron (Forestage)	The area of the stage located just in front of the proscenium.
Arbor	A carriage or rack that contains weights, usually flame cut steel or cast iron, in sufficient quantity to balance a load.

Arbor Pit	An area located below an opening in the stage floor that permits greater travel for counterweight arbors and pipe battens.
Arbor Release	A part of the fire curtain rigging that permits the fire safety curtain arbor to move and the fire safety curtain to close. The release is usually controlled by the fire line system.
Arena	A performance space with seating all round the performers. Examples include theaters, basketball courts, and indoor rodeos.
ASA	Acoustical Society of America
As Built Drawings (Final Drawings)	Equipment or layout drawings that show equipment as it was actually built and intended to be installed. They may not reflect actual, as installed, conditions.
ASME	American Society of Mechanical Engineers
ASTC	American Society of Theater Consultants
ASTM	American Society for Testing of Materials
Audience	The area of the theater where visitors sit to view a stage performance.
Auditorium	A hall or seating area within the hall where the audience views a performance.
Austrian Curtain	A curtain that is raised (opened) with brailed lifting lines and is sewn with both vertical and horizontal fullness.
AWG	American Wire Gauge (formerly Brown & Sharp) – Used to identify wire diameters.

B

Backstage	The stage area that is located beyond the sight of the audience. Usually behind curtains and other masking devices.
Balcony	A raised platform extending out from a wall, often used for additional rows of seats in an auditorium.
Banner Hoist	A hoist with a smooth drum designed to roll up a cloth banner. Usually used with curtains intended to modify the acoustic properties of a space.
Bar Joist	A beam fabricated using lightweight rolled or fabricated sections that is used for long spans under light loading conditions.
Batten	A bar, usually made from steel pipe, from which scenery, lights and curtains are hung.
Batten Clamp	See "Pipe Clamp."
Beam	A structural member (usually horizontal in a building structure) that resists bending.
Beam Clamp	A device from which a load is hung, attached to the flange of a steel beam without altering the beam in any way.

Bearing	A device that supports a shaft or other machine part while minimizing friction.
Belaying Pin	A wood or steel rod, inserted into a hole in a pin rail, that secures ropes attached to a load. They are typically removable.
Bi-Parting Drape	A curtain that opens from the center to either side.
Black Box	A room (often painted black) that is intended for performance and lacks a permanent configuration, seating, or fixed performance area. Provision for performance lighting and props or curtains is often made.
Block	An assembly that consists of one or more sheaves and axles in a housing.
BOCA	National Building Code. Has been superseded by the IBC.
Boom	A vertically mounted pipe used for stage lights.
Border Curtain	A curtain used to define the top limit of the stage and to mask or hide lights and unused scenery and curtains.
Box Boom	Originally a vertical pipe in a seating box used for stage lights, but now used to indicate any side lighting position.
Brail Curtain	A curtain that is raised (opened) with brail type lift lines and is sewn flat or has horizontal fullness.
Brail Lines	Lifting lines that pass through a row of rings sewn to the back of the curtain and attach at the curtain bottom. The curtain folds up when the lines are pulled.
Brail Winch	A winch designed to work as part of a rigging system to raise and lower a curtain from its bottom support using cables run through rows of rings on the back of the curtain.
Breaking Strength	The load at which a failure occurs.
Bridge-Lighting	A catwalk that crosses from one side of the stage to the other, used for lighting fixtures and operator access. It may be dead hung or flown.
Bridle	An assembly that splits a lift line into two separated attachment points. Used to support trusses or to provide extra support along a pipe batten to limit deflection.
Building Code	A set of municipal, state, or federal guidelines for the design and construction of buildings.

C

Cable Clip	A device to mechanically fasten cables, consisting of bolts, nuts, and pads that bear against the cable to prevent crushing and slippage.
Cable Cradle	A device that supports an electrical cable loop and prevents sharp bends. It often has a hole for attachment of a lifting line.

Cable Reel	A drum for holding hose or various types of electrical cable that winds using springs or a motor. The hose or cable is connected at the hub of the drum so the connection to other systems is maintained as the drum rotates.
Cable Roller	A roller assembly designed to prevent moving cables from contacting any part of a building or adjacent rigging. Not intended to change cable direction or carry loads.
Capstan Winch	A winch, usually portable, with an un-grooved drum designed to assist in moving heavy loads. An operator wraps a rope around the drum and pulls to tighten the rope on the drum. Friction causes the rope to travel with the rotating drum.
Carriage	See "Arbor."
Catwalk	A walkway for access to a distant point (usually overhead).
Certificate of Occupancy	Certificate issued by a building inspector with local jurisdiction that certifies that a building meets codes and is safe to use.
Certified Rigger	A rigger who has passed the "Entertainment Technician Certification Program" (etcp) exam and is recognized as competent to do rigging for a period of time. This certification is based on both experience and a written test. Regular re-certification is required.
Clew	Device that connects several ropes or cables to one, usually stronger, rope or cable.
Clutch	Clutches are couplings that permit selective engagement and disengagement of shafts, such as a gearbox shaft from a drum.
Compensating Line	A system of light and heavy chains or cables that balances lift line weight as it transfers from the batten to the arbor side of a moving counterweight set.
Competent Person	The ESTA/ANSI Series E1 standards definition is a person who is capable of identifying existing and predictable hazards in the workplace, and who is authorized to take prompt corrective measures to eliminate them.
Continental Seating	A seating arrangement with access aisles only at the ends.
Contour Curtain	A brail or Austrian curtain rigged so that each lift line may be operated separately to form different shaped openings.
Counterweight	(n) Weights, usually flame cut steel or cast iron, that are placed in counterweight arbors to balance the weight of loads hung on battens. (v) The act of adding or removing weight from a set in order to achieve a balanced system.
Counterweight Arbor	See "Arbor."
Counterweight Assist Hoist	An electric hoist whose capacity is augmented by the addition of a counterweight arbor.
Counterweight Rigging	A rigging system where the load is balanced by a counterweight so that only a small force is required to overcome friction and move the load.

Counterweight Set	A rigging system where the load is balanced by a counterweight so that only a small force is required to overcome friction and move the load.
Crash Rail	See "Stop Batten."
Cross Aisle	A major aisle running parallel to the stage that is used as an entryway into the theater.
Cross Over	A hallway, outside of the stage house or behind the masking curtains, to allow performers and technicians to move from one side of the stage to the other without being seen.
CSI	Construction Specifications Institute
Curtain	Any fabric panel that is hung as part of a scene or to mask unwanted views.
Curtain Track	A formed or extruded shape that contains moving carriers and supports drapery. They often have a cord or other means to open and close the drapes.
Cyclorama	(1) Curtain at the rear of the performance area used to represent the sky or distant areas. (2) Set of borders, legs, and drops used to define the limits of a performance area.

D

D/d Ratio	It is the ratio between the tread diameter (D) of the drum or sheave and the cable diameter (d). Smaller ratios reduce the service life of cables.
Dash Pot	An adjustable, hydraulic ram that smoothly slows and stops a moving object.
Dead End	The end of a rope or part of a device that is not active or load carrying.
Dead Haul	Pulling a load that is not counterbalanced.
Dead Hung	Directly fixed to the structure or attached at a fixed elevation using chain, rods, or cable.
Dead Load	The permanent or non-removable part of a system load (i.e. the weight of a batten versus the load hung from it).
Design Life	The minimum expected life of the system expressed in hours or cycles of operation.
Design Load	The load that a system or equipment item is designed to carry. This load can be made up of dead loads, live loads, dynamic loads, and environmental forces.
Direct Struck Limit	A limit switch that is actuated directly by a moving device passing by the switch location.

Diversity	A factor applied to power requirements for dimming and stage machinery. This reduces the amount of available power because it is very unlikely that all dimmers and stage machines will be in use, or at full power, at the same time.
Double Purchase	A rope or cable that passes from a **lifting** device (arbor, winch, or person) over a **block**, to a block attached to the load, and tied off at the previous block, is double purchased. The system allows twice as much load to be raised for a given effort, but the rope or cable must be pulled twice as far, so total work done remains the same.
Down Stage	The area of the stage that is closest to the audience. See "Raked Stage."
Drive Shaft	A rotating component that conducts power from an engine or other power source to a drum, pulley, or gear.
Drop Curtain	A curtain that is painted or constructed in a manner that makes it a part of the scenic environment.
Drum Hoist	A hoist with a drum for wrapping cable as it is taken up. One end of the drum is typically supported by a bearing while the other end is connected to the output shaft of the gear box.
Dynamic (Live) Load	The loads in a system that change in magnitude, direction or location over time.

E

Egress	A path or walkway leading to an exit.
Electric	A name given to a pipe batten used to support lighting lighting equipment in a theater.
Elevation	The height above or below an arbitrary point in a building (generally the stage floor).
Elevation Drawing	A drawing that shows the vertical face of an object or system..
Emergency Stop Circuit	This should be a failsafe, separately wired circuit in rigging control that stops any and all controlled machinery in an emergency. The circuit can be triggered by depressing Emergency Stop pushbuttons and by various automatic sensors and limit switches. To re-start it is necessary to take one or more specific actions to begin motion.
Environmental Forces	Conditions in the environment which have an affect upon the strength, size, or effective life of equipment. Examples of forces include snow loads on roofs and wind against the side of a building.
Equal Pitch	All grooves in the sheave have the same pitch diameter so that the center of each line travels the same distance as the sheave rotates one revolution.
ESTA	Entertainment, Service and Technology Association.

ETL Link	Electro Thermal Links are fusible links which react (melt) when the ambient temperature reaches 165º F or when subjected to an imposed electrical impulse.

F

Factor of Safety	The ratio between the rated working load of a component or system and its minimum ultimate breaking strength.
Failsafe	A device or design that fails to a safe state. It does not mean that it will not fail.
Fail Safe Brake	A brake that will fully engage and resist motion of the device if power or control signal is lost. For example: a spring applied, electrically released brake.
Fall Arrest System	A device that engages to halt a person or other load that has exceeded a predetermined speed, indicating a falling condition.
Field Check	A visit made to an installation project for the purpose of obtaining project measurements, checking its status, and finding potential conflicts.
Fire Safety Curtain	A curtain that closes automatically in event of a fire to prevent heat, smoke and flames on the stage from reaching the audience. The curtain may be closed when the space is not occupied to prevent unauthorized access and to prevent falls from the edge of the stage.
Fireline	Firelines are installed around the perimeter of a stage-proscenium arch to hold the fire safety curtain open. Firelines connect the curtain to all manual electrical and heat activated devices that release the safety curtain.
Fixed Speed	A winch that operates at a single speed with no ability to modify the speed. Fixed speed winches are typically used for low speed setup or heavy load applications.
Fleet Angle	The angle formed between the centerline of a sheave or drum and another sheave or fixed point.
Floor Block	Pulley mounted at the floor to hold a rope or cable in position and to reverse its direction. Floor blocks meant for rope often incorporate a means of adjustment to accommodate changes in length due to loads or environmental conditions.
Flown	Suspended in a manner that permits the equipment to be raised and lowered.
Fly	The act of lifting scenery, lights, and curtains.
Fly Gallery	A gallery or catwalk above the stage floor from which counterweight and hemp (rope) rigging is operated.
Fly Loft	The space between the roof and the performance area that is not visible to the audience.
Forestage	The portion of the stage located in front of the proscenium or main curtain line.

Free End Ball	A heavy ball that is attached to the end of a fire line and wrapped around the fire safety curtain operating line to prevent closure of the curtain. When tension is release in the fire line the weight of the ball causes it to fall free, releasing the curtain.
Front Curtain (House Curtain)	A curtain used to define the stage location to the arriving audience. It is often the curtain closest to the audience and may also perform the function of an "Act Curtain."
Front of House (FOH)	A generic term for areas of the theater other than the stage, usually referring to the audience and lobby areas.
Fullness	Additional fabric that is added to a curtain to be sewn into pleats. 100 percent fullness means that the curtain would be double its finished width before the pleats are made.
Fusible Link	A device consisting of two metal parts that are soldered together. The solder melts at a predetermined temperature allowing the two halves to separate.

G

Gallery	Any platform above and to the side of the stage floor.
Gearmotor	The combination of a gearbox and motor in a single unit. The motor may also incorporate a brake.
Grade 5 Bolt	A medium carbon steel bolt that has been quenched and tempered for increased hardness and tensile strength in accordance with SAE Specification J429. The heads of bolts rated as Grade 5 have three lines at 120º intervals on their heads.
Green Room	A lounge for performers and/or technicians.
Gridiron (Grid)	An open floor, usually made from light steel channels or grating, that is located near the roof steel. It provides mounting locations for rigging equipment and access to that equipment for inspection and maintenance.
Guide	To control the movement of rigging devices by means of slides or rollers moving in tracks or on stretched cables.
Guide Shoe	A rolling or sliding device that connects a counterweight arbor or sliding tension block to guide rails in order to guide its travel.
Guide Rails	Components that confine and control the movement of counterweight arbors and tension floor blocks. See "J-Guide, A-Guide, Lattice Track, T-Guide, and Wire Guide."
Guillotine	A curtain that runs the width of the proscenium.

H

Hand Line	A line, usually rope, that is pulled by hand to lift or control the movement of a load.
Hand Winch	A device that consists of a hand crank that rotates a drum or pulley through a torque multiplying / speed reducing mechanism.

Head Block	A pulley mounted to support steel that changes the direction of lift and operating lines between the loft blocks and an arbor or winch.
Head Block Beams	Structural framing designed to support the head blocks and all related loads. Usually consisting of one or two beams and associated bracing members.
Heat Resisting Border	A curtain that is placed between stage masking curtains and a heat source, such as a stage light, to prevent a fire. The heat resisting curtain employs a fabric which is fire proof, rated for high temperatures and spreads the heat from hot spots.
Hemp (Rope or Spotline) Rigging	A rigging system that employs ropes and sandbags instead of counterweight arbors or other devices. Usually used for temporary rigging.
Hoist	A geared mechanism, either hand operated or motorized, for use in raising (vertical movement only) equipment. The gearing produces a mechanical advantage in speed and load capacity.
Hoisting Machine	A powered machine used for raising, lowering, and holding objects.
Holding Brake	A brake use to hold a load in a static condition as opposed to decelerating a load to a stop and holding the load.
House	See "Auditorium."
House Curtain	See "Act Curtain"
House Left/Right	The sides of an auditorium as seen by an audience member while facing the stage.
HVAC	Air handling equipment in a building which consisting of Heating, Ventilation, and Air Conditioning.
Hydraulic Descent Control	A device used to control the speed of a closing fire curtain. These devices include hydraulic dampers, speed regulators, and dashpots.

I

IBC	The International Building Code. A model national building code that was created to replace regional building codes such as BOCA and UBC.
Idler	A pulley designed to support one or more cables but not to make direction changes.
Incremental Block	A multi-grooved pulley that supports and changes the direction of cables between the load and the head block and that supports other, more distant, lines in the set.
Index Light	A series of lamps in a special housing designed to illuminate the locking or pinrail area.
Index Strip	A device located at the front of a locking rail to hold line set identification labels.

J

J-Guide

J-shaped aluminum members fixed in parallel rows for the purpose of guiding arbors or clews.

K
L

Lattice Track

A parallel pair of angles or other structural members that guide an arbor or clew. Low friction slides or roller guides are placed on both sides of the device to be guided.

Lead Line

See "Lift Line."

Leg Curtain

A curtain used to define the side limit of the stage and to mask or hide actors, lights, and unused scenery in the off stage area (wings).

Lift Line

Any rope or cable located between a load and a winch or counterweight arbor.

Lighting Bridge

A walkway across the stage (fixed or flown) where lights are hung and where they may be adjusted and maintained.

Line Set

A system consisting of one or more lift lines and related components operating together to lift, lower, or suspend a load.

Limit Switch

An electro-mechanical switch that trips (changes state) when contacted by a moving device. They are used to halt the motion of a winch or other electro-mechanical device.

Line Shaft Winch

Winch with a series of cable drums connected to a gearbox by a common shaft.

Live End

The end of a rope or part of a device that is active or load carrying.

Live Load

That part of a system load that may be added or deleted (i.e. lights hung from a pipe batten).

Load Side Brake (Load Brake)

A brake in the power train of the winch that is attached to the same shaft as the load, at the output side of the gearbox.

Loading Gallery (Loading Bridge)

A gallery above the stage floor where technicians add and remove counterweights from the arbors. Usually located so technicians have access to arbors when battens are at their lowest positions.

Load Sensing

A mechanical or electrical device that senses the load in a cable or block and produce a signal that can be read by a controlling device.

Locking Collar

A fastening device located on the counterweight arbor rods above the upper spreader plate and counterweights and intended to help keep the weights in the arbor during a hard impact.

Locking Rail (Loading Rail)

A structural railing designed to support rope locks in a way that allows them to be easily operated. It holds the out of balance loads from the rigging system held by rope locks. It also serves as a safety railing for operators and other personnel.

Loft Block	A pulley mounted to the gridiron or support steel that supports and changes the direction of a lift line cable between the load and the head block.
Loft Well	(1) An opening in the gridiron designed for the attachment of loft blocks so that lift lines can pass through it. 2) An opening in the gridiron designed so cables can pass through from blocks mounted above without rubbing against the opening.
Loge	The part of a theater mezzanine closest to the stage.

M

Main Curtain	See "Front Curtain."
ManualMaker™	This software program from Clancy facilitates the creation custom operation and maintenance manuals for stages using Clancy hardware. Sections are written in Microsoft Word for most standard Clancy products.
Masking	A set of curtains or scenic elements used to define the visual limits of a performance area.
Mechanical Systems	Equipment needed to make a building structure functional, including plumbing, fire protection, and HVAC.
Mezzanine	1. The lowest balcony in a theater. 2. A low-ceilinged story located between two main stories in a building.
Motor (Primary) Brake	A brake that is mounted at the motor. It has a low torque capacity and fast response. Used for normal stopping and holding duty on a motorized hoist.
Motorized Rigging	A theatrical rigging system using powered winches and other devices to move equipment rather than muscle power.
Mouse	To wrap the end of a rope, cable or turnbuckle to prevent it from unwinding.
Mule Block	A pulley that supports and changes the direction of one or more cables traveling between loft blocks and head block.
Mule Winch	See "Capstan Winch."
Multi-Cable	Electrical cable (borderlight cable) with multiple conductors that conducts electrical power to multiple circuit wire ways and boxes on the stage. At least one conductor must be used as a grounding wire.
Multi-Line Block	Any block that can support more than one line. See "Incremental Block" and "Multi-Sheave Block".
Multi-Sheave Block	A block with more than one sheave, each of which can support and change the direction of a rope or cable. Sheaves can be held by a common shaft or by multiple shafts within a common housing.

N

NEC	The National Electrical Code (USA)
NEMA	National Electrical Manufacturers Association.
NFPA 101	The Life Safety Code.

Nicopress® — A registered trademark of the National Telephone Supply Company, used to describe compression type sleeves placed at the end of a wire rope to interconnect two ropes or to form an eye at the end.

O

Off Stage — The stage floor area that is not a part of the acting area and is not visible to the audience.

Olio Curtain — A curtain located between the "Front" or "Act" curtains and the "Rear" curtain that closes off a portion of the acting area for more intimate presentations. It is often colored or decorative.

On Stage — The portion of the stage area visible to the audience, usually defined by masking curtains, scenery, an orchestra shell, or by lighting.

Orchestra — (1) A group of musicians who play instrumental selections (2) The portion of the auditorium on the main floor that is closest to the musicians and the acting area.

Orchestra Lift — A moving platform that is used to adjust the elevation of the musicians in relation to the stage and auditorium. Usually operates within the confines of an orchestra pit.

Orchestra Pit — A depressed area between the stage and audience seating area where musicians sit, so the audience can hear the music and see the performance over the heads of the musicians.

Orchestra Pit Filler — Removable platforms that are used to close off the orchestra pit at the level of the stage or auditorium.

Orchestra Pit Lift — A section of the orchestra pit floor that may be raised and lowered by some mechanical (typically motorized) means.

Orchestra Shell — An enclosure on stage, consisting of walls and a ceiling that reflects sound into the auditorium. Usually decorative in nature.

Over Balance Bar System — In this system the curtain and counterweight are balanced so that the curtain can be raised and lowered manually with a minimum of effort. A weighted bar is held above the upper batten of the fire safety curtain by a hinged mechanism. The hinged mechanism opens when the fire line is released, so that the weighted bar slides down the center lift lines to rest on the upper batten. This makes the curtain heavier than the counterweight and causes it to close.

Over Speed Brake — Any brake that is controlled to recognize when the speed exceeds a preset threshold and then acts to stop the controlled load.

Out-of-Balance	A condition that exists when the weight of a batten, fittings, and attached loads do not equal that of counterbalancing equipment such as counterweight and an arbor. For safe and efficient use, manually operated sets should be balanced to within 50 pounds of neutral.
Outrigger	A barrier device that protects counterweight arbors from scenery, etc. that may be leaned against them. Often also supports index lights.

P

Paint Frame	A rigid frame, usually made of wood, to which drops and flats may be attached vertically for painting. They are normally rigged to be raised and lowered so painters can reach all areas of the frame.
Parking Brake	See "Holding Brake".
Pendant	A hand held controller that is attached to an electrical cable so the operator can move about to obtain better visibility of the devices being controlled.
Pileup Winch	Winch with a drum that has a narrow slot to contain the cable in a single vertical layer. The speed and load capacity varies with each layer of cable. Also called a Yo-Yo winch.
Pinrail	A railing with holes to accept belaying pins. May also act as a safety railing at the edge of a gallery or walkway.
Pipe Clamp	Clamping device that bolts around a pipe for attachment of chain or cable hangers.
Pipe Grid	Horizontal structure hung over a stage or auditorium to support lights and scenery. Made from pipes crossing on right angles at set intervals.
Pipe Weight	The counterweight needed in an arbor to keep an empty batten evenly balanced.
Pitch Diameter	Diameter of a sheave or drum measured from the center line of the cable wrapped around it.
Pivot Block	A pulley designed to adjust to structures at odd angles.
Plan Drawing	A drawing that shows the layout or top view of a construction or object.
Point Hoist	A single line winch, used singularly or in groups, to hold a load at a specific point over the stage. They are the motorized equivalent of spot lines, providing the greatest flexibility possible in automated rigging (Similar to a dimmer per circuit in lighting).
Portal	A portal consists of a header (border) and tabs (legs) that can be moved to adjust the size and shape of the proscenium opening to fit various performance needs. It is usually located just up stage of the front curtain and may have provision for mounting lights.
PowerAssist®	These hoists are designed to drive existing or new counterweight sets by using a closed loop, proprietary rope/chain arrangement to operate between zero pounds up to 1,000 pounds out of balance from the arbor.

PowerLift®	A J.R. Clancy Product. See "Zero Fleet Angle Hoist."
Purchase Line	See "Hand Line."
Proscenium	The dividing wall or barrier between the audience and the stage.
Proscenium Arch	The opening in the proscenium through which the audience views a performance.

Q

R

Raked Stage	A sloped platform that is lower near the audience for better visibility and higher at the rear, providing the illusion of distance. This is the source for the terms "Down Stage" and "Upstage."
Recommended Working Load	The maximum load which J.R. Clancy, Inc. recommends be applied to current, listed products which are in "like new" condition and which have been properly installed, maintained, and operated. "Rated Load," "Safe Working Load," and "Working Load Limit" are similar terms used by other manufacturers.
Resultant Load	A single load resulting from the combination of two, or more, forces acting on an object.
Reverse Bend	Passing a rope over a series of blocks so the rope is bent in opposing directions.
Rigging	All of the hardware used to lift, lower, and hold performance equipment on or above a stage.
RiggingWriter®	This software program from J.R. Clancy facilitates the creation of custom rigging specifications based on using J.R. Clancy hardware. Sections are written in Microsoft Word and are available for most standard J.R. Clancy products.
Riser	(1) The vertical distance between one step and the next. (2) Platforms located one step apart so that standing or seated people can see or be seen. (3) An electrical diagram indicating wiring for systems, e.g. power supply for a hoist.
Road House	A theater used for touring attractions that stay for a short period and bring some, or all, of their theatrical equipment with them.
Rope Lock	A cam operated device that clamps the hand line that is attached to an arbor in order to prevent movement. Designed to hold the unbalanced load in a set.
Rotary Limit Switch	A device containing a driven rotating shaft that contacts one or more switch contacts as it rotates.
Run-Away	Theater jargon which indicates an out of balance batten that is out of the operator's control.

S

Safe Working Load	See "Recommended Working Load (RWL)."

366

Safety Chain	1) A secondary support line, usually of chain, that supports a fire curtain or other device when the primary support cable becomes slack for any reason. (2) The extra weight of fire curtain safety chains helps the fire curtain accelerate at the start of its travel.
Safety Factor	This is the ratio between "Recommended Working Load" and minimum, or average, failure rating that must be furnished above the RWL to account for all of the uncertainties. These can include the actual operating load, shock loads, variations in materials and manufacturing processes, environmental conditions, accuracy of the design theory, and whether failures would endanger human lives.
Safety Inspection	A term used to identify the inspection of theater and entertainment spaces and equipment for the purpose of finding possible safety hazards and the need for maintenance or possible replacement of equipment.
Sag Bar	A support rail, usually of wood or plastic, that keeps cables from sagging over a horizontal span due to their own weight. Sag bars don't carry any loads.
Sandbag	A fabric bag that can be filled with sand and attached to rope rigging as a counterbalance to the load hung from the set.
SceneControl®	J.R. Clancy SceneControl rigging controllers use industrial grade PLC computers, touch screen 3-D displays, and industrial grade operators that require an operator to be present at the console when any equipment is moving. An optional load monitoring system stops motion with the detection of any change in load. Cues and presets can be created, modified, stored, and replayed. Targets, speeds, and positions are displayed. Displays show metric units, decimal feet or feet and inches.
Scrim	A curtain made from a semi-transparent material that looks solid when lit from the audience side and becomes almost invisible when back lit.
Section Drawing	A drawing that reveals an imaginary view obtained by making a cut through an object.
Self-Climbing	A pipe grid or batten that has an integral device for raising and lowering.
Set	A system of cables, pulleys, lifting devices and battens that holds a specific set of scenic elements, curtains or lights.
Shackle	A U-shaped device with holes at each end to accommodate a pin or bolt; used to connect a rope, cable, or chain to another device or a hanging point.
Sheave	A component with a groove around its circumference to support and contain a rope or cable and a bearing at its center to permit rotation about a shaft.
Shock Load	Loads generated by the rapid application of a force or motion to an object or by the collision of moving bodies.

Side Line Pulley	A light duty block that mounts by its side to a surface. They are normally used to support fire lines and operating cords for curtain tracks.
Sight Line	The edge or line of view, of what can be seen on stage from the location of the audience.
Single Point Failure Proof	Equipment designed to provide multiple load paths so that an equipment failure at any point will provide alternative load paths and not allow the load to fall.
Single Purchase	A rope or cable passing from a lifting device (arbor, winch, or person) over a block, or series of blocks, to a load is single purchased. Force must be exerted equal to the load to be held or raised.
Slack Line	A cable that droops or leaves the sheave or drum groove because it lacks tension in the line.
Smoke Pocket	A slot, usually of fabricated steel that supports a guide system at the edges of a fire safety curtain and that helps to prevent smoke passing around the edges of the curtain.
Smoke Seal	A fabric flap that mounts on the proscenium wall and contacts the fire curtain in order to form a barrier that reduces the passage of air and smoke between the stage and auditorium.
Snub Line	A short piece of rope used to tie down a hand line to prevent movement.
Spot Block	Any block that is designed for temporary, and easily movable connection to a gridiron or other theatre structure.
Spotline Rigging	A single line rigging system designed to be easily installed, relocated, and removed. They are often rigged with rope and are frequently motorized.
Spreader Plates	A thin plate located on counterweight arbor rods, spaced by the user at 2 foot intervals between counterweights, to prevent the rods from spreading apart under a sudden impact load and releasing the counterweights.
Stage	A platform on which performances are given.
Stage Left/Right	The left and right sides of a stage as seen by an actor standing on stage facing the audience.
Stage Lift	A section of the stage floor that may be raised or lowered to different levels above and below the stage by some mechanical (typically motorized) means.
Staggered Seating	An arrangement whereby the seats in alternating rows are offset to permit sightlines.
Starter	An electrical device that consists of a contactor, overload protection, and other control devices to power a motor. Many starters have dual contactors that are mechanically and electrically interconnected to cause the motor to run in either direction.

Static (dead) Load	A load that does not change position or magnitude over time.
Stop Batten (Bumper Angle)	A member mounted to the T or J-Guides that limits the travel of arbors at their top and bottom trim. They are often provided with a wood or rubber bumper to reduce noise and shock due to sudden stops of the arbors.
Stopping Brake	A brake that is activated while the load is in motion and is used to decelerate the load to a controlled stop and hold it.
Straight Lift Curtain	A curtain that can be raised (opened) without folding in any way.
Structural Drawing	An engineering drawing that describes the size, location, and attachment details of the building structure.
Submittal Drawings	Drawings that are prepared by the equipment supplier or installer to describe the equipment and details of the installation to the client. Approval of the drawings by the client indicates his acceptance of the proposed equipment, locations, and conditions of the installation.
SureBrake®	This variable torque brake is always applied, acting directly upon the winch drum, ensuring an immediate stop with no engagement shock and no need for electricity or external sensors.
SureGrip®	This rope, available exclusively from J.R. Clancy, is constructed using a 3-strand construction combining filament and staple/spun polyester wrapped around fibrillated polyolefin. One strand contains an identifying tape showing the manufacturer's name and address with the year of manufacture.
SureGuard II®	A device that accepts input from sensors and control devices and releases a fire safety curtain in response to these signals. It contains a battery and charger so a short term power loss will not result in a curtain closure. The name is a trademark of J.R. Clancy, Inc.
SureLock®	A special rope lock made by J.R. Clancy, Inc. designed so it cannot be opened when the counterweight set is more than 50 pounds out of balance in either direction. Also see "Rope Lock."
Swaged Fitting	A fitting that is squeezed in a die so that the material in the fitting cold flows around the strands in the cable to form a tight connection. The excess material will flow out around the edges of the die.
Swivel Block	A pulley that allows the sheave to rotate and align itself in the plane of the cable.

T

Tab	(1) A masking leg that is mounted at right angles to the front of the stage. (2) See "Portal."
Tableau	A curtain that is drawn open by a line running through rings located diagonally across the rear of the curtain from the leading edge up to the top on the offstage edge.

Tag Line	A line attached to a load to assist in controlling its movement.
Tandem Block	A block with two or more sheaves on separate shafts within a common housing.
Teaser	Another name for a border curtain. It often refers to the first masking curtain on stage and is paired with the "Tormentor" legs.
T-Bar (T-Guide)	"T" shaped members placed in parallel rows to guide arbors or clews. Guides may consist of low friction slides or rollers.
Tension Block	See "Floor Block."
Theater (Theatre)	A place for the exhibition of dramatic, music, or dance performance presentation of information or for discussion with a group, (ex., a classroom).
Theater Rigging	Equipment that is used to hold or move people or other equipment in a theater space.
Thimble	A grooved fitting around which a rope or cable is bent to form an eye. It supports the rope or cable and prevents kinking and wear.
Thrust Stage	A room with seats arranged on three sides around a performance space located against the fourth wall. This wall may be used for scenery, back drops, and acting space.
Tieoff Bracket	A bracket attached to rigging blocks, gridiron, or other structure to hold one end of wire ropes or chains.
Tormentor	Another name for a leg curtain. These are the first masking legs located after the main curtain.
Traction Drive Hoist	Hoist with a V-grooved drum that uses friction between cables and the sides of the grooves to engage the pulling cables. Increasing the cable tension causes the cables to jam tighter in the v-grooves.
Travel	The path of moving stage equipment and the distance moved.
Traveler	A curtain on a track that can be opened or closed to reveal or mask a portion of the stage.
Tread Diameter	The diameter of a sheave measured at the bottom of its groove.
Tread Pressure	This indicator of the radial bearing pressure (P) of a rope against a sheave groove is taken as the Tension (T) in the rope divided by the tread radius (R) of the sheave times the rope diameter (d). $$P = 2T\,Dd$$
Trigger Arbor Release	This is an auxiliary system that is added to a fire safety curtain rig so the curtain can be in balance for normal operation but also allow automatic closure in an emergency by adding weight to the curtain. It basically consists of a guided auxiliary weight arbor, a catch arbor that is tied to the curtain and receives the auxiliary weight arbor (trigger arbor), and a triggering device that releases the trigger arbor in response to a loss of tension in the fire line.

Trim	(1) A load is "in trim" when the equipment load equals the counterbalancing weight. (2) A set or element is trimmed when it has been placed in the desired position within the performance area.
Trim Chain	A length of chain placed between a lift line and a pipe batten or scenic element to connect them and to facilitate minor height adjustment of the load.
Tripped	A curtain or scenic element is lifted by a second set of lines attached at the bottom or intermediate point on the piece. Pulling the lines will cause the piece to fold in half or thirds. Note: If the piece is counterbalanced, the weight balance will shift as the piece is tripped.
Truss Batten	Two or more pipes or other linear members fabricated together with cross bracing in a trussed configuration. Used in place of a pipe batten for heavy loads or extended distances between lift lines.

U

UBC	The Uniform Building Code (USA). Has been superseded by the IBC.
Under Hung	Hung from the bottom of a beam or structure.
Up Stage	The portion of the stage that is furthest from the audience. See "Raked Stage."
Upright	Resting on top of a beam or structure.

V

Valence	See "Border Curtain." Usually a special border associated with the "Front Curtain." May be permanently fixed within the proscenium arch.
Variable Frequency Drive	An electronic device that can vary the speed of an AC motor by varying the frequency of the current supplied to the motor. Speeds can typically be varied over a limited range of speeds.
Upright	Resting on top of a beam or structure.
Variable Speed	A device that is capable of operating at various speeds. The time required to ramp up to the operating speed and back to zero may be adjustable.
Vector Drive (also Flux Vector Drive)	An AC variable speed drive that offers greatly increased performance over variable frequency drives. A processor in the drive develops the correct vectors of magnetic flux within the motor to provide the required performance. A closed loop vector drive can provide full torque at zero speed, allowing it to hold the load while not moving. These drives provide the best low speed performance of an AC drive.

W

Wall Batten	Horizontal structural members to which guide tracks are attached.
Wall Knee	Bracket that attaches a wall batten to the building structure.

Well	Gaps between gridiron members intended for the mounting and support of loft blocks on boundary channels and for allowing the free passage of cables.
Winch	A machine for pulling and holding equipment using a rope or cable.
Wings	The portion of the stage area located to either side of the acting area.
Wire Grid	An open floor that supports lights or provides access to theatrical equipment. It is formed of woven cables attached to, and supported by, a structural frame.
Wire Guide	Wires placed to control the location and travel of arbors, clews and curtains.
Wire Rope	A wire rope consists of a number of strands laid helically about a metallic or non-metallic core. Each strand consists of a number wires also laid helically about a center.
Working Load Limit (WLL)	See Recommended Working Load (RWL).

X

Y

Yo-Yo (Pile-up) Hoist	A hoist type used when space is tight and fleet angles are difficult. The drum contains a narrow slot(s) where the lift line piles up in a single layer. The hoist capacity, speed, and distance traveled vary with each cable wrap.

Z

Zero Fleet Angle Hoist	A hoist with cables that exit the winch at fixed points so that fleet angles do not need to be considered in the rigging layout. This is accomplished by incorporating a moving head block or by making the drum move in relation to the head block per Izenour / J.R. Clancy designs dating from the early 1960s.
Zetex®	Registered Trade name for a woven, high temperature, silica glass fabric used in the making of fire safety curtains. The name is a trademark of Newtex Industries, Inc.

Appendix 2:
Reference Data

Sometimes you just need data about a piece of equipment or hardware. While manufacturers provide data on their products, some things you should just know as a rigger. Below are tables of reference data that may be helpful.

Round Slings

Code	Color	Capacity Vertical (lb)	Capacity Choker (lb)	Capacity Basket (lb)
EN30	Purple	2,600	2,100	5,200
EN60	Green	5,300	4,200	10,600
EN90	Yellow	8,400	6,700	16,800
EN120	Tan	10,600	8,500	21,200
EN150	Red	13.200	10,600	26,400
EN180	White	16,800	13,400	33,600
EN240	Blue	21,200	17,000	42,400
EN360	Grey	31,000	24,800	62,000
EN600	Brown	53,000	42,400	106,000
EN800	Olive	66,000	52,800	132,000
EN1000	Black	90,000	72,000	180,000

Pipe Weight

Size	Schedule 40 LB per Foot	Schedule 80 LB per Foot
1"	1.68	2.17
1-1/4"	2.27	3
1-1/2"	2.72	3.63
2"	3.65	5.02

Welded Chain

Grade 30

Nominal Chain Size		Material Diameter		Minimum Breaking Strength		Working Load Limit	
in	mm	in	mm	lb	kN	lb	kg
1/8	4.0	0.156	4.0	1,600	7.2	400	180
3/16	5.5	0.217	5.5	3,200	14.4	800	365
1/4	7.0	0.276	7.0	5,200	23.2	1,300	580
5/16	8.0	0.331	8.0	7,600	33.8	1,900	860
3/8	10.0	0.394	10.0	10,600	47.2	2,650	1,200
7/16	11.9	0.488	11.9	14,800	65.8	3,700	1,680
1/2	13.0	0.512	13.0	18,000	80.0	4,500	2,030
5/8	16.0	0.63	16.0	27,600	122.6	6,900	3,130
3/4	20.0	0.787	20.0	42,400	188.6	10,600	4,800
7/8	22.0	0.866	22.0	51,200	228.2	12,800	5,810
1	26.0	1.02	26.0	71,600	318.2	17,900	8,140

Grade 80

Nominal Chain Size		Material Diameter		Minimum Breaking Strength		Working Load Limit	
in	mm	in	mm	lb	kN	lb	kg
7/32	5.5	0.217	5.5	8,400	38.0	2,100	970
9/32	7.0	0.276	7.0	14,000	61.6	3,500	1,570
5/16	8.0	0.315	8.0	18,000	80.6	4,500	2,000
3/8	10.0	0.394	10.0	28,400	126.0	7,100	3,200
1/2	13.0	0.512	13.0	48,000	214.0	12,000	5,400
5/8	16.0	0.63	16.0	72,400	322.0	18,100	8,200
3/4	20.0	0.787	20.0	113,200	504.0	28,300	12,800
7/8	22.0	0.866	22.0	136,800	610.0	34,200	15,500
1	26.0	1.02	26.0	190,800	850.0	47,700	21,600
1-1/4	32.0	1.26	32.0	289,200	1,288.0	72,300	32,800

Alpha Chain

Nominal Chain Size		Material Diameter		Minimum Breaking Strength		Working Load Limit	
in	mm	in	mm	lb	kN	lb	kg
1/4	7.0	0.276	7.0	13,000	57.83	3,250	1,477.3
Meets ASTM B633 FE/ZN5 specifications.					DF = 4		

STAC Chain

Size	Inside Length	WLL (lb)
1/2"	3.74"	12,000

Bolt Markings/Data

Grade	Radial Bolt Markings	Material	Nominal Size Diameter/Inches	Proof Load psi	Tensile Strength minimum psi	Yield Strength minimum psi
Grade 2 No Radial Lines		Low or Medium Carbon Steel	1/4" to 3/4"	55,000	74,000	57,000
			Over 3/4" thru 1 1/2"	33,000	60,000	36,000
Grade 5 3 Radial Lines		Medium Carbon Steel	1/4" to 1"	85,000	120,000	92,000
			Over 1" thru 1 1/2"	74,000	105,000	81,000
Grade 8 6 Radial Lines		Medium Carbon Alloy Steel	1/4" thru 1 1/2"	120,000	150,000	130,000
Metric 8.8		Medium Carbon Steel	All sizes under 16mm	580	800	640
			16mm thru 72mm	600	830	660
Metric 10.9		Alloy Steel	5mm thru 100mm	830	1040	940

Forged Scaffolding Clamps (Cheeseboroughs)

Grade	Torque	Slippage Capacity	Tension Capacity
Industrial	50 ft/lb	4,000 lb	16,000 lb
Military	50 ft/lb		25,000 lb

7X19
Galvanized Aircraft Cable

7X7
Galvanized Aircraft Cable

Diameter (in)	Min. Breaking Strength (lb)	WT/1000 feet (lb)	Diameter (in)	Min. Breaking Strength (lb)	WT/1000 feet (lb)
3/32	920	17.5	3/64	270	-
1/8	2,000	29	1/16	480	7.5
5/32	2,800	45	3/32	920	16
3/16	4,200	65	1/8	2,000	28.5
7/32	5,600	86	5/32	2,800	43
1/4	7,000	110	3/16	4,200	62
5/16	9,800	173	7/32	5,600	86
3/8	14,400	243	1/4	7,000	106
Meets Fed. Spec. RR-W-410D for dimension			Meets Fed. Spec. RR-W-410D for dimension		
Meets MIL-W83420D for strength			Meets MIL-W83420D for strength		

6X25
Galvanized Wire Rope
IWRC EXIPS

6X37
Galvanized Wire Rope
IWRC EXIPS

Diameter (in)	Min. Breaking Strength (lb)	WT/Ft (lb)	Diameter (in)	Min. Breaking Strength (lb)	WT/Ft (lb)
3/8	6.8 T	0.26	1/4	3.1 T	0.116
7/16	9.2 T	0.35	5/16	4.7 T	0.18
1/2	12 T	0.46	3/8	6.8 T	0.26
9/16	15.1 T	0.59	7/16	9.12 T	0.35
5/8	18.5 T	0.72	1/2	12 T	0.46
3/4	26.5 T	1.04	9/16	15.1 T	0.59
7/8	35.8 T	1.42	5/8	18.5 T	0.72
1	46.5 T	1.85	3/4	26.5 T	1.04
			7/8	35.8 T	1.42
			1	46.5 T	1.85
Meets Fed. Spec. RR-W-410D			Meets Fed. Spec. RR-W-410D		

Swaging

Nicopress Cavity Code	Wire Rope Size	Number of Nicopress Swages	Number of Locoloc Swages
C	3/32"	1	2
G	1/8"	3	3
M	5/32	3	3
P	3/16"	4	4
F2	7/32	2	4
F6	1/4"	3	4
G9	5/16"	3 or 4	5A/4C

Pear Rings

Crosby A-341 Alloy Pear Shaped Links

Size (in)	WLL (lb)
1/2	7,000
5/8	9,000
3/4	12,300
7/8	15,000
1	24,360

Design Factor = 5

Crosby G-341 Carbon Steel Pear Shaped Links

Size (in)	WLL (lb)
3/8	1,800
1/2	2,900
5/8	4,200
3/4	6,000
7/8	8,300
1	10,800

Design Factor = 6

Shackles

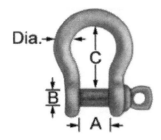

Black-Oxide Steel Shackles

Dia.	A	B	C	WLL (lb)
1/4"	15/32"	5/16"	1-1/8"	1,000
5/16"	17/32"	3/8"	1-1/4"	1,500
3/8"	21/32"	7/16"	1-7/16"	2,000
7/16"	23/32"	1/2"	1-11/16"	3,000
1/2"	13/16"	/8"	1-15/16"	4,000
5/8"	1-1/16"	3/4"	2-1/2"	6,500
3/4"	1-1/4"	7/8"	3"	9,500
7/8"	1-7/16"	1"	3-1/4"	13,000
1"	1-11/16"	1-1/8"	3-3/4"	17,000

DF = 6

Hot-Dipped Galvanized Carbon Steel Shackles

Dia.	A	B	C	WLL (lb)
3/16"	3/8"	1/4"	7/8"	666
1/4"	7/16"	5/16"	1-1/8"	1,102
5/16"	1/2"	3/8"	1-1/4"	1,500
3/8"	5/8"	7/16"	1-7/16"	2,204
7/16"	3/4"	1/2"	1-11/16"	3,306
1/2"	13/16"	5/8"	1-7/8"	4,409
5/8"	1-1/16"	3/4"	2-3/8"	7,165
3/4"	1-1/4"	7/8"	2-13/16"	10,471
7/8"	1-7/16"	1"	3-5/16"	14,330
1"	1-11/16"	1-1/8"	3-3/4"	18,739
1-1/8"	1-13/16"	1-1/4"	4-1/4"	20,943
1-1/4"	2"	1-3/8"	4-11/16"	26,455
1-3/8"	2-1/4"	1-1/2"	5-1/4"	29,762
1-1/2"	2-3/8"	1-5/8"	5-3/4"	34,000
1-3/4"	2-7/8"	2"	7"	50,000
2"	3-1/4"	2-1/4"	7-3/4"	70,000

DF = 6

Hot-Dipped Galvanized Alloy Steel Shackles

Dia.	A	B	C	WLL (lb)
3/8"	5/8"	7/16"	1-7/16"	4,000
1/2"	13/16"	5/8"	1-7/8"	6,600
5/8"	1-1/16"	3/4"	2-3/8"	10,000
3/4"	1-1/4"	7/8"	2-13/16"	14,000
7/8"	1-7/16"	1"	3-5/16"	19,000
1"	1-11/16"	1-1/8"	3-3/4"	25,000
1-1/4"	2"	1-3/8"	4-11/16"	36,000
1-1/2"	2-3/8"	1-5/8"	5-3/4"	50,000
1-3/4"	2-7/8"	2"	7"	68,000
2"	3-1/4"	2-1/4"	7-3/4"	86,000

DF = 6

Truss Data

Thomas Engineering

GP 12" x 12" | Maximum Center Point Load

Lbs Per Ft	10'	20'	30'	40'	50'	60'	70'	80'
5.5	4,497	1,550	865	428	-	-	-	-

ST 12" x 12" | Maximum Center Point Load

Lbs Per Ft	10'	20'	30'	40'	50'	60'	70'	80'
8.7	7,348	3,628	1,662	848	445	-	-	-

GP 15" x 15" | Maximum Center Point Load

Lbs Per Ft	10'	20'	30'	40'	50'	60'	70'	80'
6.2	4,600	2,250	1,450	1,000	650	-	-	-

ST 15" x 15" | Maximum Center Point Load

Lbs Per Ft	10'	20'	30'	40'	50'	60'	70'	80'
9.6	9,372	4,626	2,770	1,466	739	304	-	-

GP 20.5 x 20.5 | Maximum Center Point Load

Lbs Per Ft	10'	20'	30'	40'	50'	60'	70'	80'
8.8	2,870	2,870	1,858	1,322	957	-	-	-

Tomcat

Super beam 13.7 x 10 spigoted — Maximum Center Point Load

Lbs Per Ft	10'	20'	30'	40'	50'	60'	70'	80'
7.7	3,831	1,863	1,184	827	-	-	-	-

Core truss 12 x 12 plated — Maximum Center Point Load

Lbs Per Ft	10'	20'	30'	40'	50'	60'	70'	80'
6.0	2,483	1,200	753	516	-	-	-	-

Core truss 12 x 18 plated — Maximum Center Point Load

Lbs Per Ft	10'	20'	30'	40'	50'	60'	70'	80'
6.2	2,481	1,195	746	506	-	-	-	-

Core truss 20.5 x 20.5 plated — Maximum Center Point Load

Lbs Per Ft	10'	20'	30'	40'	50'	60'	70'	80'
6.9	5,289	2,925	1,927	1,278	1,066	655	-	-

Light duty truss 12 x 12 plated — Maximum Center Point Load

Lbs Per Ft	10'	20'	30'	40'	50'	60'	70'	80'
6.1	1,673	1,063	650	426	-	-	-	-

Light duty truss 12 x 12 spigoted — Maximum Center Point Load

Lbs Per Ft	10'	20'	30'	40'	50'	60'	70'	80'
9.2	7,785	3,099	2,089	824	-	-	-	-

Light duty truss 12 x 18 plated — Maximum Center Point Load

Lbs Per Ft	10'	20'	30'	40'	50'	60'	70'	80'
6.7	2,229	1,058	643	6.7				

Ballroom truss 12 x 30 spigoted — Maximum Center Point Load

Lbs Per Ft	10'	20'	30'	40'	50'	60'	70'	80'
12.6	11,361	6,299	5,106	3,036	2,942	1,897	1,229	697

Medium duty truss 20.5 x 20.5 plated — Maximum Center Point Load

Lbs Per Ft	10'	20'	30'	40'	50'	60'	70'	80'
8.5	4,744	2,306	1,464	1,021	737	-	-	-

Medium duty truss 20.5 x 20.5 spigoted — Maximum Center Point Load

Lbs Per Ft	10'	20'	30'	40'	50'	60'	70'	80'
11.5	9,204	5,797	3,781	2,748	2,109	-	-	-

Heavy duty truss 30 x 20.5 spigoted   Maximum Center Point Load

Lbs Per Ft	10'	20'	30'	40'	50'	60'	70'	80'
13.2	17,780	8,775	5,725	4,163	3,195	2,359	-	-

Heavy duty 30 x 20.5 plated   Maximum Center Point Load

Lbs Per Ft	10'	20'	30'	40'	50'	60'	70'	80'
9.4	5,840	3,704	2,387	1,703	1,273	970	-	-

Extra heavy duty truss 36 x 24 spigoted   Maximum Center Point Load

Lbs Per Ft	10'	20'	30'	40'	50'	60'	70'	80'
24.9	20,683	20,220	17,077	10,264	9,877	6,458	4,649	2,733

Stacking truss 25 spigoted   Maximum Center Point Load

Lbs Per Ft	10'	20'	30'	40'	50'	60'	70'	80'
9.0	10,206	5,033	3,278	2,377	1,818	1,430	-	-

Tyler Truss Systems

Centerline 16" x 20"   Maximum Center Point Load

Lbs Per Ft	10'	20'	30'	40'	50'	60'	70'	80'
-	4,916	3,176	2,288	1,737	1,354	-	-	-

12" x 12"   Maximum Center Point Load

Lbs Per Ft	10'	20'	30'	40'	50'	60'	70'	80'
-	1,360	741	665	316	-	-	-	-

12" x 12" AV   Maximum Center Point Load

Lbs Per Ft	10'	20'	30'	40'	50'	60'	70'	80'
-	3,273	1,605	1,034	632	-	-	-	-

12" x 12" Custom Spigot Truss   Maximum Center Point Load

Lbs Per Ft	10'	20'	30'	40'	50'	60'	70'	80'
-	5,398	2,635	1,658	850	-	-	-	-

12" x 18"   Maximum Center Point Load

Lbs Per Ft	10'	20'	30'	40'	50'	60'	70'	80'
-	3,180	2,160	1,170	630	-	-	-	-

12" x 18" AV   Maximum Center Point Load

Lbs Per Ft	10'	20'	30'	40'	50'	60'	70'	80'
-	2,647	1,287	818	571	-	-	-	-

20" x 20" Bolt Plate   Maximum Center Point Load

Lbs Per Ft	10'	20'	30'	40'	50'	60'	70'	80'
-	6,060	2,975	1,924	1,380	1,039	-	-	-

20" x 20" Spigoted   Maximum Center Point Load

Lbs Per Ft	10'	20'	30'	40'	50'	60'	70'	80'
-	4,720	2,700	2,500	1,776	1,600	1,060	-	-

Threaded Rod and Bolts

Size	Stress Area (Sq. inches)	Grade 2 Tensile Strength (pounds)	Grade 5 Tensile Strength (pounds)	ASTM A193 B-7 Tensile Strength (pounds)	Grade 8 Tensile Strength (pounds)
1/4" - 20	0.0318	2,350	3,800	3,975	4,750
1/4" - 28	0.0364	2,700	3,800	4,550	5,450
5/16" - 18	0.0524	3,900	6,300	6,550	7,850
5/16" - 24	0.0580	4,300	6,300	7,250	8,700
3/8" - 16	0.0775	5,750	9,300	9,700	11,600
3/8" - 24	0.0878	6,500	9,300	11,000	13,200
7/16" - 14	0.1063	7,850	12,800	13,300	15,900
7/16" - 20	0.1187	8,800	12,800	14,850	17,800
1/2" - 13	0.1419	10,500	17,000	17,750	21,300
1/2" - 20	0.1599	11,800	17,000	20,000	24,000
9/16" - 12	0.1820	13,500	21,800	22,750	27,300
9/16" - 18	0.2030	15,000	21,800	25,400	30,400
5/8" - 11	0.2260	16,700	27,100	28,250	33,900
5/8" - 18	0.2560	18,900	30,700	32,000	38,400
3/4" - 10	0.3340	24,700	40,100	41,750	50,100
3/4" - 16	0.3730	27,600	44,800	46,650	56,000
7/8" - 9	0.4620	27,700	55,400	57,750	69,300
7/8" - 14	0.5090	30,500	61,100	63,650	76,400
1" - 8	0.6060	36,400	72,700	75,750	90,900
1" - 12 & 14	0.6630	39,800	7,900	84,900	99,400
1-1/8" - 7	0.7630	45,800	80,100	95,400	114,400
1-1/8" - 12	0.8560	51,400	89,900	107,000	128,400
1-1/4" - 7	0.9690	58,100	101,700	121,150	145,400
1-1/4" - 12	1.0730	64,400	112,700	134,150	161,000
1-3/8" - 6	1.1550	69,300	121,300	144,400	173,200
1-3/8" - 12	1.3150	78,900	138,100	164,400	197,200
1-1/2" - 6	1.4050	84,300	147,500	175,650	210,800
1-1/2" - 12	1.5810	94,900	166,000	197,650	237,200

Turnbuckles

THE CROSBY GROUP
HG-226 EYE & EYE   **DF 5:1**
Recommended for Straight or in-line pull only.
Meets the performance requirements of Federal Specifications FF-T-791b, Type 1, Form 1 — CLASS 4
Except for those provisions required of the contractor

THREAD DIAMETER & TAKE UP	WWL (LBS)
1/4" x 4"	500
5/16" x 4-1/2"	800
3/8 x 6	1200
1/2" x 6"	2200
1/2" x 9"	2200
1/2" x 12"	2200
5/8" x 6"	3500
5/8" x 9"	3500
5/8" x 12"	3500

BREWER-TITCHENER
780 – G EYE TO EYE   **DF 5:1**
Recommended for Straight or in-line pull only.
Meets design requirements of federal specifications, FF-T791, Type 1, Class 4.
Drop forged carbon steel with galvanized finish.
Galvanizing meets ASTM A-153 specifications.
Weldless

THREAD DIAMETER & TAKE UP	WWL (LBS)
1/4" x 4"	500
5/16" x 4-1/2"	800
3/8" x 6"	1200
1/2" x 6"	2200
1/2" x 9"	2200
1/2" x 12"	2200
5/8" x 6"	3500
5/8" x 9"	3500
5/8 x 12"	3500
5/8" x 18"	3500

THE CROSBY GROUP
HG-227 JAW & EYE   **DF 5:1**
Recommended for Straight or in-line pull only.
Meets the performance requirements of Federal Specifications FF-T-791b, Type 1, Form 1 — CLASS 8,
Except for those provisions required of the contractor.

THREAD DIAMETER & TAKE UP	WWL (LBS)
1/4" x 4"	500
5/16" x 4-1/2"	800
3/8 x 6	1200
1/2" x 6"	2200
1/2" x 9"	2200
1/2" x 12"	2200
5/8" x 6"	3500
5/8" x 9"	3500
5/8" x 12"	3500

THE CROSBY GROUP
HG-228 JAW & JAW   **DF 5:1**
Recommended for Straight or in-line pull only.
Meets the performance requirements of Federal Specifications FF-T-791b, Type 1, Form 1 — CLASS 7,
Except for those provisions required of the contractor.

THREAD DIAMETER & TAKE UP	WWL (LBS)
1/4" x 4"	500
5/16" x 4-1/2"	800
3/8 x 6	1200
1/2" x 6"	2200
1/2" x 9"	2200
1/2" x 12"	2200
5/8" x 6"	3500
5/8" x 9"	3500
5/8" x 12"	3500

All rigging equipment and hardware should be inspected periodically
for wear, abuse and general adequacy.

Weight Chart for Theatrical Lighting Instruments*

* add 2.3 lb for C-Clamp

Manufacturer	Instrument Type	Weight w/o clamp	
ETC	Source 4- 5 degree	19.2	lb
	Source 4- 10 degree	15	lb
	Source 4- 19 degree	14	lb
	Source 4- 26 degree	14	lb
	Source 4- 36 degree	14	lb
	Source 4- 50 degree	14	lb
	Source 4- 15-30 degree Zoom	21	lb
	Source 4- 25-50 degree Zoom	17	lb
	Source 4 Junior- 26 degree	10	lb
	Source 4 Junior- 50 degree	10	lb
	Source 4 Junior- Zoom	10	lb
	Source 4- HID 5 degree	23	lb
	Sourcc 4- HID 10 degree	19.3	lb
	Source 4- HID 19 degree	18	lb
	Source 4- HID 36 degree	18	lb
	Source 4- HID 50 degree	18	lb
	Source 4- HID Zoom 15-30 degree	25	lb
	Source 4- HID Zoom 25-50 degree	20.8	lb
	Source 4- HID Junior 26 degree	13.6	lb
	Source 4- HID Junior 36 degree	13.6	lb
	Source 4 Junior- 50 degree	13.6	lb
	Source 4- HID Junior Zoom	15	lb
	Source 4 Parnell	8	lb
Altman	6" Fresnel	9	lb
	8" Fresnel	15	lb
	6" ERS	14 to 15	lb
	Shakespeare ERS	15 to 17	lb
	Shakespeare Zoom	21	lb
	Baby Zoom	15	lb
	575W Star PAR	8	lb
	PAR 64 Aluminum	8	lb
	PAR 64 Steel	11	lb

Colortran	4-1/2" ERS	20.2	lb
	6" ERS	20.2	lb
	8" ERS	20.2	lb
	10" ERS	30	lb
	Mini ERS	13	lb
	6" Fresnel	11	lb
	8" Fresnel	19.5	lb
	8" Studio Fresnel 2kW	31	lb
	Far Cyc , 3 units	30	lb
	3 unit Striplight	35	lb

Weight of Lighting Cable

Cable	Weight per Foot
19-pin 12/14 Multi	0.6
19-pin 12/19 Multi	0.8
12/3 SO	0.23
12/3 SJ0	0.15
14/1 SJO	0.11
7-pin Socapex 14/7	0.34
7-pin Socapex 16/7	0.19
12/3 SOOW	0.22
12/2 SJOOW	0.12
12/5 SOOW	0.13
10/5 SOOW	0.46

Weight of Metal

An online weight calculator for metal can be found at
http://www.onlinemetals.com/calculator.cfm

Appendix 3:
Overhead Lifting

What does "overhead lifting" mean?

Let's begin with the National Association of Chain Manufacturers (NACM) and their definition as adopted on Sept. 28, 2005:

> *Overhead lifting: that process of lifting that which would elevate a freely suspended load to such a position that dropping the load would present a possibility of bodily injury or property damage.*

The NACM definition is very clear and concise. Let's see what OSHA has to say about overhead lifting since OSHA, unlike NACM, is federally mandated. The only reference on overhead lifting we have comes from Table H-1, *Rated Capacities for Alloy Steel Chain*- 29 CFR 1929.251 (f)(1). In a footnote, OSHA states,

> *"Other grades of proof tested steel chain include Proof Coil, BBB Coil and Hi-Test Chain. These grades are not recommended for **overhead lifting** and therefore are not covered by this code."*

This doesn't give us much to go on, nor is it likely to be all that helpful especially in our industry. For many years theatre industry professionals have followed the OSHA mandates written for <u>Overhead and Gantry Cranes</u>, CFR 1910.184, and <u>Cranes and Derricks,</u> CFR 1926.550. These regulations were the only guidance we had to lifting operations in a *totally unrelated* industry.

In reading CFR 1910.184, the use of non-alloy steel chain for overhead lifting is not prohibited, but chain *manufacturers* recommend only *alloy* steel chain. Non-alloy chain such as proof coil and high-test chain should only be used for overhead lifting in accordance with the manufacturer's recommendations.

OSHA does govern the use and manufacture of steel chain slings. They do not specify what chain can be used for overhead lifting; they leave that to the manufacturer. They DO state, however, that alloy chain must NOT be used with loads in excess of their rated capacities. OSHA's 29 CFR, 1910.184(e)(5) states,

Sling use. Alloy steel chain slings shall not be used with loads in excess of the rated capacities prescribed in Table N-184-1. Slings not included in this table shall be used only in accordance with the manufacturer's recommendations.

TABLE N-184-1

RATED CAPACITY (WORKING LOAD LIMIT), FOR ALLOY STEEL CHAIN SLING; RATED CAPACITY (WORKING LOAD LIMIT), POUNDS							
Chain Size, Inches	Single Branch Sling 90 Degree Loading	Double Sling			Triple & Quadrupal Sling (3)		
		Vertical Angle (1)			Vertical Angle (1)		
		30 Degrees	45 Degrees	60 Degrees	30 Degrees	45 Degrees	60 Degrees
		Horizontal Angle (2)			Horizontal Angle (2)		
		60 Degrees	45 Degrees	30 Degrees	60 Degrees	45 Degrees	30 Degrees
1/4"	3,250	5,650	4,550	3,250	8,400	6,800	4,900
3/8"	6,600	11,400	9,300	6,600	17,000	14,000	9,900
1/2"	11,250	19,500	15,900	11,250	29,000	24,000	17,000
5/8"	16,500	28,500	23,300	16,500	43,000	35,000	24,500
3/4"	23,000	39,800	32,500	23,000	59,500	48,500	34,500
7/8"	28,750	49,800	40,600	28,750	74,500	61,000	43,000
1"	38,750	67,100	54,800	38,750	101,000	82,000	58,000
1 1/8"	44,500	77,000	63,000	44,500	115,500	94,500	66,500
1 1/4"	57,500	99,500	81,000	57,500	149,000	121,500	86,000
1 3/8"	67,000	116,000	94,000	67,000	174,000	141,000	100,500
1 1/2"	80,000	138,000	112,500	80,000	207,000	169,000	119,500
1 3/4"	100,000	172,000	140,000	100,000	258,000	210,000	150,000

This clause is commonly interpreted to mean that OSHA would approve for overhead lifting a non-alloy sling that the *manufacturer* approved. Another recommendation from ASME B30.9-2006 section 9-1.2.3 states:

> *Other Materials and Components*
> *"Chain or components other than those listed in paras. 9-1.2.1 and 9-1.2.2 (i.e., alloy) may be employed. When such materials are employed, the sling manufacturer or a qualified person shall provide specific data. These slings shall comply with all other requirements of this Chapter.*

Again ASME defers to the manufacturer on the use of non-alloy slings for overhead lifting. In some industries, outside of the theatre, corrosive conditions warrant the non-use of alloy metals.

Freely suspended

Our definition above stated overhead lifting is *"that process of lifting that which would elevate a freely suspended load to such a position that dropping the load would present a possibility of bodily injury or property damage."* It would now seem that we now have to determine whether a load is being *"freely suspended"* in order for the definition to apply. Basically, the term *"freely suspended*" implies that an overhead object is being hung without restraints of any kind and is left to freely rotate. Remember, these definitions were originally written for the Crane, Derrick, and Gantry industry. It becomes easy to see how these rules and recommendations were simply followed by theatre architects and engineers in the process of theatre building installations.

In Chapter One we discussed the differences between running rigging and standing rigging. We also noted that anything running through a cog or wheel must be rated for *overhead lifting*. The question now remains, is it *"freely suspended?"* Unlike the single lift cables found in a crane or gantry, counterweight lift lines and their components ***are*** *restrained* simply by the design of the system. The batten load is being held in place by *multiple* lift lines. The strains on the lift lines and working components caused by the rotation of *freely suspended* loads are simply not present in a theatre lineset. In addition, the load rating on the manufactured components of a counterweight system are much higher than the actual working load limit of the theatre lineset because these components meet the standards written for the crane and gantry industry.

Alloy or non-alloy trim chains

The issue is chain use in theatres really hits home when we deal with trim chains on battens. When theatre consultants began specifying alloy chain be used for trim chains on battens, it really did not matter that trim chain did not meet OSHA's definition of slings or not. Manufacturers and installers of counterweight systems found chain manufacturer who would make alloy chain that would work for this need (probably partially to meet the specification and probably partially for public relations reasons). The question is, "For this use, is alloy trim chain safer and needed?" Let's look at the facts.

In looking at a safety issue like this one, we need to look at the weakest link in the system. So, what is the breaking strengths we need to consider?

- 1/4" - 7x19 wire rope has a breaking strength of approximately 7,000 pounds
- 1/4" - Grade 30 Proof-coil chain (non-alloy) has a breaking strength of approximately 5,200 pounds
- 1/4" - Grade 63 alloy chain has a breaking strength of approximately 15,000 pounds

Since most lift lines are made of 1/4" - 7x19 wire rope, its breaking strength is the first number we need to consider. If the breaking strength of the chain is greater than 7,000 then the wire rope is the weakest link. Since the the breaking strength of the alloy chain is more than twice the breaking strength of the wire rope, alloy chain is clearly not going to be the weakest link. But what about the non-alloy chain?

Let's continue looking at the wire rope for one more minute. The 7,000 pound breaking strength is based on a cable termination that is 100% efficient, such as copper swaging sleeves. But what if the wire rope is terminated with cable clips? If so, the breaking strength is reduced by 20% to approximately 5,600 pounds. This is still greater than the 5,200 pound breaking strength of the chain, but not by a lot.

What we have not looked at is how the chain is being used to create the trim chain. Below is a drawing how a trim chain is typically installed.

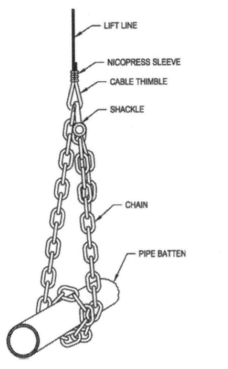

LIFT LINE

NICOPRESS SLEEVE

CABLE THIMBLE

SHACKLE

CHAIN

PIPE BATTEN

-photo courtesy of JR Clancy

As you can see, one end of the trim chain is permanently attached to the thimble on the end of the lift cable. The chain then wraps around the batten twice before being attached back to the thimble with a shackle.

What this does is essentially mean that the batten, and the load hanging on it, is hanging on two legs of chain, just like on a bridle, and divides the load in half, or doubling the capacity of the chain. This means that the breaking strength of a 1/4" Grade 30 chain, used in this manner, is now 10,400 lb – significantly greater that the breaking strength of the wire rope lift line. Destructive test that we have done verifies that in this configuration, the wire rope will break before the chain or the shackle.

So, what is the problem with this method? Nothing, as long as you use it as show above. However, a problem could develop if, instead of attaching the shackle to the thimble, it is attached to a link in the chain. If this is done, then two problems occur. First, the entire load is now on one part of chain, reducing its breaking strength back to 5,200 pounds. Second, this problem is compounded by the fact that the shackle is sitting on top of a link, causing it to be pinched between the shackle and the link below. This reduces the breaking strength by 20 percent, making the breaking strength now 4,160 pounds. Destructive tests have proven that this point is the weakest part of the system and will break first.

When the both ends of the trim chain are connected to the thimble, 1/4" Grade 30 (non-alloy) chain is a perfectly safe and acceptable material for trim chain, in our opinion. However, because the cost of 1/4" alloy chain is so close the cost of 1/4" Grade 30 (non-alloy) chain, it makes good sense to install alloy chain in a new installation.

Summary

Safety is the ultimately the goal in our understanding of anything related to overhead lifting. In theatre rigging, and production in general, we often adopt products and materials from other industries. If there is any doubt on how a piece of lifting equipment is to be used, it is best to contact the manufacturer directly. [1] Grade 30 Proof Coil chain, for example, when properly

[1] Note that suppliers are not manufacturers. When questions arise concerning the proper use of any lifting equipment, it is best to contact the manufacturer directly.

installed has been used for many years to attach loads to battens; all are perfectly acceptable within the definition of overhead lifting as adopted by the NACM.

Appendix 4:
Bibliography

Animated Knots. http://www.animatedknots.com

ANSI (American National Standards Institute). http://tsp.plasa.org/tsp/documents/published_docs.php

Automatic Devices Company. http://www.automaticdevices.com/

Budworth, Geoffery and Dalton, Jason, The Book of Knots. Ivy Press Limited (2003).

CCOHA (Canadian Centre for Occupational Health and Safety) http://www.ccohs.ca/

Conner, William, Burning Issues in Fire Curtain Regulation, ESTA Protocol, (March 2001).

Core Slings. http://CoreSlings.com

Culhane, Dan., Basic Straight-Lift Fire Safety Curtain Operation, TD&T, Vol. 41 No. 4 (Fall 2005).

Entertainment Technician Certification Program. http://etcp.esta.org/cert_recognized/training_programs/electrical_list.htm

Fire Safety in Theaters – A New Design Approach Part I, Assessment of Fire Safety Measures in Proscenium Theaters, Ove Arup & Partners Consulting Engineers PC, (September 10, 2009).

Glerum, Jay O., Stage Rigging Handbook, Third Edition. Carbondale: Southern Illinois University Press, (2007).

Hall, Delbert L., Rigging Math Made Simple, 3rd Ed. Spring Knoll Press, (2014).

James Thomas Engineering. http://jthomaseng.com/pdffiles/Product 20Range 202014_merged.pdf

JR Clancy. http://jrclancy.com

McMaster-Car. http://McMaster.com/

Mutual Hardware. http://www.mutualhardware.com

OSHA (The Occupational Safety and Health Administration). https://www.osha.gov/

PLASA (Professional Lighting and Sound Association. https://www.plasa.org/

RigStar. http://rigstar.com

Sapsis, Bill, editor. *Entertainment Rigging for the 21st Century.* Focal Press, (2014).

The Crosby Group. http://www.thecrosbygroup.com/html/default.htm#/en/calc/snatchblockrigcalc.htm

The Flywire. http://www.eepurl/T7gMf

The Journal of Emergency Medical Services. http://www.jems.com/articles/print/volume-34/issue-8/patientcare/dangerous-suspension-understan.html

The Stagecraft Institute of Las Vegas. htttp://stagecraftinstitute.com

TomCat Truss. http://www.tomcatglobal.com/Tomcat/media/tomcat/Catalogue/TOMCATUCATU (pdf).pdf?ext=.pdf

Tyler Truss. http://www.tylertruss.com

USITT (United States Institute for Theatre Technology) http://www.usitt.org/

Wire Rope Technical Board. *Wire Rope User's Manual*, 4th ed. 2005.